American Monetary Policy, 1928-1941

American Monetary Policy
1928-1941

LESTER V. CHANDLER

Atlanta University

Harper & Row, Publishers
New York, Evanston, San Francisco, London

Contents

Preface

This volume examines American monetary policies from early 1928 to the time of America's entry into World War II in December 1941. This longer period breaks naturally into three parts, each including a major episode in American monetary history. Part I covers the period extending from the reversal of the easy-money policies of 1927 to the stock-market collapse in October 1929. Its central focus is on the vain attempt of the Federal Reserve to curb stock-market speculation, or at least the use of credit for this purpose, and at the same time to avoid or reduce adverse effects on the domestic and international economies.

Part II covers the period of the Great Slide—the tragic decline of national income, employment, and price levels to the nadir of the depression, symbolized by the collapse of the banking system at the beginning of March 1933. This, too, is a story of frustration and failure. Whether or not it could have been otherwise, the Federal Reserve failed to stop the Great Slide or even to prevent a nationwide banking panic.

Part III covers the period of the New Deal from March 1933 to the end of 1941. During the first two periods, the Federal Reserve occupied the center of the stage; the federal government played almost no role in monetary policy. To say that roles were reversed in the third period would be an exaggeration, but the relative role of the Federal Reserve was reduced markedly as the federal government seized the initiative, adopted radically new gold and silver policies, and established a wide variety of new financial institutions that affected the functioning of the monetary and credit systems. This, too, was a period of frustration and partial failure. The economy was still plagued with excessive unemployment and unused capacity when the nation accelerated its rearmament program in 1940.

For many years after its end, this period was largely neglected by economists, perhaps partly because they became absorbed in the problems of World War II and the postwar period. As a result, many earlier analyses, interpretations, and conclusions went unchallenged. Information that had later become available, theoretical advances, and the advantages of longer perspective were not exploited to increase our understanding of events during these troubled years. Recently, however, interest in the period has revived and many valuable contributions have appeared, the most important of which is the *Monetary History of the United States, 1867-1960,* by Milton Friedman and Anna J. Schwartz. Economists are deeply indebted to these authors for the wealth of information and analysis that they have provided. Yet there is, I believe, a place for further examination of this period. Additional information is becoming available, and further analysis may modify or supplement the interpretations already available.

The following pages provide little information that is new concerning actual policy actions, since what the Federal Reserve did and did not do has long been a matter of record. They do, however, offer some new interpretations and attempt to shed additional light on the reasons for the monetary policies of both Federal Reserve and government officials. Such questions as these are raised: What were the explicit or implicit monetary, banking, and business-cycle theories of these officials? How did these affect their perception and interpretation of developments and events? In what terms did they conceive their principal purposes, objectives, and responsibilities? How did they view the potentialities and limitations of the instruments at their command? How were their thinking and their policies affected by the attitudes, modes of thought, and economic understanding of economists, officials, and the public?

Though it draws upon the works of other writers, this study relies primarily on original sources, including both published and archival materials. In making all relevant materials available, the Federal Reserve has been of immeasurable assistance, for which I wish to record here my deep gratitude.

So many people have been helpful in the preparation of this study that I cannot mention them all. I must, however, record my thanks to Katharine Guroff, who so cheerfully and efficiently served as research assistant.

Lester V. Chandler

Last Years of the New Era

_____

I

1

Prologue

This story begins in early 1928. At that time the Federal Reserve was in its 14th year. During most of its early formative years it had operated under conditions far different from those that had been anticipated when the Federal Reserve Act was drafted and adopted in 1913, and much of its experience during those years had not been very helpful in developing policies for "normal" peacetime periods. When the Reserve banks opened for business in November 1914, the country was still suffering from the financial crisis and interruption of transatlantic shipping following the outbreak of World War I in August. By mid-1915 the economic tide had turned, and an inflationary boom developed even before America's entry into the war. Rising demands for American exports induced large gold imports and increased domestic expenditures for both investment and consumption purposes. The Federal Reserve was powerless to prevent the resulting inflation. Possessing only a handful of earning assets to sell and having no power to raise member bank reserve requirements, it could not stem the rise of bank credit and the money supply. When the United States entered the war in April 1917, wholesale prices had already risen nearly 75 percent since mid-1914 and more than 35 percent in the preceding 12 months.

From that time until the end of the war in November 1918, the overriding objective of Federal Reserve policy was to assure the success of Treasury financing—to enable the federal government to borrow all the money it needed on terms fixed by the Congress and the Treasury. Neither the end of the war nor the end of federal deficits in mid-1919 freed the Federal Reserve from this objective. The Treasury still faced large refinancing needs and was reluctant to permit the declines of bond prices that would accompany credit restriction and rising interest rates. Not until the early months of 1920 was the Federal Reserve free to take effective action to halt the inflation. At the peak of the inflation in May 1920, both wholesale prices and the money supply (currency plus demand deposits) were more than double their levels in 1914.

The ensuing deflation and depression were sharp and painful. Prices plummeted, unemployment mounted, and business failures were widespread. Farmers and many others would not soon forget or forgive the sharp deflation

3

of the values of their products and assets. For the first time the Federal Reserve was widely criticized. Some accused it of precipitating the depression by raising its discount rates sharply in May 1920. Still more blamed it for its failure to take effective action to lessen pressures for credit and monetary liquidation. Fortunately, however, the depression was relatively short. After reaching their low points in early 1921, employment and industrial production began to recover and by late 1922 had surpassed their 1920 peaks.

Thus it was not until 1922, about eight years after its establishment, that the Federal Reserve came to operate under anything like "normal peacetime conditions," with freedom to develop and pursue peacetime objectives. Even in 1922 economic and political conditions were far from "normal" in any prewar sense of the term. The war had wrought profound changes—destruction of productive power, shifts in the balance of economic and financial power, shifts in the volume and patterns of international trade, economic and political instability, and so on. For many, all this was symbolized by widespread monetary and fiscal disorders, and especially by the breakdown of the international monetary system. In 1914 the gold standard was truly international; every major country kept the value of its currency stable in terms of gold. The war shattered these arrangements. In 1922 the United States was the only major country on a gold standard; the currencies of all other countries had depreciated in terms of gold, and their values were fluctuating both in terms of gold and in terms of other currencies in exchange markets.

These conditions affected Federal Reserve policies in at least two ways. For one thing, they made the prewar "rules of the international gold standard game" inapplicable. We can only conjecture whether Federal Reserve officials would have followed such rules, or how they would have interpreted them, even if an international gold standard had existed. But in the absence of such a system, and in the face of fluctuating exchange rates, there was no logical reason for allowing domestic supplies of money and credit to be dominated by changes in the nation's monetary gold stock. Federal Reserve officials therefore faced the problem of developing and pursuing new objectives and policy guides, at least until such time as a new international system could be established.

In the second place, the reestablishment of some sort of international gold standard became an important objective of Federal Reserve policy. Like most others of the day, Federal Reserve officials considered a network of stable exchange rates to be essential for promoting international trade and capital movements and believed that for this purpose there was no practical substitute for gold standards. Some also professed to long for the day when monetary policies would again be subjected to the discipline of an international gold standard. In assisting other countries to return to gold, there was at least some element of altruism. Those Federal Reserve officials most influential in these efforts were convinced that foreign countries returning to gold would thereby increase their economic stability and prosperity. However, there were also large elements of American self-interest in this policy. These officials strongly believed that American exports and prosperity in general would be enhanced by greater prosperity and stability abroad and by the advantages of stable exchange rates. It was not impolitic to stress the resulting gains for American agricultural exports.

By the beginning of 1928 the restoration of an international gold standard was almost complete. Progress had been slow until mid-1925, but after Britain's return to gold at that time many others followed. France stabilized *de facto* in 1926 and *de jure* in mid-1928. Only a few stragglers had not stabilized by late 1928 and 1929. The job of monetary reconstruction appeared to be complete. But this was by no means the end of the matter. To maintain these gold standards and to help them function in a viable manner remained an important consideration for the Federal Reserve.

In short, though the Federal Reserve had been in operation more than 13 years by the beginning of 1928, only the last 5 or 6 of those years had been characterized by anything like "normal peacetime conditions." The System had made real progress in gaining acceptance, in formulating objectives, in developing facilities and personnel, and in gaining understanding of its powers. But it was still very much in a formative stage, with many unresolved issues and widely differing views among its officials. Some of these issues were basic, relating to such problems as the division of power and responsibility within the System, the objectives to be pursued, and the instruments to be employed. Many critics of Federal Reserve policies in the late 1920s and early 1930s have pointed to their indecisiveness, vacillations, and outright errors. However one may judge them, these policies can be understood only if one bears in mind the youth and short experience of the System at that time and the persistence of wide differences in views, convictions, and understanding within it.

POWER AND RESPONSIBILITY

Which powers and responsibilities did the authors of the Federal Reserve Act intend to give to the Federal Reserve Board in Washington, and which to the directors and officers of the 12 Federal Reserve banks? Even the closest reading of the legislative history of the Act and of the Act itself as it existed in the late 1920s cannot yield a precise answer. A considerable decentralization of power was clearly intended. Congress had, after all, rejected proposals for a single central bank and had provided for a system of 8 to 12 regional Reserve banks. Two of the most potent arguments for decentralization were directed to the fear of concentrated control, and especially of "political" control, over the financial system and to the desire to adapt the credit policies and practices of the Reserve banks to the peculiar conditions of their respective districts. Moreover, various sections of the Act specifically gave to the directors and officers of the regional Reserve banks powers which appeared sweeping, especially if the language were interpreted broadly. However, the Act also established the Federal Reserve Board and gave it both general and specific powers to supervise, regulate, and restrict the Reserve banks. In many cases the language was ambiguous. If very narrowly constructed, the powers of the Board over the Reserve banks would be much like the powers of the Comptroller of the Currency over national banks. If very liberally interpreted, the powers of the Board would be broad indeed. To illustrate the issues let us consider the division of power and responsibility for three important policy instruments—discount rates, open-market operations in United States government securities, and open-market operations in acceptances or bills of exchange.

In effect, the Federal Reserve Act conferred on the directors of each Reserve bank the power "to establish a discount rate or rates subject to review and determination by the Federal Reserve Board." This language suggests what became normal practice: A Federal Reserve bank would take the initiative in proposing a rate or set of rates for review by the Board. By 1920 the Attorney General had ruled that no Reserve bank could put a rate into effect without Board approval, and that the Board could not only disapprove a proposed rate but also determine the rate to be established by that bank in place of the proposed rate. This policy still left unanswered a set of important legal questions: Did the Board have the legal power to initiate changes in discount rates—to force a Reserve bank to change a rate which had already been established with Board approval? The Board did just that in October 1927, when it ordered the Federal Reserve Bank of Chicago to lower its rate from 4 to 3 1/2 percent. Reactions both within and outside the system were adverse. Several Reserve bank officials who favored the rate reduction nevertheless protested the procedure, Senator Glass found it "wanton," and many others questioned not only the wisdom but also the legality of the Board's action. The legal power of the Board to force rate changes was clarified only in the Banking Act of 1935, which added the provision that each Reserve bank ". . . shall establish such rates every fourteen days, or oftener if deemed necessary by the Board." In the meantime, the Board refrained from taking the initiative.

The Act was even less specific in allocating authority over open-market purchases and sales of U.S. government obligations and certain other governmental securities. It provided only that each Reserve bank should have the power to purchase and sell these securities, "such purchases to be made in accordance with rules and regulations prescribed by the Federal Reserve Board." Note the implication that each Reserve bank would carry out its own purchases and sales and that the Board's specific power to prescribe rules and regulations applied only to purchases and not to sales. This left several questions unanswered: Did the Board have power to regulate sales and even to force Reserve banks to sell? How far could it go under its power to prescribe rules and regulations applicable to purchases? Could it merely prescribe general principles and procedures, or could it go so far as to determine the amounts of securities to be purchased by each Reserve bank?

As the Reserve banks began to purchase government securities in some volume in 1922, the disadvantages of uncoordinated operations by the 12 banks became apparent. Prices and yields on these securities were affected in ways considered undesirable by Reserve bank officials and by the Secretary of the Treasury. The governors of the Reserve banks, and especially Governor Benjamin Strong of the Federal Reserve Bank of New York, therefore took the initiative in establishing, in May 1922, "The Committee of Governors on Centralized Execution of Purchases and Sales of Government Securities by Federal Reserve Banks." This committee was composed of the governors of the Federal Reserve Banks of Boston, New York, Philadelphia, Chicago, and

Cleveland. Benjamin Strong was its chairman and J. Herbert Case, Deputy Governor of the New York Bank, its vice-chairman. The initial function of the committee is indicated by its title; it was merely to execute orders. Power to determine the volume and timing of purchases and sales remained with the individual Reserve banks. Gradually, however, the committee began to make recommendations to the Reserve banks and to exert an important influence on their open-market policies.

Members of the Federal Reserve Board viewed with misgivings the growing influence of the committee, and at least one member, Adolph Casper Miller, opposed the rising importance of open-market operations. In April 1923 the Board abolished the committee formed by the governors and established a new body to be called "The Open-Market Investment Committee" (hereafter referred to as the OMIC). The OMIC, with the same membership as the old committee, was to operate "under the general supervision of the Federal Reserve Board" in carrying out purchases and sales for the System account, called "The Open-Market Investment Account" (or OMIA). Though this action by the Board tended to increase both the degree of centralized influence over open-market operations and the Board's jurisdiction and power, it did neither in a clear-cut way. (1) Each Reserve bank still retained the right to refuse to participate in purchases or sales made by the OMIC for the System's Open-Market Investment Account. Several Reserve banks did refuse to participate in such purchases, especially in the early 1930s, either because of their reserve or free-gold positions or because they disapproved of System policies. (2) Each Reserve bank retained freedom to buy and sell for its own account, and several exercised this power on various occasions, usually in conformity with a gentleman's agreement among the Reserve banks to refrain from purchases or sales that would be at cross-purposes with System policy. Purchases by the Federal Reserve Bank of New York for its own account were to play important roles at the time of the stock-market crash and on several occasions in the early 1930s. (3) The powers of the Federal Reserve Board over purchases and sales by the OMIC and by the individual Reserve banks for their own accounts remained ambiguous. The Board rarely tried to seize the initiative and order the OMIC to buy or sell, but it did assert its right to supervise, regulate, and restrict operations proposed by the OMIC. The latter did not carry out operations disapproved by the Board, but its members and several of the Reserve bank governors insisted that the Board should deal only with general policy, leaving to the OMIC discretion to execute purchases and sales conforming to that policy. At least some members of the Board wanted more detailed control, even to the point of determining the exact amounts to be bought or sold and the exact timing of transactions. There were similar disagreements concerning the Board's powers over transactions by individual Reserve banks for their own account. For example, in November 1929 the Board, irked by the large purchases made by the New York Reserve Bank after the stock-market crash, voted to prohibit every Federal Reserve bank from buying or selling government securities without the Board's approval. However, it rescinded its action when advised by counsel "that there is considerable doubt of the legality of the regulation."

These issues were never fully resolved prior to 1935 and remained subjects of controversy. However, the indecisiveness, vacillations, and delay in open-market policy did not result solely from controversies over the location of control powers; they reflected also wide differences of opinion both within the Federal Reserve Board and among the Federal Reserve banks concerning the appropriate role of open-market operations in government securities.

The Federal Reserve Act also empowered each Reserve bank to purchase and sell acceptances and bills of exchange in the open market, "under rules and regulations prescribed by the Federal Reserve Board." Here again the Act implied that the initiative lay with the Reserve banks, with the Board acting in some sort of regulatory role. As it turned out, operations in acceptances were carried out largely by the Federal Reserve Bank of New York for its own account or the accounts of the other Reserve banks; these were not put under the control of the OMIC. Though the other Reserve banks made some direct purchases, most of them could find only a small volume of acceptances in their own regional markets and they had to adjust their bill-buying rates (the rates of discount at which they bought) to the rate in effect at the New York Reserve Bank.

The normal procedure that developed early was that the Reserve banks proposed rates for review and approval by the Board. Up until 1918 the Board approved both minimum and maximum buying rates for acceptances of prime quality, leaving the Reserve banks free to fix actual buying rates within these limits. After that time the Board approved only minimum buying rates, thus allowing the Reserve banks to fix actual rates at or above the minimum level. By the late 1920s, however, some members of the Board felt that this gave the Reserve banks, and especially the New York Bank, too much freedom to determine acceptance policy for the System and proposed that the Board should have power to approve actual as well as minimum rates. Officials of the New York Bank and of several other Reserve banks objected, claiming that they needed flexibility to adjust to changing market conditions. The Board did not go so far as to require approval of actual rates above the minimum, but it did narrow the discretion of the Reserve banks and on several occasions delayed approval of proposed minimum rates.

Thus we find that the Federal Reserve Act was at best ambiguous in allocating power and responsibility for the System's three most powerful policy instruments—discount rates and open-market operations in government securities and acceptances. Moreover, it provided no means for the quick and effective resolution of differences in interpretation or for the settlement of conflicts. These remained to be resolved through cooperation and, in some cases, through competitive behavior of Federal Reserve officials. Some conflict and delay would probably have occurred even if all Federal Reserve officials had been in complete agreement on their objectives, on the appropriate instruments to use in promoting these objectives, and in their understanding of the effects of their policies. But conflict and controversy were assured by the fact that at the beginning of 1928 there was no such general agreement throughout the System, or even within the Federal Reserve Board or among the Reserve banks. Differences were numerous, persistent, and in some cases crucial. For this the ambiguity of the Act was in part, although not wholly, responsible.

OBJECTIVES AND POLICY GUIDES

The Act came closest to prescribing policy guides in providing that discount rates should be "fixed with a view of accommodating commerce and business." A. C. Miller found this language admirable:

The phrase "accommodation of commerce and business" has always struck me as one of the rare inventions that occur occasionally in American statesmanship. Whoever was the author of that phrase did a magnificent thing. It is great language. The word "accommodation" is susceptible of the wisest interpretation and reaches to the noblest of economic purposes.[1]

This language certainly had the merit of affording maximum freedom of interpretation, whether wise or not, and ample flexibility and adaptability to changes in conditions and aspirations. By the same token it provided virtually no guidance to policy-makers. Even those with diametrically opposed views as to the purposes and policies of the System could conscientiously pay lip service to it. For example, Benjamin Strong and George Harrison of the New York Reserve Bank believed that the Federal Reserve should on its own initiative exercise positive control of the money markets, opposing and countering destabilizing forces. This, they believed, was "accommodation of commerce and business" in the broadest and most useful sense of the term, because it contributed to the overall stability of the economy. Toward the other extreme were those who believed that "accomodation" required the Federal Reserve to respond more or less passively to the needs of business and commerce as evidenced by their demands for bank credit. The Federal Reserve should respond and "accommodate," not initiate or resist. The legislative history of the Act and certain provisions of the Act itself lent more support to the second group than to those who believed the Federal Reserve should take the initiative and regulate the market in a positive way.

One of the major issues involved, though not the only one, was the validity of the "real bills doctrine" or the "commercial loan theory of banking." At least two of the men who were influential in determining the content of the Federal Reserve Act were adherents of the commercial loan theory. H. Parker Willis, who helped draft the Act and was a principal advisor to Carter Glass, became the most widely known and most unbending advocate of the theory, and Glass never abandoned it.

Influences of the theory appear in several provisions of the Act. (1) Paper conforming to this theory was given preferential treatment as a basis for borrowing at the Federal Reserve banks. The Act provided that each Federal Reserve bank might discount for its members, or lend to them on notes collateraled by, "notes, drafts, and bills of exchange arising out of commercial transactions; that is, notes, drafts, and bills of exchange issued or drawn for agricultural, industrial, or commercial purposes, or the proceeds of which have been used or are to be used, for such purposes." Specifically excluded were instruments with maturities exceeding 90 days at time of dis-

---

[1]Hearings before the House Banking and Currency Committee on H.R. 11806, 70th Congress, 1st Session (May 2, 1928), p. 193. Hereafter cited as Hearings on H.R. 11806.

count and those "covering merely investments or issued or drawn for the purpose of carrying or trading in stocks, bonds, or other investment securities, except bonds and notes of the United States." Senator Glass later declared that the Federal Reserve Act would never have permitted the Reserve banks to lend on government security collateral if its proponents had not believed that the federal debt would continue to decline.[2] The purpose was clearly to discriminate against all earning assets of member banks that did not conform to the commercial loan theory. (2) Reserve banks were empowered to buy and sell in the open market bills of exchange and acceptances of types eligible for discount. These were considered prime examples of short-term paper based on real transactions. One purpose was to develop an acceptance market in the United States and thus to make more funds available for "legitimate" business and less for the stock market. (3) Federal Reserve notes had to be fully backed by collateral, and the only Federal Reserve assets that could be used as collateral were gold and discounted eligible paper. This was considered necessary to ensure that note issues would be appropriately elastic and would not exceed the "needs of trade." We shall see later that even in 1932 Senator Glass was very reluctant to allow government securities to be used as collateral for Federal Reserve notes and that H. Parker Willis and some other commercial loan theorists were sharply opposed to doing so.

It is difficult to assess precisely the extent to which the commercial loan theory influenced the thinking and policy positions of Federal Reserve officials in the 1920s and 1930s. Some Reserve officials seem to have rejected it completely and none accepted it in its most extreme and most indefensible form—that no quantitative control of money and credit is necessary because their quantities will be automatically adjusted to the needs of trade, with neither excesses nor deficiencies, if the Federal Reserve and commercial banks make only short-term, self-liquidating loans to finance production, distribution, and trade in real goods and services. All recognized that some quantitative regulation was necessary, if only through adjustments of discount rates. However, large elements of the commercial loan theory—elements of language, of preoccupation with the form of bank credit rather than the total stock of money, and of more or less passive accommodation—persisted and strongly influenced Federal Reserve thinking and policies. This statement will later be supported with some examples.

For one thing, Federal Reserve officials tended to think in terms of "credit" rather than "money." Their speeches abounded with references to the supply of credit, credit conditions, and credit policies. References to the supply of money and to monetary policies were much less frequent.[3] The

---

[2]Hearings before the Senate Banking and Currency Committee on S. Res. 71, 71st Congress, 3rd Session (January 20-23, 1931), p. 53. Hereafter cited as Hearings on S. Res. 71.

[3]One interesting example is W. Randolph Burgess, *The Reserve Banks and the Money Market*, Harper & Row, New York, 1927. Burgess refers to the supply of credit many times and never to the supply of money; he consistently uses the term "credit policy" rather than "monetary policy." Lauchlin Currie, *Supply and Control of Money in the United States*, Harvard University Press, Cambridge, Mass., 1934, provides one of the earliest and best diagnoses of the importance of distinguishing clearly between money and

difference was not merely semantic; it both reflected and affected ways of thinking. Those who used the terms "money" and "monetary policy" tended to concentrate their attention on the supply of money. The former term is not, of course, unambiguous—one of the major issues being whether it should include only currency and demand deposits or time and savings deposits as well. But however they defined "money," those who concentrated their attention on it tended to give the center of the stage to the total stock of money and to its velocity of circulation, and to consider of only secondary importance the types of assets acquired by the Federal Reserve and commercial banks in the process of creating money. Thus, they were likely to be less concerned about the types of loans and investments made, the types of collateral offered, or the professed purposes of loans. In assessing the "needs of trade" they tended to think less about the demands for bank loans by certain segments of industry or for certain types of purposes and more about the quantities of money balances demanded to support optimum levels of economic activity. Many of them also tended to think in quantity-theory terms.

On the other hand, those who thought in terms of "credit" and "credit policy" faced from the outset difficult problems of definition and precision of communication, for "credit" has meanings ranging all the way from creditworthiness to stocks of outstanding debts or credits. In some cases it includes all types of credit, in others only bank credit. Even the term "bank credit" was often used ambiguously, sometimes to refer to bank liabilities, especially deposits, and sometimes to the earning assets of banks. It was most common for those who thought in terms of "credit" and "credit policies" to center their attention on bank loans and investments. Many paid special attention to particular types of investments and loans, rather than to the total stock of money—to the maturity of loans, the collateral or other security offered, and the professed purpose for which the loan funds would be used. They tended to ask, "For what purpose will the borrower from the bank spend the funds initially?" The unwary were prone to forget that the money created by the loan might be re-spent several times during the life of the loan for purposes quite unrelated to the form of the loan. They tended to believe that the uses to which money would be put were closely related to the form of loan paper acquired by the banks, and that the "needs of legitimate trade" were best reflected in loan demands based on short-term, self-liquidating paper arising out of real transactions. Conversely, proceeds of loans based on security collateral were thought more likely to be used for speculation in securities.

A few examples will illustrate the wide differences in the understanding and attitudes among Federal Reserve officials in the late 1920s and help to explain some of the difficulties of securing prompt agreement on policies. By this time the New York Reserve Bank had moved far from a stance of "passive accommodation" and toward one of positive regulation, if not control, of monetary and credit conditions. This position developed under Governor Strong but was shared by his successor, George L. Harrison, and by other influential officers of the bank, such as W. Randolph Burgess and J. Herbert

---

credit and demonstrates the dangers inherent in thinking in terms of "credit policy." See especially Chapters 4 and 5.

Case. They believed that under many circumstances the Federal Reserve should lead, rather than be led by, the market—that it should itself take the initiative in regulating credit conditions to promote its objectives. This was evidenced to some extent in the New York Bank's discount rate policy; its rates were changed oftener and over a wider range than those of the other Reserve banks. It was especially evident in the bank's strong advocacy of open-market operations as a policy instrument. This instrument enabled the System on its own initiative, without relying on the willingness of member banks to borrow, to increase or decrease the supply of member bank reserves in order to promote selected objectives. By the standards of some 40 years later, the purposes and scope of the open-market operations advocated by New York officials in the late 1920s and early 1930s may not seem very ambitious, but to many contemporary critics they appeared bold indeed.

Also, officials of the New York Bank emphasized, perhaps more than any other group in the System, the fluidity of credit, and especially its fluidity among the various branches of the open markets for money and securities. They pointed to the large number and variety of lenders and borrowers, the numerous channels connecting them, and the wide repercussions resulting from an insertion or withdrawal of funds at any point. From this they drew the conclusion that it was impossible for a Federal Reserve monetary or credit policy—one relying on discount rates or open-market operations—to make funds scarce or plentiful for one purpose without affecting credit conditions in other branches of the market. They also stressed the impossibility of regulating the types of purposes to which the overall supplies of money and credit would be put by regulating the types of assets acquired by the Federal Reserve in supplying bank reserves. Their argument was usually in two stages. (1) The Federal Reserve could not in this way control even the initial uses to which funds would be put by the member bank borrowing from it or selling other assets to it. Consider first the case of a borrowing member. It usually does not borrow to make a specific loan or investment; rather, it borrows to cover a deficiency of reserves which it usually claims has resulted from deposit withdrawals, but which in any case reflects the net result of many types of receipts and payments by the bank. The type of collateral offered by the borrowing bank is determined not by the nature of any prospective loan or investment but by convenience and cost. Something similar is true when a bank or other entity gains funds from the Federal Reserve by selling to it acceptances or government securities. The seller may have sold for any number of reasons, and there is no reason to presuppose that he will buy other assets similar to the ones he sold. (2) In any case, the initial recipient of reserves resulting from Federal Reserve loans or purchases in the open market will ordinarily account for only a fraction, often a very small fraction of the resulting total expansion of money and credit. As the bank which initially received the reserves expands its loans and investments, it loses deposits to other banks and has to transfer reserves to them in payment. These recipient banks usually do not know the ultimate sources of these reserves, and even if they do they are under no special obligation to the Reserve banks and are free to use their increased lending and investing power as they see fit.

All this is, of course, of crucial importance to Federal Reserve attempts to determine the uses to which money and credit will be put by regulating the types of assets that it acquires.

A. C. Miller, member of the Federal Reserve Board from 1914 to 1936, found many of these ideas and attitudes quite unacceptable. Miller's own ideas and attitudes are important in understanding both Federal Reserve policies during this period and later assessments of them. As a member of the Board, Miller exerted a significant influence on these policies, sometimes as innovator but more often as a cautious cooperator or as a member of the opposition. He influenced later assessments of these policies through his own testimony before numerous congressional committees, through his other speeches and writings, and also through his personal friendship with Herbert Hoover. There can be little doubt that President Hoover's many public comments on Federal Reserve policies, mostly after the fact and mostly adverse, were strongly influenced by Miller and Miller's views and prejudices.

Miller's policy stance was generally unambitious and cautious, tending toward passive accommodation. He was vigorously opposed to open-market policy except on those "rare occasions when resort to it may be truly necessary."[4] He much preferred rediscounting:

I believe that our troubles will be enormously minimized—in fact I think we will pretty nearly get rid of most of them—if the Federal Reserve banks are operated as institutions of rediscount.[5]

In the spring of 1928 he proposed that open-market operations be permitted only on an affirmative vote of at least five members of the Federal Reserve Board in order to assure that they would be resorted to "only under the pressure of an exigency so real or so important that prudence would advise against awaiting the slower action through discount rates."[6] He was still of the same opinion in January 1931, "more so than ever."[7] He believed that overexpansion or inflation of credit was likely when the Federal Reserve supplied funds on its own initiative by purchasing securities, but that this was unlikely to result from rediscounting because member banks would not like to borrow or show indebtedness. He also contended that the insertion of funds on the initiative of the Federal Reserve was especially likely to divert credit into investment securities, loans on such securities, and call loans. In his supporting arguments Miller revealed a faulty understanding of banking processes, as evidenced in the following quotation.

... when the Federal reserve banks operate as investment banks, by buying investments, they force the member banks of the country also to operate as investment banks by buying investments or loaning against investments or by making loans of the kind here described as loans on real estate.[8]

---

[4]Hearings on S. Res. 71, p. 150.

[5]Ibid.

[6]Hearings on H.R. 11806, p. 190.

[7]Hearings on S. Res. 71, p. 139.

[8]Ibid.

... When the reserve system puts money into the market by open market purchases, the money goes eventually to the highest bidder, and inasmuch as the open money market of the country is first and foremost in New York where the great call market is, that is the market to which the Federal Reserve money tends to go. And where it first tends to go, it has a tendency to stay. We talk much of the fluidity of money and credit. The fact is that it is sometimes very sluggish in its movement and tends to remain where it is first put out—that is the New York call-loan market. It will stick there if there is a good demand for it. [9]

Every element of these arguments is suspect. (1) There is no reason to believe that increasing member bank reserves through Federal Reserve purchases of "investments" will "force the member banks also to operate as investment banks" any more than would an increase of bank reserves through gold imports, currency inflows, or overflows of reserves from banks that had borrowed from the Federal Reserve. (2) Banks did indeed adjust their reserve positions to a considerable extent by increasing and decreasing their funds in the open markets. But it is surely an exaggeration to suggest that the largest part of each addition to a bank's reserves will go into call loans. The bank may also meet customer's demands that would otherwise be refused, purchase acceptances or commercial paper, and so on. (3) Even if money does go initially to the New York call-loan market it is very doubtful that "where it first tends to go, it has a tendency to stay." Brokers and dealers increase their borrowings primarily to cover the excess of their payments to sellers of securities over their receipts from buyers of securities. There is no reason to believe that the sellers who receive money, including the proceeds from call loans, will elect to use a major part of it to make further call loans. They may use it instead to finance production or consumption or to purchase mortgages or other securities. (4) Miller seriously underestimated the fluidity of funds among the various branches of the financial markets. This helps account for his belief in early 1929 that the System could significantly decrease total loans to brokers merely by limiting brokers' loans by those member banks that were currently borrowing from the Federal Reserve, leaving all other banks and all other lenders free of control.

Miller believed not only that increased bank lending power resulting from open-market purchases would be used in large degree to increase the supply of call loans, but also that a fall of call-loan rates would induce increases in security speculation and the quantities of call loans demanded.

The call-loan market will in ordinary times take all the money offered it at a price.[10]

Richard N. Owens and Charles O. Hardy found no support for this thesis.

One of the most universally accepted principles of finance is that stock market speculation is primarily governed by variations in interest rates. According to the prevailing view, low interest rates cause increased borrowing for stock exchange speculation and a consequent rise in stock values, while high interest rates check speculation and produce a fall

---

[9]Ibid., p. 149.

[10]Hearings on S. Res. 71, p. 135.

in stock prices . . . . The conclusion reached is that neither economic analysis nor historical research reveals any foundation for the accepted theory.[11]

Miller did not, however, believe that increases in the call rate would effectively curb stock speculation, and he doubted the effectiveness of a cheap-money policy in countering business recessions.

. . . it is a debatable question whether or not in a period of business recession, business recession can be arrested by making money cheap. My opinion is that it can't be done to any appreciable extent, if at all.[12]

With these ideas and attitudes, it is no wonder that Miller opposed vigorous Federal Reserve actions on its own initiative, and especially large open-market purchases. He condemned the easy-money policies of 1924 and 1927 and opposed both the sizable purchases by the New York Bank at the time of the stock-market crash and further proposed purchases in the early months of 1930. But as the depression deepened he came to believe that one of those rare occasions had arrived when resort to open-market operations was truly necessary.

Roy A. Young, Governor of the Federal Reserve Board from October 1927 to September 1930 and from that time Governor of the Federal Reserve Bank of Boston, differed with Miller on many points, but he became a vigorous opponent of the active open-market policies advocated by the New York Bank and favored a much more passive approach. Edward H. Cunningham, an Iowa farmer who was the agricultural member of the Federal Reserve Board from May 1923 until his death in November 1930, seems never to have taken a broad view of the functions of the Federal Reserve. He was interested primarily in maintaining "reasonable" interest rates for legitimate business, and especially for agriculture. His successor, Wayland W. Magee, a Nebraska farmer, appears to have followed much the same line.

The governors and directors of the Reserve banks other than the New York Bank were by no means in full agreement, but most of them tended toward a policy of passive accommodation. For example, Governor Norris of the Philadelphia Reserve Bank made the following statement for himself and his directors to a meeting of the Open-Market Committee in September 1930:

We have always believed that the proper function of the System was well expressed in the Tenth Annual Report of the Federal Reserve Board—"The Federal Reserve supplies the needed additions to credit in times of business expansion and takes up the slack in times of business recession." We have therefore necessarily found ourselves out of harmony with the policy recently followed of supplying unneeded additions to credit in a time of business recession, which is the exact antithesis of the rule above stated.

The other Reserve bank governors probably did not accept all these points, but a clear majority opposed the creation of "artifically easy" credit conditions through purchases of government securities.

These few examples illustrate the wide differences in the understanding,

---

[11]*Interest Rates and Stock Speculation*, Macmillan, New York, 1925, pp. vii and viii.

[12]Hearings on H.R. 11806 (April 30, 1928), p. 114.

attitudes, and concepts of the System's functions that still prevailed among Federal Reserve officials in the late 1920s. We shall later encounter many more.

We shall now survey very briefly Federal Reserve objectives and guide-posts as they had evolved by 1928. These will be discussed more fully in later chapters. As already indicated, gold imports and exports and the gold reserve positions of the Federal Reserve banks were not major guides or determinants of Federal Reserve policies during the period from early 1922 to late 1931. Concern about their low reserve ratios may have been one reason for post-poning the adoption of more liberal policies in 1920-1921, and worry about their small amounts of "free gold" became a reason, but by no means the only one, for credit restriction in the latter part of 1931. In the intervening period, when the actual reserve ratios of the Reserve banks were about double the legal minimum, Federal Reserve officials did not restrict credit for the purpose of preventing actual or threatened gold exports, nor did they uni-formly allow gold imports to ease credit conditions. They had evolved other guides and objectives. These included: (1) "credit conditions," (2) prevention of "excessive" uses of credit for speculation in securities, (3) promotion of stability of business activity and price levels, and (4) reestablishment and maintenance of gold standards abroad. The very multiplicity of these guides, with the probability of conflicts among them, would have presented difficult policy problems even if all Federal Reserve officials had been in full agree-ment on their appropriateness as guides and on their relative importance, but the lack of any such agreement magnified the problem.

During 1928-1929 the major conflict was between the objective of re-stricting the amount of credit used in security speculation and the objectives of maintaining high levels of domestic business activity and of helping the international gold standard operate in a viable manner. Throughout the period covered by this volume there remained wide differences of viewpoint both within and outside the System concerning the degree of responsibility and power of the Federal Reserve for promoting high and stable levels of econom-ic activity.

CONCLUSIONS

As Federal Reserve officials faced the problems of 1928, with more problems to follow, the System was still in a formative stage. Federal Reserve officials were still in the process of formulating peacetime objectives and developing ways to implement them. The Federal Reserve Act provided vir-tually no specific directions and little useful guidance. It was vague concerning the allocation of power and responsibility within the System and even vaguer about the objectives toward which Federal Reserve powers were to be di-rected. Nor was specific direction provided by the federal government's own economic policy or a public consensus on the relevant issues. The federal government itself admitted no responsibility for promoting economic stability at home or for reestablishing and maintaining workable gold standards abroad. There was neither an "employment act" nor any strong support within government for the types of commitments that such legislation implies. Federal Reserve officials knew well that a repetition of the war and postwar cycle of inflation-deflation would bring strong protests or worse, but they were not narrowly constrained by an exacting public consensus.

Such conditions almost assured conflict, indecisiveness, and delay in the formulation and execution of Federal Reserve policies. The Federal Reserve Board was usually unwilling to take the initiative in formulating policies and in imposing them on the Reserve banks, however much it might restrict and delay action on proposals made by those banks. A. C. Miller later wrote with respect to policies in 1928:

A partial explanation for the hesitancy on the part of the Board at this time, in the absence of proposals for action from the Reserve banks, may be found in the Federal Reserve Act itself and in the tradition that had grown up in the system. This tradition was that initiative in credit policy should originate with the federal reserve banks, and that the Board's function ordinarily should be to approve or disapprove proposals brought forward by the banks.[13]

A similar view of the Board's role was stated in 1928 by Roy A. Young, then Governor of the Federal Reserve Board:

At the present time we have 12 banks that are autonomous in their operation, and we have one board in Washington that is a supervisory rather than an administrative body.[14]

A Board composed of more forceful men with stronger leadership and stronger convictions concerning the importance of positive Federal Reserve policies might have been more successful in seizing the power of initiative, by persuasion if not by force.

While the Board failed to take the lead, a large part of this power almost inevitably accrued to the Federal Reserve Bank of New York. It was by far the largest bank in the System, located at the very center of the nation's monetary and financial system, and it had the advantage of having a succession of very able governors. First Benjamin Strong and then George Harrison became leaders in policy-making, not only for their own bank but also as members and officials of the OMIC and the Governors' Conference. When they were in full agreement, the Board and the New York Bank could usually persuade the other Reserve banks to agree quickly and cooperate fully, though there were some occasions, notably in the early 1930s, when the other Reserve banks vetoed policies advocated by both New York and the Board. But disagreements between the Board and New York were not infrequent. Some undoubtedly reflected, at least in part, personality clashes and jealousies of institutional prerogatives, but most were based on differences of opinion on policy. Indecisiveness and delay became almost inevitable when New York and the Board disagreed. New York could not act without Board approval, the other Reserve banks were usually unwilling to take the initiative in proposing ambitious positive policies, and the Board rarely tried to persuade the other Reserve banks to propose the policies that it favored.

---

[13]"Responsibility for Federal Reserve Policies: 1927-1929," *American Economic Review*, September 1935, p. 452.

[14]Hearings on H.R. 11806 (May 29, 1928), p. 143.

2

The Economy in the 1920s

To provide a background for later discussions of Federal Reserve policies in 1928 and the years immediately following, this chapter will outline some of the most relevant economic and financial developments during the decade of the 1920s. The first step will be to reexamine some widely accepted views about the American economy, and especially about monetary and financial developments.

INFLATION IN THE 1920s?

Many accounts of this period picture the American economy as one permeated by "inflation" resulting from "excessive supplies of cheap credit." Largely, though not solely, because of the Federal Reserve easy-money policies of 1924 and 1927, amounts of credit "far in excess of the needs of legitimate business" were allegedly forced into the economy, thus creating artificially cheap money, generating speculation, and inducing serious imbalances. As one writer put it, "The economy became a sick patient, sent off on a debauch, maintained on bootleg supplies, from which he will not recover for some time."[1] Most of those holding such views concluded not only that overexpansion of credit and widespread inflation were responsible for the subsequent depression but also that recovery could come only after liquidation and deflation had corrected the imbalances generated earlier.

---

[1]C. Reinold Noyes, "The Gold Inflation in the United States, 1921-1929," *American Economic Review,* June 1933, p. 197. Among the many sources stressing the overexpansion of credit in this period and its inflationary effects are the following:

Charles E. Persons, Credit Expansion, 1920-1929," *Quarterly Journal of Economics,* November 1930, pp. 94-130.
Benjamin M. Anderson, Jr., *The Chase Economic Bulletin* May 16, 1932, p. 307.
Lionel Robbins, *The Great Depression,* Macmillan, London, 1934, pp. 48-54.
A. C. Miller testimony in Hearings on S. Res. 71, pp. 134-135.
Walter E. Spahr testimony in Hearings on H.R. 5357 (Banking Act of 1935), House Banking and Currency Committee, 74th Congress, 1st Session (March 27, 1935), p. 734. Hereafter cited as Hearings on H.R. 5357.

After reading such accounts one would expect to find, on turning to the facts, that the economy was straining its productive capacity, that prices of goods and services were rising rapidly, that the money supply and bank credit were increasing at extraordinary rates, and that interest rates were abnormally low. The actual statistics, though difficult to interpret, paint a rather different picture.

OUTPUT AND ITS PRICES

TABLE 2-1

National Income and Price Levels,
1920-1929 Index Numbers, 1926 = 100

				Wholesale Price Indexes			
Year	Index of GNP at constant prices (1)	Index of GNP at current prices (2)	Implicit price deflator of GNP (3)	All commodities (4)	All commodities other than farm products and foods (5)	Farm products (6)	Consumer price index (7)
1920	73.5	93.2	126.8	154.4	161.3	150.7	113.4
1921	67.3	71.3	105.9	97.6	104.9	88.4	101.1
1922	78.0	76.1	97.6	96.7	102.4	93.8	94.7
1923	87.4	87.4	100.0	100.6	104.3	98.6	96.4
1924	87.2	87.1	99.9	98.1	99.7	100.0	96.7
1925	94.7	95.8	101.2	103.5	102.6	109.8	99.2
1926	100.0	100.0	100.0	100.0	100.0	100.0	100.0
1927	99.8	97.9	98.1	95.4	94.0	99.4	98.1
1928	100.6	100.2	99.6	96.7	92.9	105.9	97.0
1929	106.4	105.9	99.5	95.3	91.6	104.9	97.0

Source: U.S. Bureau of the Census, *Historical Statistics of the United States, Colonial Times to 1957*, Washington, D. C., 1960, pp. 116, 126, and 139. Indexes have been converted by the writer to a 1926 base.

No such excess demand or price inflation was evident in markets for currently produced goods and services. The first column of Table 2-1 shows that real output (GNP at constant prices) fell 8 percent from 1920 to 1921 and then rose with interruptions only in the recession years, 1924 and 1927. Measuring from 1923, the first year of full recovery from the postwar depression, the percentage increases of real output were 14 percent to 1927 and 22 percent to 1929. Though these were sizable increases, the annual rate of increase, compounded, was 3.5 percent, about equal to the long-term growth rate. The economy achieved these increases with no unusual strain on either its capital facilities or the labor force. Though the unemployment rate was low—only 3.2 percent in 1929—there was no general excess demand for labor, and money wage rates did not rise as fast as labor productivity.

Price levels of goods and services were virtually stable after 1923. The "Implicit Price Deflator of GNP" (an index of prices of the total output of goods and services) fell 23 percent from 1920 to 1922, rose slightly to 1923, and then remained remarkably stable, with a slight downward trend, through

1929. Other broad price indexes tell much the same story. Wholesale prices, and especially those for commodities other than farm products and foods, trended slightly downward after 1925, and consumer prices were virtually stable.

In the face of these facts, how could anyone argue that there was price inflation in markets for goods and services? Some replied that there was hidden or implicit price inflation because prices failed to decline as much as costs of production. The latter fell as technological advances increased productivity more rapidly than wage rates and prices of other inputs rose. The result, they claimed, was "profit inflation." A case can indeed be made for a declining price level reflecting increasing productivity per unit of inputs, but it is by no means clear that a stable price level under these conditions represents "price inflation" in any injurious sense of the term.

THE MONEY SUPPLY

TABLE 2-2

The Money Supply, 1920-1929
(amounts in millions of dollars)

June 30	Demand deposits adjusted plus currency outside banks (1)	Percentage change of (1) in preceding year (2)	Demand deposits adjusted plus currency outside banks and time deposits at commercial banks (3)	Percentage change of (3) in preceding year (4)
1920	$23,271		$34,230	
1921	20,790	−12.4%	31,707	−7.4%
1922	21,391	+ 2.9	32,983	+4.0
1923	22,697	+ 6.1	36,071	+9.4
1924	23,062	+ 1.6	37,554	+4.1
1925	24,949	+ 8.2	40,923	+9.0
1926	25,601	+ 2.6	42,726	+4.4
1927	25,539	− 0.2	43,845	+2.6
1928	25,881	+ 1.3	45,683	+4.2
1929	26,179	+ 1.2	45,736	+0.1

Source: Board of Governors of the Federal Reserve System, *Banking and Monetary Statistics,* Washington, D. C., 1943, p. 34.

Contentions that the money supply rose at an "excessive" rate are also hard to support with facts. Column 1 of Table 2-2 shows the money supply, narrowly defined to include only currency outside banks plus demand deposits adjusted. The money supply in this sense declined 12.4 percent in the year following June 1920, but by mid-1923 had regained three-quarters of its losses. From that time through June 1929 there was only one annual increase that could be termed extraordinarily large—the 8.2 percent rise during the year ending in June 1925. In only one other year was the increase as great as 2.6 percent. In the years ending in June 1928 and 1929, the increases were only 1.3 and 1.2 percent, respectively. The annual average rate of increase, compounded, was 2.8 percent from June 1923 to June 1927, 2.7 percent from June 1923 to June 1928, and 2.4 percent from June 1923 to June 1929. These average growth rates were clearly less than that of real output during the period, which we found earlier to be 3.5 percent. One who believes that the money supply, thus defined, should grow proportionally with the nation's productive capacity would argue that monetary policy was not too liberal but too restrictive, especially after 1927.

An examination of the money supply more broadly defined to include not only currency and demand deposits adjusted but also time and savings deposits at commercial banks reveals a somewhat different picture. (See Column 3 of Table 2-2.) This is because time and savings deposits grew more rapidly than demand deposits. The average annual rate of increase, compounded, of the money supply, more broadly defined, was 5 percent from June 1923 to June 1927, 4.8 percent from June 1923 to June 1928, and 4 percent from June 1923 to June 1929. Thus the money supply, defined in this way, grew slightly faster than real output.

However, the significance of the growth of time and savings deposits and their effects on the rate of total spending were then, and remain, difficult to assess. Some tended to believe that dollar-for-dollar they were as powerful as demand deposits as stimulants to spending. Those who thought in terms of credit rather than money pointed out that banks could lend and purchase securities on the basis of time deposits as well as demand deposits. Even some of those who thought in terms of the money supply and the velocity of money, or the demand for money balances, thought that an increase of time deposits could stimulate spending almost as much as an equal amount of demand deposits, even though the time deposits themselves were not used for spending. This could occur because the public held more time deposits and fewer "idle" demand deposits, thus tending to increase the income velocity of money. This increase probably did occur to some extent, since the public could thus get more interest on its funds, and in some cases the banks probably encouraged it because of the lower legal reserve requirements against time and savings deposits or to retain deposits that they might otherwise lose.

It would be a mistake, however, to assume that the entire growth of time deposits represented a shift of the public's preference away from demand deposits—merely a substitution of time deposits for demand deposits. The 1920s witnessed a rapid growth of financial intermediation in general—a tendency of the public to hold a larger part of its assets in the form of claims against financial intermediaries rather than holding directly the securities of the ultimate issuers. This was evidenced by the growth of savings and loan associations, mutual savings banks, insurance companies, and investment trusts. To at least some extent, therefore, the growth of time deposits at commercial banks represented not a shift of the public away from demand deposits, but a preference for holding time deposits rather than other securities or claims. In effect, the public elected to hold more time deposit claims, and the banks were thus enabled to hold the securities and other claims that would otherwise have been held by the public.

That the growth of time and savings deposits represented largely a substitution for other securities and claims rather than for demand deposits receives some support, though not necessarily confirmation, from the data in

TABLE 2-3

The Money Supply and Income Velocity
(amounts in billions of dollars)

Year	GNP at current prices (1)	Demand deposits adjusted plus currency (2)	Income velocity of money (1) ÷ (2) (3)
1920	$ 88.9	$23.5	3.78
1921	74.0	21.2	3.49
1922	74.0	21.5	3.44
1923	86.1	22.7	3.79
1924	87.6	23.5	3.73
1925	91.3	25.5	3.58
1926	97.7	25.9	3.77
1927	96.3	25.9	3.72
1928	98.2	26.2	3.75
1929	104.4	26.4	3.94

Sources: Data for GNP from U.S. Bureau of the Census, *U.S. Historical Statistics from Colonial Times to 1957*, Washington, D.C., 1960, p. 139. The money supply, which reflects annual averages of monthly figures, was computed from data in Friedman and Schwartz, *A Monetary History of the United States, 1869-1960*, Princeton University Press, Princeton, N.J., 1963, pp. 710-712.

Table 2-3. If these deposits were largely a substitute for demand deposits, one would expect that as they grew more rapidly than demand deposits, the income velocity of money, narrowly defined, would rise significantly. Column 3 indicates that this did not occur. Income velocity showed no upward trend from 1923 through 1928, and the small increase in 1929 might well be explained by the high level of interest rates at that time. In view of these facts and the failure of the rate of spending for output to rise as fast as real output, it is difficult to argue persuasively that the money supply, however defined, was increased too rapidly.

However, these data would not have been persuasive to those observers who thought in terms of credit and credit conditions rather than in terms of the money supply. Their use of the term "credit" was sometimes ambiguous, but when they referred to "bank credit" they ordinarily meant total bank loans and investments. Table 2-4 shows the behavior of these at all commercial banks.

Their total moved in a manner roughly parallel with total bank deposits, of which it is the major counterpart. It fell 7 percent from June 1920 to June 1922, but by June 1923 had risen to slightly above the 1920 peak. During the following 6 years it rose 32 percent. The average compound annual rate of increase was 5.2 percent from June 1923 to June 1928, and 4.8 percent from June 1923 to June 1929. Was this, in some meaningful sense, an "excessive" rate of increase of bank credit? This question is difficult to answer, partly because the more relevant quantity is the behavior of the total supply of credit, of which bank credit is only a part, and the share of banks in the total supply is variable. The most significant criterion for judging the behavior of the total supply of credit is to be found in the behavior of such quantities as interest rates, real output, employment, and price levels. We have already seen that demands for output did not overtax productive capacity or induce increases in the prices of output.

TABLE 2-4

Loans and Investments of All Commercial Banks
(amounts in billions of dollars)

June 30 Year	Total Loans and Investments		Total Loans		Total Investments	
	Amount	Percentage change from preceding year	Amount	Percentage change from preceding year	Amount	Percentage change from preceding year
1920	$37.0		$28.6		$ 8.4	
1921	34.7	−6.2%	26.4	−7.7%	8.4	0.0%
1922	34.4	−0.9	25.0	−5.3	9.4	+11.9
1923	37.7	+9.6	27.4	+9.6	10.3	+ 9.6
1924	39.0	+3.4	28.3	+3.3	10.7	+ 3.9
1925	42.0	+7.7	30.2	+6.7	11.8	+10.3
1926	44.3	+5.5	32.1	+6.3	12.2	+ 3.4
1927	46.1	+4.1	32.9	+2.5	13.2	+ 8.2
1928	49.0	+6.3	34.5	+4.9	14.5	+ 9.8
1929	49.8	+1.6	36.1	+4.6	13.7	− 5.5

Source: Board of Governors of the Federal Reserve System, *All Bank Statistics;
United States, 1896-1955*, Washington, D.C., 1959, pp. 34-35.

INTEREST RATES ·

Turning to the facts after reading lurid accounts of "excessive supplies of cheap credit" in the 1920s, one would expect to find "abnormally low" interest rates. Again, one finds no persuasive supporting evidence for such conclusions. One might judge rates on two different bases: Were they low by historical standards? Were they so low as to induce inflationary increases of demands for output? Meaningful historical comparisons of interest rates are difficult to make, partly because financial instruments do not remain unchanged through time and partly because relative heights of interest rates change. However, there is no evidence that interest rates in the 1920s were low by historical standards. In fact, long-term rates, represented by yields on the highest grade of corporate bonds, were high. Sidney Homer concluded that, "This decennial average of prime bond yields for the 1920s was the highest in the eight decades of which it occupied approximately the center."[2] These rates were clearly higher than they had been in the prewar decade, 1904-1913. In fact, the lowest average annual rate in the 1920s was above the highest average rate during any year of the prewar decade. The lowest annual average in the later period was 4.05 percent, and the average for the years 1924-1929 was 4.36 percent. Short-term open-market rates, represented by 4-6-month prime commercial paper, were slightly lower than they had been in the earlier decade. Even at that, they averaged well over 4 percent, and in only one year—1924—did they average as low as 3.98 percent. The second

---

[2]*A History of Interest Rates*, Rutgers University Press, New Brunswick, N. J., 1963, p. 346.

question—"Were rates so low as to induce inflationary increases in demand for output?"—has already been answered in the negative.

OTHER CRITERIA

After examining broad averages and aggregates relating to GNP at constant and current prices, the price level of output, wholesale prices, consumer prices, the money supply, the volume of bank credit, and interest rates, we have found no firm support for the many allegations that the economy of the 1920s was permeated by inflation resulting from excessive supplies of cheap credit. Why, then, were such statements made so frequently during the period and even more frequently in the early 1930s? The answer is complex and probably in several parts. To some extent they reflected inverted reasoning, such as this: "Depressions are brought on by excessive supplies of cheap credit. A depression did begin in 1929. Therefore the preceding period must have been characterized by excessive supplies of cheap credit." However, there were at least two other reasons for these allegations: (1) the "quality" of bank credit, in the sense of the form of bank loans and investments, and (2) the use of credit for speculative purposes, especially in the securities markets and in certain types of real estate.

TABLE 2-5

*Indexes of Loans and Investments in All
Commercial Banks Index, June 1923 = 100*

	Loans				Investments			
June 30 year	*Total*	*Real estate*	*Colla- teral*	*All Other*	*Total*	*USG's*	*Obligations of state and political sub- divisions*	*Other securi- ties*
1920	104.3	76.0	103.5	113.5	81.3	79.0	79.9	84.1
1921	96.3	79.0	94.9	102.7	81.0	70.9	88.2	89.3
1922	91.4	86.5	93.5	91.5	90.6	83.5	97.0	96.2
1923	100.0	100.0	100.0	100.0	100.0	100.0	100.0	100.0
1924	103.2	111.0	103.3	100.7	103.4	92.5	116.9	111.0
1925	110.3	124.3	116.1	102.0	113.8	96.7	129.2	127.2
1926	117.1	136.2	125.3	105.4	118.4	95.9	145.8	134.1
1927	120.2	141.2	133.2	104.6	127.5	97.6	161.8	148.9
1928	125.9	146.0	146.2	105.5	140.1	107.1	169.1	166.0
1929	131.8	148.8	143.0	118.8	132.5	105.8	165.4	151.0

Source: Board of Governors of the Federal Reserve System, *All Bank Statistics*, Washington, D.C., 1959, pp. 34-35.

As noted earlier, adherents of the commercial loan theory, who were most likely to be concerned with the "quality" of credit, held that commercial banks should make only short-term, self-liquidating agricultural, industrial, and commercial loans based on real transactions in goods and services. Such loans were considered greatly superior to any other earning assets for banks. In the first place, they were alleged to be highly liquid for the lending bank.

The unwary assumed that they also provided liquidity for the banking system as a whole. In the second place, the demand for such loans was believed to be the best indicator of the legitimate needs of business. Bank credit was unlikely to exceed the "needs of trade" if confined to this form, but likely, almost by definition, to be "excessive" if extended in other forms. In Table 2-5, loans conforming to this theory are included under the column headed "all other loans," though these figures also include some nonconforming loans. It will be noted that these loans increased far less rapidly than other forms of bank credit after mid-1923. For example, during the next 6 years they rose 18.8 percent, while total bank loans and investments rose 31.8 percent. Increases of the other components during this period were 48.8 percent for loans on real estate, 43 percent for collateral loans, and 32.5 percent for total bank investments.

The failure of these "commercial" loans by banks to increase more rapidly does not seem to have resulted from any decreased willingness of banks to make them. Rather, it reflected a decrease of business demands for such loans relative to the scope of their operations. Many reasons have been given for this decline of demand. Most commonly mentioned were the greater speed of transport and better inventory controls that lessened the need for goods in process relative to output; growth in the size of business firms that gave more firms access to the long-term securities markets; a growing preference for financing at least minimum working capital needs by long-term issues; and the favorable terms on which stock issues could be sold. Yet the commercial loan advocates insisted that banks should acquire only this type of asset. One shudders to contemplate the inadequate growth of the money supply that would have resulted if bankers had followed their advice. But the commercial loan advocates themselves shuddered as they saw that a major part of the expansion of bank credit was in mortgages and other loans on real estate, loans based on securities and other collateral, obligations of state and local governments not "related to production and trade," and corporation bonds and other securities. To them two conclusions were obvious. First, the banks, individually and collectively, were becoming illiquid and could easily become "frozen." Second, bank credit was expanding excessively; it was excessive because it exceeded the increase in demands for commercial loans.

Another reason for the allegation that credit expansion was excessive was the use of credit for speculative purposes, especially in real estate and securities. The most spectacular speculation in real estate was in Florida in the mid-1920s, but real estate speculation was far from absent in other areas. There had been a real shortage of dwellings and commercial buildings in the early years of the decade because of such factors as the interruption of construction during the war, the continued increase of population, urbanization, and rising incomes. Large profits and capital gains were realized by construction companies and real estate developers, and these led in some cases to excessive optimism, speculation, and even outright fraud. We shall later discuss in some detail the use of credit for speculation in securities.

To many, the very availability of credit for speculative purposes was *prima facie* evidence that the total supply of credit was excessive. They seemed to reason that "legitimate" demands for credit would be met first, and that only the excess supply would go into speculative uses. The policy implication was that the total supply of credit should be so restricted that none would be left over for undesirable types of speculation. These inferences are of doubtful validity.

If the preceding section has not proved conclusively that there was not in any sense an overexpansion of the total supply of credit before 1928, it should at least have shown that those who contended that the whole economy was permeated by inflation and that the total supply of credit was clearly and grossly excessive have not proved their case. Especially suspect are those judgments based on the types of credit extended by the banks or on the fact that credit came to be used for speculative purposes. My own judgment is that a significantly smaller expansion of the money supply, however defined, and of bank credit during the period before 1928 might indeed have resulted in less speculative activity, but only at the cost of lessened employment and production.

STOCK SPECULATION

As already mentioned, a major objective of Federal Reserve policies in 1928 and 1929 was to curb "excessive" uses of credit for speculation in common stocks. This was no new consideration for the Federal Reserve. To lessen the importance of the New York call-loan market and to divert funds away from stock speculation and into "legitimate business" was an important purpose of the Federal Reserve Act. During World War I and the postwar inflation of 1919-1920, stock speculation and the use of credit for this purpose became major issues within the System. Moreover, there were few months after 1923 when the Federal Reserve ignored stock-market behavior in making its policies.[3] The influence of this consideration was usually toward a policy of less ease or more restriction.

Many accounts of stock-market behavior in the 1920s, and especially in the later years of the boom, are more dramatic than analytical. There were certainly elements of drama—human greed and hopes of getting rich quick without work, feverish gambling, financial swashbuckling by bulls and bears, pool operations and manipulations, buying on slim margins, great newspaper headlines, and, most dramatic of all, the final crash. On reading some of these accounts one gets the impression that the entire market and its participants were insane, completely out of touch with reality. The crash itself and the following long decline of stock prices seemed to confirm this view. No one can deny that excesses did occur, with serious consequences, or that the prices of many stocks rose to unrealistic levels. But such dramatic accounts tend to exaggerate and to ignore basic forces and developments in the economy which justified large increases in stock prices during the decade. It is even possible that the levels of prices reached in 1928, though not at the peak in 1929, might have proved to be quite justified if the economy had continued to

---

[3]See Lester V. Chandler, *Benjamin Strong, Central Banker*, Brookings, Washington, D. C., 1959, various citations in the index under "stock market."

TABLE 2-6

Index of Common Stock Prices, 1915-1929
Annual Averages, 1926 = 100

Year	Total (1)	Industrials (2)	Railroads (3)	Public utilities (4)
Ave. 1910-1914	70.7	46.7	95.1	79.6
1915	66.2	51.7	80.9	76.0
1916	76.2	67.2	86.9	82.6
1917	68.3	62.6	76.3	74.4
1918	60.7	56.7	68.7	59.9
1919	70.7	72.6	70.1	60.3
1920	64.2	66.1	64.0	54.5
1921	55.2	51.6	61.8	57.8
1922	67.7	64.7	72.7	70.9
1923	69.0	66.6	71.9	73.8
1924	72.8	69.7	76.7	78.9
1925	89.7	88.4	89.5	94.9
1926	100.0	100.0	100.0	100.0
1927	118.3	118.5	119.1	116.0
1928	149.9	154.3	128.5	148.9
1929	190.3	189.4	147.3	234.6

Source: Cowles Commission for Research in Economics, *Common Stock Indexes,*
1871-1937, Bloomington, Ind.: Principia Press, 1938, pp. 67-73.

grow, interrupted by no more than minor depressions. In any case, a brief look at some of the relevant facts will be useful.

Column 1 of Table 2-6 shows that in the depression year 1921 the average of all stock prices included in the index had fallen to a level 22 percent below the average for the 5 year prewar period, 1910-1914. In 1923, when stock prices had barely regained their prewar level, some observers were already claiming they were excessive. Then they continued to climb. Increases from the 1923 average were 71 percent to 1927, 117 percent to 1928, and 176 percent to 1929. Shares of public utilities rose even more. These are indeed large and rapid increases, especially those in 1928 and 1929. However, the level, and changes in the level, of stock prices without any reference to actual or prospective dividends and earnings have almost no significance. Shares are, after all, only pieces of paper whose value is presumably based upon the income that will accrue to them. Increases in actual and prospective earnings and dividends per share would normally justify price increases. Both increased markedly during this period. Average dividends per share increased about 38 percent from 1923 to 1927 and 61 percent from 1923 to 1929.[4]

The most meaningful test of the "reasonableness" of stock prices would be to compare current prices with future dividends or earnings per share, but since the future is not known, a more common practice is to compare current prices and current dividends or earnings per share. In Table 2-7 "dividend yield" for any year is arrived at by dividing dividends for the year by the average price of stocks for the year; this is the percentage of dividends to

[4]Cowles Commission for Research in Economics, *Common Stock Indexes,*
1871- 1937, Bloomington, Ind., Principia Press, 1938, p. 389.

TABLE 2-7

Dividend Yields and Earnings-Price Ratios for Common Stocks, 1915-1929

Year	All Stocks		Industrials		Railroads		Public Utilities	
	Dividend yield	Earnings-price ratio[a]	Dividend yield	Earnings-price ratio[a]	Dividend yield	Earnings-price ratio[a]	Dividend yield	Earnings-price ratio[a]
1915	4.96%	10.57%	4.14%	13.46%	5.21%	9.27%	6.01%	9.37%
1916	5.62	16.17	6.16	24.75	5.13	11.01	5.72	9.77
1917	7.90	15.11	9.78	21.89	6.12	10.50	6.75	8.92
1918	7.24	13.15	7.71	15.86	6.32	10.49	7.57	8.48
1919	5.75	10.63	5.18	11.30	6.26	9.85	7.37	8.56
1920	6.13	10.08	5.54	12.06	6.81	5.84	8.06	10.67
1921	6.49	4.22	5.84	d 0.61b	7.08	10.10	8.29	12.23
1922	5.80	8.25	5.37	7.26	5.95	8.70	7.62	12.30
1923	5.94	11.38	5.40	10.70	6.29	12.77	7.59	11.41
1924	5.87	10.27	5.25	9.36	6.44	11.91	7.35	10.84
1925	5.19	11.19	4.75	11.22	5.66	11.95	6.13	9.60
1926	5.32	10.05	5.24	9.56	5.52	12.23	5.57	9.99
1927	4.77	7.57	4.72	7.20	4.89	8.68	4.96	8.24
1928	3.98	7.30	3.82	7.02	4.76	8.98	4.09	7.15
1929	3.48	6.23	3.65	6.31	4.29	8.83	2.29	4.45
Sept. 1929c	2.92		3.19		3.96		1.69	

[a]Data for the earnings-price ratio apply to a smaller number of stocks because earnings are not available for all stocks included in the broader price index.

b d = loss

c Data in the last line are from Standard Statistics Company, *Standard Statistical Bulletin*, January 1932, pp. 120-121.

Source: Cowles Commission for Research in Economics, *Common Stock Indexes, 1871-1937*, Bloomington, Indiana: Principia Press, 1938, pp. 373, 405.

current prices. Similarly, the "earnings-price ratio" is simply the percentage of earnings per share to the average price per share during the year. Note that these do not include any expected increases in dividends or earnings.

In 1923 the average dividend yield was 5.94 percent, and the earnings-price ratio 11.38 percent. In 1927, the year preceding the period that we shall study and a year in which many were already saying that stock prices were at unsustainable levels, the dividend yield was 4.77 percent and the earnings-price ratio 7.57 percent. Even in retrospect it is impossible to say with certainty that these prices were "unreasonably" high. Defenders of existing, or even higher, price levels pointed out that dividend yields alone were about equal to yields on high-grade corporate bonds, that dividends were protected by undistributed corporate profits, that dividends could be expected to grow because of both plowed-in earnings and the progress of the economy, and that the public had become willing to hold stocks at lower yields because it was now more familiar with these securities and had more faith in the future stability of the economy.

In 1928 and 1929 stock prices rose relative to both dividends and earnings. The average dividend yield was 3.98 percent in 1928 and 3.48 percent in 1929. The last line in Table 2-7 shows that in September 1929, the last full month before the crash, prices had risen so much that average dividend yields had fallen to 2.92 percent on all stocks in the index, to 3.19 percent on industrials, to 3.96 percent on railroads, and to 1.69 percent on public utilities. These are, of course, averages; the prices of speculative favorites rose far more and their yields were indeed vulnerable. Anything that shook confidence in the future growth of earnings, dividends, and prices could bring a tumble.

In trying to assess Federal Reserve policies during this period one faces these questions: "At what stage in the rise of stock prices did they become 'unreasonably' high? When did prices become so high that they would have proved unsustainable even if the nation had avoided a serious depression?" Though no one can answer with confidence, I would put the date no earlier than mid-1928 and probably later.

These questions may appear irrelevant to Federal Reserve policy in view of the many statements by Federal Reserve officials that the behavior of stock prices, and even stock speculation as such, were none of their concern; and that their job was to regulate credit, to prevent "absorption of credit in the stock market" and "abuses of Federal Reserve credit." They insisted repeatedly that they were not "arbiters of stock values." It is difficult to take these protestations at face value; the thinking and policy decisions of Federal Reserve officials must have been influenced to some extent by the rise of stock prices and fear of a later sharp decline of prices that would have serious economic repercussions. However, since Federal Reserve officials insisted that their concern was with credit, and their policies related to money and credit, we shall now turn our attention to the use of credit for security speculation during this period.

There can be no doubt that large amounts of credit were used for speculation in stocks during the late 1920s, but it is impossible to say how much. This problem confounded Federal Reserve officials, especially in the first half of 1929 when they embarked on a program of direct action to prevent the use of Federal Reserve credit for speculative purposes. To distinguish "speculation" from other motives and activities was only one of their problems. They could not estimate accurately the total amount of credit used for "speculation" nor identify the particular loans made for this purpose. One way out was to define speculative loans as those loans made with securities as collateral. But this was an inadequate and even misleading indicator of the amounts borrowed for speculative purposes. If one believes the stories of the day, some speculated with money derived not from loans with security collateral but from loans on their unsecured notes, their businesses, their houses, and their other assets. How pervasive this practice was or what amounts were involved we do not know. On the other hand, by no means all the proceeds from loans collateraled by securities were used for speculative purposes. Many were put directly to consumption or business uses.

TABLE 2-8

Principal Loans on Security Collateral Selected Dates, 1920-1929
(amounts in millions of dollars)

	Loans to Brokers in New York City				Other Loans on Security Collateral by Member Banks			
Date	Total (1)	By New York City banks (2)	By outside banks (3)	By others (4)	Total (5)	To brokers and dealers outside New York City (6)	Other (7)	Grand Total (8)
June 30, 1920	1,400	465	395	560	4,185			5,585
June 30, 1921	1,000	365	255	380	3,780			4,780
June 30, 1922	1,670	790	370	510	3,340			5,010
June 30, 1923	1,730	800	420	510	3,730			5,460
June 30, 1924	1,740	950	380	410	4,020			5,760
June 30, 1925	2,660	1,150	770	740	4,798			7,458
June 30, 1926	2,930	1,060	780	1,090	5,481			8,411
June 30, 1927	3,570	1,130	970	1,470	6,056			9,626
Dec. 31, 1927	4,430	1,550	1,050	1,830	n.a.			n.a.
June 30, 1928	4,900	1,080	960	2,860	7,028			11,928
Dec. 31, 1928	6,440	1,640	915	3,885	7,348	975	6,373	13,788
June 29, 1929	7,070	1,360	665	5,045	7,734	921	6,813	14,804
Oct. 4, 1929	8,525	1,095	790	6,640	8,109	939	7,170	16,634
Dec. 31, 1929	4,110	1,200	460	2,450	8,488	803	7,685	12,598

Source: Board of Governors of the Federal Reserve System, *Banking and Monetary Statistics,* Washington, D.C., 1943, pp. 76, 79, and 494. These figures are only approximate and do not include all loans on security collateral. The most obvious omission is nonmember bank lending on collateral other than to brokers and dealers in New York City.

Table 2-8 shows the principal types of loans on security collateral. The first columns relate to borrowings by brokers and dealers in securities in New York City from all types of lenders—from banks and from various nonbank sources. Most of the proceeds of these loans were used to purchase and carry securities on margin for the accounts of brokers and dealers themselves or, in much larger amounts, for the accounts of their customers. Most of these were

properly considered "speculative." However, some were, in effect, for the
"business purposes" of dealers—to carry inventories of commercial paper, acceptances, government obligations, and other securities, and to finance the
holding of new issues until they could be sold. In the late 1920s, when new
security flotations were large, the amounts of loans demanded for such purposes must not have been insignificant in amount.

Loans to New York City brokers and dealers were only a part of total
loans based on security collateral. As shown in Column 5 of Table 2-8, member bank loans on security collateral to borrowers other than New York City
brokers and dealers exceeded bank loans to those brokers and dealers during
most of the period. This form of lending was quite common before the war
and it grew in the 1920s. For what purposes were the proceeds of these loans
used? Some assumed that virtually all were used to purchase and carry the
securities which served as their collateral or other similar securities, and that
most of them were "speculative." This was clearly true of some, perhaps the
larger part, but certainly not of all. Many borrowers offered security collateral
to get loans for consumption or for various types of business uses. However,
no one knew in what proportions the proceeds of collateral loans were used
for the various types of purposes, or how to identify speculative loans. These
issues became of real importance as the Federal Reserve tried to discourage
speculative loans. Some officials wanted to discourage all loans on security
collateral, while others believed that they should concentrate on loans to
brokers.

Before turning again to the data in Table 2-8, it will be useful to
consider briefly the two principal methods used by the Federal Reserve in its
attempts during 1928-1929 to curb the "absorption of credit" in stock speculation: (1) general credit restriction through open-market operations in government securities and increases in discount and bill buying rates; and (2) "direct action" aimed specifically at limiting speculative loans. The first tended
to restrict the total supply of credit and left to competition among private
lenders and borrowers the function of determining the extent to which the
various specific types of credit, speculative and nonspeculative, would be restricted. The second put member banks currently borrowing from the Federal
Reserve under pressure to reduce, or even to eliminate, their loans of this
type. Note that direct action was confined to member banks in debt to the
Federal Reserve, and that these banks could conform either by reducing their
speculative loans or by paying off their borrowings from the Federal Reserve;
they could do the latter in various ways, including borrowing from other
sources, selling investments, or reducing other loans. Direct action did not
apply at all to those member banks not in debt to the Federal Reserve, or to
nonmember banks, or to loans by others.

Table 2-8 provides several important facts about loans to brokers and
dealers in New York City. Perhaps most striking are their rapid growth during
the 1920s and their magnitude in early October 1929, just before the crash.
During the depression year 1921 they were abnormally low, only $1 billion in
June. In the next 3 years they rose to $1.74 billion, and by the end of 1927
they had reached $4.4 billion. Then they grew $2 billion during 1928 and
another $2.1 billion during the first 9 months of 1929. Thus, they nearly

doubled after the end of 1927. At $8.5 billion on October 4, 1929, they were indeed large, both in absolute amount and in relation to any previous levels. However, their relative size should not be exaggerated. For example, at their peak in 1929 they were equal to only 9.8 percent of the total value of shares listed on the New York Stock Exchange.[5] This hardly confirms the view that most stocks were being held with borrowed money. Moreover, it should be borne in mind that at the peak bank loans to New York brokers and dealers, at $1.9 billion, were equal to less than 4 percent of total bank loans and investments.

The table also shows the great importance of brokers' loans by "others." These are, of course, brokers' loans by all lenders other than commercial banks and were often referred to disapprovingly as "bootleg loans." We have only limited information about the sources of these loans. However, answers to a questionnaire addressed to 7 large New York banks suggest that when these loans were at their peak in 1929, about 58 percent came from business corporations, 18 percent from individuals, 8 percent from investment trusts, 7.5 percent from foreign banks, and 2 percent from other foreign sources.[6] Column 4 shows that at the peak on October 4, 1929, these loans by others accounted for 78 percent of total loans to brokers. Brokers' loans by banks rarely rose above their level at the end of 1927, and in 1929 they were below that level. Thus loans by others accounted for the entire increase of brokers' loans after 1927 and for 92 percent of the increase after mid-1924. These facts are highly relevant to Federal Reserve attempts to curb total loans to brokers through curbing loans by banks in debt to their Reserve banks.

Why was the Federal Reserve so concerned with curbing the volume of "speculative loans"? Federal Reserve officials might have given several answers, but the one emphasized in 1928-1929 was that "The use of credit for speculative purposes absorbs credit and tends to reduce the supply and raise the cost of credit for legitimate business purposes." References to the "absorption of credit in the stock market" were widespread.[7] The whole issue became obscured by definitional problems and muddled thinking.

Because of its crucial importance to an understanding and assessment of Federal Reserve policies, we shall consider briefly this question: "Do loans to brokers 'absorb credit' in the meaningful sense of decreasing the supply and raising the cost of funds for business and other uses?" It is, of course, true that with any given amount of bank reserves and a given level of reserve requirements, the more the banks lend to brokers, the less can they lend to others or use to purchase securities. This is because loans to brokers create deposits against which reserves must be held. It is also true that a "nonbank" lender to brokers cannot lend the same money to someone else. However, this

---

[5]Report of the President of the New York Stock Exchange, Year Ending May 1, 1930, p. 107.

[6]Hearings on S. Res. 71, p. 1024.

[7]For a discussion of the issues and for citations of relevant literature, see Charles O. Hardy, *Credit Policies of the Federal Reserve System*, Brookings, Washington, D. C., 1932.

statement concentrates attention on the form of the loan and ignores the use of the money proceeds of the loan. Where does the money go? It does not disappear. In the first instance it goes into the deposit balances of brokers, and many have assumed that it stayed there. However, they ignore the fact that brokers' deposit balances are extremely small relative to the value of their transactions and that they can handle very large increases in transactions with only very small increases in their deposits. In general, brokers borrow not to make net additions to their deposit balances, but only to meet the excess of their outpayments over their receipts. Thus we can be fairly confident that virtually all the borrowed money will be transferred quickly to the sellers of shares, who can use it as they see fit. They could, of course, add it to their idle balances, but they also have the attractive alternatives of using it for consumption, to finance their own business needs, to buy bonds, or to purchase such short-term liquid assets as call loans, acceptances, and so on. In some cases the sellers of shares may lend indirectly to the buyers.

Thus we find that the money proceeds of loans to brokers are not "absorbed or locked up in the stock market." Borrowers buying stock serve as intermediaries, borrowing money to be transferred to sellers of shares, and these recipients determine the uses to which the money will be put. Moreover, it is not at all clear that a rise in demands for brokers' loans, and in the actual amount of brokers' loans, will tend to raise the general levels of interest rates. For example, the sellers of shares may use the money to finance their own business needs, thus reducing their own demands for loans, or to increase their loans to others.

What is likely, however, is that rising optimism concerning the future of share prices will tend to change the relative levels of interest rates and current dividend yields. Expecting compensation in the form of capital gains, buyers become willing to buy stock at lower current dividend yields, borrowing more for the purpose if necessary. This does not necessarily mean that the absolute level of interest rates will be increased, only that interest rates will be higher relative to the falling current dividend yields on shares. For example, rising share prices decrease the current cost of equity financing, and increased financing through share issues tends to decrease business demands for loans.

In view of the complexity of the subject it would be rash to assert that rising demands for loans on securities contributed nothing to the rise of interest rates in 1928 and 1929. However, one thing is clear: A far more powerful force toward higher interest rates was the Federal Reserve's restrictive monetary policy.

INTERNATIONAL MONETARY RELATIONSHIPS

Another important consideration in Federal Reserve policy, noted earlier, was the reestablishment of an international gold standard and the maintenance of viable monetary conditions abroad. Most countries had returned to gold by the beginning of 1928. Under this new gold standard system, many central banks held at least a part of their international reserves in the form of foreign exchange, mostly as claims against the British pound sterling and the American dollar. After the reestablishment of stable exchange rates and under the relatively prosperous conditions of the late 1920s, short-term funds became internationally mobile.

By 1928 the new system had already begun to show strains, and more appeared later. These were related to inappropriate exchange rate relationships and to tendencies toward maldistribution of the world's monetary gold. We shall confine our attention to three countries—Great Britain, the United States, and France.

Monetary conditions in Britain were of worldwide importance for several reasons: Sterling was one of the two principal currencies held as reserves by other central banks; London was one of the great international money and capital markets; and Britain was a major international trader. Soon after Britain's return to gold in mid-1925 it became increasingly apparent that the exchange rate on sterling was too high. Throughout this period, Britain was unable to reconcile satisfactorily her objectives of promoting employment and growth at home and of maintaining equilibrium in her balance of payments. To achieve the latter she had to follow monetary and fiscal policies so restrictive that a large residue of unemployment remained. To make matters worse, she had only a slender gold reserve and owed large short-term liabilities to foreigners. Britain thus had a strong interest in the maintenance of relatively easy monetary and credit conditions in other countries, and especially in the United States.

The latter was in a far stronger position. In 1924, before other countries returned to gold, the United States held 40 percent of the world's monetary gold and tended to gain more when her capital exports were small. The balance of trade and services account was favorable every year. When her capital exports were large, the United States increased the gold and dollar reserves of the rest of the world, but when her capital exports dwindled, as they did in the latter half of 1928 and in 1929, the rest of the world lost reserves to the United States. Britain was one of the principal sufferers, but not the only one.

The *de facto* stabilization of the French franc in mid-1926 introduced new stress in the international situation. Before that time, France had suffered from monetary and fiscal disorders at home, the franc had depreciated sharply in exchange markets, and French people and business firms had accumulated large amounts of foreign exchange. The tide turned abruptly when the French achieved stabilization, ending domestic inflation and making it clear that the exchange rate on the franc would fall no further and would probably rise. There was a veritable flight to the franc as Frenchmen, and probably others as well, rushed to buy francs and supply foreign currencies. To stop the rise of the franc, which was having adverse effects on French exports, the Bank of France supplied francs in exchange for foreign currencies. Well before the *de jure* stabilization of 1928, the Bank of France had accumulated very large holdings of foreign exchange, chiefly claims on sterling and dollars. Moreover, it was soon discovered that the new exchange rate on the franc, 3.92 cents, undervalued this currency. Thus her favorable balance of payments enabled France to increase still further her holdings of gold and foreign currencies. To make matters worse, France proved to be a very reluctant holder of foreign exchange as international reserves, feeling that a first-rate country should hold her international reserves in the form of gold, not claims against foreign currencies. She therefore tried intermittently to withdraw gold from New York and London. The former could lose gold without embarrassment; London could not. Actual and threatened French withdrawals of gold from London were a source of disquiet throughout the period under review. Also, many other countries were disturbed by the tendency for monetary gold to be concentrated in the United States and France.

The Federal Reserve assisted the restoration and maintenance of gold standards abroad in several ways. (1) The first was by extending stabilization credits. Several countries received such aid at the time of their stabilization in the 1920s and again when their currencies came under stress in the early 1930s. (2) The second was by purchases of currencies, chiefly sterling, when these were weak in exchange markets. The Federal Reserve purchased sterling on several occasions, usually in the autumn. (3) The last was through its general monetary and credit policies. The influence of this consideration on the Federal Reserve was usually toward more liberal, or less restrictive, policies. To promote capital exports and avoid more restrictive monetary conditions abroad were clearly two purposes, though not the only ones, of the

TABLE 2-9

Foreign Security Issues in the United States, 1924-1929
(amounts in millions of dollars)

Period	For new capital	For refunding	Total	Change in U.S. gold stock
1924—1st half	270	94	364	+244
2nd half	700	153	853	+ 11
1925—1st half	449	109	558	−139
2nd half	636	124	760	+ 39
1926—1st half	529	92	621	+ 48
2nd half	597	72	669	+ 45
1927—1st half	682	103	785	+ 95
2nd half	655	137	792	−208
1928—1st half	858	192	1,050	−270
2nd half	405	34	439	+ 32
1929—1st half	460	19	479	+183
July-Sept., 1929	80	1	81	+ 48
Oct.-Dec., 1929	134	14	148	− 88

Source: Board of Governors of the Federal Reserve System, *Banking and Monetary Statistics,* Washington, D.C., 1943, pp. 488-489, 536-537.

famous easy-money policies of 1924 and 1927. However, we shall find that such considerations were not powerful enough to prevent the Federal Reserve from adopting highly restrictive policies in 1928 and 1929, policies which were very painful for Britain and many other countries.

Table 2-9 shows the behavior of foreign security issues in the United States and of the nation's monetary gold stock during the period 1924–1927. These foreign issues do not, of course, include all international long-term capital movements of the United States, but they will serve as a rough indicator of changes in those movements. During the early years of the decade, when American capital exports were small, the country's gold stock rose almost continuously, reaching a peak of $4.2 billion in late 1924. Then capital exports rose sharply, partly because of the easy-money policy of 1924 and partly because of improved conditions abroad. The United States actually lost $139 million of gold to the rest of the world in the first half of 1925, but gold imports were resumed during the next 2 years. At the end of June 1927 the American gold stock was only $88 million above its peak in 1924. At least partly because of the easy-money policy of 1927, American capital exports during the year following June 1927 were at their highest levels of the decade. Net gold exports amounted to $478 million during this one year. Note that restrictive Federal Reserve policies did not result in either a decline of capital exports or a halt in the redistribution of American gold during the first half of 1928. However, foreign issues declined sharply in the latter half of 1928 and in 1929, and virtually ceased during the period July–September 1929. To make matters worse, funds from other countries flowed to the United States, some to be lent in the call-loan market and some to purchase stocks. Gold exports ceased, and gold imports amounted to $263 million in the period from June 1928 to October 1929. However, these gold losses to the United States are inadequate indicators of the monetary restriction suffered by other countries. Probably more powerful were the restrictive monetary policies imposed by those countries to prevent their gold losses from becoming even larger.

The dwindling flows of loan funds from the United States, actual gold losses, and restrictive monetary policies imposed to prevent even larger gold losses undoubtedly served to weaken economies abroad and to make them vulnerable to depression. Federal Reserve officials, at least those in New York and Washington, recognized these adverse effects of their policies, though they may have underestimated their magnitude. It was largely because of fear of these effects, as well as concern for the consequences for business conditions at home, that Federal Reserve officials did not take even more vigorous actions to curb stock speculation.

3

1928—Year of Restriction

At the end of 1927 the Federal Reserve was still operating under the easy-money policy adopted on July 27 of that year and reaffirmed at the meeting of the Open-Market Investment Committee on November 1. Discount rates at all the Reserve banks were 3 percent, and buying rates on prime bankers' acceptances ranged from 3 percent on those with maturities of 1-15 days to 3 3/4 percent on the longest maturities. System holdings of government securities had increased about $225 million since the end of July, and bill holdings had risen $220 million, the two together supplying about $425 million of reserve funds to the banking system. However, $350 million of these funds had been absorbed by a $200 million decrease in the country's monetary gold stock and a $150 million increase of currency in circulation, most of the latter occurring during the Christmas period. Member bank reserves had risen $210 million, or about 8 percent, but member bank debts to the Reserve banks had increased $140 million. Partly because of the Federal Reserve's policies, but partly also because of the current business recession, interest rates in the market were somewhat below their levels during the early part of the year. Rates on 4-6-month commercial paper were at 4 percent, those on 90-day acceptances at 3.25 percent, and those on call loans ranged between 3.50 and 4.18 percent during December.

When the OMIC met in Washington on January 12, 1928, it reviewed developments since its last meeting on November 1. It was generally pleased with the results, and especially those on the international front. As a memorandum prepared for the Committee stated:

> When Federal Reserve discount rates were reduced last August and September, money conditions abroad were an important consideration. Sterling and other European exchanges were weak and stringent money conditions abroad, with increasing discount rates and consequent pressure on unemployment and declining purchasing power for our own goods, appeared inevitable unless money were easier in this country.
>
> Now the situation is quite changed. Much that was hoped to be accomplished by our rate action has been accomplished. Most of the European exchanges are above par and European countries have both taken gold from us and increased their holdings of dollars. Since the first of the year the exchanges have declined as bills drawn in dollars have come due and short coverings have become less of an influence. Firmer money here would put more pressure on the exchanges and might possibly lead to some rate advances abroad, but

European money markets are now more firmly entrenched and much more able to take care of themselves.

The business outlook at home was hopeful but not yet rosy. In December, the latest month for which Federal Reserve officials could have had information, the industrial production index had risen only slightly from the low point reached in November and was still 10 percent below the peak levels reached in the spring of 1927 and the autumn of 1926. Factory employment was 8 percent and factory payrolls 6 percent below their earlier peaks. Officials at the meeting did not believe that existing levels of unemployment were serious or that the recession would develop into a depression, but they were not certain that recovery had begun or that it would continue. For this reason they were disposed to be cautious in moving toward a firmer credit policy.

However, they were disquieted by two other developments. One was the large increase in bank credit during the preceding six months, the largest in any half-year since 1924. Total bank loans and investments had risen over 3.5 percent since mid-1927. The other disquieting development was the rise of stock prices and brokers' loans. Stock prices had risen nearly 14 percent and brokers' loans 24 percent since June. Increases since December 1926 were 26 percent for stock prices and 36 percent for brokers' loans.

It was under these conditions that Federal Reserve officials decided to move toward a firmer policy, but to do so cautiously in view of the business situation. They were especially cautious about increasing discount rates. The Federal Reserve Board, meeting on January 11 with Secretary of the Treasury Andrew Mellon in the chair, arrived at a "consensus of opinion that no increase of rates should be made within the next week or ten days. . . ." Members of the OMIC, meeting in Washington the next day, expressed similar judgments. Deputy Governor Case reported that some directors of the New York Bank believed that no action should be taken to raise rates until they had further opportunity to study the apparent beginning of an upward trend in business. Governors E. R. Fancher of Cleveland and James B. McDougal of Chicago also referred to the apparent improvement in business but were apprehensive that advances in discount rates might retard this tendency. Deputy Governor William H. Hutt stated that the officers and directors of the Philadelphia Reserve Bank were not so optimistic about business and would probably not raise its discount rate unless others raised theirs and forced the issue. The consensus was that there should be no immediate increase in the discount rate at any Federal Reserve bank, that the situation should be watched carefully during the next few weeks, and that "in the interim any correction in money market tendencies should be through operations in the Open-Market Investment Account."

The resolutions adopted by the OMIC at the conclusion of the meeting reflected these judgments:

1. The object of the policy adopted on November 1, 1927, has been accomplished.
2. The Committee program should now work towards somewhat firmer money conditions as far as necessary to check unduly rapid further increases in the volume of credit.

3. In order to accomplish this program the Committee would expect to sell further amounts of Government securities and if necessary to deal with gold movements in such manner as is necessary to carry out the program.

In fact, the first steps toward such a policy had been taken even before the meeting, as the OMIC had sold $50 million of government securities that had been purchased earlier to offset the restrictive effects of gold exports. Policies were to become more restrictive, and increases in discount and bill-buying rates were to come sooner than expected.

THE FIRST PHASE OF ACTIVE RESTRICTION, JANUARY-AUGUST 1928

For analytical purposes it will be useful to divide the longer period of restriction extending from the end of 1927 to the stock-market crash in October 1929 into four subperiods: (1) the first phase of active restriction, January-August 1928; (2) period of inaction, August 1928-January 1929; (3) direct action, February-June 1929; and (4) the final phase, July-October 1929.

It will be helpful to summarize briefly some of the principal monetary developments in the first 7 months of 1928. During this period 8 of the Reserve banks increased their discount rates in 3 equal steps from 3 1/2 to 5 percent, and the other 4 raised their rates in 2 steps from 3 1/2 to 4 1/2 percent. Bill-buying rates were increased 7 times, the rate applicable to the shortest maturities rising from 3 to 4 3/4 percent. The reserve positions of member banks were put under pressure both by gold losses and by decreases in Federal Reserve holdings of government securities and acceptances.

Table 3-1 presents information relating to the reserve position of member banks. Column 1, indicating the total volume of member bank reserves, shows that in July 1928 these had fallen $102 million, or 4 percent below their average level in January, though they were still slightly above their average levels in 1926 and 1927. However, the banks were able to avoid much greater losses of reserves only by sharply increasing their debts to the Federal Reserve. Column 2 shows that member bank borrowings, which averaged $465 million in January, rose steadily to more than $1 billion in June and then remained above that level through September. This was far above their average levels in 1926 and 1927. In fact, this was their highest level since 1921. During the 4 months, June-September 1928, member bank borrowings from the Federal Reserve were equal to more than 45 percent of their total reserves. We shall find that there were only 3 months during the entire period from May 1928 to September 1929 when average member bank borrowings amounted to less than 40 percent of their total reserves. Column 3 tells the same story in different terms. "Unborrowed reserves" reflects the amounts of reserves that banks have acquired from sources other than borrowing at the Federal Reserve. These averaged $1,637 million in 1926, $1,848 million in 1927, and $1,961 million in January 1928. Yet by August 1928 they had fallen to $1,213 million, representing decreases of 38 percent from the January level, 34 percent from the 1927 average, and 26 percent from the 1926

TABLE 3-1

Member Bank Reserve Positions, 1928-1929
(In millions of dollars, averages of daily figures for period shown)

	Member Bank reserves (1)	Member Bank borrowings at the Federal reserve (2)	Un-borrowed reserves (1) − (2) (3)	Excess reserves (4)	Net free reserves (4) − (2) (5)
1926	2,209	572	1,637		
1927	2,290	442	1,848		
1928					
January	2,426	465	1,961		
February	2,368	471	1,897		
March	2,365	513	1,852		
April	2,396	661	1,735		
May	2,388	836	1,552		
June	2,355	1,019	1,336		
July	2,324	1,090	1,234		
August	2,274	1,061	1,213		
September	2,314	1,064	1,250		
October	2,331	975	1,357		
November	2,352	897	1,455		
December	2,367	1,013	1,354		
1929					
January	2,387	849	1,538	53	− 796
February	2,357	875	1,482	46	− 829
March	2,337	956	1,381	41	− 915
April	2,308	990	1,318	36	− 954
May	2,296	951	1,345	33	− 918
June	2,314	974	1,340	42	− 932
July	2,334	1,090	1,244	42	−1,048
August	2,322	1,040	1,282	36	−1,004
September	2,335	961	1,374	34	− 927
October	2,386	878	1,508	42	− 836
November	2,521	950	1,571	65	− 885
December	2,395	801	1,594	48	− 753

Source: Board of Governors of the Federal Reserve System, *Banking and Monetary Statistics,* Washington, D.C., 1943, pp. 368-371. Data on excess reserves not available for the period before 1929.

average. The supply of unborrowed reserves to member banks remained far below 1926-1927 levels throughout the period to October 1929.

Table 3-2 shows the principal factors accounting for the reduction of unborrowed reserves and the sharp increase of member bank borrowings during the period January-August 1928. One was the $298 million reduction of the nation's monetary gold stock. Gold losses, which had amounted to $200 million during the last 5 months of 1927, were ended and reversed only in July. Most of this gold was taken by France. The Federal Reserve drained off another $396 million of reserve funds by selling government securities in the open market. In August, total Federal Reserve holdings of these securities had fallen to $210 million. Of these, $130 million were held for the individual accounts fo the Reserve banks; most of these had been acquired originally for earnings purposes. Only $80 million remained in the Open-Market Investment Account. Still another $200 million of bank reserves had been drained off by

TABLE 3-2

Changes in Member Bank Reserves and Related Items, January–August 1928
(Monthly averages of daily figures in millions of dollars)

Changes during month	Reserve Bank Credit Outstanding					Gold stock	Treasury currency outstanding	Money in circulation	Treasury cash holdings	Treasury deposits with Federal Reserve Banks	Non member deposits accounts	Other Federal Reserve accounts	Member bank reserve balances total
	Bills discounted	Bills bought	USG's	All other	Total								
January	− 64	− 5	− 94	− 17	− 180	− 39	0	− 263	+ 9	+ 9	0	− 1	+ 27
February	+ 6	− 13	− 106	− 11	− 124	− 4	0	− 76	− 5	+ 7	− 1	+ 5	− 58
March	+ 42	− 17	+ 9	− 3	+ 31	− 38	+ 1	+ 1	− 1	− 3	− 2	+ 3	+ 3
April	+ 148	+ 15	− 64	+ 11	+ 110	− 80	+ 1	+ 20	0	− 4	+ 4	+ 5	+ 31
May	+ 175	− 9	− 94	− 5	+ 67	− 88	+ 1	+ 8	+ 3	− 3	0	+]4	+ 8
June	+ 183	− 105	− 25	+ 6	+ 59	+ 6	− 1	+ 14	− 3	− 11	+ 1	+ 1	+ 33
July	+ 71	− 59	− 19	+ 7	0	+ 5	− 2	+ 10	+ 2	+ 6	+ 2	+ 1	− 31
August	− 29	− 7	− 3	− 7	− 46	+ 5	+ 1	+ 3	+ 1	+ 9	− 2	+ 6	+ 50
Total Change, January–August	+ 532	− 200	− 396	− 19	− 83	− 298	+ 1	− 305	+ 6	+ 18	+ 1	+ 26	− 125

Source: Board of Governors of the Federal Reserve System, *Banking and Monetary Statistics*, Washington, D.C., 1943, p. 370.

a reduction of Federal Reserve holdings of acceptances. This decrease was achieved principally by increasing the buying (discount) rates at which the Federal Reserve stood ready to purchase acceptances.

Thus we find that the supply of unborrowed member bank reserves was decreased by three principal factors: the gold drain, Federal Reserve sales of government securities, and the decrease of Federal Reserve holdings of acceptances. These three drained off $894 million of reserve funds. The principal factor tending to supply more bank reserves was the $305 million net decrease of currency in circulation, but most of this occurred in January. These factors together account for most of the $657 million decrease of unborrowed bank reserves during the January-August period. Federal Reserve officials believed that discount rates had been made "more effective" in two principal ways: by increasing member bank indebtedness and by raising the rates that banks had to pay on these increased borrowings.

Let us now examine more closely Federal Reserve thinking and policy-making during this period, looking first at the policies discussed and followed from the time of the OMIC meeting on January 12 until its next meeting on March 25. In accordance with his instructions, the manager of the Open-Market Investment Account proceeded to sell government securities. System holdings declined $65 million from January 18 to February 1, only $26 million during February, and $22 million in the first 28 days of March. A memorandum to the OMIC on March 24 explained:

A somewhat restricted volume of business was an influence in the decision not to carry sales of securities further in January and February.

Other communications within the System refer to the effects of gold exports, to the desirability of proceeding slowly enough to observe the effects of past sales, and to reluctance to sell securities at falling prices. No official in the System seems to have objected to sales in this volume.

In the meantime, increases in discount rates came sooner than expected. First to propose an increase to 4 percent was the Chicago Bank, which had reduced to 3 1/2 percent in October 1927 only when ordered by the Board to do so. This rate became effective on January 27; it was followed by Richmond and New York by February 3 and by all the Reserve banks by March 1. The Federal Reserve Board approved all these recommendations, with only one dissenting vote—Edward H. Cunningham, the agricultural member of the Board. Cunningham's dissent foreshadowed both his own future attitudes and the issues which would plague the System until late 1929. In voting against the proposed Chicago increase, he explained to his colleagues:

... There is nothing in the credit situation of the country that would indicate any inflationary tendency other than the large increase in the so-called brokers' loans in the stock market.

The mandate of the Congress expressed in the Federal Reserve Act is that the discount rate at a Federal Reserve bank shall be fixed with a view of accommodating business and commerce. The action taken in raising the discount rate at the Chicago bank commits the Federal Reserve Board to a policy of rate-making whereby stock market activities become the major consideration regardless of the economic conditions. I do not wish to be committed to such a policy; therefore, I vote "no."[1]

Two days later, in voting against a similar increase for Richmond, he elaborated:

...I feel that increases in the discount rate for the purpose of restricting stock market activities should only be resorted to when other means within the power of the Board have failed to accomplish the objective. I am not in favor of penalizing agriculture and business because of the indirect use of credit for investments in brokers loans; therefore, I vote "no."[2]

Though sometimes absent because of illness, Cunningham never voted for a rise in discount rates before August 1929. He favored limiting the use of credit for speculative purposes, but doing so by some sort of direct action rather than by general credit restriction. Reflecting an attachment to commercial loan ideas, he found sales of government securities less objectionable than increases of discount rates.

Cunningham was not the only Federal Reserve official opposed to a general restriction of credit to combat stock speculation. For example, A. L. Austin, Chairman of the Board of Directors in Philadelphia, wrote to W. R. Burgess in New York on February 25:

Permit me to say, in reply to your letter of February 20th, that I understood the "bugaboo" of the stock market, in connection with fixing the discount rates, was waved aside last August by Governor Strong, when evidently it was the desire of some parties to lower rates and make money easier, notwithstanding the very great speculative activity in the stock market at that time. Four or five months later that seems to have been forgotten. Fixing the rates to accommodate commerce and business applies to all kinds of business besides stock exchange trading, and the business reports coming into the System certainly suggest that all businesses, except the Stock Exchange, which probably only uses twelve or fifteen percent of the credit of the country, needed stimulating, and not repression. I have never seen the benefit of sacrificing the general business of the country for the New York Stock Exchange, and I thought Governor Strong's suggestion of last August was proper.

Some others in the System shared these apprehensions, if not the positive policy conclusions.

At its meeting on March 24, the OMIC reviewed developments since January 12. It found foreign security issues in the American market still at a high level and gold outflows continuing. Trends in domestic business were favorable:

In more recent weeks the available evidence indicates a continued tendency toward business recovery, and this improvement has gone far enough so that Federal Reserve policy may be considered more independently of the conditions of business than for some weeks past.

However, the industrial production indexes for February and March had not yet returned to their highest levels of 1926 and 1927. The volume of bank credit had declined more than seasonally in January and February but was

---

[1]Minutes of the Federal Reserve Board, January 24, 1928.

[2]*Ibid.*, January 26, 1928.

increasing again in March. Stock prices had behaved erratically, showing no definite trend in January, declining slightly in February, and rising again in March. The rise in March was about 11 percent, and this was accompanied by a more rapid rise of brokers' loans.[3] Market rates of interest had risen, but not yet sharply, from their levels in late 1927.

After considering such factors, the OMIC concluded that:

> While it appeared for a time that the purposes set forth in the Committee's recommendations on January 12 were being accomplished, there has recently been a renewed tendency towards what seems an unnecessary expansion of credit, indicating that the 4 percent discount rate in the larger money markets is not as effective as had been contemplated.

If the existing discount rate lacked effectiveness because bank borrowings were too small, especially borrowings by banks in the big money centers, the appropriate remedy was for the Federal Reserve to sell more government securities. Governor Strong explained, in the meeting with the Federal Reserve Board, that

> ... in the opinion of all the members of the Open Market Investment Committee, immediate sales of securities would be necessary to insure a more effective 4 percent rate unless further gold exports had taken place and accomplished the same purpose.

Strong assured the Board that such sales, if approved,

> would be conducted with a view to making more effective the prevailing rediscount rates of the Federal Reserve banks and not with a view to bringing about an increase in Federal Reserve bank rates.

Every member of the OMIC supported this view.

The Board approved these recommendations, with only A. C. Miller voting "no."

> Mr. Miller stated that he voted "no" because of (1) the absence of any evidence of expansion of borrowings for commercial purposes beyond what is seasonal and proper in character; (2) the uncertainty still characteristic of the business outlook following the recent recession of the autumn and winter; (3) the adverse influence on business recovery that increased money rates may be expected to exert; and (4) the almost certain influence that firming of money conditions such as is contemplated by the program of the Open Market Committee may be expected to have in firming money rates. "I am of the opinion," said Mr. Miller, "that the adoption or the approval by the Board of a policy of further firming money conditions will be inadvisable until the whole situation with respect to the probable course of trade and industry is clearer. The present status of the stock exchange loan account of the banks is not, in my opinion, sufficient justification for a policy of further firming of money at this time."[4]

Having received Board approval, the OMIC increased its sales of government securities. It sold $96 million between March 28 and April 30, $76 million in May, and $5 million in June and July. Losses of monetary gold during this period were $195 million. In addition, Federal Reserve holdings of acceptances declined $184 million, largely because of increases of the mini-

---

[3]These data refer to the Standard Statistics index for 90 stocks, including industrial, railroad, and public utilities.

[4]Minutes of the Federal reserve Board, March 26, 1928.

mum bill-buying rate, in 5 steps, from 3 1/4 to 4 1/2 percent. All these developments served to decrease the unborrowed reserves of the banking system and to raise market rates of interest. (See Table 3-1, above.)

Though the OMIC had assured the Board on March 26 that the purpose of open-market sales would not be to pave the way for further increases of discount rates, the latter were not long in coming. The rate was raised from 4 to 4 1/2 percent at Chicago and Boston on April 20, at 3 other Reserve banks before the end of the month, and at all by June 7. New York did not increase its rate until May 18, when 7 other Reserve banks had already acted. This did not reflect any reluctance of New York to increase its rate; instead it was an experimental attempt to discourage the flow of funds to New York. It was hoped that the maintenance of higher discount rates in other major financial centers would keep funds there and inhibit their flow to the stock market. These hopes were apparently not realized.

The Board approved all these increases, but some of its members were becoming increasingly unhappy about using general credit restriction, and especially increases of discount rates, to combat stock speculation. We have already noted that Cunningham refused to vote for rate increases. Now another member, George R. James, took the same position. When Boston proposed a 4 1/2 percent rate on April 18, James stated to the Board:

> While sharing the desire to check the inflationary tendency of the stock market and the flow of Federal Reserve credit in that direction, I am strongly of the opinion that the security holdings of the Federal Reserve System should be substantially reduced, if not entirely disposed of, prior to making any increase in discount rates.
>
> I, therefore, vote "no" on the proposal of the directors of the Federal Reserve Bank of Boston to increase the discount rate of that bank today.[5]

At a Board meeting on May 2 to consider OMIC recommendations, he elaborated his views and proposed a program that failed of adoption.

> In view of the abnormal increase in brokers' loans and other evidences of an inflationary tendency in the money market, I desire at this time to offer suggestions in the hope that the Board may adopt them as a part of its policy:
>
> *First:* That daily settlements as to reserve requirements be ordered for all reserve bank or branch cities. Deposits computed as at the opening of the day's business to govern.
>
> *Second:* Liquidate the System's Open Market Account and suspend temporarily all activities of the Open Market Committee.
>
> *Third:* Establish a rate same as discount rate for buying of bills and for repurchase agreements.
>
> *Fourth:* The Board to suggest or request the reserve banks to make no loans on collateral notes to banks having money on call after duly notifying the member banks of this policy.
>
> As I see it, there is nothing in the present business situation that warrants the raising of discount rates so long as the reserve banks are loaning money to member banks having money employed in the call market. When the open market account is liquidated it will, in my judgment, be time to consider the rediscount rates.[6]

---

[5]Minutes of the Federal Reserve Board, April 18, 1928.

[6]*Ibid.*, May 2, 1928.

J. W. McIntosh, Comptroller of the Currency until his resignation in November 1928, attended Board meetings only infrequently, but he never voted for a rate increase during this period. On July 10 he explained to the Board:

I can see nothing in business or agricultural conditions that would justify any increase of the discount rate in any district at this time.

If it is intended to effect any decrease in the amount of money loaned on call, I would still be opposed to it as I do not believe that increasing rediscount rates would have any effect on this condition over any period of time.[7]

Thus at least three members of the Board—Cunningham, James, and McIntosh—were adamantly opposed to rate increases.

The third round of discount rate increases, this one from 4 1/2 to 5 percent, was also initiated by Chicago. The new rate was proposed on July 2 but not approved until July 10, owing to the Board's difficulty in assembling a quorum. By August 1, 7 other Reserve banks had followed suit. Only 4 retained 4 1/2 percent rates—Minneapolis, Kansas City, Dallas, and San Francisco. These banks did not propose further rate increases until the early months of 1929.

The end of July marked the end of the first phase of active restriction. Changes from the relatively easy money conditions prevailing at the end of 1927 had been sharp indeed. The Federal Reserve had sold $400 million of government securities and reduced its acceptance holdings more than $200 million. The monetary gold stock had fallen $266 million. Minimum bill-buying rates had been increased in 7 steps from 3 to 4 1/2 percent. Eight of the Reserve banks had increased their discount rates from 3 1/2 to 5 percent and the other 4 to 4 1/2 percent. Discount rates were now at their highest level since 1921. Member bank borrowings, now above $1 billion, were also at their highest level since 1921, and were equal to 45 percent of their total reserves. Unborrowed reserves had declined $667 million, or 36 percent. Largely because of these restrictive measures, but perhaps partly because of rising demands for credit, market rates of interest had risen, as illustrated below.

Average yields on	December 1927	Week ending July 28, 1928
Prime commercial paper, 4-6 months	4.00%	5.25%
Prime bankers' acceptances, 90 days	3.25	4.50
Rate on new call loans	4.43	5.50
Yield on Aaa corporate bonds	4.46	4.61

PERIOD OF INACTION, AUGUST 1928-JANUARY 1929

Federal Reserve behavior during the period from the end of July 1928 to January 1929 contrasts sharply with that in the period just examined. The System did only a little during this period to relieve the degree of restriction imposed by its earlier actions, but it did nothing to increase the degree of

[7]*Ibid.*, July 10, 1928.

restrictiveness. It sold no more government securities. Not one Reserve bank proposed an increase in its discount rate during the period from July 18, 1928, to February 14, 1929. Bill-buying rates remained unchanged from July 26, 1928, until January 1929. Yet the period was one of rapidly increasing stock speculation. Stock prices, which had shown little net change during the 4 months preceding August, rose 25 percent during the remainder of the year, and the volume of brokers' loans rose $1.4 billion, or 29 percent.

Why did the Federal Reserve remain so inactive in the face of such developments? The answer is complex and difficult to unravel. I am inclined to discount heavily, if not to deny completely, the relevance of the fact that 1928 was a presidential election year. More relevant to policy in this period and later was a hiatus in the leadership and coordination of the Federal Reserve System. This was closely related to the passing of Benjamin Strong. Strong's period of imaginative, ambitious, and forceful leadership ended in 1927. During the first seven months of 1928 he was ill and tired most of the time and made long trips to Europe. Even before his return to the United States in early August he knew that he would have to retire soon. His death on October 16 removed the most powerful and influential official in the System. On Strong's death, the New York directors appointed Gates W. McGarrah as Acting Governor, and he served in this capacity for more than a month until George L. Harrison was elected Governor on November 22.

In both experience and ability Harrison was well qualified for the job. He had worked six years at the Federal Reserve Board before going to the New York Bank in 1920, and after arriving in New York rose rapidly to the top. He often represented Strong, both abroad and at home. He shared Strong's ambitious concepts of the purposes of the Federal Reserve and learned much from Strong and from the many capable officials and staff members assembled at the New York Bank. He was intelligent, hard-working, and courageous. But capable as he was, Harrison could not reasonably be expected to assume quickly the position that Strong had occupied in the System or to use it as effectively. For one thing, he did not have the prestige that Strong had accumulated over a period of 14 years. Moreover, he lacked some of the powers that had enabled Strong to become so influential—forcefulness sometimes bordering on ruthlessness, imagination in conceiving projects and in devising means of implementing them, and unusual persuasiveness. Not less relevant was the fact that when Harrison assumed office there was strong and rising opposition to the power and influence of New York in System affairs. Some of this involved personal feelings and institutional prerogatives. Strong had sometimes stepped on sensitive toes, and in some areas any policy originating in New York was immediately suspect. Also involved, however, were substantive differences of view concerning the appropriate objectives of the System and methods of promoting them. We have already noted that some Federal Reserve officials, both at the Board and the other Reserve banks, did not accept Strong's principle of positive control and were especially suspicious of open-market operations undertaken on the Federal Reserve's own initiative. The New York Bank's position was especially vulnerable in late 1928 and 1929 because the 1927 easy-money policy which that bank had sponsored was coming under wide attack as the cause of the speculative mania.

This hiatus in Federal Reserve leadership is highly relevant to Federal Reserve policies in late 1928 and the years immediately following. Yet the major reason for the inactive policy of the Federal Reserve during the six months following July 1928 is to be found in the System's conflicting objectives and its inability to find ways of reconciling them. Officials could think of no effective and acceptable way of curbing the use of credit for speculation without undue injury to domestic business and monetary conditions abroad.

Many writers have asserted that the Federal Reserve discontinued its restrictive activities in the autumn of 1928 in order to accommodate the seasonal increases of business demands for credit. This was indeed one reason for the decision, but the concern was not only for seasonal effects. Federal Reserve officials also became deeply worried that further restriction, and even the maintenance of existing conditions over a long period of time, would seriously injure the domestic and international economy.

Some evidence of this concern appeared at least as early as July. For example, a memorandum prepared for the meeting of the OMIC on July 17 stated in part:

> The present high rates are testing the credit situation and it seems reasonable to believe that pressure will be felt at the weakest point, whether this is the prices of industrial securities, the volume of new issues, the amount of new building, or whatever else. . . .
> If the present high interest rates are continued for several months it seems possible that business activity may be affected six months or a year from now . . . .
> From the various considerations and other aspects of the current situation, it would appear that some further period of testing credit situation might not be undesirable. But it would also appear that too extended a period of high money rates would be detrimental to business and would react unfavorably on the world financial position.

Apprehension seems to have increased in August. A memorandum prepared for the OMIC meeting on August 13 points out that interest rates were higher, the total volume of bank credit somewhat reduced, banks were selling some government securities, bond prices had declined, and markets for new issues were congested.

> European exchanges have weakened further and those of England, France, Italy, and Holland are only slightly above the points at which gold will move to this country, unless prevented by higher rates abroad or sale of their balances here to support the exchanges . . . .
>
> . . . there are some reasons for believing that the present amount of member bank borrowing is too large to be continued over an extended period without some unfortunate results. (1) Almost regardless of the discount rate, it keeps severe pressure on the credit situation. (2) By keeping open-market rates high relative to the discount rate, it tends to make the cost of financing through acceptances higher than direct borrowing at banks and tends to dry up the bill market. (3) By keeping open-market rates high relative to the discount rate, it makes borrowing profitable and creates difficulty in dealing with borrowing banks. "Good" banks work out of debt taking losses; less cooperative banks use the Reserve System for profit.

At the end of this meeting Harrison presented the report and recommendations of the OMIC to the Board:

> The policy recommended by the Committee in most of its meetings since January has been to check or prevent unduly rapid or unnecessary increase in the volume of bank

credit. While the total volume of loans and investments of reporting member banks is now considerably above what it was at the low point in February, nevertheless, it is approximately $300,000,000 below the high point of May, and there is evidence that member banks are making continued efforts to reduce their borrowings at Federal Reserve banks.

The Committee does not believe that conditions necessitate an immediate purchase of securities by the System. It is of the opinion, however, that as pointed out at the last meeting, an extended period of high money rates and heavy pressure resulting from large borrowings by member banks would not be wholesome and that there are some indications that with the approaching fall demands for credit it may soon be possible or necessary to take steps looking towards the reduction, or at least the avoidance of the necessity of any substantial increase, in the volume of member bank discounts. With these facts in view and realizing that if and when the time arrives undue delay may be hurtful to the situation, the Committee recommends that it should be the policy of the System to purchase securities whenever that should become necessary to avoid undue credit stringency.

In the ensuing discussion, Harrison stressed that securities would be purchased only as a last resort if a dangerously tight money situation should arise despite efforts to prevent it through purchases of acceptances, exchange operations, and other methods.

All officials appear to have been in agreement that at the very least steps should be taken to prevent seasonal increases in demands for credit from adding to the heavy pressures already existing, but there were wide differences of opinion concerning the methods to be used. Miller proposed the creation of a new class of paper, "Seasonal Crop-Moving Paper," on which the Reserve banks would lend at rates 1/2 to 1 percent below their regular discount rates. James was in hearty sympathy with Miller's objectives but countered with a proposal that buying rates on bankers' acceptances and trade bills, regardless of origin, be set at 1/2 to 1 percent below the rate for other classes of paper. The OMIC reacted adversely to these suggestions; Harrison reported to the Board that all members of the Committee, with the exception of Governor Harding of Boston,

felt that preferential rates on special classes of paper would probably not accomplish what is desired and that the Committee feels that the question whether the season's crops can be moved expeditiously and reasonably involves the bigger question of the whole credit structure and will have to be dealt with through open market operations rather than through preferential rates on commodity paper. He expressed the opinion of the Committee that to reduce the bill rates would undoubtedly result in the dumping of a vast volume of acceptances on the Federal Reserve banks, which though it might have the effect of easing the credit situation would undo the work of many years in developing a bill market.

Cunningham, absent because of illness, wrote to the Board:

Personally, I feel, with large crops now coming on, that prices are bound to go lower and anything that can be done to assist in bringing a net return to the producer would be helpful. I would favor easing up on the discount rate, but would not favor easing the situation by open market purchases. A lower discount rate would be welcomed by all legitimate business interests. Easing the situation through open market purchases looks too much like effort to help big interests only, and the country would be likely to resent it.

Hamlin, also absent, telegraphed:

... feel personally that pressure should not be relaxed for some time at least. Would, however, favor discretionary authority to Committee to buy acceptances as usual, and, in case of sudden emergency, or of conditions under which continuous pressure would injure crop moving and penalize business more than it would be of help in controlling existing tendencies, to purchase securities up to a fixed amount, but, if reasonably possible committee should consult with Governor Young before buying securities; if not possible, the Committee should have discretionary authority to act.

James moved that Chicago be requested to review its 5 percent discount rate with a view to reducing it, but his colleagues on the Board defeated his motion.

On the other hand, Miller and James were adamantly opposed to purchases of government securities. The outcome is indicated in the Board's letter to the OMIC on August 16.

... The Board would not care to agree to the purchase of Government securities, except as a last resort. We understand from the discussion had with your Committee that you favor easing through the bill market, if possible, and through the Government security market only if unavoidable. With this understanding, the Board approves the purchase of Government securities by the Committee but limits the amount to $100,000,000. If a situation should develop which will require reconsideration, the Board will be glad to meet the Committee at any time for that purpose.

As it turned out, the Federal Reserve bought no government securities during this period; its purchases were confined to acceptances. Its holdings of acceptances rose from $162 million at the end of July to $284 million at the end of September, and to an average level of more than $450 million during the last 3 months of the year. It did not lower its bill-buying rate, but it did buy freely all the good acceptances offered. Thus the market rate came to be the same as the Federal Reserve buying rate, which was 4 1/2 percent for maturities not in excess of 90 days. It was largely because of this injection of nearly $300 million of funds that member banks were able to improve their reserve positions slightly. (See Table 3-1). But the new policy was hardly one of "ease." During the last 3 months of the year member banks still owed the Federal Reserve over $900 million on the average, and their unborrowed reserves remained considerably below their levels during the early part of the year.

As Federal Reserve holdings of acceptances rose, some officials came to feel that the bill-buying rate was slightly too low. In mid-October a Deputy Governor of the New York Bank wrote to the Board that the policy of supplying autumn credit requirements through bill purchases had been entirely successful and that

bill holdings will probably increase in October and November faster than demand for reserve bank credit, in which event discounts for member banks will tend to decline and money rates are likely to be easier than in recent weeks.

The Board replied:

... members of the Board are not quite clear as to the meaning of the last paragraph of his letter and wish that it could be clarified ... one or two members have so interpreted it as to reach the conclusion that it involves an abandonment of the policy which the System has been following of keeping certain pressure on the money market.

At the OMIC meeting on November 13 all the governors present expressed the opinion that, though they had no jurisdiction over the matter, it might be advisable for New York to increase its buying rate for bills of all maturities by one-eighth of 1 percent in the near future. The New York directors discussed this at length on November 15 but decided not to increase the rate. The question came before the Board again on December 15 when it was informed by New York that dealers were advancing their buying rates on acceptances one-eighth of 1 percent to protect against a possible rise of rates later. Miller reiterated his view that the Federal Reserve buying rate was too low and moved that it should be increased, beginning with one-eighth. His motion lost on a tie vote. Young explained that he voted "no" because an increase of one-eighth of 1 percent would have little effect, and the latest figures indicated that money was working out of the call-loan market, not into it.

Views in New York changed around the end of the year as larger amounts of bills were offered to the Reserve bank. On January 3 the directors voted an increase in the bill-buying rate and requested Board approval. The latter decided to postpone action until after the OMIC meeting scheduled for January 7, but New York made the rate effective on January 4. Young, Miller, and perhaps also some other members of the Board were angered by the action and were but little mollified by Harrison's explanation that this conformed to the procedure followed consistently since 1918, under which the Board approved only minimum rates, leaving the Reserve banks free to set actual rates at or above the approved level. The Board adopted Miller's motion that the Governor should draw up a new regulation applying to bills the same procedure applicable to discount rates, but Young seems to have taken no such action.

Policies and procedures relating to open-market operations in government securities also became controversial. One incident related to OMIC recommendations on November 15. In effect, the Committee recommended continuation of its existing authorization, under which it was empowered to purchase up to $100 million of government securities, but to use this power only in the event of an emergency or to prevent any undue stringency of credit. The Board withheld its decision for 12 days and then disapproved, explaining:

If the Board approves this recommendation it will give approval to a policy of buying an indefinite amount of Government securities. It does not care to give this approval for three reasons:
1. It would not be in harmony with expressions and actions already taken by certain reserve banks.
2. It is not prepared at this time to say definitely that an emergency should be handled by the purchase of Government securities, or whether other avenues should be resorted to.
3. It believes that if any real emergency develops in the country, it might be advisable to have another meeting of the Committee.
During the interim, however, adjustments of temporary credit situations, which would not be in the nature of serious emergencies, may be advisable and the Board will

hold itself in readiness to act promptly upon written or telephone request from the Committee in an amount not to exceed $25,000,000.[8]

Thus the Board refused permission to buy any government securities; it merely indicated its willingness to act promptly on future requests, and even this commitment applied only to a very small amount of securities—an amount too small to meet any significant emergency or to constitute a significant shift in policy.

This incident was not unrelated to a Board proposal considered by the Conference of Governors of the Federal Reserve banks on November 15-16, 1928. This called for sweeping changes in the composition and procedures of the OMIC. The major features of the Board's proposal were these: (1) Membership on the OMIC would be expanded to include representatives of all 12 Reserve banks. This committee would select an Executive Committee of 5 members to carry out its policies. (2) The Governor of the Federal Reserve Board would be chairman of the expanded OMIC. (3) The OMIC would meet with the Federal Reserve Board before it arrived at its recommendations. Under the prevailing procedure the OMIC met with the Board only after it had formulated its recommendations. (4) The power of the Board to approve or disapprove would be expanded to include not only general policy but also the timing and specific amounts of purchases or sales. The Governors' Conference approved only one major change proposed by the Board—expansion of membership on the OMIC to include representatives of all 12 Reserve banks. It rejected all the others, voting in effect to maintain prevailing procedures and powers. Since this action was unacceptable to the Board, no change was made until 1930. Relations between the Board and the OMIC continued to be ill-defined and frequently frictional.

CONCLUSIONS

By late January 1929 the Federal Reserve's policy of restriction had been in effect about a year. Monetary and credit conditions had changed markedly during the period. Member bank borrowings at the Federal Reserve had nearly doubled, rising to nearly $900 million, equal to 37 percent of total bank reserves. Unborrowed bank reserves had fallen more than $400 million, or 22 percent. The total volume of bank credit was barely above its level of a year earlier. Interest rates had risen sharply, especially short-term rates. Call-loan rates averaged above 7 percent in December 1928 and frequently reached considerably higher levels. However, the Federal Reserve had not achieved its objective of curbing stock speculation. Share prices rose 38 percent in the year, with four-fifths of the increase in the last 6 months. Brokers' loans reached the unprecedented level of $6.4 billion; this reflected an increase of 45 percent for the year. However, some of the feared consequences of the protracted period of restriction were already appearing. Foreign security issues in the American market had fallen to only a small fraction of their rate in

---

[8]Minutes of the Federal Reserve Board, November 27, 1928.

1927 and the first half of 1928. Gold outflows had ended in mid-year and given way to gold inflows, which would have been even larger if some foreign banks had not sold some of their dollar balances or embarked on restrictive policies. Domestic business activity was still at high and rising levels, but even here there were warning signs in the form of a decreasing availability of mortgage money, a downturn in construction, and increasing difficulties in floating long-term bond issues.

4

The Direct Action Controversy

This chapter examines Federal Reserve policies from the first of February 1929 to August of that year. The first four months of this period witnessed dramatic controversy within the System. On February 2 the Board began its now-famous program of "direct action" to combat the "seepage of Federal Reserve credit into speculative uses." The various Reserve banks cooperated in varying degrees, some unable to hide their dislike for the program, especially when it was not coupled with an increase in discount rates. The Board, on its part, refused to allow discount rates to be raised from 5 to 6 percent. Week after week the New York Bank and several others voted such increases only to have them disapproved by the Board. The controversy ended only in late May when an agreement was reached to work out a new program, but the new program was delayed until early August.

Failure to raise discount rates to 6 percent did not mean that no generally restrictive actions were taken during the period. Discount rates at the Minneapolis, Kansas City, Dallas, and San Francisco Reserve banks, which were 4 1/2 percent at the end of 1928, were increased to 5 percent. Federal Reserve holdings of government securities were decreased further from an average of $229 million in January to $147 million in July, a decrease of $82 million. In the latter month, holdings in the Open-Market Investment Account were only $18 million; the remainder was in the individual investment accounts of the various Reserve banks. Most restrictive of all was the $398 million decrease in Federal Reserve holdings of acceptances. These holdings averaged only $75 million in July. This reduction was effected largely by raising bill-buying rates above prevailing discount rates. The lowest bill-buying rate was increased in 4 steps between January 3 and March 25 from 4 1/2 to 5 3/8 percent. Thus during much of the period it was from one-fourth of 1 percent to three eighths of 1 percent above the discount rate. This was unprecedented in Federal Reserve history.

Largely because of these Federal Reserve policies, and despite gold inflows of $220 million, the reserve position of banks was put under heavy pressure, comparable to that in mid-1928 before the Federal Reserve began to increase its acceptance holdings. (See Table 3-1, above.) Member bank borrowings averaged $1,096 million in July, equal to 47 percent of their total reserves. As would be expected under such circumstances, interest rates rose sharply, The weekly average rate on call loans never fell below 6 percent during the first 7 months of the year, and for several weeks it was above 11 percent. On occasions the rate rose as high as 20 percent. Bond yields rose and their prices decreased. For long-term federal obligations the price decline was 5 percent from early 1928 to July 1929, and for high-grade corporate bonds it was 9 percent. New bonds became hard to sell in the declining market.

The controversy that plagued the System during this period did not spring from differences in ultimate objectives. All Federal Reserve officials wanted to decrease "the excessive use of credit for speculation in stocks," all wanted more plentiful supplies of credit and lower interest rates for "legitimate" uses, and all wanted to decrease the pressure on monetary conditions abroad. The questions at issue were, "How can we best promote and reconcile these various objectives? What instruments should we use and how much reliance should be placed on each?" On such questions there were wide differences of views throughout the System. This was not a controversy between a unified Board on the one side and unified Reserve banks on the other. The Board was sharply divided, as were officials of the various Reserve banks.

Those who favored increases of discount rates were not opposed to the use of direct action or moral suasion to prevent "abuses" of Federal Reserve credit. They had long insisted that borrowing from the Reserve banks was a privilege and not a right and that this privilege should not be abused by borrowing continuously, or too much, or for improper purposes. At least some had refused or curtailed loans to banks that lent for clearly speculative purposes and in excessive amounts. However, most believed that direct action alone could not achieve the objectives sought, especially not when discount rates were kept so low relative to market rates. Time and again during this period they insisted that the maintenance of discount rates at levels so far below short-term market rates presented almost irresistible temptations to banks to borrow for profit and insured the failure of a direct action program. Some also believed that general credit restriction, including increases in discount rates, could somehow chill the speculative fever quickly, so that it would then become safe for the System to liberalize credit for legitimate purposes. However, they did not explain persuasively how this could be achieved. Stock speculation could, of course, be curbed by credit restraint so sharp and prolonged as to plunge the country into depression, but this was not the route they hoped to follow. They hoped that speculation would prove to be much more sensitive than legitimate business to credit restraint and higher interest rates, at least partly because the first and heaviest impact of credit restraint would fall on speculative loans. Strong believed this to be true.

The minute we have a very large loan account at the Reserve Bank of New York, the large member banks are continually calling the Stock Exchange loans. This calling of loans is a process of selection or discrimination. Each bank picks out the weak house or the house which has loans with pool stocks or stocks which have advanced rapidly in price, or those which are less well regarded. Every day this turning process takes place. The less desirable borrowers are harassed to death by the need for borrowing money. The better borrowers are harassed by the discrimination against certain types of collateral. They in turn go to their customers for more margin or to take up the stocks that are complained of, and it is not very long before the whole psychology changes. I admit that this very process does itself inevitably effect an alteration in the general level of the money market but it involves much less danger than . . . direct action.[1]

Harrison later argued much the same way. This line of argument is not persuasive. For one thing, it is not clear that banks would decrease their call loans to such a great extent before curtailing their other loans and investments. Moreover, Strong probably underestimated the extent to which a decrease of bank loans to brokers would be offset by increased loans from others.

Advocates of direct action believed that a simpler and more effective way of curbing speculation was to apply pressure on member banks that were simultaneously borrowing from the Federal Reserve and making speculative loans. They assumed that such banks would respond by calling their speculative loans rather than by reducing their other loans and investments, and that the reduction of speculative loans by these banks would not be offset by increases in such loans by other banks and other types of lenders. The problem and the response turned out to be more complex than anticipated.

The direct action program was initiated by the Federal Reserve Board, not the Reserve banks, and Miller was its principal sponsor. It was Miller who in December 1928 first advanced the idea of sending a letter to the Reserve banks. He also did most of the work on the letter sent to the Reserve banks on February 2 and on the statement released to the public on February 7. The Board was divided on the issue. Governor Young was clearly opposed. Platt was no more than lukewarm in supporting it and consistently voted to approve increases in discount rates. James and Cunningham probably supported it primarily because they were adamantly opposed to increases in discount rates.

Because of its importance, the Board's letter of February 2 to all the Reserve banks is reproduced in full.

> The firming tendencies of the money market which have been in evidence since the beginning of the year—contrary to the usual trend at this season—make it incumbent upon the Federal reserve banks to give constant and close attention to the situation in order that no influence adverse to the trade and industry of the country shall be exercised by the trend of money conditions, beyond what may develop as inevitable.
>
> The extraordinary absorption of funds in speculative security loans which has characterized the credit movement during the past year or more, in the judgment of the Federal Reserve Board, deserves particular attention lest it become a decisive factor working toward a still further firming of money rates to the prejudice of the country's commercial interests.
>
> The resources of the Federal Reserve System are ample for meeting the growth of the country's commercial needs for credit, provided they are competently administered and protected against seepage into uses not contemplated by the Federal Reserve Act.
>
> The Federal Reserve Act does not, in the opinion of the Federal Reserve Board, contemplate the use of the resources of the Federal reserve banks for the creation or extension of speculative credit. A member bank is not within its reasonable claims for rediscount facilities at its Federal reserve bank when it borrows either for the purpose of making speculative loans or for the purpose of maintaining speculative loans.
>
> The Board has no disposition to assume authority to interfere with the loan practices of member banks so long as they do not involve the Federal reserve banks. It

---

[1]Strong letter to O. M. W. Sprague, May 7, 1928.

has, however, a grave responsibility whenever there is evidence that member banks are maintaining speculative security loans with the aid of Federal reserve credit. When such is the case the Federal reserve bank becomes either a contributing or a sustaining factor in the current volume of speculative security credit. This is not in harmony with the intent of the Federal Reserve Act nor is it conducive to the wholesome operation of the banking and credit system of the country.

You are desired to bring this letter to the attention of the directors of your bank in order that they may be advised of the attitude of the Federal Reserve Board with respect to this situation and the problem confronting the administration of Federal Reserve banks. The Board would like to have from them an expression as to (a) how they keep themselves fully informed of the use made of borrowings by their member banks, (b) what methods they employ to protect their institution against the improper use of its credit facilities by member banks, and (c) how effective these methods have been.

The Board realizes that the problem of protecting the credit situation from strain because of excessive absorption of credit in speculative security loans is attended with difficulties. It also realizes that there are elements in the situation which are not readily amenable to recognized methods of banking control. The Board nevertheless believes that, however difficult, the problem can be more completely met and that the existing situation admits of improvement.

The Federal Reserve Board awaits the reply of your directors to this letter and bespeaks their prompt attention in order that it may have their reply at an early date.

Several points in the Board's letter stand out clearly. (1) The Board accepted the idea that speculative loans "absorb credit" and that such an "absorption of credit" had in fact been a major reason for the firming of money rates. It did not even hint that the major source of tightened credit has been the System's own policies. (2) "The Board has no disposition to assume authority to interfere with the loan practices of member banks so long as they do not involve the Federal reserve banks." The context indicates that the Board was assuming such authority only with respect to those member banks borrowing from the Federal Reserve, not with respect to all the other member banks, nonmember commercial banks, or other types of lenders. (3) The directors of all 12 Reserve banks were expected to reply promptly to 3 questions:

(a) how they kept themselves fully informed of the use made of borrowings by their member banks,

(b) what methods they employed to protect their institution against the improper use of its credit facilities by member banks, and

(c) how effective these methods had been.

The implication soon became clear: The Reserve banks should do a better job on these matters.

On some things the letter was extremely vague, and this vagueness was to lead to frictions and difficulties. One question was the meaning of "speculative credit" and "speculative security loans." These terms were of key importance for operational purposes, yet they were not defined in the letter and had no specific definition in common usage. They could have meant several different things, including: (1) only loans made to brokers and dealers in securities, (2) these loans plus all other loans on security collateral where the proceeds were used for "speculative" purposes, (3) all loans on security collateral, or (4) all loans, regardless of collateral, whose proceeds were used for speculation. To which of these categories of "speculative loans" was the Board's letter directed? Some Reserve bank officials assumed that the Board meant only brokers' loans, or only brokers' loans in New York City. Others

thought the Board meant to include all loans on securities. There was evidence
to support both views and others as well. It is not even clear that members of
the Board were in full agreement on the meaning of these terms, though the
weight of the evidence is that the Board intended a broad interpretation.

For example, Cunningham wanted to restrict Federal Reserve loans to
every bank carrying collateral loans. In January, believing that the Board
lacked adequate power under existing legislation, he asked his colleagues to
approve the following resolution with a view to having it enacted as an
amendment to the Federal Reserve Act.

> Except with the approval of the Federal Reserve Board, which is concurred in by
> the affirmative vote of not less than five members of the Board, no member bank shall
> be entitled to the privilege of rediscounting with the Federal Reserve Bank of its District
> while simultaneously having an investment in notes, drafts or bills covering merely invest-
> ments or issued or drawn for the purpose of carrying or trading in stocks, bonds or other
> investment securities.[2]

After being informed by counsel that the Board already has adequate legal
power, Cunningham proposed in August that the Board issue the following
regulation:

> Except with the permission of the Federal Reserve Board, no Federal Reserve
> Bank shall discount or rediscount any note, draft or bill of exchange for, or make any
> loan or advance to, or purchase any bills of exchange, bankers' acceptances, or govern-
> ment, State or municipal securities (under repurchase agreement or otherwise) from, any
> member bank which at the time (a) has outstanding loans to any person, firm, partner-
> ship, corporation, company or association, whose principal business it is to negotiate
> purchases or sales of or to purchase, sell or otherwise deal in, stocks, bonds or other
> investment securities (other than bonds or notes of the Government of the United States)
> either for its own account or for the account of others, or (b) has outstanding loans to
> or deposits with any other bank, which at the time has outstanding loans to any such
> person, firm, partnership, corporation, company or association.[3]

The motion lost by a vote of 4 to 2, with only James and Cunningham voting
for it and Miller abstaining.

The Reserve banks had still other reasons for believing that the Board
wished to define "speculative loans" in a broad way. For example, the Board's
letters to most of the Reserve banks in late April and early May, urging them
to improve their efforts, referred not to brokers' loans but to security loans,
and the statistics cited to show that the Reserve banks had not achieved the
desired results applied to total loans on securities. The Federal Advisory
Council, approving the Board's policy at a meeting on February 14, referred
not to speculative loans but to "loans based on securities."

> The Federal Advisory Council approves the action of the Federal Reserve Board in
> instructing the Federal Reserve Banks to prevent, as far as possible, the diversion of
> Federal Reserve funds for the purpose of carrying loans based on securities. The Federal
> Advisory Council suggests that all member banks in each district be asked by the Federal
> Reserve Bank of the district to co-operate in order to attain the end desired . . . .[4]

---

[2]Minutes of the Federal Reserve Board, January 19, 1929.

[3]*Ibid.*, August 8, 1929.

[4]*Annual Report of the Federal Reserve Board*, 1929, p. 218.

Deputy Governor Worthington of the Kansas City Reserve Bank commented in a letter to Governor Bailey on February 21:

> You will note that in that statement the terms "speculative loans" or "speculative securities" are not used but that they refer to "loans based on securities." That was the intention. Mr. Goebel gives as an illustration a case where one of his customers desired to borrow $50,000 on some Cities Service stock, worth at present market more than $100,000, and his bank declined to make the loan on the grounds that their funds were needed for legitimate commercial borrowings.[5]

Governor Seay of Richmond felt that this language was "right broad." Many member bankers knew of the council's recommendation, for at least four of the Reserve banks sent it to all their members and it was widely publicized.

The vagueness of the Board's reference to "speculative loans" led to much confusion and to wide differences in the standards applied in the various Federal Reserve districts. Another statement in the Board's letter also posed comparable problems:

> A member bank if not within its reasonable claims for rediscount facilities at its Federal Reserve bank when it borrows either for the purpose of making speculative loans or for the purpose of maintaining speculative loans.

What did this mean in operational terms? Under what conditions should a Reserve bank lend or refuse to lend to a member? Under one strict interpretation it should refuse to lend at all to any bank which had any "speculative loans" on its books, however these might be defined. This, however, would virtually close the discount window to many banks, especially if "speculative loans" were construed to include all loans based on securities. A less rigid rule, followed by some Reserve banks, was to refuse to make or renew loans to banks which had "excessive amounts" of speculative loans and had been borrowing too long, or too frequently, or too much. However, such rules of reason were hard to formulate and administer in a nonarbitrary manner. A third course, which some Reserve banks thought they were being asked to follow, was to inquire into the reasons for a bank's borrowing—into the types of transactions that led to the need for borrowing and the specific uses to which the borrowed funds would be put.

It is not possible to examine in detail the functioning of the direct action program, the precise nature of the actions taken by the various Reserve banks, all the problems encountered, and the successes or failures of the program. However, a few examples will throw light on some of these areas.

Several of the Reserve banks found it difficult to discover the purpose for which members were borrowing. New York gave what was by then its standard answer—that a bank borrows not to make a specific loan or investment but to cover a deficiency in its reserves, which often reflects losses of deposits and in any case is the resultant of a large number of transactions. Governor Seay said that borrowing banks

unanimously give shrinkage of deposits as the reason, and they always assure us that they

---

[5]P. W. Goebel, a Kansas City banker, was the member of the Federal Advisory Council from that district.

are making no new loans, or at least, are restricting new loans to those which are small and essential.[6]

Cleveland stated:

as a purely practical matter it is not possible to analyze the cause of bank borrowings in each instance, for the reason that frequently such action is necessitated by a multiplicity of causes.[7]

San Francisco found that

All parties claim continuous rediscounting due to overpurchases of bonds and certificates and that decline in value prohibits sale except at considerable loss.[8]

Philadelphia reported that to get out of debt many banks would have to sell government securities at significant losses, which would materially reduce their surplus accounts.

As our banks have always been liberal subscribers to these issues, in good times and bad, we feel that it would be an undue hardship to enforce immediate sale at such a sacrifice.[9]

Several other Reserve banks referred to the unwillingness of members to sell their government securities at depreciated prices.

Most of the Reserve banks seem to have been more willing to bring pressure on borrowing banks that were lending to brokers and dealers in New York than to put pressure on borrowing banks with other collateral loans. It seems unlikely, however, that any Reserve bank applied rigidly a rule that it would not lend at all to a bank with call loans on its books. Account was taken of the frequency, duration, and amount of the bank's borrowings and sometimes the nature and location of the borrower. For example, Chicago wrote to the Board in late February:

We have made it very clear to our members that we will not advance Federal Reserve credit to a bank having money on call.

Yet it made an exception for loans to brokers and dealers to finance transactions on the Chicago Stock Exchange, apparently on the theory that these were, in effect, loans to customers to finance business transactions. Cleveland, in its letter to the Board on February 9, commented that:

In our opinion the continuous use of reserve bank credit facilities on the part of banks which at the same time are lending on the street is a gross misuse of our funds, and member banks, in the few instances where such conditions have obtained, have been told that existing loans with us must be liquidated at maturity, provided that on that date funds are still being loaned for speculative use. It is pertinent to point out that our definition of the term "continuous borrowing" in cases like the above has been applicable to banks which have been indebted to us for a period of thirty days.

---

[6] Letter to the Federal Reserve Board, February 16, 1929.

[7] Letter to federal Reserve Board, February 9, 1929.

[8] Telegram to Federal Reserve Board, March 20, 1929.

[9] Letter to the Federal Reserve Board, April 16, 1929.

Kansas City concentrated on discouraging loans to New York brokers and dealers.

There have been no efforts made to persuade member banks to curtail their use of Federal Reserve credit because of loans on stocks and bonds carried by such member banks for brokers and dealers in securities outside New York City, or carried for others than brokers or dealers. The position of our directors in this respect has been that such loans in our district are almost entirely made up of loans to local dealers in investment securities and to individuals who are more or less regular customers of the banks, and that such loans, while inevitably involving some speculative use of credit, should not be placed in the same category as open market noncustomer loans.[10]

New York, to the annoyance of the Board, consistently took the position that it should not deny loans to a member simply because that bank was making loans to brokers or dealers in securities. What was to be prevented was not the making of such loans by borrowing banks but "excessive" borrowings and "excessive" loans to brokers. Moreover, for the large city banks many of these loans were, in effect, customer loans for business rather than speculative purposes.

Several Reserve banks attempted to discourage borrowing members from making collateral loans to borrowers other than brokers and dealers, and in doing so encountered serious problems. Some of these loans were clearly for speculative purposes, some were for productive or consumption purposes, and most were hard to identify as to purpose without very extensive research. The Philadelphia Reserve Bank protested attempts to control these loans,

Inasmuch as Philadelphia is an old city where capital has been accumulating for over two centuries, where there have always been large holdings of securities, and where such securities have always been used as collateral for loans made for all sorts of purposes, productive and otherwise . . . .[11]

It also reported that approximately half of the total loans made on securities by 40 reporting member banks were issued by trust companies, whose collateral loans had always constituted the bulk of their lending business. Some had no commercial loans at all. Governor Seay of Richmond was also unhappy about discrimination against collateral loans in general. The Boston Reserve bank faithfully asked its members to reduce collateral loans of all types; most pledged their cooperation, some with obvious reluctance. A banker in Norwich, Connecticut, replied portentously, "We beg to say that we will heartily cooperate with you in the request you made . . . and refuse all collateral loans, so far as we can without detriment to our business."

The Reserve banks soon discovered an important reason why their members were so reluctant to curtail collateral loans to customers: Some of these customers were among the bank's largest depositors and valuable to the bank for other reasons. Governor Harding of Boston informed the Board on February 25:

There is keen competition between banks throughout New England and many of our

---

[10]Letter to Federal Reserve Board, February 14, 1929.

[11]Letter to Federal Reserve Board, February 13, 1929.

banks tell us that it has been necessary to make such loans in order to prevent shifting of good accounts.[12]

Governor Seay believed that a bank would in most cases be unwilling to refuse collateral loans to a customer, explaining in an involved way that the bank

would probably sell its investments rather than lose the customers, because if it lost those customers, it would probably lose deposits and would be compelled to borrow, in any event, or sell its investments.[13]

These examples illustrate some of the problems encountered in interpreting and administering the direct action program. Others will appear as we review some of the principal events of the period.

As already indicated, Governor Young was the only member of the Board to vote against sending the February 2 letter to the Reserve banks; he also voted against issuing the public statement of February 8 and against release of the Federal Advisory Council recommendation on February 14. Hamlin stated that he voted "aye" because the letter was not a ruling of law but merely a declaration of good banking policy and did not advocate or suggest drastic liquidation. Platt did not vote against the program, but his support was unenthusiastic and he voted consistently for increases of discount rates. The Board held throughout this period that no Reserve bank shoud raise its discount rate above 5 percent until the direct action program had been given a chance to show what it could accomplish.

Recommendations for rate increases from 5 to 6 percent were not long in coming. New York acted on February 14, asking for a Board decision the same day. The Board disapproved. New York repeated its recommendation 9 more times between February 14 and May 23, always with the same result. Chicago made the same recommendation 4 times, Philadelphia 3 times, and Boston 6 times. They would have acted oftener if they had not known in advance that the Board would disapprove. Some of the other Reserve banks also wanted higher rates, but they did not act, partly because they knew the Board would disapprove and partly because they did not want higher rates while discount rates in the major financial centers remained at 5 percent.

The period of disagreement dragged on. At least some members of the Board felt, not without good reason, that several of the Reserve banks were less than fully cooperative in the direct action program, and the Reserve banks considered the Board's continued disapproval of rate increases unreasonable. Visits of Governor Young to New York and of Harrison and some of his directors to Washington brought no solution. In the meantime, monetary conditions abroad were deteriorating and strains were appearing in domestic business. These were noted in a memorandum for the OMIC meeting on April 1:

The higher money rates do not appear to have restricted short-term commercial borrowing but in a number of other ways the present high level of money rates is beginning to have a detrimental effect upon business. (1) The volume of building opera-

---

[12]Letter to Governor Young, February 25, 1929.

[13]Seay memorandum to the directors of the Richmond Bank, February 9, 1929.

tions has been declining, largely because of difficulty in obtaining second mortgage money and loans for building operations and also difficulty in selling real estate bonds . . . . (2) A good many state, municipal, railway and other projects ordinarily financed through bonds and notes have been postponed because of difficulty in securing funds at reasonable prices . . . . (3) Reduced foreign financing in the United States, together with rising money rates and stringent money conditions in England, Holland, Germany and Italy due largely to our high call loan rates, are diminishing the purchasing power of those countries for our products, a tendency which is likely to be reflected sooner or later in reduced exports.

It thus seems reasonably certain that present money conditions, if long continued, will have a seriously detrimental effect upon business conditions, and the longer they are continued the more serious will be the effect.

Harrison communicated his deep concern to Owen D. Young, the great industrialist, who was Deputy Chairman of the Board of Directors of the New York Bank and was at that time in Paris negotiating what later came to be the Young Plan for Reparations. He mentioned, among other things, an impending Treasury refinancing operation. Young cabled his reply on March 12.

In course of our discussions here with Hjalmar Schacht, Montagu C. Norman, Emile Moreau, Pierre Quesnay and others certain facts and points of view as to the general monetary situation are emerging. While these are probably familiar to you it may be helpful for me to summarize them as they appear for me.

The British position is increasingly difficult to maintain and Norman expects to have to raise his rate within a week or two. Amsterdam will probably follow shortly and Schacht indicates that he may have to follow London but in any event would follow an increase in Amsterdam.

The French position continues strong and for two weeks they have sold no devisen and they probably would not find it necessary to increase their rate.

The Belgian position is also believed to be strong but they might follow a general rate increase.

While a short period of the very high rates now in prospect may not be serious there seems reason to be apprehensive of the results of the continuance of these rates over an extended period particularly if there is no relief before autumn.

It seems quite apparent that the call money rate in New York is dominating the world's monetary position and is menacing the reserve of central banks.

Thus as I see the position it is essential that the Federal Reserve System should take prompt and decisive control of its own market not only to preserve its own prestige but also because failure to do so would risk the impairment of European monetary systems so recently returned to the gold basis.

One might anticipate the rise in European rates and the cleaning up of your Treasury operations as coming about the same time. If so it should present a good opportunity to take hold of our situation with a strong hand.

From this distance I hesitate to make any suggestions as to methods which might be employed. While it is desirable that the methods employed should be the best ones this now seems to me much less important than that some methods be adopted and followed through. The important thing is to accomplish the result.[14]

Young sent a private cable to Harrison on the same day, suggesting strategy.

This is to supplement my other cable which is intended for whatever use you care to make of it whereas this is intended for you alone unless you would like to show it to

---

[14]Schacht, Norman, and Moreau were the governors of the Reichsbank, the Bank of England, and the Bank of France, respectively. Quesnay was a Deputy Governor of the Bank of France.

C. M. Woolley. So far as I am able to judge the situation there seems to me no hope of control over the New York market without complete agreement between the Federal Reserve Bank of New York and the Federal Reserve Board as to the policy they are willing to back. If it is impossible for the New York Bank to come to agreement with the Federal Reserve Board direct the situation is serious enough to warrant seeking the intervention of the Secretary of the Treasury and the President of the United States. If I should make a recommendation as to methods it would be to have C. M. Woolley either see the President of the United States direct or if that were embarrassing get Henry M. Robinson to see him. Any approach to the President of the United States should of course be first approved by Andrew W. Mellon. I am cabling you fully to give you all that is on my mind on this matter and with the hope it may aid you in your difficult position.[15]

Harrison and Woolley did visit Washington, but Harrison reported:

While I have been informed that President is concerned I understand he prefers to keep hands off at this juncture. In circumstances both C. M. Wooley and I have felt that we might only embarrass him by seeking an audience just now.[16]

Secretary Mellon's testimony supported Harrison's:

In reply to questions, Secretary Mellon said today that the credit situation throughout the country had not yet reached the point where it had attracted the attention of President Hoover.

The Secretary said that he had discussed the credit status with the President casually, but that Mr. Hoover had not exhibited unusual interest in the matter.[17]

There is no evidence that Hoover conveyed his views to Federal Reserve officials at any time during this period.

Harrison and Wooley agreed with Owen D. Young that some definite policy should be adopted and carried through but puzzled as to what that policy should be. In mid-March Woolley was inclined to favor a shift toward easier money, as his cable to Owen Young indicated:

... immediate reduction of rate to 4 1/2 percent might correct the scourge of high call rates, (a) which continue to suck deposits out of banks by "all others," now nearing the three billion mark, (b) to attract gold from abroad, which is the greater menace so convincingly pointed out by you.

If such rate reduction were followed by call rates of 5 1/2 per cent the logical effect, as I view it, would impel "all others" to call their loans and transfer gradually to bond and other investments, thus affording needed relief to banks and reinstate their control of street loans.

Lower call rates would doubtless intensify speculation, but in such event the inevitable break would all the sooner occur, and conceivably within a few days due to the possibility of pool distribution ... at which point it might be feasible to reduce the bank rate to 4 per cent in the interest of commerce and industry in this country and in the interest of central banks abroad.

If our rate is advanced to 6 per cent call rates would inevitably advance, aggravating present embarrassment to American banks and increasing the grave menace of further gold shipments by foreign banks. Both evils require lower call rates for their correction.

While my colleagues do not agree with this reasoning, I cannot in all conscience

---

[15]C. M. Woolley, a director of the New York Reserve Bank, was working closely with Harrison in trying to come to an agreement with the Board.

[16]Harrison cable to O. D. Young, April 10, 1929.

[17]*The New York Times*, March 22, 1929, p. 6.

retire from the opinion that lower call rates are absolutely essential for the security of banking situation at home and abroad . . . .

Business in general is flowing at a high rate of advance over last year, but the classic thing has happened for the past 3 months. Building contracts awarded are heavily decreasing. This has always been the precursor of a general decline in business activity . . . .

These factors impel me to believe that lower interest rates for commerce and industry in this country are quite as imperative as such lower rates are for central banks abroad.

If you and your colleagues and Gates will consider the reasoning herein set forth, and thereafter if you will cable me through the bank that in your judgment the immediate increase in our bank rate is the safer and wiser course to pursue, I will immediately buckle down to work for an advance in the rate, and if 7 per cent would seem to be more effective I will work as hard for that.[18]

Young cabled his reply on March 18:

. . . my own view is that whether wise or not we are committed to the policy of the high rate program by the announcement of the Federal Reserve Board and our own action. To change our policy now would be misunderstood or at least not understood both at home and abroad. The central bank heads here and the others all seem to be agreed that the traditional method for controlling our market through rate increase is the wise one. The fact that they are willing to take the increased strain on their resources which will inevitably come from our rate increase indicates their sincere belief in the method . . . . They expect it to come quickly otherwise their position will be more dangerous than at present. Therefore in view of our policies at home up to date and the unanimous opinion here I would personally hesitate to take responsibility on a low rate program now. It is essential however that we adopt one program or the other and act on it promptly and firmly because we cannot stay where we are. Whatever policy is adopted should be agreed upon in advance and firmly followed through. I doubt if you can secure such agreement without getting the support of the President of the United States and the Secretary of the Treasury. If they will support the high rate program and procure the cooperation of the Federal Reserve Board I would adopt that policy and carry it through just as quickly and strongly as I could. If the President of the United States and the Secretary of the Treasury will not support a high rate policy then I would adopt the low rate policy which you recommend and carry that out as the only practical alternative. If you wish to show this message either to the President of the United States or the Secretary of the Treasury I have no objection.

At this point Harrison was not yet ready to move toward an easier policy and continued to recommend increases in the New York discount rate. The stalemate continued.

The stock market showed signs of weakness in March. After drifting slowly downward for nearly two weeks, stock prices dropped sharply on March 26, more than 8.2 million shares changed hands on the New York Stock Exchange, and the call-loan rate jumped to 20 percent. To many this looked like the end of the stock-market boom and the beginning of a financial crisis. At this point the National City Bank of New York intervened, offering enough call loans to prevent the rate from going above 20 percent. The incident became of special interest because the head of that bank, Charles E. Mitchell, was a director of the Federal Reserve Bank of New York. Members of the Federal Reserve Board were furious, and a Congressman demanded that

---

[18]Cable on March 15, 1929. The reference to "Gates" is to Gates W. McGarrah, Chairman of the Board of Directors of the New York Bank.

Mitchell resign his directorship at the New York Reserve Bank. Mitchell replied that his bank had merely met the normal responsibility of a major bank in New York in time of threatened crisis, and in doing so had promoted rather than conflicted with Federal Reserve purposes.

By May, shifts in attitudes began to appear at the Board and some of the Reserve banks. Among the Board there was less support for direct action without increases of discount rates. For this there were several reasons. One was probably the recommendation of rate increases by the Federal Advisory Council at its meetings on April 19 and May 21. Another was the growing unhappiness with the direct action program. Many Reserve bank officials probably shared the feelings expressed by Governor Norris of Philadelphia in his letter to Charles Hamlin on April 25:

> This whole process of "direct action" is wearing, friction-producing, and futile. We are following it honestly and energetically, but it is manifest, beyond the peradvanture of doubt, that it will never get us anywhere. It is like punching at a mass of dough. You make a dent where you hit, but the mass swells up at another point. As long as we maintain a discount rate which is absurdly low, and out of proportion to all other rates, the present conditions will continue. Our 5 per cent rate is equivalent to hanging a sign out over our door "Come in," and then we have to stand in the doorway and shout "Keep out." It puts us in an absurd and impossible position.

Unhappiness increased when the Board wrote to nine of the Reserve banks in late April and early May admonishing them to make the direct action program more effective. Platt dissented vigorously.

> ... I desire to place in the Board's records an emphatic protest against the continuance of this method of seeking control without supplementing it, and giving it force, by approving the rate increases, which in the judgment of the directors and officers of the Federal reserve banks of all the financial districts, supported by the unanimous judgment of the Federal Advisory Council, should be made.[19]

Governor Young, who was then out of town, also reacted vigorously after Platt informed him of the incident.

> I am bitterly opposed to any such intimidation and coercion as proposed by one of my colleagues and outlined in your letter of April 27th. I want to be so recorded. I will appreciate it if you will see that a copy of this telegram gets to every member of the Board....
> I have consistently backed the Board in its policy of February 6th, frequently when it was extremely difficult from my point of view, but it seems to me that if that policy in the opinion of the Board has been productive of such unsatisfactory results that the Board now feels that it must again reprimand nine of the reserve banks, such a nagging program is inadvisable. Therefore, if the Board feels that more should be done it should at least follow market rates for money.[20]

Thus support for rate increases strengthened within the Board. In the early weeks only Platt supported them; by May 23 Platt was joined by Young and Mellon. However, they could not carry the day against Miller, Cunningham, Hamlin, and James.

By this time, however, some Reserve bank officials who had been the

---

[19]Minutes of the Federal Reserve Board, April 30, 1929.

[20]Young telegram to Platt, May 6, 1929.

most ardent advocates of rate increases were beginning to think that such increases would be too late and too dangerous. They noted that the autumn seasonal increase in demands for credit was only three months away and dwelt at length on the deteriorating economic situation at home and abroad. As early as May 17, Norris wrote to Harrison that though he had earlier favored an increase in the discount rate he was becoming more doubtful about its expediency. He pointed to the falling prices of crops and the tightening situation abroad, adding prophetically:

I have a feeling that things are shaping themselves for a very decided business slump in the fall.

Harrison was moving toward the same view. The situation was especially dangerous because banks were becoming increasingly unwilling to borrow from the Federal Reserve, partly because of the pressure of the direct action program. One evidence of this was a rate for outside federal funds 1 to 2 percent above the discount rate.

At their meeting on May 28, the directors of the New York Bank discussed the entire situation at length. They decided not to propose a rate increase but to try to work out an overall program on which agreement might be reached. In a long letter to the Federal Reserve Board on May 31, McGarrah outlined the main points which he and his directors believed necessary in such a program.

They believe that at the moment the agreement upon a mutually satisfactory program is far more important than the discount rate . . . . In view of recent changes in the business and credit situation, we believe that a rate change now without a mutually satisfactory program might only exaggerate existing tendencies.
With this in view, and in the interest of trade, industry and agriculture, we believe it may soon be necessary:

(1) To establish a less restrictive discount policy in order that member banks may more freely borrow for the proper conduct of their business.
(2) To correct the widely understood intimation of the Federal Reserve Board that collateral loans are not a proper function of legitimate banking.
(3) To be prepared to increase the Federal reserve bank portfolios if and when any real need of doing so becomes apparent.

These steps may be necessary in order to restore business confidence, permit of reopening of a bond market, and to make funds more freely available to finance our export trade, especially in agricultural products at the time of crop movement.
Whether all this can be safely done without a firm rate control policy we are prepared to discuss, but a longer discussion as to the discount rate without a real understanding regarding a future program we regard as futile. Our directors, therefore, refrain from rate action in the hope that a general policy in which we and the Board can concur may be quickly determined.

. Harrison, McGarrah, and three directors of the New York Bank went to Washington on June 5 for a long discussion with the Federal Reserve Board. Harrison wrote to Governor Talley of Dallas the next day:

As a result of our meeting there several things seem clear: (a) that there is no chance of any immediate approval of a rate increase; (b) that we are in agreement that we may soon have to take care of the mid-year turnover as well as the late summer and fall demands for credit; (c) that we shall have to adopt a discount policy which will permit banks to borrow from us whenever they need to do so for the safe and proper conduct of their business regardless of whether or not they happen to have collateral loans in their portfolio.

At a meeting on June 11 the Federal Reserve Board considered two long memoranda, one by Miller and the other by Cunningham. Both praised the direct action program, contending that it had produced good results, that it provided precedents that would be useful in the future, and that it should not be abandoned. They agreed, however, that it should be "tempered." At the end of the discussion Young and Cunningham were appointed as a special committee to outline future policy. The result was the Board's letter of June 12 to all the Reserve banks.

The Federal Reserve Board has given further consideration to the question of future program. The Board thoroughly realizes that many factors now unforeseen may enter into the credit situation during the coming months. However, it believes that at the moment there is a possibility of carrying out a program for the future months without an immediate rise in the discount rate or, at this writing, easing the situation either by the purchase of bills or Government securities . . . .

Since February the policy of the Federal Reserve System has expressed itself primarily through what is called "direct action" and this position was taken deliberately by the Federal Reserve Board. To this position it holds fast. It is satisfied with the reasonableness of its policy and with its necessity, even though the methods and degree of application may be controversial.

The Board, after a careful review of the credit situation, finds that the increased demand for credit to meet mid-year requirements and also the credit demand for early autumn will probably require member banks to increase their rediscounts at the Federal Reserve Banks. This situation will be better served by a temporary suspension of a rigid policy of direct pressure, which, however, should not be abandoned, but rather tempered in order to permit member banks that have not found it practicable to readjust their position in accordance with the Board's principle, to avail themselves of the rediscount facilities of the Federal Reserve Banks for the purpose of avoiding, as far as possible, any undue strain or any unnecessary increase in the cost of credit in meeting the seasonal needs of agriculture, industry and commerce.

If such rediscounts become excessively large so as to unduly tighten the credit situation to a point where it acts as a deterrent to business and there are no other unsatisfactory factors in the situation, relief should be given through some release of Federal Reserve credit, preferably through the purchase of bills, but if it should appear at the time that such relief is not adequate or practicable, then, the Federal Reserve Board would be glad to give consideration to supplementing the relief through the purchase of short-time Government securities.

In suggesting this program for the future months, the Board is not unmindful that a limited number of member banks may expand undesirable loans upon Federal Reserve credit to a point which would not be justified by conditions and circumstances surrounding these institutions, and in such cases the Board would expect the Federal Reserve Banks to resort to the usual direct action.

Again, if such increase in rediscounts and Federal Reserve portfolios leads to an undue increase in loans having the earmarks of unsound banking practice in any great number of member banks where direct action cannot be applied simultaneously and quickly enough to protect the general credit situation, the Board would be glad to consider other corrective measures.

One has to sympathize with Governor Seay's reaction to this letter:

It is rather a strange and mixed course of procedure which the Board expects Federal Reserve banks to follow. Having told member banks that they are not within their reasonable rights for rediscounts while they are lending under certain conditions, we are now not to abandon that position but to temper it, and permit such banks which have not found it practicable to readjust their position in accordance with the Board's principle to avail themselves of rediscount facilities for the purpose of avoiding undue strain, etc. Then if they overdo the matter we are to tell them that they have overdone it and resume pressure. It is difficult to pilot the ship with such a variable compass.[21]

Yet for all its obscurity, the letter did permit the Reserve banks to suspend temporarily and to temper the rigid policy of direct pressure. How much this changed the actual policies of the Reserve banks is not known. It seems a safe guess, however, that most of the Reserve banks happily seized the opportunity to relax direct pressures.

Thus, June 12 marked the end of the rigid direct action policy. The rest of the easing program, except for a one-quarter of 1 percent decrease in the bill-buying rate, was delayed for almost 2 months to August 9.

CONCLUSIONS

The twin purposes of the direct action program initiated on February 2 and formally "tempered" and "temporarily suspended" on June 12 were to curb speculative loans and stock speculation while maintaining adequate supplies of credit at reasonable rates for legitimate uses. How successful was the program? Should we conclude with Miller and Cunningham that it proved to be "a practicable technique" which yielded useful results? Or should it be adjudged largely a failure? A review of actual developments during the period cannot provide definitive answers because there is no way of isolating the effects of the direct action program from others, such as those emanating from the increase of discount rates from 4 1/2 to 5 percent at 4 of the Reserve banks, the increase of bill-buying rates, and the decrease of Federal Reserve holdings of acceptances and government securities. Nor can we know how different the results might have been if other policies had been followed—for example, if discount rates had gone to 6 percent, or even higher.

A brief look at some of the actual developments during the period may nevertheless be of limited usefulness. Stock prices showed no upward trend during this time; in fact, they were almost 1 percent lower on June 12 than on February 6. Bank loans to brokers actually declined $530 million during the first half of 1929, but brokers' loans by others rose $1,160 million; the net increase was $630 million. These figures might suggest that the direct action program did in some degree encourage banks to shift from speculative to other loans. Perhaps it did, but it certainly did not succeed in preventing increases in interest rates on other types of credit. As already noted, the general structure of short-term interest rates reached its highest level since 1921 and bond prices fell.

Without denying that the direct action program had some effect, I suggest that the decline of bank loans to brokers and other developments in credit markets were influenced to a greater extent by the tight reserve positions of the banks in the face of high customer demands for bank credit. Member bank borrowings during June averaged $975 million, equal to 42

---

[21]Letter to Harrison, June 27, 1929.

percent of their total reserves. At the same time customer demands for bank loans were high. Under such circumstances it is usual for banks to favor customer loans and to try to adjust their reserve positions by selling assets of an "open-market" type—those that do not involve a customer relationship. The data in Table 4-1 suggest that this occurred in the period under review.

TABLE 4-1

Member Bank Loans and Investments
(amounts in millions of dollars)

	Decem- ber 31, 1928	June 29, 1929	Change, in millions	Per- centage change
Total Loans and investments	$35,684	$35,711	+$ 27	+ 0.08%
Open-market-type assets				
Investments				
U.S. government securities	4,312	4,155	− 157	− 3.6
All other investments	6,217	5,897	− 320	− 5.1
Total	$10,529	$10,052	−$ 477	− 4.5
Loans				
Loans to brokers and dealers	$ 3,531	$ 2,946	−$ 585	−16.6

Open-market paper (accept-
    ances, commercial paper,
    etc.)
	602	447	− 155	−25.7

Total loans	$ 4,133	$ 3,393	−$ 740	−17.9
Total open-market-type assets	$14,662	$13,445	−$1,217	− 8.3
Customer-type assets				
Loans on securities to others than brokers and dealers	6,373	6,813	+ 440	+ 6.9
All other loans	14,469	15,452	+ 1,243	+ 5.5
Total	$21,022	$22,265	+$1,243	+ 5.9

Source: Board of Governors of the Federal Reserve System, *Banking and Monetary Statistics,* Washington, D.C., 1943, pp. 74-78.

Total loans and investments of member banks changed very little in the first half of 1929. However, customer-type loans—including both collateral loans to others than brokers and dealers and "all other loans," which include commercial loans to customers—rose about $1.2 billion. This was almost exactly offset by reduced bank holdings of open-market assets. Banks reduced not only their loans to brokers and dealers but also their holdings of investments and short-term open-market paper, such as acceptances and commercial paper. In fact, the reduction of their holdings of these other assets were greater than the decrease of their loans to brokers and dealers. Thus banks contributed to the general rise of interest rates and the fall of bond prices.

5

The End of the New Era

When the direct action program was suspended on June 12, 1929, the Federal Reserve Board and the New York Reserve Bank were agreed that other steps should be taken to relieve the degree of credit restriction, or at least to prevent the autumn's seasonal increase in demands for credit from tightening credit conditions further. These other steps were slow in coming. The bill-buying rate applicable to maturities up to 120 days was reduced from 5 3/8 to 5 1/4 percent on July 12. However, since this still left it one-fourth of 1 percent above the discount rate, Federal Reserve bill holdings did not increase. The other parts of the easing program were not adopted until August 8.

The delay probably resulted in part from a perplexing set of economic developments during the summer. On the one hand, there was an upturn in stock speculation. Stock prices, which had shown little net change in the two months preceding mid-June, began to rise again and by early August had increased about 15 percent. Brokers' loans also rose, largely reflecting increased loans by others. On the other hand, domestic business conditions had begun to deteriorate. Industrial production reached a peak in June, leveled off, and began to decline slowly. New construction fell below earlier levels, and there were increasing complaints about shortages of mortgage money and difficulties in floating new bond issues. Restrictive impacts on other countries were becoming more apparent. These were closely related to the decrease of foreign bond issues in the American market, which by now was only a trickle, but it was accentuated by flows of foreign funds to New York. Governor Norman cabled Harrison from the Bank of England on June 14:

... if for further period your money rate continues firm and bond market dead then Europe will face the autumn in a weakened and worsened condition .... Since prospect of readjustment on your side appears to be increasingly uncertain we now expect to be forced sooner or later to increase our rate to 6 1/2 per cent.

Harrison was also worried, as he wrote to Governor Calkins on July 20:

I am also much concerned about the foreign situation and the effect of our high money rates not only upon our own export business but also upon monetary conditions general- ly abroad. Since the first of January eleven principal European banks of issue have lost approximately $310,000,000 in gold and devisen. In an effort to protect their reserves many of these banks have already increased their discount rates and face further increases. These higher rates of discount abroad are being found necessary not because of any inflation in their own credit position but because of the need to protect their reserves which are being drained away largely by conditions in this market.

In these circumstances some of the foreign banks of issue face penalty rates of discount or even some sort of suspension of gold standard unless conditions are quickly alleviated through an easing in our rate position here and an opening of our bond market. The effect of a continuance of these tendencies upon our export trade needs no elaboration.

By this time central bank discount rates had already risen to 5 1/2 percent in Britain and the Netherlands, 7 percent in Italy, and 7 1/2 percent in Germany.

Under such conditions, Federal Reserve officials began in early August to reconsider existing policies. Meeting with the Federal Reserve Board on August 2, Harrison outlined the general alternatives as he saw them:

(1) to adopt a policy of pressure reflected through sharp and repeated rate advances; (2) to do nothing but maintain the present position, or (3) to adopt a policy of relaxation which would let Federal Reserve credit out into the market as needed during the fall, if possible to do so safely.[1]

All present agreed that the third course was the most appropriate. On August 7 and 8 the governors of all 12 Reserve banks met with the Federal Reserve Board in Washington. Governor Young said that the Board had received the following suggestions and asked for comments and other proposals.

1. That the System do nothing, taking care of seasonal requirements through rediscounts or purchases of bills as offered.
2. That the System ease the situation by reducing the bill rate to a point where it will accumulate bills and, at least, maintain rediscounts where they are.
3. That the System ease the situation through the purchase of government securities if it feels that the acquisition of bills is not proceeding or will not proceed quickly enough.
4. That the System lower the bill rate, accumulate bills, and also purchase Government securities, raising the rediscount rate, not at the moment, but later if the open market operations should invite speculative demand for credit to any great extent.
5. That the System raise the rediscount rate in the larger centers, simultaneously reducing the bill rate and possibly going so far as to buy some government securities, thus building up the bill portfolio and reducing the large line of rediscounts.[2]

Everyone present except representatives of three Reserve banks—Seay of Richmond, McKay of Chicago, and Martin of St. Louis—favored easing in some degree. However, views differed more widely as to how this objective should be achieved. James proposed the creation of a special class of commodity paper which the Federal Reserve would purchase at a preferential rate, but his proposal was not accepted. Everyone voting for a policy of easing favored a reduction of bill-buying rates, which would increase Federal Reserve holdings of acceptances. Purchases of government securities were favored only in case purchases of acceptances proved to be inadequate. Most controversial was the

---

[1]Minutes of the Federal Reserve Board, August 2, 1929.

[2]*Ibid.*, August 7, 1929.

proposal that the discount rate be increased at one or more of the Reserve banks. James and Cunningham wanted no increase anywhere. All the governors except Harrison were opposed to increases at their own Reserve banks, but eight favored an increase in the New York rate. A crucial question was whether a rate increase in New York would force the other Reserve banks to raise their rates. Nine thought it would not, but the representatives of Atlanta, Chicago, and St. Louis were apprehensive.

At the end of their meeting on August 8, the governors submitted their recommendations to the Federal Reserve Board.

It is the judgement of the Governors that the demand for increased credit incident to the autumn requirements of crop moving and business should be met, so far as possible, by an increase in the bill portfolio of such banks as care to participate in bill purchases.

The Governors are also of the opinion that this procedure can best and most safely be undertaken, and with least risk of abuse in the use of Federal reserve credit, under the protection of an effective discount rate in the New York district.

They are further led to this conclusion by the expressed belief that an increase in the discount rate of the Federal Reserve Bank of New York would necessitate increases in few, if any, of the other Federal reserve banks during the period of seasonal business demand; and the desire of the directors and officers of all other reserve banks to avoid increases, if possible. It is, therefore, recommended that the Reserve Board act favorably on any application that may be made by the Federal Reserve Bank of New York for an increase in its existing rate.[3]

On the same day New York voted to increase its discount rate from 5 to 6 percent and to lower from 5 1/4 to 5 1/8 percent its bill-buying rate applicable to maturities up to 120 days. The Board approved the rates the same day and they became effective on August 9. Approval of the reduction of the bill-buying rate was unanimous, but Cunningham and James opposed the increase in the discount rate. Cunningham feared that a 6 percent rate in New York while discount rates remained at 5 percent at the other Reserve banks would suck funds from the interior to the stock market. Moreover, he contended, to raise the discount rate to combat security speculation violated the Federal Reserve Act, which provided that rates should be such as to accommodate commerce, agriculture, and industry.

This action of the Federal Reserve in raising the New York discount rate while at the same time lowering the bill-buying rate has raised many questions, among which are these: (1) Was the net effect of this combination of actions expected to be restrictive, easing, or neutral? The discussion preceding the action indicates clearly that the overall purpose was to ease somewhat. Federal Reserve officials explicitly rejected policies aimed at further restriction or even at maintenance of the status quo and voted for some relaxation. (2) Was the objective only to meet seasonal needs? Increased seasonal demands for credit in the autumn and a desire to prevent these from increasing interest rates were certainly mentioned prominently in the discussion and may alone have led some to favor the policy. Yet it is hard to believe that this was the only purpose. Also mentioned prominently were the need to relieve pressures on domestic business and on the international situation. Moreover, sever-

---

[3]*Ibid.*, August 8, 1929.

al officials expressed their hope that the policy would not only prevent further strains on credit but would also have a net easing effect. (3) If the purpose was to ease, why was the New York discount rate raised from 5 to 6 percent? The effect of this action, considered by itself, was certainly not to ease credit for legitimate business or any other purpose. The objective seems to have been to avoid the appearance of a sharp shift of Federal Reserve policy toward ease, to warn stock speculators, and somehow to inhibit the flow of credit into speculative loans. Just how this was to be accomplished is not clear, but the following two communications throw some light on the motivations. Deputy Governor Burgess of the New York Reserve Bank wrote to the manager of the Buffalo branch on August 9:

> The present hope is that the low bill rates will bring us a sufficient quantity of bills so that as we go into the autumn member banks will not have to increase their indebtedness but may, in fact, perhaps decrease it somewhat so that there will be no difficulty of a credit shortage. The high discount rate gives added assurance that any money that is put into the market through purchase of bills will be used to repay indebtedness here rather than for an expansion of credit for speculative uses.

On August 10 Harrison cabled a longer explanation to the governors of several important European banks.

> As you know our discount rate has been below open market rates for many months. To obtain a better control of our market we have been anxious to establish a more normal relationship between our rate and private rates. The need for this readjustment has been accentuated by the approach of the autumn in as much as (a) the usual autumn demands for credit (b) the tendency of our present high market rates to attract gold from abroad both make it desirable for us to put additional funds into the market by the purchase of bills and possibly later if necessary by the purchase of government securities. We have felt however that it would be unwise to take this apparently necessary step without first safeguarding the use of our credit by an increase in our discount rate to a level more nearly in line with market rates. Having increased our discount rate we are now hopeful that we may be able to buy sufficient bills to satisfy the usual autumn needs without additional money stringency and even possibly to relieve the money market somewhat. While our domestic situation calls for such a policy we of course have in mind the need of the European economy also for lower interest rates in New York and believe that our present program will work towards that end more quickly and more safely than a program of relaxation without the protection of an effective discount rate.

To correct "abnormal" rate relationships was probably an important consideration. For one thing, as noted earlier, discount rates had for months been abnormally low relative to short-term market rates. Reserve bank officials complained that this encouraged banks to borrow and remain in debt and weakened the tradition against continuous borrowing. Moreover, discount rates had been abnormally low relative to Federal Reserve bill-buying rates. Since February the bill-buying rate had been from one-fourth to three-eighths of 1 percent above the discount rate. This was the principal reason for the sharp decline of Federal Reserve holdings of acceptances. When the New York discount rate was raised to 6 percent and the lowest bill-buying rate reduced to 5 1/8 percent, a more normal relationship was established. Offerings of acceptances to the Federal Reserve could be expected to increase. Federal Reserve holdings rose from only $79 million on August 7 to $264 million on September 25 and to $379 million on October 23, the eve of the stock-market crash.

Thus the increase from August 7 was $300 million. This, together with a $40 million increase in the monetary gold stock, eased slightly the reserve positions of member banks. Member bank borrowings from the Federal Reserve declined from $1,064 million to $796 million and their unborrowed reserves rose $323 million. However, market rates of interest did not fall and some rose slightly.

The New York Bank began to buy acceptances almost immediately after approval of the new policy on August 8. Within a few weeks its officials could report that bill purchases were more than sufficient to offset seasonal increases in demands for credit and that member banks had been able to reduce their borrowing slightly. It now seemed likely that purchases of government securities would not be needed. Thus on this occasion, as in the latter part of 1928, the bill-buying rate became a highly important policy instrument. Because of this, some members of the Board, especially Miller, wanted a review of policy-making procedures. Miller asserted that this was a national policy problem too important to be left largely to New York; that the other leading Reserve banks should have a voice and the Board more precise control. Specifically, he felt that the Board should approve or disapprove each actual buying rate. New York again objected, insisting that it needed flexibility to adjust to changing market conditions. Miller's proposal was not adopted, but New York did begin to propose both minimum and maximum rates; these were set in August at 5 and 6 percent respectively, this leaving New York with a wide range of discretion.

At a meeting in Washington on September 24, the OMIC reviewed existing policies and recommended, in effect, that these be continued.

> During the past eighteen months interest rates in this country have gradually risen and money, especially for new undertakings, has become more difficult to obtain. While business continues at a high level, there are some indications of a possible impending recession.
>
> Rates in many foreign centers have risen even more markedly and the loss of reserves of central banks threatens further increases in rates and probable curtailment of Europe's capacity to buy this country's products.
>
> In accordance with the System policy adopted on August 8th seasonal requirements for Federal Reserve credit have been met by bill purchases, and in fact such purchases have been sufficient to reduce rediscounts to some extent.
>
> For the purpose of avoiding any increase and, if possible, facilitating some further reduction in the total volume of member bank discounts during the fall season, if this can be done without stimulating unnecessary or abnormal expansion of member bank credit, the committee favors a further increase of the open-market holdings of the Federal Reserve Banks. It favors an increase of these holdings by the continued purchase of bills if they can be obtained in sufficient amounts to accomplish this purpose. If bills cannot be obtained in sufficient amounts without interfering with the present desirable distribution, it favors the purchase of Government certificates of the short maturities.
>
> The committee therefore recommends that it be authorized to purchase not to exceed 25 million dollars a week of such certificates for account of such banks as care to participate, with the understanding that there be careful current review of the consequences of such purchases, in order that there may be another meeting with the Board at any time that . . . . . may seem advisable either to the Board or to the committee. In any event, the committee feels that there should be another such meeting not later than November 1st.[4]

[4]Minutes of the OMIC, September 24, 1929.

Governor Young indicated the Board's approval a week later.

> The Board approves of your program to continue the purchasing of bills, and if necessary supplement the program by purchasing short-time Government securities for those Reserve Banks that desire to participate for the purchase mentioned in your recommendation, to wit:—"For the purpose of avoiding any increase and, if possible facilitating some further reduction in the total volume of member bank discounts during the fall season, if this can be done without stimulating unnecessary or abnormal expansion of member bank credit." The Board, to this end, grants the authorization requested to purchase short-time Government securities at not to exceed 25 million dollars a week.
> In authorizing such purchases, the Board is approving mainly for seasonal reasons and such approval should not be interpreted as a reversal of former policy.
> The Board welcomes and adopts the suggestion contained in the recommendation of the committee that there be careful review of the consequences of such purchases, and you will be advised promptly by the Board if at any time it believes that purchases should be discontinued or the procedure changed.[5]

Two things about this policy are noteworthy. (1) Neither the OMIC nor the Board was yet ready for a real reversal of policy. Both wanted to avoid any increase, and if possible to facilitate some decrease, of member bank borrowings, but neither wanted to shift toward a significantly less restrictive policy. (2) The authorization to purchase government securities was very small—no more than $25 million a week. This was far too small to permit a significant reversal of policy and it was to prove inadequate during the stock-market crisis. Reserve officials could not know that such a crisis was less than a month away, and that it would call for a sharp reversal of policies.

THE STOCK-MARKET CRASH

The stock market's rise and fall in 1929 was no smooth, uninterrupted climb followed by a vertical plunge into an abyss. A chart of stock prices in that year is like the silhouette of a rugged mountain, with the rise on one side interspersed with flat areas and shallow declines and the descent on the other side interrupted by several minor peaks. We have already mentioned the erratic behavior of stock prices in March, including some sharp declines; the failure of the general level of prices to change significantly during the two months prior to mid-June; and the 15 percent increase from mid-June to early August. The rise continued through that month. By the first of September the average of stock prices was 30 percent above the level at the beginning of the year.[6] This figure refers to the average level; speculative favorites had risen much more while many others had actually declined.

Stock prices behaved quite erratically in September, sometimes rising, sometimes falling, but showing a net decrease of about 5 percent for the month. The number of shares changing hands on the New York Stock Exchange rose above 4 million on many days and sometimes above 5 million.

---

[5]Young letter to Harrison, October 1, 1929.

[6]These data refer to the Standard Statistics index, which includes the stocks of 90 industrial, railroad, and public utilities corporations.

Wide differences of view concerning the future course of stock prices were obviously developing. There were still many optimists, as indicated by the amount of buying when price breaks occurred. However, increasing numbers were becoming less optimistic and even pessimistic. These were some of the sources of weakness most often cited at that time: (1) the height of stock prices relative to current and immediately prospective dividends and earnings; (2) the great rise of brokers' loans, which was considered an indication that stocks were "falling into weaker hands"; (3) the persistence of high interest rates and bond yields; (4) the flamboyant and widely publicized operations of pools and other manipulators; (5) rising concern about the future course of business acitvity. Current newspaper reports referred to downturns in steel buying, steel production, auto production, and other evidences of weakness. The National City Bank letter concluded consolingly that ". . . a slackening of trade and industry should be beneficial at this time in correcting undesirable tendencies and thus pave the way for renewed expansion later on."[7]

The market became even more erratic in October, as indicated in Table 5-1. On October 3 came what *The New York Times* described as "the worst break of the year." Sales on the New York Stock Exchange were 4,747,000 shares, with 1,500,000 shares traded in the last hour. Prices continued to decline the next day with a volume of 5,624,000 shares. Then they rallied for a week, rising to levels above those prevailing at the beginning of the month, only to lose all these gains and more by October 22. Up to this point the highest number of shares traded in any one day had been 6,092,000 shares. Then came October 23. Prices dropped sharply with 6,375,000 shares traded. Newspaper headlines proclaimed, "Prices of stock crash in heavy liquidations. Total drop of billions. Paper loss $4,000,000,000. 2,600,000 shares sold in final hour in record decline. Many accounts wiped out."[8] The next day brought a huge wave of selling, with 12,894,560 shares traded. Prices declined sharply but rallied toward the close on an announcement that bankers were going to support the market. Prices remained relatively stable during the next two days, leading some to conclude that the worst was over. Then came two days of disaster; the number of shares traded was 9,213,000 on October 28 and 16,410,000 on October 29. It was estimated that the value of 240 representative stocks had declined nearly $16 billion since October 1 and that the decline for all 1,279 issues listed on the New York Stock Exchange was probably 2 or 3 times that amount.[9] The market then rallied again as the principal New York banks reduced margin requirements and as Morgan, Rockefeller, and others announced their intentions to buy. However, the respite was brief. Prices broke sharply again on November 4 and then continued irregularly downward until November 13, when they reached their low point.

At this point, average stock prices were far below their level on September 1. On the earlier date the value of all stocks listed on the New York Stock Exchange was $90 billion; on December 1 it was only $64 billion.

---

[7]*The New York Times*, October 1, 1929, p. 36.

[8]*The New York Times*, October 24, 1929, p. 1.

[9]*Ibid.*, October 30, 1929, p. 1.

These were indeed huge losses, but it should be noted that even at the lowest point in November average stock prices were still as high as they had been in March 1928. In effect, the crash merely wiped out the gains since that time.

FEDERAL RESERVE POLICIES DURING THE CRASH PERIOD

The erratic behavior of stock prices during September and the declines during the first three weeks of October evoked no change in Federal Reserve policy. The declines beginning on October 23 were a far different matter, for they raised the danger that the stock-market crash would bring a full-scale banking and financial crisis. This was primarily because of the size of brokers' loans and the danger that they would be withdrawn. On October 4 total loans to brokers in New York City were $8,525 million; of these, $1,095 million were by New York City banks, $790 million by outside banks, and $6,640 million by others. Outside banks and others began to withdraw their funds immediately after the stock-market decline on October 23, and their withdrawals had become very rapid by October 28. Their total withdrawals appear to have been approximately $2 billion during the week ended October 30.[10] New York City banks faced dangerous problems. To prevent the sharp decline of stock prices from turning into a rout, perhaps leading to a closing of the exchanges, they would have to lend more to replace at least some of the funds withdrawn by others. To make matters worse, New York City banks lost reserves as deposits were transferred from them to banks in other areas. They would be able to cope with the situation only if the Federal Reserve provided them with more reserves. The Federal Reserve was willing to do this, but uncertain as to the best means.

For several days after October 23 New York City banks had to meet their needs by borrowing from the Federal Reserve. Within 5 days their borrowings had risen from only $40 million to more than $150 million. To ease the strain, the directors of the New York Reserve Bank voted on October 24 by the narrow margin of 4 to 3 to reduce the discount rate from 6 to 5 1/2 percent. This action was predicated on Board approval or disapproval the same day ". . . because in the present circumstances the directors believe it would be unwise to hold the matter in abeyance." The Board disapproved unanimously. However, Hamlin stated that he would probably have voted for the reduction if the vote in New York had not been so close. When New York proposed a reduction to 5 percent on October 31 the Board approved immediately and unanimously.

In the meantime, purchases of government securities by the New York Bank had created friction between it and the Board. It will be remembered that after its September meeting the OMIC had been authorized to buy no more than $25 million of government securities in any week. During the night of October 28, following a day on which stock prices had fallen sharply and

---

[10]Data on total brokers' loans on these two dates are unavailable. The figure cited is derived from member banks' weekly reports.

large amounts of brokers' loans had been withdrawn, Harrison feared that a catastrophe threatened and that call rates would soar unless assistance were given. He concluded that the Federal Reserve should ease the situation by purchasing government securities before the market opened and the call-loan rate was announced. He did not, however, have time to consult the Federal Reserve Board or the other members of the OMIC, and he was able to reach only 2 of his directors at 3 o'clock in the morning. Early on the morning of October 29 New York purchased for its own account $50 million of government securities and added another $65 million to its holdings during the next 2 days. Several members of the Board were very annoyed when Harrison infomed them on October 29 of his actions and the reasons for his haste. They supported unanimously Cunningham's resolution that further purchases of government securities should be suspended, that the most effective method of meeting the situation would be to reduce the New York discount rate to 5 percent, and that under the circumstances all the Reserve banks should lend freely. The angered Board was in a mood to tighten its control over open-market operations. James asserted that the New York action without prior approval by the OMIC and the Board was "contrary to the letter and spirit of the so-called 'gentlemen's agreement' under which the OMIC was formed and has functioned during the last five years or more," and recommended that counsel be instructed to draw up and submit to the Board a suitable recommendation putting final approval of open-market operations with the Federal Reserve Board.[11] Hamlin proposed that all operations in government securities, whether for the open-market investment account or for the accounts of the individual Reserve banks, be brought under such control. Miller thought acceptances should also be included.

On November 5, with only Platt dissenting, the Board approved the following regulation which was to be sent to the Reserve banks with a request for their reactions.

Except with the approval of the Federal Reserve Board, no Federal Reserve Bank shall (a) buy any bonds, notes, certificates of indebtedness or Treasury bills of the United States, having a maturity in excess of fifteen days, or (b) sell any bonds, notes, certificates of indebtedness, or Treasury bills of the United States.[12]

This regulation was never put into effect, however, because two days later Young advised the Board that its counsel thought there was considerable doubt of its legality. The Board's attitude toward open-market operations was still negative when it considered the recommendations of the OMIC at the conclusion of its meeting on November 12. In effect, the committee recommended that its existing authority to purchase up to $25 million a week be replaced with one authorizing purchases up to $200 million in total. When this recommendation came before the Board, Miller offered a motion which canceled the existing authority to purchase up to $25 million a week, authorized no specific amount, stated the Board's feelings that conditions were still

---

[11]Minutes of the Federal Reserve Board, October 25, 1929.

[12]*Ibid.,* November 5, 1929.

TABLE 5-1

Common Stock Prices and Shares Traded on the New York Stock Exchange, October and November 1929

Day of month		Index of stock prices 1926 = 100	Number of shares traded on the New York Stock Exchange (amounts in millions)
October	1	238.1	4.525
	2	239.8	3.368
	3	229.9	4.747
	4	227.5	5.624
	5	238.1	2.452
	6	S[a]	S
	7	241.7	4.262
	8	240.9	3.758
	9	240.4	3.157
	10	244.7	4.000
	11	244.3	3.964
	12	C[b]	C
	13	S	S
	14	242.6	2.756
	15	240.6	3.107
	16	232.2	4.088
	17	235.8	3.864
	18	229.0	3.508
	19	222.4	3.488
	20	S	S
	21	220.2	6.092
	22	224.5	4.130
	23	211.2	6.375
	24	204.5	12.895
	25	207.4	5.923
	26	206.0	2.088
	27	S	S
	28	180.6	9.213
	29	162.2	16.410
	30	182.6	10.727
	31	191.8	7.149
November	1	C	C
	2	C	C
	3	S	S
	4	181.7	6.203
	5	H[c]	H
	6	163.7	5.915
	7	169.7	7.184
	8	168.2	3.215
	9	C	C
	10	S	S
	11	157.7	3.367
	12	148.7	6.453
	13	140.2	7.761
	14	152.8	5.569
	15	161.2	4.340
	16	C	C
	17	S	S
	18	159.5	2.747
	19	164.4	2.718
	20	168.9	2.829
	21	171.6	3.139
	22	171.0	2.929
	23	C	C
	24	S	S

TABLE 5-1 - Continued

Day of month	Index of stock prices 1926 = 100	Number of shares traded on the New York Stock Exchange (amounts in millions)
November 25	169.0	3.020
26	164.1	2.634
27	166.1	2.432
28	H	H
29	C	C
30	C	C

aS = Sunday, bC = Closed, cH = Holiday

Source: *Standard Statistics Basebook*, 1932, Standard Statistics, Inc., New York.

too unclear to permit the formulation of a permanent policy, and empowered the Governor of the Board to act in an emergency. However, it continued,

if emergency should arise with such suddenness and be so acute that it is not practicable to confer with the Governor, the Board will interpose no objection to a purchase operation being undertaken with the understanding, however, that prompt advice of such purchase be furnished the Board.[13]

The motion was adopted with only Platt voting "no." His vote was negative because the existing $25 million authorization was canceled. Thus the OMIC was left with no authority to act without prior consultation with the Governor of the Board.

Directors and officials of the New York Bank were quite upset by the Board's action, both because of the implied limitation on their powers and because they wanted the System to be in a position to buy securities quickly if necessary. There followed several discussions between Governor Young and Harrison and a committee of the directors of the New York Bank. Harrison urged Young to leave questions of procedure and jurisdiction for determination after the difficult period had ended, and he promised that if the Board would approve the OMIC recommendations of November 12 he would suggest to his directors that as a matter of policy the New York Bank refrain from making pruchases for its own account for credit-policy purposes without the Board's approval. However, this would not apply to emergencies or to small purchases purely as a local market matter.[14]

Young told his colleagues on November 25 that he was willing that the Board content itself with approving general policy, reserving the right to express itself if purchases were made too rapidly. He then moved that the OMIC be authorized to buy up to $200 million of government securities with the understanding that if the Board felt that purchases were being made too rapidly it would so inform the committee. Young's motion was adopted, but Miller, James, and Cunningham voted against it.

13*Ibid.*, November 12, 1929.

14Minutes of the Board of Directors of the Federal Reserve Bank of New York, November 27, 1929.

There can be no doubt that the purchases made by New York for its own account played a major role in precipitating this controversy. However, more basic issues were involved. We have already noted that on several earlier occasions some Board members had expressed dissatisfaction with existing procedures and had also stated their hope and even their determination, that reliance on open-market operations for policy purposes would be reduced. These attitudes persisted into the depression, as we shall see later.

By mid-November the Federal Reserve had taken several easing actions. The New York discount rate had been reduced from 6 to 5 percent on November 1 and to 4 1/2 percent on November 15. Its bill-buying rate had been reduced in 4 steps from 5 1/8 to 4 percent. System holdings of government securities had risen $177 million. The reserve positions of member banks had improved somewhat but were still far from "easy" by normal standards. Member bank borrowings from the Federal reserve still amounted to $970 million, equal to 37 percent of their total reserves.

Market rates of interest began to fall immediately after the crash, partly because of Federal Reserve actions and partly because of declining demands for funds. Even at the end of the year, however, they were still as high as they had been in mid-1928. With the fall of interest rates in New York, the strain on monetary conditons abroad was lessened. The flow was now away from New York. Several foreign central banks were now, at long last, able to lower their discount rates and to lessen other credit restrictions. For example, the Bank of England, which had been forced to raise its bank rate to 6 1/2 percent in September, reduced it to 6 percent in November and 5 1/2 percent in December. Central bank rates were reduced in Germany from 7 1/2 to 7 percent in December, in the Netherlands from 5 1/2 to 5 percent in November and to 4 1/2 percent in December, and in Belgium from 5 to 4 1/2 percent in December. The relief was indeed welcome but for some it was perhaps too late.

Thus the stock-market boom, which for nearly 2 years had been the principal reason for the Federal Reserve's restrictive policies, had ended. The Federal Reserve's problem was now very different and even more challenging—to deal with what became the greatest depression that America and the capitalist world had ever experienced.

6

An Appraisal of Policies in 1928–1929

In attempting to evaluate American monetary policies in 1928 and 1929, one immediately encounters a number of difficult questions: What were the results of the policies actually followed? What alternative policies were available? How much different would the outcome have been if policies had been different in specified ways and degrees? These questions involve still others relating to objectives and their ranking and compatibility with each other, the appropriateness and adequacy of the instruments used, and the skill of Federal Reserve officials in using the instruments at their disposal to promote their objectives.

ACTUAL RESULTS

On the basis of their own objectives, Federal Reserve policies in 1928 and 1929 must be judged a failure. Their major purposes were to curb the "excess" of stock-market speculation and the same time avoid deleterious effects on domestic economic activity and on monetary and economic conditions abroad. They achieved none of these. Stock speculation continued to grow for nearly two years after the Federal Reserve began to restrict credit to curb it, and when the crash came it could hardly have been worse. If the Federal Reserve played a role in ending the speculative boom it was probably by creating, or by helping to create, a downturn in economic activity.

I also conclude that Federal Reserve policies in the last two years of the 1920s must bear a heavy responsibility for precipitating the great depression in the United States and the rest of the world, though I do not believe that policies in this period were responsible in large degree for the severity and duration of the depression. This is not to say that Federal Reserve policies were solely responsible for the onset of the depression. Other developments undoubtedly contributed to the vulnerability of prosperity. For example, the long period of prosperity and high rates of investment in the United States during the 1920s had brought huge increases in the nation's stock of real capital. The housing shortage had been alleviated, and there was no longer such a large backlog of unsatisfied demand for construction at profitable

83

prices. The stock of capital in many industries had also grown greatly. Under these conditions, the marginal efficiency of investment was probably falling somewhat. To prolong the prosperity period and to maintain investment at levels sufficient to absorb the very large flow of saving that would accompany "full employment" levels of national income probably called for lower interest rates. Under such conditions, credit restriction and rising interest rates could be fatal to prosperity.

No matter how it may be measured, credit restriction during this period, and especially from mid-1928 to the stock-market crash, was severe and prolonged. For nearly 18 months following May 1928 member bank borrowings at the Federal Reserve were rarely below $900 million, or 39 percent of their total reserves, and during nearly half of these months borrowings were above $1 billion. Unborrowed reserves were throughout this period at least 10 percent below their level at the end of 1926, and most of the time they were even lower. The money supply grew very slowly. In mid-1929 the money supply, narrowly defined to include only currency and demand deposits, was only 1.2 percent above its level a year earlier and 2.5 percent above its level 2 years earlier. More broadly defined to include time deposits at commercial banks as well, the money supply had grown only one-tenth of 1 percent in a year and 4.3 percent in 2 years. Both short-term and long-term interest rates rose, and there were increasing complaints about shortages of mortgage money and difficulties in floating new bond issues. The increasing cost of loan funds probably did not restrict investment spending by those corporations in a position to issue common stock on favorable terms, but it must have had repressive effects on others, and especially on construction.

The restrictive credit policy in the United States and the accompanying increase of interest rates and deterioration of the bond market certainly tightened monetary conditions abroad and made many countries more vulnerable to depression. The sharp decline of American foreign lending and the flow of foreign funds to the United States in 1929 tightened credit conditions abroad in several ways—by decreasing the supply of loan funds from America, by draining off reserves in the form of gold and dollars, and by inducing central banks to raise discount rates and take other restrictive measures. Other factors also probably contributed to the economic downturns in several other countries in late 1929 and 1930, but the tightening of credit during the period before the stock-market crash was at least a contributing and perhaps a decisive factor.

CONFLICTING OBJECTIVES

The primary reason for the failure of Federal Reserve policies during this period to achieve any of their objectives stems from the great weight given to the objective of preventing "absorption of credit in stock speculation." This mistake, in turn, stemmed from failure to define objectives clearly and in operational terms, lack of understanding and even misunderstanding, and the inadequacies of the instruments used. As indicated earlier, Federal Reserve officials repeatedly took the position that they were not arbiters of stock values or concerned with stock speculation *per se;* their job was to regulate credit and their concern was to prevent the absorption of credit in speculation which would raise the cost of credit for legitimate uses. I have already expressed my agreement with the conclusion reached by most of the economists who have studied the issue—that the rise of brokers' loans and other loans on security collateral did not significantly "absorb credit" in the sense of decreasing the supply of funds available for other uses and of raising the general level of interest rates. Thus Federal Reserve officials were fighting a nonexistent, or at most a weak, force and doing so in ways that promoted the very results they wished to avoid—decreases in the supply and increases in the cost of funds for "legitimate" uses.

To contend that the Federal Reserve should not have pursued its professed purpose of preventing the "absorption of credit" is not to say that it should not have concerned itself with stock speculation and the behavior of stock prices. A central bank whose controlling objective is to promote economic stability may properly take actions to regulate a stock-market boom, for at least two reasons. (1) High and rising stock prices and falling yields on stocks may generate excessive spending for output and especially excessive spending for investment during the boom period. The behavior of spending for output and of employment and price levels during the late 1920s did not indicate that this was happening, however. (2) The fall of stock prices after they have risen to levels that cannot be sustained is likely to generate depressive forces on the economy by increasing the cost of business financing through equity issues, by reducing consumption because of the decrease of wealth as measured in money terms, and by damaging business expectations as to the profitability of new investment. Despite their public protestations to the contrary, I believe that many Federal Reserve officials were strongly motivated by just such fears as these. They failed to say so because they were not convinced, or at least thought the public did not believe, that it was the proper function of the Federal Reserve to regulate stock speculation or the behavior of stock prices, no matter what might be the impact on the economy. Its jurisdiction was over credit, and its purpose was to regulate credit so as to accommodate commerce, industry, and agriculture. Only if rationalized in these terms would its intervention be condoned.

Moreover, the instruments that the Federal Reserve used were simply inappropriate and inadequate to achieve the dual objectives of limiting the use of credit for stock speculation and preventing decreases in the supply of credit for other uses. The two principal methods that were used—the direct action program and general credit restriction through open-market sales of securities and increases in discount and bill-buying rates—failed to achieve their objectives not because of minor errors of degree and timing in their use but because they were basically inadequate for the task.

The almost inherent inadequacy of the direct action program as conceived in 1929 can best be suggested by comparing it with the margin requirements authorized in October 1934. Under this legislation the Federal Reserve Board was empowered to set and change minimum margin requirements for loans made for purchasing or carrying securities listed on the national securities exchanges. To put the same thing another way, the Board was empowered to stipulate maximum loan values, these being stated as a percentage of the values of the securities. It is illegal for any borrower to borrow or any lender to lend more than this stipulated percentage. Two points about this device are noteworthy. (1) It provides a way of limiting effective demands for such loans. By decreasing maximum loan values, the Board can decrease the effective demands for loans of this type and thus perhaps tend to increase the supply of credit flowing through other channels. (2) It applies not only to banks but also to other lenders.

The direct action program of 1929 had neither of these important characteristics. It made no attempt to curb demands for such loans, and it applied to only one type of lender—those member banks currently in debt to the Federal Reserve banks. No more than a third of the member banks borrowed during any one month in 1929, though over 60 percent borrowed at some time during the year.[1] The program was not directed at member banks which were not borrowing from the Federal Reserve or at nonmember banks or at nonbank lenders.

Partly because of its limited coverage, the program was doomed to failure from the beginning. Miller and its other supporters underestimated the general mobility of funds among the various branches of the money market, and they grossly underestimated the mobility of funds into brokers' loans. The call-loan market was widely known, such loans could be placed quickly and at small cost, and the call loan was considered one of the safest and most liquid earning assets in the entire financial market. Together with acceptances, open-market commercial paper, and short-term government obligations, call loans had long been the prime investments for short-term funds. It was almost inevitable that any significant rise of call-loan rates relative to others would attract large flows of funds to that market. Banks might indeed hesitate to refuse loans to customers in order to lend at call, but they and other lenders had no such reason to favor other types of open-market loans. In fact, many undoubtedly sold these other types of open-market paper, or at least refrained from buying them, in order to take advantage of favorable call rates. Thus it was impossible to insulate rates in the rest of the open market from those in the call market.

Moreover, as was noted earlier, a bank which was admonished for holding brokers' loans or other collateral loans while borrowing from the Federal Reserve could adjust by calling the criticized loans or by repaying its borrowings at the Federal Reserve. Faced with such alternatives, some undoubtedly reduced their criticized loans, but at least some repaid their debt at the Federal Reserve, doing so by borrowing elsewhere or by selling acceptances, open-market commercial paper, government securities, or other open-market assets. Some may even have made marginal reductions in their other loans to customers. Also plausible is Harrison's contention that the direct action program tended to strengthen the tradition against borrowing and made some banks unwilling to borrow from the Federal Reserve for any purpose.

Thus the direct action program as conceived and executed was incapable

---

[1]*Annual Report of the Federal Reserve Board,* 1929, p. 66.

of achieving its dual objectives. The same was true of general credit restriction. There can be no doubt that much more restrictive actions could have killed the speculative mania. By selling their few remaining government securities and raising discount and bill-buying rates sharply, the Reserve banks could have slowed speculation to a crawl. What is extremely doubtful is that they could have achieved this without precipitating a depression. Harrison and the other advocates of more restrictive policies, including higher discount rates, realized fully that they could not avoid raising the cost of credit for "legitimate" business while the restrictive policy was in effect. However, they hoped that the period of restriction could be short because speculation would be affected much more quickly and permanently than business activity, thus permitting an early shift to easier money. They relied heavily on two ideas: that general credit restriction would have a quicker and heavier impact on speculative credit than on credit for other uses and that speculation would prove to be more sensitive to increased interest rates and changes in expectations than would business activity. They were probably wrong on both counts.

Though not to the same degree as Miller, they underestimated the mobility of credit among the various branches of the credit market, and especially among the branches of the open market, and thus overestimated the extent to which interest rates on speculative loans, however defined, could be raised relative to other interest rates. They also overestimated the vulnerability of speculation relative to that of business activity. A highly restrictive policy could affect both speculation and business activity in two principal ways: by increasing the cost of credit and by altering expectations as to the future course of prices and profits. It was hoped that speculation would be quieted for a long period, both by the increased cost of credit for carrying securities and by eradication of bullish expectations concerning future stock prices. This position underestimated the strength and resiliency of these expectations. Most of those who borrowed to carry stocks were not expecting appreciation of a mere 5 or 10 percent a year; they were expecting much more, and an increase of a few percentage points in interest rates would not deter them as long as their expectations remained so rosy, which would be as long as they did not expect a business depression. Under other circumstances in which expectations as to stock prices were less durable, a policy of general restriction might have succeeded in achieving its dual objectives, but in the New Era of optimistic bullishness it could not.

Investment in such areas as construction, plant and equipment, and inventory was more vulnerable on both counts. Since they were generally not expected to yield such high rates of return, they were more sensitive to increases in interest rates, and thus a deterioration of expectations would surely threaten investment spending.

In short, this was a case in which the Federal Reserve failed primarily because it was pursuing multiple objectives which it could not reconcile with the instruments that it used. The failure was not primarily because it administered these instruments ineptly; it was because neither the direct action program, nor general credit restriction, nor the two combined, was adequate for the job.

POLICY ALTERNATIVES

What were the policy alternatives? One would have been to discard one or more objectives and concentrate on those remaining. For example, the Federal Reserve might have disclaimed responsibility for stock-market behavior and shaped its policies solely with a view to promoting economic stability and growth. This policy would have called for more liberal monetary expansion. In this event, stock speculation would have been at least as great and a crash would have come sooner or later, which would probably have had unfavorable effects on investment and consumption. However, the impact would not have fallen on an American and a world economy already weakened and made vulnerable to depression by a long period of monetary restraint.

Another general alternative would have been for the Federal Reserve to concern itself with stock-market behavior as well as other objectives, but to develop instruments appropriate and adequate for the purpose. Some of these might have been developed by the federal government. In criticizing Federal Reserve policies in the period, it is only fair to recall the environment in which the System operated. In dealing with speculative excesses, it had little help from the federal government. President Coolidge's optimistic statements about brokers' loans and stock prices in early 1928 are less important for the small fillip they gave to speculation than as symbols of the lack of concern and sense of responsibility of his administration for developments in this area. Herbert Hoover was apparently concerned and communicated his worries to a few associates, but neither as Secretary of Commerce nor as President during the last six months of the stock-market boom did he do or say anything publicly to alleviate the situation. Moreover, the federal government did little to regulate practices that contributed to the speculative fever. It did not concern itself with such stock-exchange practices as pool operations, other types of manipulations, and circulation of false rumors and reports. It was almost equally inactive in regulating various investment banking abuses, mergers, stock watering, and so on. More federal regulation in these areas might have presented the Federal Reserve with a somewhat less intractable problem.

An instrument very useful for reconciling objectives would have been margin requirements of the type instituted in 1934. It is an interesting commentary on the times that no official either within or outside the Federal Reserve advanced such a proposal in this vexing period. This is especially interesting in view of the fact that such a device was actually used by the Federal Reserve, acting through the New York Reserve Bank, in 1917-1919.[2] For the dual purpose of curbing stock speculation and facilitating Treasury issues, agreements were made with brokers and dealers to limit their borrowings and with New York City banks to raise margin requirements. Since this policy depended on voluntary cooperation and did not have the force of law, it had a checkered and short life, but it was useful. In the environment of the late 1920s there was little chance that either the administration or the Congress would approve such legislation, but Federal Reserve officials did not

---

[2]See Lester V. Chandler, *Benjamin Strong, Central Banker*, Brookings, Washington, 1958, pp. 124-132.

even propose it. Nor did they try to develop a voluntary program with bankers and members of the stock exchanges. The reasons are unclear. Perhaps Federal Reserve officials were averse to such selective controls, or perhaps they knew that there was little chance of getting voluntary cooperation.

LEADERSHIP

Some critiques of policy during this period have laid great stress on the hiatus in Federal Reserve leadership, and some have emphasized the generally low quality of Federal Reserve officials. The latter cannot be denied; too many Federal Reserve officials lacked adequate understanding and other qualities required for effective leadership. A younger man with Benjamin Strong's imagination, enterprise, forcefulness, and persuasiveness could have made a real difference, especially in developing and gaining acceptance for new approaches. As already indicated, I do not deny the validity or relevance of these facts. However, I would also stress the factors which made it extremely difficult to achieve such leadership and a unified and constructive program. Since these have already been discussed they will be mentioned only briefly here. (1) The first was the vagueness of the Federal Reserve Act as to the purposes of the System. Since neither the Act nor any other mandate specified objectives or priorities, it was easy for Federal Reserve officials to continue to have differing objectives. (2) The second was the regional structure of the System, with its vague distribution of power between the Board and the Reserve banks and some implications that the Board's powers were largely to review, supervise, and regulate. However undesirable the results, the Board's tendency to refrain from initiating and leading in an active, constructive way is understandable in light of the Act and its legislative history. (3) The lack of any superior body both able and willing to force agreements within the System in cases of conflict and continuing disagreement. A vigorous President, acting either directly or through his Secretary of the Treasury, could have done this, but the Presidents during the period did not essay this role. Neither did they take steps to improve decision-making and administrative arrangements within the System.

Experience during this period and the following years demonstrated the dangers of a system in which power and responsibility were diffused in an ambiguous way among the Board and the 12 Reserve banks, with no one body clearly empowered to take the initiative for the System as a whole or to force unified action. More satisfactory arrangements were developed only in 1935.

The Great Slide, 1929-1933

II

II

7

A Profile of the Great Slide, 1929–1933

We turn, in this section, to an examination of American monetary policies during the fateful 40 months between the stock-market crash in late October 1929 and the collapse of the commercial banking system at the beginning of March 1933. Federal Reserve actions and inaction can best be understood and evaluated in the context of the economic, financial, political, and intellectual environments of the period. To this end, the present chapter will outline the principal economic and financial developments, the next will describe the state of economic and political thinking concerning depressions and monetary policy, and the one following will examine the thinking of Federal Reserve officials.

The general pattern of conditions and developments during this period are, of course, well known—widespread unemployment of labor and underutilization of other productive factors, marked reductions of real output and real income, sharp declines of prices of output and assets, a large deflation of the money supply, widespread defaults on mortgages and other debts, thousands of failures of commercial banks and some other types of financial institutions, and a breakdown of the international monetary system. The nation had never before experienced such serious deflation of economic activity and prices nor such widespread disruption of its financial processes.

Though it is now clear that the economic recession began even before the stock-market crash, it is still difficult to fix precisely the dates of the downturns in the United States and other countries. For example, one study concluded that the downturn began in Germany in April 1929, in the United States in June, in Great Britain in July, and in other industrialized Western countries within a few months. Another found that it began during the first half of 1929 in Poland, Canada, and Argentina; in the third quarter in the United States, Belgium, and Italy; and within the next few months in most other Western countries.[1] However, almost all agree that the United States was among the first to slide into recession and that most other Western nations had joined by early 1930. By the middle of that year the depres-

---

[1] R. A. Gordon, *Business Fluctuations*, Harper & Row, New York, 1952, pp. 387-388.

sion was world-wide in scope. Almost the only economically important nation to escape was the Soviet Union, with its antarchic policies and its reliance on centralized physical planning. That nation suffered during the period, but its problems emanated not from inadequacy of effective demands for its output but from droughts and from mistakes in planning and execution.

In the United States, business activity began to decline somewhat more rapidly after October 1929, and then continued downward, almost without interruption but not at a uniform pace, until the summer of 1932. The decline was especially rapid for several months in the latter part of 1931 and early 1932. An increase of business activity in the autumn of 1932, largely confined to nondurable consumer goods, proved to be short-lived; by March 1933 output and employment had sunk to new lows. That marked the nadir of the depression, but recovery proved to be painfully slow and did not become complete until after America entered World War II. Let us now look more closely at some of the developments during the great slide, beginning with the behavior of the money supply.

THE MONEY SUPPLY

One striking development was the large decrease of the money supply. Table 7-1 shows that the money supply, defined narrowly to include only currency and demand deposits, declined about 23 percent in the 3 years following June 1929. Defined more broadly to include also time and savings deposits at commercial banks, the money supply fell 25 percent in this 3 year period. The decline was almost uninterrupted after the end of 1929, but its speed varied considerably. At first the decline was relatively slow; less than 28 percent of the total decline had occurred by the end of 1930 and only 44 percent by mid-1931. However, 28 percent of the total decline came in the last 6 months of 1931 and another 28 percent in the first half of 1932. The entire monetary system was placed under severe strain in the latter part of 1931, primarily by the breakdown of the international gold exchange standard and attendant gold outflow, but also by surges of actual and threatened bank failures which accelerated currency withdrawals from the banking system. These strains continued into 1932. At times during this period the money supply was falling at an annual rate of 25 percent or more.

The money supply, narrowly defined, increased slightly in the latter half of 1932, only to fall again as the banking crisis of 1933 developed. In June 1933 the money supply, narrowly defined, was 27 percent below its level of 4 years earlier, and the money supply more broadly defined was down 34 percent. Such declines may not have been the sole cause of decreased demands for output, but they were at least powerful contributing factors.

The sharp decline of the money supply, broadly defined, was accompanied by, and largely reflected, a sharp reduction of bank credit. As shown in Table 7-2, total loans and investments of all commercial banks declined by $13.5 billion, or 27 percent, from mid-1929 to mid-1932, and by $19.5 billion, or 39 percent, from mid-1929 to mid-1933. To facilitate comparisons, Table 7-3 presents these data in the form of index numbers. Several important

TABLE 7-1

The Money Supply in the United States, 1929-1933
(amounts in millions of dollars)

Date	Currency plus demand deposits (1)	Index of (1) June 1929 = 100 (2)	Currency plus demand deposits plus time deposits at commercial banks (3)	Index of (3) June 1929 = 100 (4)
June 29, 1929	$26,179	100.0	$45,736	100.0
Dec. 31, 1929	26,366	100.7	45,558	99.6
June 30, 1930	25,075	95.8	44.780	97.9
Dec. 31, 1930	24,572	93.9	43,584	95.3
June 30, 1931	23,483	89.7	42,174	92.2
Dec. 31, 1931	21,882	83.6	37,248	81.4
June 30, 1932	20,241	77.3	34,290	75.0
Dec. 31, 1932	20,397	77.9	34,028	74.4
June 30, 1933	19,172	73.2	30,021	65.6

Source: Board of Governors of the Federal Reserve System, *Banking and Monetary Statistics*, Washington, D.C., 1943, p. 34.

TABLE 7-2

Loans and Investments of All Commercial Banks in the United States, 1929-1933
(Data are of June 30, in millions of dollars)

	1929	1930	1931	1932	1933
Total loans and investments	49,797	49,435	44,993	36,278	30,535
Loans—total	36,114	35,043	29,307	22,001	16,457
Real Estate	6,313	6,146	5,757	4,955	4,202
Collateral	13,572	13,434	10,807	7,260	5,358
All other	16,229	15,463	12,743	9,786	6,897
Investments—total	13,683	14,392	15,686	14,277	14,078
U.S. government obligation	4,872	4,874	6,011	6,250	7,496
State and local obligation	1,955	2,111	2,434	2,299	2,267
Other securities	6,856	7,407	7,241	55,728	4,315

Source: Board of Governors of the Federal Reserve System, *All Bank Statistics*, Washington, D.C., 1959, pp. 34-35.

facts stand out. (1) Though total bank loans and investments had already declined 10 percent by mid-1931, the decline accelerated thereafter. More than 43 percent of the total decline from mid-1929 to mid-1933 occurred in the year following June 1931. (2) Total bank loans had fallen 39 percent by mid-1932 and 54 percent by mid-1933. Percentage reductions were even larger for loans on security collateral and for "all other loans," which include commercial loans. Real estate loans would undoubtedly have been reduced more if banks had been able to collect on them. (3) Total bank investments actually increased until mid-1931 and then declined. Shifts in the composition of bank investments indicate a mounting desire to avoid increasing risks and to protect safety and liquidity. Bank holdings of U. S. Treasury obligations rose through-

TABLE 7-3

Indexes of Loans and Investments of All Commercial Banks in the United States, 1929-1933
(Data are of June 30 for each year; June 30, 1929 = 100)

	1929	1930	1931	1932	1933
Total loans and investments	100	99	90	73	61
Loans—total	100	97	81	61	46
Real estate	100	97	91	78	67
Collateral	100	99	80	35	39
Investments—total	100	105	114	104	103
U.S. government obligations	100	100	123	128	154
State and local obligations	100	108	124	118	116
Other securities	100	108	106	84	63

Source: Computed from the data in Table 7-2.

out the period. Holdings of obligations of state and local governments rose until mid-1931 and then declined, at least partly because of the deteriorating creditworthiness of many of these debtor units. Holdings of "other securities," chiefly corporate bonds, declined after mid-1930, and especially after mid-1931. These declined more than 40 percent during the 2 years following June 1931.

Reflecting reductions in the income velocity of money, the percentage decline of total spending for output was greater than that of the money supply. (See Table 7-4.) For example, percentage declines from 1929 to 1932 were 46 percent for GNP at current prices, 22 percent for the money supply, and 28 percent for the income velocity of money.

TABLE 7-4

Gross National Product at Current Prices, the Money Supply,
and the Income Velocity of Money, 1929-1933 (amounts in billions of dollars)

	(1)	(2)	(3)	Indexes, 1929 = 100		
	GNP	Money supply	Income velocity (1) ÷ (2)	GNP	Money supply	Income velocity
1929	$103.1	$26.4	3.91	100	100	100
1930	90.4	25.5	3.55	88	97	91
1931	75.8	23.6	3.21	74	89	82
1932	58.0	20.6	2.82	56	78	72
1933	55.6	19.5	2.85	54	74	73

Sources: GNP data are from U.S. Department of Commerce, *The National Income and Product Accounts of the United States, 1929-1965*, Washington, D.C., p. 2. The money supply, narrowly defined, is stated as annual averages of monthly data from Friedman and Schwartz, *A Monetary History of the United States, 1869-1960*, Princeton University Press, Princeton, N.J., 1963, pp. 712-714.

OUTPUT, INCOME, AND EMPLOYMENT

Falling demands for output were reflected in decreases in real output, price levels, employment, and rates of utilization of plant and equipment. As shown in Table 7-5, gross national output in real terms was below its 1929 level by 10 percent in 1930, 16 percent in 1931 and 29 percent in 1932.

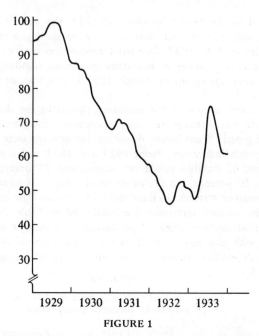

FIGURE 1

Federal Reserve Index of Industrial Production, 1929-1933.
(Average June-July 1929 = 100).

TABLE 7-5

The Gross National Product of the United States in Constant (1954) Dollars, 1929-1933
(amounts in billions of dollars)

Year	Total GNP	Change from preceding year (in billions of dollars)	Index 1929 = 100
1929	$181.8		100
1930	164.5	−$17.3	90
1931	153.0	− 11.5	84
1932	130.1	− 22.9	71
1933	126.6	− 3.5	70

Since the GNP data are annual aggregates they cannot show movements within years. The latter are indicated very approximately in Figure 1, which presents monthly indexes of industrial production, seasonally adjusted. Industrial production reached its peak in June 1929, declined slowly for 3 months, and then fell rapidly for 3 months. At the end of the year it was 18 percent below its peak. The beginning of 1930 brought an actual increase and hopes that the depression had been halted. There was even a strong revival of stock-market activity; by April stock prices had regained 60 percent of their losses from their September peak to their low point in November. However, in May 1930 the decline resumed and industrial production fell almost continuously, with only a brief interruption in the spring of 1931, until July 1932. At this point it was 54 percent below its 1929 peak. Note that the decline was especially rapid in the year following mid-1931—the year in which the deflation of the money supply and bank credit were also most rapid. After reaching a low point in July 1932, industrial production rose until October, with most of the recovery being in industries producing nondurable goods. From that point it declined again; by March 1933 it had lost all of its gains since July.

   Almost every sector of the economy shared in the decline of real output. Agriculture was virtually the only exception. However, the extent of the decline varied greatly from sector to sector. Hardest hit were construction and the durable goods industries. From 1929 and 1933 real construction fell 88 percent, output of durable producers' equipment 75 percent, and consumer durable goods 50 percent. On the other hand, output of nondurable consumer goods and consumer services declined only 15 percent. The wide differences in impacts on the various industries are illustrated in Table 7-6. The industries with the smallest declines were all producers of consumer nondurable goods. All of those with the largest declines were producers of durable goods, and most of them depended heavily on demands for capital formation purposes.

TABLE 7-6

Changes in Real Output in the United States,
1929-1933, by Industrial Classification

Industry	Percentage decline, 1929-1933
Shoe production	3.4
Textiles and products	6.4
Cigarette production	6.6
Leather and products	7.4
Gasoline production	7.4
Woolen and worsted cloth production	7.7
Cotton consumption	11.4
Tobacco products	16.7
Manufactured food products	17.8
Cigar production	34.4
Tire and tube production	34.8
Polished plate glass production	42.7
Ship-building	53.1
Furniture production	55.6
Nonferrous metals and products	55.9
Lumber production	57.9
Iron and steel	59.3
Machinery	61.6
Cement production	63.1
Nonferrous metal smelting	63.5
Transportation equipment	64.2
Automobile production	65.0
Railroad-car production	73.6
Copper production	78.9
Common and face brick production	83.3
Locomotive production	86.4

Source: Computed from Federal Reserve indexes of industrial production.

   The decline of real output was accompanied by sharp increases in unemployment. The percentage of the labor force totally unemployed, which had averaged 3.2 percent in 1929, was 8.7 percent in 1930, 15.9 percent in 1931, 23.6 percent in 1932, and 24.9 percent in 1933. At the bottom of the depression nearly 13 million, or about 1 out of every 4 members of the labor force, were totally unemployed. This understates the wastage of labor because millions more had only part-time jobs.

Decreased money demands for output were reflected not only in re-duced real output and employment but also in sharp decreases in price levels. The average price level of output fell 22 percent from 1929 to 1932, and wholesale prices fell even more. (See Table 7-7.) GNP at current prices, or the money value of output, reflects the declines of both real output and the price level of output. This had fallen 26 percent by 1931 and 44 percent by 1932. These declines of the money value of output brought, of course, equal reduc-tions in the gross national money income at the nation's disposal. In other words, in 1932 the nation as a whole had 44 percent less gross money income to consume, to save, and to meet its debts and other obligations that were relatively fixed in terms of money.

Losses of money income were indeed pervasive, but they were highly uneven among sectors of the economy, and even within sectors. To measure impacts on various industries we shall use not GNP but "national income." This is simply the money value of GNP minus depreciation allowances and all taxes on business except income taxes. (A few other minor adjustments need not concern us here.) In effect, this measures the net income of the nation—

TABLE 7-7

Gross National Product and Price Levels, 1929-1933

| | GNP at current prices (in billions) | Indexes, 1929 = 100 | | | | |
		GNP at current prices	Real GNP	GNP price deflator	Whole-sale prices	Consumer prices
1929	$103.1	100	100	100	100	100
1930	90.4	88	90	96	90	97
1931	75.8	74	84	87	76	88
1932	58.0	56	71	78	68	79
1933	55.6	54	70	77	69	75

all the value of output accruing to owners of business and to labor and other factors of production working for business and the government. This can also be viewed as the sum of the values added by all the individual industries. The "value added" by an industry is simply the value of output sold by that industry minus the value of components included in the output that were purchased from other industries. This difference, or "value added," measures the amount of net money income available to that industry to pay wages, salaries, rentals, and interest, and to provide profits—if any—to firms in the industry.

Table 7-8 shows that by 1932 total national money income had fallen by more than 51 percent, but that the decline was shared quite unequally among industries. Money income actually rose in government and government enterprises. This income was mostly in the form of wages and salaries of government employees. Some government employees did become unemployed, and many experienced decreases in their wages and salary rates. In general, however, employment remained high in the government sector, and in many

TABLE 7-8

U.S. National Income by Industrial Origin

	Money income in 1929 (in millions) of dollars)	Money income in 1932 as percent of 1929	Money income in 1933 as percent of 1929
All industries—Total	$87,814	48.5%	45.7%
Government and government enterprises	5,093	101.1	104.6
Communications and public utilities	2,864	79.8	69.8
Agricultural services, forestry, and fisheries	195	68.2	63.1
Services	10,338	59.3	53.8
Transportation	6,636	48.4	45.8
Finance, insurance, real estate	12,693	53.2	45.3
Farms	18,083	39.6	44.4
Wholesale and retail trade	13,358	47.6	41.1
Rest of world	810	48.5	39.9
Manufacturing	21,888	32.9	34.5
Mining	2,048	32.9	31.6
Contract construction	3,808	27.7	19.8

Source: U.S. Department of Commerce, *U.S. Income and Output,* Washington, D.C., 1958, p. 130. This source provides a much more detailed breakdown.

cases wage and salary rates fell less than the cost of living. Money income declined for all major classes of private industry, but by widely differing percentages. For example, money incomes in communications and public utilities fell only 20 percent. Toward the other extreme, percentage declines were 72 in contract construction, 67 in mining, 67 in manufacturing as a whole, 52 in wholesale and retail trade, and 60 percent in farming. A more detailed breakdown by industry and region would reveal even greater disparities. Note that money incomes had generally declined even more by 1933.

Table 7-9, showing the behavior of the various types of income shares, again indicates both the pervasiveness of declines and their highly uneven impacts. Note, for example, the sharp declines in the net incomes of business firms. Incomes of proprietors of unincorporated enterprises fell 64 percent from 1929 to 1932, and total corporate profits before taxes, which had been about $10 billion in 1929, were actually negative in the years 1931-1933, inclusive.

Several of the developments outlined above have important implications for the probability of success of an ambitious expansionary monetary policy, if one had been undertaken, in stopping and reversing the economic decline. (1) The continuing drop of real output created increasing amounts of unused capacity in industry and militated against a revival of new investment in plant and equipment. A militantly expansionary monetary policy might have succeeded if it had been instituted in 1930 when unused capacity was still relatively small. However, by late 1931 excess capacity was both very large and widespread. (2) The grinding deflation of money incomes and of asset prices virtually wrecked the financial structure.

TABLE 7-9

U.S. National Income by Type of
Income Share, 1929-1933

Type of income	Money income in 1929 (in millions of dollars)	Money income in 1932 as percent of 1929	Money income in 1933 as percent of 1929
National income—Total	$87,814	48.5%	45.7%
Compensation of employees	51,085	60.8	57.8
Rental incomes of persons	5,425	50.0	35.3
Net interest	6,445	84.3	78.2
Proprietor's incomes—Total	14,759	36.0	37.9
Of farms	5,968	32.4	40.8
Of other business and professional	8,791	38.5	36.0
Corporate profits before income taxes	10,100	a	a

aNegative.

Source: U.S. Department of Commerce, *U.S. Income and Output,* Washington, D.C., 1958, p. 126.

THE DEBT AND CREDIT STRUCTURE

With the sharp decline of money incomes and the accompanying fall in asset prices, the whole structure of credit and debt deteriorated and many parts could not bear the strain. Some debtors had undoubtedly assumed obligations in the 1920s which they would have been unable to meet even if their money incomes and the prices of their assets had remained at prosperity levels. However, with the sharp decline of money incomes and prices, great volumes of debt that would have been perfectly sound under more normal conditions became uncollectable, or at best of doubtful rating. This development had many implications—for the borrower himself, for the solvency and liquidity of financial institutions and other lenders, and for the ability of the Federal Reserve or any other agency to generate a recovery of new financing. To illustrate the nature of these problems let us examine the status of four types of debts—those of corporations, homeowners, farmers, and state and local governments.

Table 7-10 shows the sharp decline of total corporate profits. From $9.6 billion in 1929, they fell by two-thirds in 1930 and were negative thereafter. Corporate profit experience varied greatly from industry to industry. In some industries total corporate profits remained positive even in the worst year, 1932. These included most public utilities—electric, gas, telephone and telegraph, and pipeline transportation; tobacco manufacturing; food manufacturing; production of petroleum and natural gas; and chemicals. In 1932, when corporations as a group had net losses of $3,017 million, corporations in these industries had net profits of $897 million. This means that all other corporations suffered net losses of nearly $4,000 million. Among the industries whose corporations suffered the largest net losses were iron and steel, other metals and metal products, railroads, machinery, retail trade and automotive services, wholesale trade, and real estate.

TABLE 7-10

Corporate Profits in the United States, 1929-1933
(amounts in millions of dollars)[a]

	1929	1930	1931	1932	1933
Corporate profits before tax	9,628	3,322	− 780	−3,017	151
Less: Tax liability	1,369	3,010	498	385	521
Equals: Profits after tax	8,259	2,480	−1,278	−3,402	− 370
Less: Dividends paid	5,813	5,490	4,088	2,565	2,056
Equals: Undistributed profits	2,446	−3,010	−5,366	−5,967	−2,426

[a]These figures include profits and losses on inventories.
Source: U.S. Department of Commerce, *U.S. Income and Output*, Washington, D.C., 1959, p. 126.

Profit-and-loss experience also varied greatly with the asset size of the corporation, smaller corporations generally suffering more than larger ones. This tendency was confirmed in an interesting study by Solomon Fabricant covering the experience of 381,000 corporations in 1931 and 392,000 in 1932.[2] He found that in both 1931 and 1932 corporations with net assets of $50 million or more still enjoyed, as a group, net profits, while all smaller-size categories suffered net losses as groups. Moreover, the rate of loss, measured by the percentage of loss to total capitalization, increased with each decrease in asset size. For example, in 1932 the percentages of losses to total capitalization were 2.7 percent for corporations with assets of $10-50 million, 6.3 percent for those with assets of $500,000-1 million, 14.0 percent for those with assets of $50,000-100,000, and 33 percent for those with assets below $50,000. The same general pattern was found in almost every industry; the smaller the size of the corporation, the greater the loss rates incurred. Even in those industries in which all corporations as a group had net profits in 1932, the smaller corporations had losses. In 1932, about 323,800 corporations, or 83 percent of all those studied, were in the smaller-size classes whose average loss rates as percentages of total capitalization were 9.9 percent or greater.

Table 7-10 also indicates the extent to which corporations, in their attempts to continue dividend payments, paid out amounts in excess of their current profits after taxes. In 1929 they had retained $2,446 million of net profits; in each of the following years they paid dividends in excess of current profits after taxes. For the 2 years 1930-1931 these excess outpayments totaled $8,376 million, and for the 4 years 1930-1933 they were $16,769 million. Thus corporations drained off their assets, working capital, and liquidity. To make matters worse, the values of their other assets were declining.

These facts about corporate experience are relevant in several ways to monetary policy and its likelihood of success. (1) Corporations had lost an important source of finance and would have to rely more heavily on outside

---

[2]*Profits, Losses and Business Assets, 1929-1934*, Bulletin 55, National Bureau of Economic Research, April 11, 1935, pp. 1-12.

financing for their operations. (2) These losses and drains, with threats of more to come, increased their difficulty in securing outside financing on acceptable terms. New common-stock issues were not feasible under existing stock-market conditions. Moreover, their ability to borrow, especially to borrow on long term, was decreased as their creditworthiness deteriorated. Many could not service even their outstanding debts, to say nothing of new borrowings.

Great numbers of unincorporated business firms suffered at least as much as the smaller corporations.

Let us now turn our attention to another type of debt—home mortgages. In 1929, about half of all urban homes were mortgaged for a total of approximately $19 billion. The status of many of these mortgates deteriorated as the industrial depression deepened. Owners became delinquent on taxes, or mortgage payments, or both; foreclosures soared; and in some areas it became difficult to find buyers for houses at any price. The situation could hardly have been otherwise in view of the rise of unemployment, the fall of urban incomes, the sharp decline of residential real estate values, and the refusal of most relief agencies to assist the unemployed in retaining their homes or paying their rents. As might be expected, the situation was worst in the most depressed cities. There are no reliable statistics on the extent of defaults on home mortages in the early years of the depression. However, a survey of 22 cities as of January 1, 1934, found that the lowest rate of default on mortgages on owner-occupied houses was 21 percent.[3] It was above 38 percent in half the cities, between 50 and 60 percent in Indianapolis and Birmingham, and 62 percent in Cleveland. Default rates on rented properties were slightly higher.

Many lenders on home mortgages suffered large losses when they foreclosed, and a large part of their remaining holdings were frozen assets of highly uncertain value. Only when this situation was somehow remedied could a flow of new funds for home financing be restored. At stake were the welfare of the homeowners, banks, and other lenders, the construction industry, and the entire economy, which ordinarily relies heavily on home construction for investment spending.

Total farm debt in 1929 was about $12.4 billion, of which $9.8 billion was in mortgages, and many farmers were already complaining about the burden of their debts. The burden became heavier, and in many cases unbearable, as farm incomes and land prices fell. Between 1929 and 1932 realized gross farm incomes, including the value of farm products consumed on farms and the rental value of farm dwellings, declined 54 percent. Since costs of production did not decline proportionally, net incomes of farm operators fell nearly 70 percent. This decline reflected not a fall of real farm output but a sharp decline in the prices received by farmers. From 1929 levels, average prices received by farmers fell 41 percent by 1931 and 56 percent by 1932. This drop was accompanied by sharp declines in the values of farm land.

---

[3]The Twentieth Century Fund, *Debts and Recovery, 1929-1937*, New York, 1938, p. 164.

Widespread delinquency in meeting debt, tax, and other fixed obligations was an almost inevitable outcome.

Table 7-11 indicates that by the beginning of 1933 delinquency rates on farm mortgages in the country as a whole were 45 percent if related to the number of mortgaged farms and 53 percent if related to the value of mortgages. Delinquency rates were even higher in some of the most important farming regions. Also, farmers were by this time organizing debtor strikes, and an increasing number of states were limiting foreclosures on farms. These facts have obvious implications for country banks and other large lenders to farmers, for the creditworthiness of farmers, and for the reluctance of lenders to expand their farm loans.

TABLE 7-11

Farm Mortgage Delinquency at the Beginning of 1933a

	Percent of mortgaged farms reported delinquent	Percent of mortgaged debt reported delinquent
New England	25.3	21.9
Middle Atlantic	29.8	35.6
East North Central	35.0	42.1
West North Central	49.2	56.3
South Atlantic	48.6	60.1
East South Central	43.5	49.0
West South Central	49.8	56.9
Mountain	49.9	56.8
Pacific	40.4	43.6
United States as a whole	45.1	52.2

aThese results are based on study of a sample of 12,000 farmers.
Source: U.S. Bureau of Agricultural Economics, *The Agricultural Situation,* December 1934, p. 4.

State and local governments encountered increasing difficulties in servicing their debts and maintaining their creditworthiness as the depression deepened, primarily because of declining tax yields, rising tax delinquencies, and mounting costs of unemployment relief. Difficulties were especially acute in areas hit hardest by the depression. Most of the governmental units did meet all their debt obligations, though many succeeded only by cutting relief and other social services. However, increasing numbers defaulted; by early 1933 nearly 1,000 were in arrears on their bonds, and by the end of the year the number was 1,300.[4] These included 303 counties, 644 cities and towns, 300 school districts, and 60 other districts. Under such conditions, new borrowing became very difficult, even for some local governments that were meeting all their obligations. In 1932, a total of 697 issues amounting to $260 million could find no buyers; of those actually sold, 38 percent bore interest rates above 5 percent. For government, too, this was no period of easy money.

---

[4]Hearings before the House Banking and Currency Committee on H.R. 3082, 73rd Congress, 1st Session (February-March 1934), pp. 584-588.

The above discussion of the four types of debts and debtors should illustrate how the whole credit and debt structure deteriorated as the deflation of money incomes and asset prices ground on. Many potential borrowers did not want to go further into debt because they saw no prospects for profitable investment. However, increasing numbers were inhibited from borrowing for other reasons. For one thing, their existing debts were becoming more burdensome relative to their incomes and asset values; to incur more might prove fatal financially. Also, they faced increasing difficulties in borrowing as their creditworthiness declined. Financial institutions and other lenders found their own solvency and liquidity damaged, some fatally.

FINANCIAL INTERMEDIARIES

We have already alluded to the widespread failures of banks and other financial intermediaries during these depression years. More than 21 percent of all commercial banks failed during the 3 years 1930-1932, and still more fell in the first months of 1933. There were also numerous failures among building and loan associations, mortgage companies, and some other types of financial institutions. These failures injured the economy in several ways. However, the economy was also damaged as many of the surviving institutions virtually ceased to perform their normal function of channeling funds from savers to those who would spend them.

Why did the financial system become so distressed? Some of the oversimplified answers popular at the time and later must be discounted as general explanations. For instance: (1) Banks and other financial institutions were distressed because during the 1920s they loaded up on foreign bonds which later lost most of their value. It is true that the values of many of these issues fell sharply, though some performed as well as many domestic issues, and that a few institutions may have been seriously damaged by this alone. But since these securities constituted less than 2 percent of the total assets of financial intermediaries, they could not account for more than a tiny fraction of total losses. (2) They were in distress because their owners or managers were dishonest, or at the very least had betrayed their trust in managing other people's money. It is true that some did engage in speculation or peculation and perhaps more were imprudent in taking loans for themselves and their friends and associates. In individual cases institutions suffered acutely because of such practices. However, it seems highly unlikely that this was a major source of the general difficulties of financial institutions. (3) They were in distress because in the 1920s they loaded up on domestic loans and securities that would have proved unsound even if prosperous conditions had continued, and that certainly could not weather even a mild depression. Such allegations are difficult to appraise. It was true that in 1929 and preceding years, as in any other period of high prosperity, some securities had been purchased and loans made on the basis of highly optimistic assumptions about the future. There were indeed many risky mortgages, mortgage bonds, and other bonds and loans. Even a mild depression would have brought some, although not widespread and large, losses.

In explaining the failures and other distress of financial intermediaries I would emphasize developments within the depression itself, developments which did not stem inexorably from financial practices in the 1920s. Of these, the sharp deflation of money incomes and asset prices was the most powerful. This affected financial intermediaries in two adverse ways. For one thing, as already noted, it lowered the value and liquidity of their assets. Also, by lowering money incomes and saving, it decreased the flow of savings to these institutions.

As is well known, a financial intermediary acquires funds by issuing claims against itself, such as deposit claims, building and loan shares, life insurance or annuity policies, and so on. It uses these funds to buy bonds, mortgages, or other claims. To attract and retain funds it must convince savers that it is solvent—that its assets are at least as valuable as its liabilities. The fall in the value of bonds and other securities accompanying the deflation of incomes and asset prices obviously threatened the solvency of financial intermediaries. Such an institution must also convince savers that it is sufficiently liquid—that it can meet promptly all its express or implied promises to pay. It has three principal sources of liquidity: (1) current receipts of funds, (2) sales of assets, and (3) borrowings from others. All three were damaged by the deflation.

During periods of prosperity, financial intermediaries can depend heavily, some almost exclusively, on current cash receipts to supply them with liquidity. These are of two principal types. One consists of receipts of interest and repayments on loans. In periods of prosperity these receipts are usually large and relatively dependable. The other consists of flows of new savings. These, too, are usually large in periods of high income. Thus in prosperous periods these two types of receipts may be large enough, or almost so, to meet all the liquidity needs of an intermediary. Both, however, dwindel in depression. Borrowers from the institution become delinquent on their interest and principal payments. Savers, whose incomes are falling, save less and decrease the flow of new savings to these institutions. Some savers whose incomes have fallen sharply become net withdrawers of funds. The extent to which saving declined during the depression is indicated in Table 7-12. For example, total personal saving amounted to $4,168 million in 1929; by 1932 it was negative. American households as a group were net dissavers, consuming more than their current incomes by borrowing and by drawing on past savings. It was inevitable that they would draw out some of their savings from financial institutions.

To illustrate the impact on a financial institution, consider the case of a building and loan association, a mutual savings bank, or the savings department of a commercial bank which has depended heavily on the savings of families whose incomes have declined sharply. Its receipts of interest and principal repayments are likely to be interrupted by delinquencies. At the same time, its depositors are likely to make net withdrawals, perhaps not because they distrust the institution but because they need the funds to support themselves. Thus the institution's assets are drawn off, it can no longer depend on current receipts to meet its liquidity needs, and it must rely more heavily on sales of assets and on borrowings. These sources, too,

TABLE 7-12

Gross Private Saving in the United States, 1929-1933
(amounts in millions of dollars)

	Personal saving	Corporate net saving[a]	Capital consumption allowances, etc.	Total private gross saving
1929	4,168	2,918	8,617	15,703
1930	3,406	2,250	8,541	12,197
1931	2,507	2,952	8,166	7,721
1932	− 646	−4,920	7.615	2,049
1933	− 648	−4,569	7,161	1,944

[a]Corporate net saving is undistributed corporate profits after inventory valuation adjustment.

Source: U.S. Department of Commerce, *National Income*, Washington, D. C., 1954, p. 164.

have been damaged by deflation. Some assets which were quickly salable at full value in prosperity can be sold only slowly or at greatly reduced values in depression. Moreover, some normal sources of borrowing become no longer available, either because lenders become unable to lend or because they distrust the creditworthiness of the institution.

It was through such processes that the deflation of money incomes and asset prices undermined financial institutions. Failures of these institutions usually appeared to come suddenly as people lost confidence in them and rushed to withdraw their funds. Back of this panic, however, were the weakening forces described above.

Let us look now at some other factors relevant to the failure rates of commercial banks and especially to differences in the failure rates for various classes of these banks. Table 7-13 shows failure rates by regions. Several important facts stand out. (1) Failure rates in the nation as a whole were indeed high. During the years 1930-1932 inclusive, failure claimed 5,096 banks, or 21.5 percent of all banks existing at the beginning of the period. (2) Failure rates differed widely by state and region. At the lowest end of the scale, the failure rate for New England as a whole was only 7.6 percent. Toward the upper end were 10 states with failure rates at least half again as high as the national average. (See Table 7-14.) All of these states were in the South or west of the Appalachians, and all were predominantly agricultural.

One reason for the high failure rate was the predominance of unit banking. Of the more than 23,000 commercial banks at the end of 1930, nearly 97 percent were unit banks. In the following 18 states, there was not a single bank with a branch:

Colorado	Kansas	South Dakota
Connecticut	Missouri	Texas
Florida	Montana	Utah
Idaho	Nevada	Vermont
Illinois	North Dakota	West Virginia
Iowa	Oklahoma	Wyoming

TABLE 7-13

Commercial Bank Suspensions by State

Geographic division and state	Number of banks at beginning of 1930	Number of failures 1930- 1932 inclusive	Failure Rate as Percent of Banks at Beginning of 1930			
			1930	1931	1932	Total, 1930–1932 inclusive
United States	23,695	5,096	5.7%	9.7%	6.1%	21.5%
New England	696	53	1.6	4.7	1.3	7.6
Maine	100	2	—	2.0	—	2.0
New Hampshire	71	2	—	2.8	—	2.8
Vermont	85	2	2.4	—	—	2.4
Massachusetts	254	24	0.8	7.5	1.2	9.4
Rhode Island	25	0	—	—	—	—
Connecticut	161	23	4.3	6.2	3.7	14.3
Middle Atlantic	2,977	320	1.0	7.7	2.0	10.7
New York	933	73	0.9	5.9	1.1	7.8
New Jersey	536	49	0.6	7.1	1.5	9.1
Pennsylvania	1,508	198	1.3	9.1	2.8	13.1
East North Central	5,263	1,349	5.4	11.6	8.7	25.6
Ohio	946	166	2.6	12.6	2.7	17.5
Indiana	859	251	10.1	11.2	7.9	29.2
Illinois	1,764	572	7.1	13.5	11.8	32.4
Michigan	741	221	2.8	15.2	11.7	29.8
Wisconsin	953	139	2.5	5.0	7.0	14.6
West North Central	6,335	1,577	6.6	11.3	7.0	24.9
Minnesota	1,041	184	2.1	9.7	5.9	17.7
Iowa	1,252	442	6.9	16.6	11.7	35.3
Missouri	1,278	305	8.1	9.5	6.3	23.9
North Dakota	410	139	14.4	16.1	3.4	33.9
South Dakota	386	151	14.2	18.9	6.0	39.1
Nebraska	803	206	5.7	13.6	6.4	25.6
Kansas	1,165	150	3.7	3.3	5.9	12.9
South Atlantic	2,317	595	9.6	11.4	4.7	25.7
Delaware	47	1	—	—	2.1	2.1
Maryland	215	27	1.4	9.3	1.9	12.6
District of Columbia	40	4	—	—	10.0	10.0
Virginia	459	66	4.4	8.1	2.0	14.4
West Virginia	297	73	3.4	19.2	2.0	24.6
North Carolina	416	187	22.4	15.1	7.5	45.0
South Carolina	205	79	13.2	16.6	8.8	38.5
Georgia	405	91	7.7	8.6	6.2	22.5
Florida	233	67	16.7	7.3	4.7	28.8
East South Central	1,606	398	9.5	9.3	6.0	24.8
Kentucky	568	95	5.3	4.8	6.7	16.7
Alabama	348	88	9.8	10.3	5.2	25.3
Mississippi	307	127	19.2	18.2	3.9	41.4
West South Central	2,562	468	7.8	6.8	3.7	18.3
Arkansas	413	204	32.4	13.8	3.1	49.4
Louisiana	225	31	4.4	3.1	6.2	13.8
Oklahoma	616	78	3.6	3.9	5.2	12.7
Texas	1,308	155	2.6	6.6	2.7	11.9
Mountain	931	183	2.7	6.7	10.3	19.7
Montana	195	30	5.6	5.6	4.1	15.4
Idaho	137	35	0.7	7.3	17.5	25.5
Wyoming	85	5	—	3.5	2.4	5.9
Colorado	273	50	1.8	7.7	8.8	18.3
New Mexico	56	2	—	1.8	1.8	3.6

TABLE 7-13 (continued)

Geographic division and state	Number of banks at beginning of 1930	Number of failures 1930-1932 inclusive	Failure Rate as Percent of Banks at Beginning of 1930			
			1930	1931	1932	Total, 1930-1932 inclusive
Arizona	46	17	10.9	10.9	15.2	37.0
Utah	104	26	2.9	8.7	13.5	25.0
Nevada	35	18	–	5.7	45.7	51.4
Pacific	1,008	153	1.2	5.4	8.6	15.2
Washington	339	53	0.9	6.5	8.3	15.6
Oregon	234	42	0.9	6.0	11.1	17.9
California	435	58	1.6	4.1	7.6	13.3

Sources: Board of Governors of the Federal Reserve System, *Federal Reserve Bulletin*, November 1937, pp. 1089-1122; *Banking and Monetary Statistics*, Washington, D.C., 1943, p. 284.

TABLE 7-14

States with High Failure Rates, 1930-1932
(failure rates as percentages of banks
in existence at the beginning of 1930)

	1930	1931	1932	Total, 1930-1932 inclusive
National average	5.7	9.7	6.1	21.5
Nevada	–	5.7	45.7	51.4
Arkansas	32.4	13.8	3.1	49.4
North Carolina	22.4	15.1	7.5	45.0
Mississippi	19.2	18.2	3.9	41.4
South Dakota	14.2	18.9	6.0	39.1
South Carolina	13.2	16.6	8.8	38.5
Arizona	10.9	10.9	15.2	37.0
Iowa	6.9	16.6	11.7	35.3
North Dakota	14.4	16.1	3.4	33.9
Illinois	7.1	13.5	11.8	32.4

Source: Table 7-13.

Note that most of these were predominantly agricultural states. Also, many of the banks in these areas were small and heavily dependent on farming and on local towns closely linked to farming.

At the beginning of 1930, there were 751 branch banks operating a total of 3,522 banking offices. However, many of these were largely confined to a single town or city. For example, 2,391 of the offices were in the head-office city, and only 1,131 outside. Of the 1,131 branches outside head-office cities, 552 were in California, leaving only 579 for all other states. There were either no branches at all outside the head-office city, or at most 3, in the following 8 states:

Michigan	Wisconsin
Indiana	New Mexico
New Hampshire	Washington
New York	Oregon

Thus we are justified in saying that most American banks operated only a single office or had branches only within their own cities.

Of course, it does not necessarily follow that a unit bank or one operating branches only within its home city must draw most of its deposits from its locality and make most of its loans there. Very large banks, such as those in New York, Chicago, and other major centers, can draw deposits from all over the country and even from abroad, and their lending can be highly diversified regionally. Small banks, which predominated, are in a far different position. They usually find it difficult to draw deposits from a distance, and similarly difficult to lend to distant borrowers. They do, of course, buy earning assets in the open market, but these usually yield less than do loans to customers. Thus the fortunes of great numbers of these banks depended largely on the status of the local economy.

A major reason for the high failure rates of country banks relative to failure rates at other banks during the early part of the great slide—say, to mid-1931—appears to have been large shifts of deposits and reserves away from country areas, these reflecting in large part an "unfavorable balance of payments" of agricultural areas. Such regional shifts might be of little significance in a system composed of a few nationwide branch banking systems, for deposits lost by a branch in one region might be gained by a branch in another. However, such shifts can have serious consequences in a system composed largely of small unit banks, with no branch system that is more than statewide. Banks located in regions losing large amounts of deposits and reserves to other areas can be weakened and made vulnerable to failure.

For example, consider the position of a "typical" unit bank located in a predominantly agricultural area, heavily dependent for its deposits on farmers and on others whose incomes depend on farmers, and with a large part of its loans in the area. During the early part of the depression, such areas tended to have "unfavorable balances of payments" with other areas on both income and capital accounts. Reflecting the early decline of the prices of farm products, farm incomes fell sharply, and farmers received less from other areas than they spent in other areas. Also, capital movements from other areas to farmers virtually stopped; in fact, farmers were asked to repay some of their debts to insurance companies and other distant creditors. To meet these net outpayments, farmers and those dependent on them paid deposits to other areas, and their banks were drained of deposits, reserves, and other liquid assets. To make matters worse, such banks found it more difficult to collect on local loans.

I believe that such interregional shifts of deposits help to explain the relatively high failure rates of banks in farm areas during the early part of the depression. Many of these banks may have lacked good management, but they were subjected to heavier drains and strains than many other banks. The data in Table 7-15 tend to support this thesis, especially for the early years of the depression. For example, total deposits at all commercial banks decreased 4 percent during the 2 years ending in June 1931. However, deposits in member banks located in cities of 500,000 or more, except Chicago, suffered no net deposit drains; in fact, their deposits increased by 8 to 10 percent. Country banks located in all the Federal Reserve districts west of the Appalachians

TABLE 7-15

*Indexes of Total Deposits at Commercial Banks,
by Classes (Index, June 1929 = 100)*

	June 1929	December 1930	June 1931	June 1932	December 1932	June 1933
All commercial banks	100	99	96	72	73	65
Member banks	100					
In New York City	100	114	110	82	91	92
In Chicago	100	106	95	64	73	79
In other cities, 500,000 and over	100	108	108	84	86	76
In cities, 100,000 -500,00	100	99	85	80	73	77
Country member banks in Federal Reserve districts of:						
Boston	100	97	94	73	75	70
New York	100	101	102	83	80	72
Philadelphia	100	100	99	85	84	72
Cleveland	100	90	85	63	60	46
Richmond	100	87	85	65	66	57
Atlanta	100	86	81	66	55	60
Chicago	100	90	83	57	52	33
St. Louis	100	84	85	66	62	51
Minneapolis	100	93	89	72	66	60
Kansas City	100	93	88	69	66	62
Dallas	100	87	81	61	62	59
San Francisco	100	92	87	64	59	49

Source: Computed from data in various tables in Board of Governors of the Federal Reserve System, *Banking and Monetary Statistics,* Washington, D.C., 1941. The data cited are for operating banks only. Thus their behavior through time is affected by bank failures. Allowance for this does not invalidate the general conclusions reached, but it does, of course, counsel cautious interpretation of the figures.

suffered losses of deposits of 10 percent or more, and losses were 15 percent or more in 6 of these districts.

Deposit behavior at the various classes of banks became more complex as the industrial depression deepened. I believe, however, that interregional shifts of deposits and reserves help to explain differential failure rates among the various cities. For example, banking disturbances were especially severe in the Detroit, Chicago, Toledo, and Pennsylvania iron and steel areas. These were all industrial centers in which unemployment and losses of incomes were extremely severe. I believe that the high incidence of bank failures in those areas is explained in part by their unfavorable balances of payments with other areas and the accompanying losses of deposits and reserves.

INTEREST RATES

We shall see later that Federal Reserve officials were much impressed by the decline of interest rates in this period, especially in 1930 and the first seven months of 1931 and again in 1932. In fact, some stated that money market conditions became so easy as to be "sloppy." The impression is left that credit became freely available to private borrowers at extraordinarily low

TABLE 7-16

Selected Interest Rates and Yields, 1929-1932
(annual averages in percent per annum)

Type of paper	1929	1930	1931	1932
3-6-month Treasury notes and certificates	4.42	2.23	1.15	0.78
4-6-month prime commercial paper	5.85	3.59	2.64	2.73
90-day prime bankers' acceptances	5.03	2.48	1.57	1.28
Average rates on bank loans to customers in leading cities	5.83	4.85	4.30	4.71
U.S. Treasury long-term bonds	3.60	3.29	3.34	3.68
Corporate bonds (Moody's ratings)				
Aaa	4.73	4.55	4.58	5.01
Aa	4.93	4.77	5.05	5.98
A	5.28	5.13	6.01	7.20
Baa	5.90	5.90	7.62	9.30

Sources: Various tables in Board of Governors of the Federal Reserve System, *Banking and Monetary Statistics,* Washington, D.C., 1943.

interest rates. Those who made this observation made two mistakes: they concentrated their attention too much on yields on very short-term assets of the highest safety and liquidity; and they paid too little attention to nonprice rationing of credit, which became of increasing importance.

Table 7-16, which presents annual averages of selected rates, obviously cannot show intra-year movements. However, it does indicate the wide dispersion in the behavior of various types of interest rates. Rates on highly safe and liquid short-term open-market paper fell sharply. Rates on banks loans to customers fell less. Yields on various types of long-term bonds behaved quite differently. Those on U.S. Treasury bonds declined until August 1931 and then rose; in 1932 they were above their level in 1929. Yields on the three highest grades of corporate bonds declined in 1930 and then rose; in 1932 all were above their 1929 levels. Yields on the lowest grade of corporate bonds did not fall at all; in 1932 they averaged 9.30 percent. Fewer and fewer bonds could qualify for the higher ratings as the great slide continued. For increasing numbers of private borrowers this was no period of easy money.

Table 7-17 suggests the extent to which corporate bond prices had fallen by 1932. In 1928, 53 percent of the number of outstanding issues and 58 percent of the par amounts of these issues were selling at par or above, and 85 percent of the number and 89 percent of the amount outstanding commanded prices at least 90 percent of par. However, by 1932 only 4 percent of the number of outstanding issues were at par or above and only 28 percent at 90 or better. About 44 percent had depreciated 30 percent or more and 26 percent had fallen more than half. These cold statistics suggest several things: the danger of judging credit-market conditions solely on the basis of short-term rates applicable to the safest and most liquid instruments, the great difficulties that increasing numbers of corporations would have encountered if they had tried to market new bond issues, and the large losses incurred by banks and other holders of corporate bonds.

TABLE 7-17

*Corporate Bonds in All Industries Classified by Their Prices
as Percentages of Par Value, 1928 and 1932*

	1928		1932	
	Number of outstanding issues	*Par amount outstanding*	*Number of outstanding issues*	*Par amount outstanding*
Total number of issues	3,854		3,793	
Total outstanding in par amounts (in millions)		$24,586		$27,369
Price classes as percent of par	*Percent of total*	*Percent of total*	*Percent of total*	*Percent of total*
Under 20	1.0%	0.4%	5.4%	3.6%
20-39	0.3	0.1	12.9	9.3
40-49	0.4	0.2	8.1	7.8
50-59	0.7	0.3	7.9	7.3
60-69	2.8	1.3	9.7	11.0
70-79	3.2	3.3	12.5	17.0
80-89	6.9	5.7	15.4	19.0
90-99	31.6	30.5	24.0	19.1
100-109	49.3	51.1	4.0	5.8
110-119	2.4	6.4	a	0.1
120 and over	1.4	0.7	a	—
Total	100.0	100.0	100.0	100.0

aLess than 0.1

Source: W. Braddock Hickman, *Statistical Measures of Corporate Bond Financing Since 1900*, Princeton University Press, Princeton, N.J., 1960, p. 71. This table includes only bonds for which there were market quotations and for which other relevant information was available.

CONCLUSIONS

The purpose of this chapter has been to describe some of the principal economic and financial developments during the 1929-1933 period, not to analyze the reasons for these developments. It may well be, as many contend, that an aggressive easy-money policy begun immediately after the stock-market crash could have stopped the decline and initiated recovery within a few months. However, such a policy was not adopted, and the economy continued to decline. As the deflation of output, employment, money incomes, and asset prices ground on, conditions became less and less favorable to the success of an expansionary monetary policy. All parts of the saving-investment process deteriorated. (1) Incentives to invest in construction, plant and equipment, and other types of capital were severely damaged in several ways. For one thing, excess capacity became widespread. With delines in demands for housing space, vacancies became numerous and prices of existing housing fell sharply. Many came to feel that dwellings would be in oversupply for years to come. In many areas the same was true of office and other commercial buildings. Plant and equipment became redundant relative to prevailing levels of utilization, and expectations regarding future rates of utilization became increasingly pessimistic. At the same time, deterioration in the net worth and liquidity positions of business firms and many other potential borrowers decreased their willingness to borrow and spend. To assume further obligations would jeopardize still more their chance of financial survival. These developments also decreased their creditworthiness and forced increasing numbers that did borrow or renew loans to pay higher premiums over prime interest rates. The latter might indeed fall, but fewer and fewer borrowers had access to them.

(2) With the declines of money incomes, the flow of both personal and business saving dwindled. The flow of positive saving into securities and financial intermediaries decreased, and net withdrawals became widespread even before confidence in the claims issued by intermediaries was damaged.

(3) Both the solvency and liquidity of financial intermediaries were seriously impaired. Their solvency was reduced, when not obliterated, by the decrease of the value of their mortgages, bonds, and other earning assets. Their liquidity was reduced in several ways. Their current flows of cash receipts were reduced by delinquencies in payments on outstanding loans and by diminished receipts of savings from depositors. Withdrawals by depositors who lost confidence added to the problem. Thus financial intermediaries could, to put it mildly, rely less on current receipts to meet their liquidity needs and had to rely more on their assets that were highly liquid in times of prosperity could not be sold only slowly and at reduced values. Moreover, some of the intermediaries' usual sources of borrowing became unreliable.

In this connection, it is important to remember that in the early 1930s many of the safeguards for financial institutions that we now take for granted did not exist. There was no system of deposit insurance for any type of financial institution to protect depositors and reduce threats of withdrawals. Such a system would have given a greater sense of security to the managers of the institutions and reduced their demands for liquidity. There were then only two types of federally sponsored institutions to lend to or buy assets from private financial institutions. One was the Federal Intermediate Credit System, which lent only on specified types of agricultural paper. The other was the Federal Reserve System, which lent only to member banks and to them only on "eligible paper" and U.S. government securities. Thus there was no "lender of last resort" for some 15,000 nonmember banks, for building and loan associations, and for various other types of nonbank financial intermediaries. Even member banks could borrow on only a fraction of their assets. Moreover, Senator Glass and other devotees of the commercial loan theory were reluctant to broaden the lending power of the Federal Reserve. Not until 1932 were steps taken to remedy these deficiencies. By then the hour was late.

There can be little doubt that banks and other financial intermediaries increases sharply their demands for money for liquidity purposes as the depression wore on. They needed more liquidity in some form because of the increased probability of withdrawals. For this purpose, they could rely less on net inflows of funds. Most types of earning assets became less liquid and less safe, and thus less satisfactory substitutes for money as a source of liquidity. Thus these institutions increased their demands for those types of short-term assets that remained highly liquid and for money itself. For commercial banks, this meant increased demands for reserves in excess of legal requirements. Many Federal Reserve officials repeatedly made the mistake of assuming that reserves in excess of legal requirements were also in excess of the amounts that banks would demand to hold, and therefore exerted pressure on banks to expand their loans and investments. They failed to realize that bank demands for liquidity in this form had increased so much that banks still felt under pressure to contract credit even though they held excess reserves in the legal sense of the term.

Such developments must also have decreased sharply the willingness of member banks to borrow from the Federal Reserve or to remain in debt in order to make new loans or to maintain outstanding loans and investments. Banks that borrow and lend must, of course, bear the risk and illiquidity of their loans and investments. In prosperous periods, when they estimate risk at a low level and place little value on the marginal change in their liquidity, they may be willing to borrow and lend at interest rates only a little higher than the discount rate they pay on their borrowings at the Federal Reserve, despite the tradition against borrowing. However, as the depression deepened they must have estimated risks on loans and investments at a higher level and have become increasingly unwilling to bear additional risk and illiquidity. The margin between market rates and the discount rate, which in prosperous periods would encourage an expansion, or at least bring little or no pressure for contraction of bank loans and investments, now became quite deflationary.

8

The State of
Economic Understanding

No matter how "independent" a central bank may be in the legal sense of the term, its policies are inevitably influenced by the contemporary state of economic and political attitudes and thinking. Its officials may not be wholly responsive to the aspirations and expectations of the community, but both their selection of objectives and their policy actions are shaped by these in some degree. A central bank can hardly avoid following appropriate and ambitious policies to promote economic stability if it operates in an environment characterized by these conditions: (1) a general consensus, expressed effectively through government or other channels, that the government itself or its agencies can and should assume heavy responsibility for maintaining economic stability; (2) a valid and generally accepted theory of the determination of the levels, and of changes in the levels, of national income and employment; (3) a valid and generally accepted theory of the relationships between policy actions and their effects on income and employment; and (4) a generally accepted view that a vigorous central bank policy can make an important contribution to the promotion of economic stability.

None of these conditions was met during the late 1920s and early 1930s. There was certainly no clear consensus that the federal government or its agencies should assume heavy responsibilities for economic stabilization. None of the three Presidents who occupied the White House between 1920 and March of 1933—Harding, Coolidge, and Hoover—admitted any such responsibility for the government, and none brought pressure on the Federal Reserve to do so. Nor were the clear and insistent demands from the public that either the government or the Federal Reserve assume such a role.

Of basic importance was the lack of understanding of business cycles and of the behavior of national income and employment, even among professional economists. There was no system of national income accounts and no statistical series on either total output or employment. Nor was there any comprehensive, valid, and generally accepted theory of the determination of the level, and changes in the level, of national income and employment. Some of the simple but basic ideas that are now generally known and accepted did not yet exist. For example, R. F. Kahn's now-famous article on the multiplier did not appear until June 1931, and thereafter gained acceptance only slowly.

116

The "Keynesian Revolution" did not begin until after 1936. There was no lack of business-cycle theories; in fact, there was a plethora of them, all incomplete and some in direct conflict with others. The lack of any rigorous and comprehensive theoretical framework made it impossible to demonstrate the relationships among these partial and competing theories, to choose among them, to synthesize them, and to reach anything like a consensus. There continued to be wide differences among economists and among others on the causes and cures of depressions, and some of these differences were basic.

In the absence of a valid and generally accepted theory of income and employment, there was naturally no agreement on a theory concerning relationships between monetary policy actions and their effects on income and employment. Wide differences in prescriptions for monetary policy resulted. For example, one group of economists urged the Federal Reserve to take vigorous actions to expand the supply of money and believed that such policies would make an important contribution to economic recovery. Prominent among these were such "quantity theorists" as Professors Irving Fisher, James H. Rogers, Wilford I. King, Harry G. Brown, and John R. Commons. Some others believed that such policies should be tried but doubted that they would do much good. A large group of commercial loan theorists and other "accommodationists" warned the Federal Reserve against "artificial" expansionary actions and urged that bank credit be allowed to decline along with the decreasing "needs of trade." Finally, many "liquidationists" thought the Federal Reserve should hasten "the orderly process of liquidation" required to provide a sound basis for later recovery. They felt that attempts to expand money and credit would only prolong the depression. If Federal Reserve officials listened to this babel, they must have been more confused than enlightened.

The following sections will provide examples of the wide differences in theories and policy prescriptions during this period.

THE LIQUIDATIONISTS AND ACCOMMODATIONISTS

According to the liquidations, depressions were caused by imbalances and maladjustments that developed during the preceding prosperous period. These maladjustments could be of various kinds—inflation of credit, overindebtedness, excessive stocks of capital goods, and so on. The proper cure for a depression, they believed, was to purge the economy of its maladjustments, letting this occur by a "natural" process of liquidation. To interfere with this process "artifically" would only make matters worse.

Lionel Robbins was one of those expressing these views most clearly.[1] He felt that the depression in the United States was brought on by the preceding inflation, which was traceable largely to the easy-money policy of 1927. He admitted that American prices did not rise, but he considered the failure of prices to fall in the face of rising productivity to be "inflation." Now there had to be deflation to purge the economy of its maladjustments.

[1] *The Great Depression*, Macmillan, London, 1935.

In the course of a boom many bad business commitments are undertaken. Debts are incurred which it is impossible to repay. Stocks are produced and accumulated which it is impossible to sell at a profit. Loans are made which it is impossible to recover. Both in the sphere of finance and in the sphere of production, when the boom breaks, these bad commitments are revealed.

Now in order that revival may commence again, it is essential that these positions should be liquidated . . . .

Now in the pre-war business depression a very clear policy had been developed to deal with this situation. The maxim adopted by central banks for dealing with financial crises was to discount freely on good security, but to keep the rate of discount high. Similarly in dealing with the wider dislocations of commodity prices and production no attempt was made to bring about artifically easy conditions. The results of this were simple. Firms whose position was fundamentally sound obtained what relief was necessary. Having confidence in the future, they were prepared to foot the bill. But the firms whose position was fundamentally unsound realized that the game was up and went into liquidation. After a short period of distress the stage was once more set for business recovery . . . .

Nobody wishes for bankruptcies. Nobody likes liquidation as such. If bankruptcy and liquidation can be avoided by sound financing nobody would be against such measures. All that is contended is that when the extent of mal-investment and over-indebtedness has passed a certain limit, measures which postpone liquidation only tend to make matters worse.[2]

Robbins specifically condemned easy-money policies.

Alvin H. Hansen, whose position was to change greatly within a few years, expressed similar views in 1932 when writing about expanded expenditures on public works as a remedy for depression.

Once the maladjustments of the boom period have developed, a process of readjustment is inevitable. A limited quantity of public works could not stop this process. Indeed, it may tend to delay the readjustment, since such a program would tend to work counter to the forces working for cost reduction. Hence, the only effect of public works thrown in at this phase of the cycle would be to employ a few more men. The depression would continue to run its course. (A large program of public works, financed by bond issues, could easily have the effect of postponing revival of business by affecting adversely the security flotations of private corporations.) Therefore, if public works on a limited scale are to be undertaken, the proper time to employ them is after the process of readjustment has been substantially completed. Public works actively prosecuted at this time will (partly be mopping up idle funds and so raising prices; and partly by restoring business confidence) tend to stimulate a revival and thus cut short what might otherwise be a long flat bottom of depression.[3]

. . . Cyclical fluctuations have the effect of given the whole economic structure a good shake-up and keeping the system reasonalby flexible and mobile.[4]

We shall not succeed in solving the depression through the soothing and agreeable device of inflation. We shall come out of it only through hard work, and readjustments that are painful. There is no other alternative. And we shall have to face the probability of having to repeat the process in the future, since, on balance, a downward trend in prices is likely.

---

[2]*Ibid.*, pp. 62-75.

[3]*Economic Stabilization in an Unbalanced World*, Harcourt, Brace, New York, 1932, pp. 188-189. The sentence in the first set of parentheses was included in a footnote.

[4]*Ibid.*, p. 192.

Inflation is not a sound remedy, since it carries within it the seeds of subsequent maladjustments.[5]

What Hansen meant by "inflation" is not clear, but it seems likely that he meant either an increase in the money supply or an increase in spending for output—two of the many meanings attached to the term at that time.

Another who found beneficial effects in depressions, or at least in recessions, was Franz Schneider, Jr.

Possibly we are inclined, in our pursuit of prosperity, to overlook the benefits of business recession. The recession undoubtedly has a cleaning effect on the physical and psychological elements of business. It puts current theories to the test, readjusts supply and demand to a firm basis, and eliminates accumulations of incompetents. It is nature's check on the errors of human judgment.[6]

A. B. Adams, a business-cycle theorist, also saw need for liquidating "the old inflation."

It would be quite undesirable to have an additional inflation of bank credit in this country at the present time. There is too much of the old inflation to be gotten rid of before business can be put on a sound basis. Temporary inflation would result only in a postponement of the inevitable deflation and readjustment and thereby result only in prolonging the present depression.[7]

The most widely used textbook in elementary economics during the period stated that liquidation served a useful, and even a necessary, function.

The period of depression, then, is one in which there is a complete rearrangement of internal and external relationships. Production necessarily becomes more efficient. The volume of production is kept at a low level until surplus stocks are disposed of, and new commitments are not made until there is a reasonable assurance of profits. In other words, the period of depression, gloomy and unpleasing as it is, serves as a breathing spell for business; it is a period when readjustments in the whole complex structure can be made.[8]

Many economists who were not so clearly members of the liquidationist school nevertheless contended that the Federal Reserve should shun "artificial" stimulants to expansion and should permit the volume of bank credit to decline. This group included most commercial loan theorists and other accommodationists. For example, H. Parker Willis—the leading commercial loan theorist, advisor to Senator Glass, professor at Columbia University, and active journalist—was adamantly opposed to an easy-money policy.

... the best Federal Reserve policy will be that of "hands off," with rates main-

---

[5]*Ibid.*, p. 378.

[6]"Some Observations on Recent Federal Reserve Policy," *American Economic Review Supplement*, March 1930, p. 106.

[7]*Trends in Business, 1922-1932*, Harper & Row, New York, 1932, p. 68.

[8]Fred R. Fairchild, Edgar S. Furniss, Norman S. Buck, *Elementary Economics*, Macmillan, New York, 1930, Revised edition, Volume I, p. 543. All three authors were professors of economics at Yale.

tained at a normal level, and no attempt to interfere artifically with the course of events.[9]

He declared that the Federal Reserve should return to the classical policies of central banking, which counseled in times of depression an attitude of "conservation and protection—to supply credit to those who needed it but at fairly high rates designed to suggest the fact that supplies of credit were not abundant."[10] It is perhaps well that Walter Bagehot did not learn that the rules which he had prescribed for times of financial crisis were now thought appropriate in a prolonged industrial depression. Willis thought that the Federal Reserve should, in line with classical practice, make every effort

to bring about the cancellation of the inflated credit, growing out of the previous periods of inflation, at as early a date as possible, in order that the dangers resulting from it might be minimized and kept within as narrow time-limits as might be. Certainly central banks have not been in the habit of making credit as cheap and easy as possible in such periods or distributing it generally.[11]

Benjamin M. Anderson, Jr., economist for the Chase National Bank of New York and editor of the widely read *Chase Economic Bulletin*, contended that

artificial manipulation of interest rates by a central bank seeking to overcome all other factors in the money market, generates troubles which lead to excessive rates in other directions at a later time.[12]

He thought that the volume of bank credit was "high above the ordinary needs of commerce until the summer of 1931" and should have been reduced faster. In his view, falling prices reduced the amount of credit needed by commerce and thus called for a decrease in the quantity of credit.[13] He strongly opposed "the purchasing power doctrine," which prescribed increases in spending for output as a remedy for depression, and supported "the equilibrium doctrine," which maintained that recovery would be induced by restoration of equilibrium relationships within the system. In mid-1931 he believed that this process was making headway.

. . . the logic of events is with the equilibrium doctrine. It does not require the sanction of governments or public popularity. Readjustment is now in process. Individuals, seeking to make gains, or to avert losses, are readjusting and shifting. Retail trade has been outrunning factory production for nearly a year. Retailers are reducing prices and getting business thereby. Men released from work in one field are seeking work elsewhere. Business men, finding certain lines unprofitable, are looking eagerly for other lines which may be made profitable. Industries are seeking to readjust their lines of production and their costs and prices so as to meet the markets' demands. The process of

---

9"Federal Reserve Policy in Depression," in Quincy Wright, Ed., *Gold and Monetary Stabilization*, University of Chicago Press, Chicago, 1932, p. 100.

10*Ibid.*, p. 81.

11*Ibid.*, p. 83.

12Hearings on H.R. 11499 and S. 4429 before the Senate Banking and Currency Committee, 72nd Congress, 1st Session (May 1932), p. 307.

13*Chase Economic Bulletin*, March 16, 1931.

reequilibration is going on. Given security of life and property, given the gold standard, given the enforcement of contracts, and given anything like untrammelled, open markets, the people themselves, individually, will finally restore equilibrium and bring back good business. The process is going on and progress is being made.[14]

Anderson opposed Federal Reserve purchases of government securities in 1930 and 1931 but approved those in 1932.

Some economists opposed extensive Federal Reserve purchases of government securities, as well as legislation permitting the Federal Reserve to lend on a broader range of assets, because they believed that such acquisitions would impair the liquidity of the Reserve Banks and lessen the elasticity of Federal Reserve notes and bank credit. They insisted that the Federal Reserve banks should always be highly liquid and that such liquidity was provided by their holdings of short-term self-liquidating paper conforming to the commercial loan theory. For example, George W. Dowrie, a professor of economics at Stanford, contended that the Reserve banks should always be extremely liquid, but that government securities and "Loans secured by obligations of the government . . . are not self-liquidating and should never comprise more than a minor part of the assets of a Reserve bank."[15] In his opinion,

The assets of the Reserve banks, aside from buildings and equipment, should consist of gold bars, short-term commercial paper, together with a strictly limited amount of short-term obligations of the government. There is no place in the Reserve System for real estate loans or other non-liquid paper. The portfolios of the Reserve banks have suffered an unfortunate deterioration.[16]

He deplored legislation permitting the Reserve banks to lend on paper that was not self-liquidating and also the loss of elasticity of Federal Reserve notes when government securities were permitted as collateral.

Somewhat similar points were made in a memorandum to Congress in 1935 from the Economists' National Committee on Monetary Policy. This was signed by 69 economists, though 7 signed with reservations. They insisted that only commercial paper should be used as collateral for Federal Reserve notes and opposed making "noncommercial and illiquid paper eligible for discount at the Federal Reserve."

. . the supply of noncommercial paper eligible for discount should be further restricted, not enlarged.
. . . It is the function of a central banking system to maintain at all times a liquid portfolio, since the system holds the ultimate reserves of the nation's banks . . . .
All measures designed to correct weaknesses in the Federal Reserve System should seek . . . to increase, not reduce, its commercial nature. They should assure, not impair, its liquidity. And they should free it from government financing rather than link it more closely to the fiscal needs of the government.[17]

Economists and others advancing such ideas about the liquidity of the Reserve

---

[14]*Chase Economic Bulletin,* June 21, 1931, p. 7.

[15]*Money and Banking,* Wiley, New York, 1935, p. 283.

[16]*Ibid.,* p. 319.

[17]Hearings before the House Banking and Currency Committee, on H.R. 5357, 74th Congress, 1st Session (March 27, 1935), pp. 760-761.

banks usually dwelt at length on the difficulties the Federal Reserve would encounter if it tried to liquidate its large holdings of government securities. They failed to give equal attention to the problems that would result if the Reserve banks tried to liquidate an equally large amount of their loans based on commercial paper.

Economists and noneconomists with ideas such as those described above thought that active easy-money policies by the Federal Reserve would be harmful. There was still another school with many members who thought that active easy-money policies were unlikely to be helpful even if they failed to do harm. Joseph Schumpeter represented this point of view.

> . . . there is not much room for central bank initiative in the course of depression. If facilities were forced upon them by open market buying member banks would thwart the intention, first by using their excess of funds in order to repay their debts and then by accumulating secondary or simply idle reserves.[18]

Edwin W. Kemmerer—world-famous "money doctor," author of a widely read book on *The ABC of the Federal Reserve System,* and a professor of economics at Princeton—expressed similar views. Referring to Federal Reserve purchases of government securities in 1932, he stated in December of that year:

> . . . to a considerable extent the very reflation operations which created these funds increased the business distrust that was making the conservative business public unwilling to borrow and conservative banks unwilling to invest.[19]

He elaborated on these views a year later.

> The business and financial worlds are afraid of inflation and they rightly look upon these extensive open market purchases as powerful governmental efforts exerted in the direction of inflation. This fact weakens confidence in the business situation and prospects, or, in other words, it is a factor in increasing business distrust . . . . In other words, there are powerful psychological forces at work that tend to cause all efforts to reflate by the expansion of our deposit currency to defeat themselves and actually to bring a net contraction of our circulation through resulting reductions in velocities.[20]

Kemmerer was by no means alone in holding such beliefs; these were shared by many economists and members of the business community. Why the business and financial community should have been so fearful of "inflation" under the conditions prevailing in 1932-1933 and why their "confidence" should have been so shaken by the prospect of increased supplies of money and credit remain unclear.

Another skeptic about the ability of monetary policy to hasten economic recovery was O. M. W. Sprague—frequent consultant to the Federal Reserve and the Treasury, Economic Advisor to the Bank of England, and a professor of economics at Harvard. In his testimony before the British Committee on Commerce and Industry in February 1931, he stated:

---

[18]*Business Cycles,* McGraw-Hill, New York, 1939, Vol. II, p. 658.

[19]*American Economic Review Supplement,* March 1933, p. 134.

[20]*American Economic Review Supplement,* March 1934, p. 99.

... if I were asked how, through monetary changes, the present decline in prices might have been in some part lessened, I should say that the most hopeful means in the past would have been the exercise of a great deal more restraint than was exercised in the granting of credit and in the lodgment of investment funds in the period of prosperity about two and three years ago.... But after what I may call a poison has been introduced in the economic system, such as overdevelopment in many branches of industry or heavy borrowings by numerous governments, then I am disposed to think that monetary agencies are almost helpless of themselves to stay the downward course of the price level, to say nothing of being able to induce an upward movement.... Mr. Keynes raises very interesting questions supported by much economic analysis as to whether it is possible by means of a sufficiently low rate of interest to induce that additional demand for loans and for investments which will bring about an upward movement in prices. I must say that I am skeptical about that at a time when there is a very serious disequilibrium about the world.[21]

Sprague concluded that an aggressive easy-money policy was practically out of the question in the United States, "for there is no general acceptance of the view in that country that additional good loans and additional good investments are available at a lower rate of interest."[22]

Sprague stated his position even more strongly in 1934:

I hold that no monetary policy, however wisely formulated, is sufficient to bring about a trade recovery. We had sound money and no doubt about the security of the currency between 1929 and 1933. There was also during those years a plentiful supply of credit available at low interest rates and at intervals widespread confidence that prosperity was at hand; and yet the country drifted more and more deeply into depression.[23]

THEORIES OF FISCAL POLICY

Just as there were no valid and generally accepted theories of income and employment and of monetary policy in the late 1920s and early 1930s, there was no well-developed and generally accepted theory of the effects of government tax and expenditure policies on the behavior of total income and employment. Treatises on public finance abounded in descriptions of various types of taxes, expenditures, and public debts, and dwelt at length on the shifting and incidence of various types of taxes. Some also cited cases of fiscal pathology in which governments brought on inflation through deficit spending, usually financed at least in part by the creation of new money. But they contained no analysis of the deliberate use of government tax and expenditures policies to regulate levels of national income and employment.

Though economists failed to provide a fiscal theory, they did provide general rules for fiscal conduct, and the principal rule was that of the annually balanced budget. Every governmental unit should match its tax revenues and expenditures in every 12 month period, and if it had outstanding debt it

---

[21]Minutes of evidence taken before the Committee on Finance and Industry, (The Macmillan Committee) Vol. II (February 19, 1931), p. 312.

[22]*Ibid.*

[23]*Recovery and Common Sense*, Riverside Press, Cambridge, Mass., 1934, p. 2.

should have a tax surplus to retire a part of the debt each year. There were, of course, permitted exceptions to the general rule. For example, deficits during a major war were conceded to be inevitable, and a government was not to be criticized for a small deficit resulting from an honest miscalculation of revenues and expenditures. It might also borrow to finance self-liquidating public works, such as water-supply systems or toll roads, which would themselves yield enough revenues to service and retire the debt. Moreover, a local government might borrow to pay for a large nonrecurring item, such as a new school, which would be useful over a long period of time. There were few other exceptions to the balanced-budget rule, and among them was not deficit spending, or tax reduction, or increases of expenditures to maintain and raise the level of output and employment.

Events tested loyalties to these rules during the early 1930s. Federal revenues, so heavily dependent on taxes on personal incomes and corporate profits, fell sharply as the depression deepened, and federal deficits began to appear. The accepted fiscal rules called for restoring a balanced budget by cutting federal expenditures or by raising taxes. In the early part of the period, most economists and others favored this course, many insisting that it be implemented immediately.

Why was there such strong opposition to budget deficits under conditions such as those prevailing in the early 1930s? Some reasons were not directly related to effects on total output, employment, or price levels. For example, it was believed, not wholly without justification, that a government which was allowed to spend without raising an equal amount of taxes would become wasteful and would misallocate resources. Budget balancing was a useful discipline for legislatures. However, many believed that deficit spending, with its attendant increase in the national debt, would actually prolong and intensify the depression. There appear to have been several reasons for this belief. One was the lack of an enlightening theory of national income and fiscal policy. Economists and others did not understand that a deficit reflecting a reduction of revenues resulting from a decline of national income could have an "automatic stabilizing effect," however small under prevailing circumstances, or that tax increases or reductions of government expenditures would have downward multiplier effects. They concentrated instead on what they believed to be the depressing effects of a deficit and an increase in the government debt. These depressing effects would result in part from an alleged damage to "confidence" caused by threats of "inflation" and impairment of the government's credit standing. It is difficult to understand why they thought the government's credit was so frail. The federal government's debt at the end of 1929 was equal to only about 15 percent of that year's gross national product and was more than $9 billion below its level at the end of World War I. Yet the fear was real, and the consequences of any impairment of the government's credit were believed to be calamitous. In a radio speech on March 12, 1932, Secretary of the Treasury Ogden L. Mills told the nation:

> ... our private credit structure is inextricably bound to the credit of the United States Government. Our currency rests predominantly upon the credit of the United States. Impair that credit and every dollar you handle will be tainted with suspicion. The foundation of our commercial credit system, the Federal Reserve banks, and all other

banks which depend upon them, is tied into and dependent upon the credit of the United States Government. Impair that credit today, and the day after thousands of development projects—they are still going on—will stop; thousands of businessmen dependent upon credit renewals will get refusals from their bankers; thousands of mortgages that would otherwise be renewed or extended will be foreclosed; merchants who would buy on credit will cancel orders; factories that would manufacture on part capacity at least will close down. Impair the credit of the United States Government and all that we have sought to accomplish in the course of the last few months is, to a large extent, nullified. The renewed courage and confidence that have replaced the fear and uncertainty, which prevailed almost universally, will once more grow weak and hesitant.[24]

Such views and fears were widely shared.[25] Though Secretary Mills spoke only of effects on confidence in the United States, he may have shared the fears of others that continued deficit spending would impair foreign confidence in the dollar, induce gold exports, and perhaps force the United States off the gold standard.

Some economists who would otherwise have favored deficit spending, perhaps on a much larger scale, became convinced that the deficit would have to be eliminated, or at least reduced, because of the widespread fears that had been created. For example, Jacob Viner reluctantly concluded in April 1933:

> For the Federal government, the campaign for balancing the budget has made it dangerous to increase the debt substantially, because of the adverse effect it would have on the morale of a scared public taught to measure the stability of government by the financial record for a single year or short period of years.
>
> Had it not been for this campaign of fear, however, it would have been sound policy on the part of the federal government deliberately to permit a deficit to accumulate during depression years, to be liquidated during prosperity years from the higher productivity of the tax system and from increases in tax rates when they would do no harm. The outstanding though unintentional achievement of the Hoover administration in counteracting the depression has in fact been its deficits of the last two years, and it was only its alleged fears as to the ill effects of these deficits, and the panic which the big business world professed to foresee if these deficits should recur which have made this method of depression finance seriously risky. Had the government and the business magnates retained their mental balance, there would have been less cause to fear net ill effects during a depression than during the war from even a ten billion dollar deficit....
>
> Deliberate inflation may involve violation of the letter or of the spirit of contracts, but the only visible alternatives are similar modification of contracts through forced deflation or through bankruptcy, or else economic collapse....
>
> If we are to have inflation, therefore, we must have it within the gold standard and without resort to budgets badly enough unbalanced to terrify Wall Street. These two conditions suffice to make impossible any policy of deliberate inflation on a large scale through unilateral action on our part. If it is to be accomplished at all, it must be accomplished by international agreement.[26]

Sumner H. Slichter arrived at similar conclusions in early 1933.

> Let me say emphatically that I am not in favor of attempting to balance the budget in the midst of depression. The Government deficit in a period of depression is valuable

---

[24]*Annual Report of the Secretary of the Treasury,* 1932, pp. 259-260.

[25]For many examples see Hearings on S. Res. 315 before the Senate Committee on Finance, 72d Congress, 2nd Session (February, 1933).

[26]*Balanced Deflation, Inflation, or More Depression,* University of Minnesota Press, Minneapolis, 1933, pp. 18, 19, 21, and 27.

because government borrowing is likely to produce inflation—or at least to offset in some measure the deflationary effect of the liquidation of private indebtedness. *But if the deficit is too large and excites too much alarm, its net effect may be deflationary rather than inflationary,* because apprehension over the fiscal policy of the government may cause many business enterprises to postpone buying and, in so far as possible, to avoid commitments . . . .

The unexpectedly large deficit which is developing this year seems to be having this effect. In order to gain the maximum inflationary benefit from the deficit, it is necessary, therefore, to reduce the deficit.[27]

Many also believed that government deficits deterred business recovery because the government's borrowing to finance its deficit would decrease the funds available for private use. Secretary Mellon wrote to Senator Vandenberg in December 1930:

The additional funds are to be obtained by borrowing. An issue of bonds for this purpose would draw money out of the bond market and make funds less available for other issues. Business recovery is in some degree at least dependent on a good market for new securities to supply the needs of various business enterprises. To the extent that funds seeking investment are diverted to the purchase of government bonds to be issued for this special purpose, to that extent is the capital market depleted of funds otherwise available for industrial and other employment . . . . Business must look to other means of recovery than the dissipation of savings.[28]

Many economists agreed that this argument had substance, though some did not believe that every dollar borrowed by the government would be fully offset by a decrease in funds available for private borrowing.

It is, of course, easy to reply that properly coordinated monetary and debt management policies could prevent continued deficits and increases of the public debt from lowering confidence in the public credit and from decreasing the supply and raising the cost of credit for private use. The Federal Reserve could do this by assuring an ample supply of credit for the purpose. It could even, if need be, buy the new government issues at "pegged" prices and yields. Such proposals would have met shocked opposition in this period. They would have been opposed by those who did not want the Federal Reserve to increase its own illiquidity by loading itself with government securities, thereby also increasing member bank reserves. Moreover, many would have replied that financing a government deficit by direct or indirect recourse to the central bank was the surest way to prevent recovery because it would create the greatest fears of inflation, thus virtually assuring a breakdown of "confidence," both at home and abroad.

There were, of course, economists and others who did not share these views. Some of them wanted even larger deficits, either to support the level of income and employment, or to meet relief and other urgent social needs, or both. They were not sufficiently powerful, however, to prevent the enactment in 1932 of the largest federal tax increase in the nation's peacetime history, or to prevent decreases in federal expenditures at that time. These restrictive

---

27"The Immediate Unemployment Problem," *Annals of the American Academy of Political and Social Science,* January 1933, p. 9. the italics were in the original.

28*Annual Report of the Secretary of the Treasury,* 1931, p. 387.

fiscal actions were approved by many economists and by both Republican and Democratic leaders. Even Franklin D. Roosevelt campaigned in 1932 on a platform of budget balancing and took some steps in that direction during the first weeks of his presidency.

CONCLUSION

If the American economy should slide into a serious recession in the 1970s, there would be widespread agreement among economists, businessmen, and other members of the public as to the general nature of the policies to be adopted to combat the decline. They would reject deflation and liquidation as being both ineffective and too costly in terms of output and employment. They would agree that the government could and should do something about a recession. Appealing to national income and fiscal theories that are widely accepted, at least in their general outlines, they would agree that the most appropriate method would be to increase total expenditures for output. They would also agree that while labor and other productive resources were under-utilized, increased demands would be reflected largely in increased output and employment rather than in price increases. There would also be widespread agreement on the methods to be used to increase effective demand. The Federal Reserve would be expected to initiate an active easy-money policy, and would be widely and roundly criticized if it failed to do so. Fiscal policy would be expected to help. The budget deficits that would almost inevitably appear as the falling national income lowered federal revenues would not cause alarm, but would be welcomed for their "automatic stabilizing" effects. If the recession threatened to become serious, there would be broad support for tax reductions, increased government expenditures, or both. The resulting deficits, far from destroying "business confidence," would be looked upon as favorable to recovery and to the profitability of production and investment. Moreover, the Federal Reserve would be expected to assure that the government's borrowing would not decrease the supply nor raise the cost of funds for private use.

There would, of course, be disagreements as to the timing and magnitude of actions, and the proper "mix" of policy instruments, but they would not concern fundamentals.

At the beginning of the 1930s there was no such consensus, either within or outside the Federal Reserve. There was no general agreement that the federal government or the Federal Reserve either could or should take action to limit and reverse a decline. Nor was there general agreement on either the causes of depression or the proper remedies. Many thought that liquidation, deflation, and readjustment were inevitable and necessary to set the stage for recovery. They felt that "artificial" interferences with such natural processes would only be harmful. Others did not share this belief. In view of these differences in theory and diagnosis, differences in policy prescriptions were inevitable. Some did favor expansionary fiscal policies, but widespread fears of government deficits, with their alleged deleterious effects on "confidence," made their adoption impossible.

Prescriptions for monetary policy also differed widely, and some of the differences were basic. There were, of course, many economists and others who from the beginning of the depression urged the Federal Reserve to adopt aggressive expansionary policies, including large open-market purchases of government securities and sharp reductions of discount and bill-buying rates. However, this counsel was sharply opposed not only by a large number of bankers and businessmen but also by many professional economists of high reput. Such "artificial" measures would, they asserted, only prolong the depression by interfering with natural and orderly processes of adjustment, by creating fears of inflation, and by destroying "confidence." The most appropriate Federal Reserve policy was therefore one of encouraging orderly liquidation by standing ready to lend freely to member banks but at high interest rates.

Outside the System as well as within it, the battle continued between those who believe that the purpose of the Federal Reserve should be to exercise control on its own initiative and those who advocated "accommodation." According to the latter, the System should "accommodate commerce, industry, and agriculture" by responding to the "needs of trade" as these were reflected in demands for loans conforming to the commercial loan theory. When demands for such loans declined, the Federal Reserve should allow the volume of credit to decline. To attempt to counter this trend would be "artificial." To add to the confusion, some counseled the Federal Reserve to look to the quality of its assets, its own liquidity, and the elasticity of Federal Reserve notes. To this end, they suggested that its earning assets be confined largely to loans on short-term, self-liquidating paper rather than such illiquid and inelastic assets as government securities and loans on such securities.

If such conflicting advice and criticism did not confuse Federal Reserve officials, it left them with no feeling that they were operating under a clear-cut mandate from either professional economists or the American people.

9

Economic Theories in the Federal Reserve

The state of economic understanding and thinking within the Federal Reserve during the late 1920s and early 1930s was as varied, confused, and conflicting as that outside. Federal Reserve officials held sharply conflicting views concerning the System's responsibilities, its proper objectives, its powers, and the effects of its policies on the economy. The failure of the Federal Reserve to adopt aggressive expansionary policies during this period resulted not from external restraints on the System's freedom of action but from internal conflicts of views, misunderstanding of its powers, mistaken assessments of developments in the economy, and misjudgments of the effects of the System's actions.

As we shall see later, the Federal Reserve's freedom to follow expansionary policies was not limited at any time before September 1931 by considerations relating to the nation's balance of payments or to its own gold reserve and "free-gold" positions. The balance of payments was almost continuously in surplus, the Reserve banks held large excess gold reserves, and their free gold was more than adequate. The situation changed during the international financial crisis which struck the United States in September 1931. Even then, however, the Federal Reserve could have followed much less deflationary and more expansionary policies if its officials had really wished to do so.

It is because the state of thinking of Federal Reserve officials is so important to an understanding of the policies adopted and rejected that we shall examine it at some length. We shall concentrate primarily on thinking during the period preceding September 1931, throughout which the Federal Reserve enjoyed wide freedom of action.

THE MONETARY AND FINANCIAL BACKGROUND

As we have seen, Federal Reserve officials differed widely in their assessment of conditions in the monetary and credit markets during this period. Some thought credit conditions remained "tight," while others thought there was "monetary ease," "extreme monetary ease," or even "sloppy conditions." Whether money was tight or easy depends in part on the criteria used. One criterion was the behavior of interest rates. If one judges "monetary ease" solely by the behavior of interest rates on short-term, open-market instruments of the safest and most liquid types, this was indeed a period of ease, for these rates fell sharply. As was noted in Chapter 7, however, these rates are misleading as indicators of the availability and cost of credit to most private borrowers. For one thing, most rates charged private borrowers declined less, and many actually rose as the creditworthiness of borrowers deteriorated. Moreover, nonprice methods of rationing credit were used more widely as the depression deepened.

Another criterion of "monetary ease," but one which was used only rarely by Federal Reserve officials, is the behavior of the money supply. As stated in Chapter 7, the money supply declined almost continuously after the end of 1929. From its level in mid-1929, the money supply, narrowly defined, had declined 4 percent by mid-1930, 6 percent by the end of 1930, and 10 percent by mid-1931. The money supply more broadly defined had fallen 8 percent by mid-1931.

Still another criterion of "monetary ease" might be the behavior of the "reserve positions" of member banks. Here one faces difficult problems of selecting the most meaningful measures of the "reserve positions" of banks and of judging whether changes in those reserve positions were on balance contractionary, expansionary, or neutral. Some of the relevant questions are these: "What is the most meaningful measure of member bank 'reserve positions': total reserves, unborrowed reserves, excess reserves, member bank borrowings, or some combination of these? What were member bank reactions to such changes as did occur?"

Table 9-1 presents some relevant data. These indicate that member bank reserve positions, however measured, improved somewhat during the period and might seem to suggest that the changes put the banks under less pressure to contract and more pressure to expand. After the end of 1929, total member bank reserves rose only very modestly, never more than $85 million, above their $2,335 million level in September 1929, but member bank borrowings fell markedly from their $961 million level in September. By June 1930 the latter were down to $250 million; during the rest of this period they remained at or below this level. Thus, the unborrowed reserves of member banks rose from less than $1,400 million in September 1929 to more than $2,100 million in June 1930 and then fluctuated slightly above this level. Excess reserves rose very little until mid-1931. Though we shall make little use of them, the data in the last column of Table 9-1 are suggestive. These relate to a concept developed after World War II—the "net free reserves of member banks," which are simply their excess reserves minus their borrowings at the Federal Reserve. It will be noted that throughout this period member bank net free reserves were negative; their borrowings exceeded their excess reserves, though by decreasing amounts.

Thus member banks were enabled to decrease their borrowings and to increase their unborrowed reserves. The principal factors making this possible were a $600 million increase in the monetary gold stock and Federal Reserve net purchases of $547 million of government securities. Net inflows of currency to the banks had also contributed reserve funds during the early part of

TABLE 9-1

The Reserve Positions of Member Banks, September 1929-August 1931
(in millions of dollars; monthly averages of daily figures)

Date	Total reserves (1)	Member Bank borrowings at the Federal Reserve (2)	Unborrowed reserves (1) − (2) (3)	Excess reserves (4)	Net free reserves (4) − (2) (5)
1929					
September	2,335	961	1,374	34	−927
October	2,386	878	1,508	42	−836
November	2,521	950	1,571	65	−885
December	2,395	801	1,594	48	−753
1930					
January	2,349	498	1,851	44	−454
February	2,305	378	1,927	53	−325
March	2,330	272	2,058	56	−216
April	2,350	231	2,119	42	−189
May	2,356	245	2,111	45	−200
June	2,392	250	2,142	54	−196
July	2,417	223	2,194	74	−149
August	2,392	214	2,178	52	−162
September	2,397	188	2,209	59	−129
October	2,407	196	2,211	59	−137
November	2,433	220	2,213	52	−168
December	2,415	337	2,078	73	−264
1931					
January	2,433	252	2,181	105	−147
February	2,370	216	2,154	57	−159
March	2,386	176	2,210	66	−110
April	2,376	154	2,222	56	− 98
May	2,387	163	2,224	67	− 96
June	2,404	187	2,217	129	− 58
July	2,407	169	2,238	124	− 45
August	2,345	222	2,123	101	−121

the period, but the flow reversed as the growing distrust of banks was reflected in net currency drains.

Discount rates were reduced at all the Reserve banks. The New York rate, which had been 6 percent before the crash and was down to 4 1/2 percent by the end of 1929, was reduced in 6 more steps to 1 1/2 percent. The other Reserve banks, whose rates had been at 5 percent before the crash, reduced less; Minneapolis lowered to 3 1/2 percent, 5 Reserve banks to 3 percent, 4 to 2 1/2 percent, and Boston to 2 percent. New York was clearly the most aggressive in its rate-reduction program; some other Reserve banks would not have gone as far as they did if New York had not led the way.

Did these developments—those which enabled member banks to reduce their borrowings and to increase their unborrowed reserves, and the reduced cost of borrowing from the Federal Reserve—exert strong pressures on the banking system to expand its loans and investments? On this question there were wide differences of opinion, both within and outside the System. Some officials insisted that the existing volume of excess reserves was sufficient to exert strong pressures toward expansion; others denied this.

For reasons already indicated, I believe that even in mid-1931 great numbers of banks felt under pressure to contract rather than to expand their loans and investments of the less liquid and less safe types. (1) Excess reserves were not very large relative to total bank reserves. They never exceeded $129 million, or about 5 percent of total bank reserves. (2) The improvement in reserve position was distributed quite unequally within the banking system. Some banks, especially those in the larger centers, did gain deposits and reserves, but others suffered large drains. (3) Banks came to demand more liquidity in the form of cash and other highly liquid assets both because of their fear of withdrawals and because of the decreased liquidity of their other assets. Thus they felt impelled to hold more reserves in excess of legal requirements, more cash in vault, and a larger part of their portfolios in the form of the safest and most liquid assets. (4) Banks became less willing to assume the risks involved in borrowing from the Federal Reserve in order to acquire or maintain lower loans and investments. This was partly because most loans and investments came to be considered riskier, and partly because the banks' solvency and liquidity had already deteriorated so much.[1]

RECONSTITUTION OF THE OPEN-MARKET COMMITTEE

One reason for examining the thinking and policy atittudes of all the Reserve bank governors is that seven of them were given an opportunity to have a greater voice in open-market policy after the Open-Market Committee was reconstituted in January 1930. The Federal Reserve Board has been contemplating changes in the membership, procedures, and powers of the old OMIC since August 1928. On January 16, 1930, Miller took the initiative, moving abolition of the OMIC and the establishment of a new body to be called the Open-Market Policy Conference (hereafter referred to as the OMPC). All members of the Board approved the change except Young, who explained that he had been negotiating with the Secretary of the Treasury and some directors of the New York Reserve Bank and had come to an agreement that nothing would be done at that time. Hamlin's motion to reconsider lost on a tie vote, with Miller, James, and Cunningham voting against it.

Under the new arrangements:

1. The OMPC was composed of one representative from each of the Reserve banks to be chosen by the directors of each bank.

2. The OMPC was to meet with the Federal Reserve Board upon call by the Governor of the Board or by the Chairman of the Executive Committee of the OMPC after consultation with the Governor of the Board.

3. The functions of the OMPC were to consider, develop, and recommend policies and plans with regard to open-market operations.

4. "The time, character, and volume of purchases and sales [were] to be governed with a view of accommodating commerce and business and with regard to their bearing upon the credit situation."

5. An Executive Committee of five governors was appointed to carry

---

[1] See pp. 666, above.

out the policies of the OMPC. This included representatives of the New York, Boston, Philadelphia, and Chicago Reserve banks throughout this period. The other member was from Cleveland in the first part of the period and from Atlanta in the latter part.

6. Each Reserve bank waived none of its rights under the Federal Reserve Act; any bank might retire as a member of the OMPC, but while it was a member it was expected to meet its obligations.

7. Once a policy was approved, each Federal Reserve bank was to decide whether it would participate, but a dissenting bank was expected to acquaint the Board and the Chairman of the Executive Committee of the OMPC with the reasons for its dissent.

These changes appear to have had two principal purposes: to increase the Board's power over open-market operations in government securities and to give representation to the Reserve banks that had not had members on the old OMIC. It failed to accomplish the first purpose; the Board continued to have power to restrict, but it was not very effective in initiating open-market actions. The second purpose probably conflicted with the first; the Board might have exerted more influence on a 5-man committee than on a committee of 12, especially when some of the new members proved to be so recalcitrant.

Enlargement of the Open-Market Committee may also have had a marked influence on the course of monetary policy, turning it away from one of active ease and toward passivity and even restriction. One cannot be sure of this because at least two members of the old OMIC had certainly not been friendly to large open-market purchases or other strong easing actions, and they alone might have succeeded in blocking more aggressive expansionary policies. However, most of the new members inclined toward restriction, passivity, or less expansionary policies.

VIEWS AT THE VARIOUS RESERVE BANKS

The official views of the various Reserve banks were usually expressed by their governors or deputy governors. In some cases, however, it is impossible to distinguish between the official's own views and those of his directors, for some felt bound by instructions from their boards. Governor Meyer of the Board once complained that there was little point in meeting in Washington for policy discussions when the governors came irrevocably bound by instructions, and he pleaded with them to come to the next meeting without prior commitments.

NEW YORK

As already indicated, officials of the New York Bank were by far the strongest and most consistent advocates of active monetary policies designed to regulate the market rather than to respond in an accommodating way to market developments. They were the System's leading advocate of open-market operations as a control device; they appear to have initiated all the pur-

chases undertaken in this period, and they proposed others that met disapproval. However, by late 1930 Harrison's proposals became less ambitious,
perhaps partly because he had by then met so many rebuffs. New York also
advocated an active use of bill-buying rates. During this period it reduced the
bill-buying rate 26 times, lowering it from 5 1/8 to 1 percent. In several cases
it proposed decreases that were delayed by the Board.

New York was also the most active of all the Reserve banks in changing
its discount rate. During this period it lowered its rate in 8 steps from 6 to 1
1/2 percent. Only Boston went as low as 2 percent, and only 4 other Reserve
banks as low as 2 1/2 percent. Moreover, New York always took the lead in
rate reductions. At least some of the other Reserve banks, perhaps most,
would have reduced less if New York had not led the way.[2]

By later standards some of the New York actions and recommendations
seem overly cautious and inadequate, but hardly so if contrasted with the
actions and views of other officials in the period.

CHICAGO

At, or certainly near, the other extreme was Governor McDougal of
Chicago, who could almost always be counted on to oppose easing actions,
especially purchases of government securities. At the OMPC meeting in
January 1930 he said that an easing policy would be worth considering if it
would benefit business, but he felt that existing rates were not restrictive and
that there should be a further liquidation of collateral loans by banks. By
June he was contending that there was a surplus of available credit, that
money rates were low and in his opinion too low, and that

under conditions now current, rather than to increase the System's holdings of securities,
he would be willing to let the market have a part of the present holdings of the System,
and, furthermore, would favor letting acceptances go to the investing public where they
are in great demand, even though the System's holdings might be materially reduced.[3]

When Harrison wrote that further purchases could do no harm, he replied that
experience had shown that long-continued abnormally low rates lead banks to
take risks and generate speculation.

Therefore, I am not in agreement with your view that the placing of additional
reserve credit in the market under conditions now current "can do no harm." ... I
believe that it should be the policy of the Federal Reserve System to maintain a position
of strength, in readiness to meet future demands, as and when they arise, rather than to
put reserve funds into the market when not needed.[4]

He was still of the same opinion in September when New York proposed

---

[2]Deputy Governor Worthington of Kansas City wrote to Governor Bailey on
January 27, 1931, "I took occasion to talk with the governors of the banks which have
not yet reduced their rates and found that none of them were in favor of or could see
any necessity for a reduction. Some of the others who did reduce also stated they did so
reluctantly but that they were forced into it by the action of New York."

[3]Minutes of the Executive Committee of the OMPC, June 23, 1930.

[4]Letter to Harrison, July 10, 1930.

purchases of securities to offset the effects of gold exports and rising seasonal demands for credit.

... it cannot be said that the prevailing rates for credit are in any sense a barrier to business recovery .... I hope you will agree with me that under the circumstances recited it would be inadvisable to force additional credit into an already oversupplied market.[5]

Later in the month he told members of the OMPC that he would like to see some of the System's bill holdings run off, even if this required some rise of the bill-buying rate. When the OMPC recommended that existing money market conditions, as measured by interest rates, be maintained at prevailing levels he dissented; he thought some firming of rates was advisable.

At the meeting of the OMPC in January 1931, MacDougal stated that the easy-money policy had not produced the desired results; instead, business had deteriorated. He therefore proposed that the System sell some of its government securities and let some of its bill holdings run off in order to eliminate "sloppiness" in the money market. He also stated that of the last three reductions of the Chicago discount rate, the first two were for the purpose of encouraging business but the last was only to narrow the differential between the Chicago and New York rates. He thought New York had lowered too much. In February he urged New York to sell more securities. In June he stated that he had been concerned about gold inflows but still questioned the desirability of putting out more credit when the market was already glutted. However, he voted for purchases of up to $50 million of securities, apparently in part because he thought the purchases might be viewed by the public as supporting President Hoover's proposal for a moratorium on reparations payments.[6]

Deputy Governor McKay, representing Chicago at a meeting of the Executive Committee of the OMPC and August 4, 1931, maintained that the Federal Reserve should strenghthen its own position against the day of possible currency withdrawals from the banks of the country, and that it was better to leave the securities in the banks so that they could borrow on them. He also noted that interest rates were low and bank incomes suffering. Governor Meyer of the Federal Reserve Board replied that banks were suffering more from loss of principal than from loss of income. McKay informed the OMPC later in the month that he, Governor MacDougal, and their directors were agreed that the System should keep itself in the strongest possible position. Further purchases would do no good and might do harm.

They feel that a little firming of money rates from present abnormally low levels would do more good than easing would do.[7]

---

[5]Letter to Harrison, September 12, 1930.

[6]Minutes of the Executive Committee of the OMPC, June 22, 1931.

[7]Minutes of the OMPC, August 11, 1931.

PHILADELPHIA

Governor Norris of Philadelphia and Richard L. Austin, Chairman of the Board of Directors of that bank, almost always took positions similar to those of MacDougal. The following report presented by Norris to the Federal Reserve Board in late January 1930 represented not only the views of a majority of the members of the OMPC but his own as well.

> The majority opinion was that what has already been done has set in motion a trend which should result in lower rates . . . .
> We feel that we should not interfere in that movement either in the direction of halting it or attempting to expedite it, unless the situation clearly calls for some action and we cannot see that it does. On the contrary, we feel it is better that the situation should clear up further, that the extent and duration of this recession should be more ascertainable than at the present moment, and that it is inexpedient for us to exhaust at the present time any part of our ammunition in an attempt to stimulate business when it is perhaps on a downward curve and we had better wait until we feel that we have reached a stable basis where the administration of some stimulant may have a distinct and good effect rather than to exhaust our ammunition now in what may be perhaps a vain attempt to stem an inevitable recession. Therefore, the recommendation is made that we see no necessity for operations in Government securities at this time either to halt or to expedite the present trend of credit. The majority of the Committee is not in favor of any radical reduction in the bill rate or radical buying of bills which would create an artificial ease or necessitate reduction in the discount rate. If that reduction comes about naturally from further liquidation or reduced demand, all well and good, but we do not feel that there should be any active effort to bring that about . . . . We distinctly feel that no operation in bills should be undertaken for the purpose of either forcing or facilitating a reduction of discount rates by any bank.[8]

Austin was thinking in the same pattern in March when he stated, after commenting on the fall of interest rates,

> . . . since it indicates such a great excess in the supply of bank credit, why should that supply be augmented by pumping more credit into an oversupplied market through the purchase of more Government securities and bills?
> If I may be permitted to express my humble opinion, the continued purchase of bills seems most illogical, and lays us open to the apparent undesirable charge that the action is not justified by the demand for credit but for some other purpose, it may be for boosting business, making a market for securities, or some other equally criticizable cause that certainly will come back to plague us.[9]

Later in the month, at a meeting with the Federal Reserve Board, Norris denied the advisability of purchasing government securities in a money market "already easy as a result of the normal trend." In June he stated the opposition of his directors to further reductions of discount rates and to purchases of government securities, giving still other reasons why such purchases would be harmful:

> He indicated that in his view the current business and price recession was to be ascribed largely to overproduction and excess productive capacity in a number of lines of business rather than to financial causes, and it was his belief that easier money and a better bond

---

[8]Minutes of the OMPC, January 29, 1930.

[9]Letter to J. H. Case, March 17, 1930.

market would not help the situation but on the contrary might lead to further increases in productive capacity and further overproduction.[10]

In August, when New York proposed buying securities to offset the effects of a small gold export, Norris disapproved and considered the action unwise. At the September meeting he objected strongly to the maintenance of artificially low interest rates and artificially high bond prices. The problem, he and his directors believed, was overproduction, not underconsumption, and this could not be cured by easy money.

> We believe that the correction must come about through reduced production, reduced inventories, the gradual reduction of consumer credit, the liquidation of security loans, and the accumulation of savings through the exercise of thrift. These are slow and simple remedies, but just as there is no "royal road to knowledge," we believe there is no short cut or panacea for the rectification of existing conditions . . . .
> We have been putting out credit in a period of depression, when it was not wanted and could not be used, and will have to withdraw credit when it is wanted and can be used.[11]

In April 1931, when the OMPC was considering further easing actions, Norris had altered his attitude somewhat. He still thought that greater ease would not accomplish much, but he felt that there was little danger of speculation or other bad results. He was therefore willing to cooperate by recommending that the Philadelphia discount rate be lowered from 3 1/2 to 3 percent. His chief fear was that the policy would not be reversed quickly enough. At a meeting of the Executive Committee of the OMPC in June he asked whether the System might not be criticized for making money easier when it was already easy and stated that the real difficulty was a "lack of demand by high grade borrowers while lenders were timid and hesitant with respect to any other type of borrower."[12] He abstained from voting on the committee's motion to purchase up $50 million of government securities. In August he told the OMPC that neither he nor his Board felt that any possible good could be accomplished by purchasing securities. Also, the Philadelphia Bank's free gold was now down to only $40 million.[13]

SAN FRANCISCO

Governor Calkins of San Francisco was another who could be counted on to oppose "artificial" easing. As early as January 7, 1930, he wrote to Harrison that the Federal Reserve was holding too many government securities.

> It is, perhaps, futile to apply the word artificial to credit conditions, but it appears to us that the policy pursued has resulted in an artificial condition, and as we are not in sympathy with the view that artificial conditions should be created for the purpose of promoting a bond market, we are still reluctant to go along.

---

[10]Minutes of the Executive Committee of the OMPC, June 23, 1930.

[11]Minutes of the OMPC, September 25, 1930.

[12]Minutes of the Executive Committee of the OMPC, June 22, 1931.

[13]Minutes of OMPC, August 11, 1931.

Later in the month, at an OMPC meeting, he observed that liquidation in his district had been more than usual, that the objectives of the open-market program begun in November had now been accomplished, that there was no need for an "acute" move toward easing, and that if more easing was necessary it should be promoted by lowering bill rates.

In June, after San Francisco had declined to participate in purchases of government securities, Calkins explained to the Federal Reserve Board:

... I think I may briefly summarize our reasons for not participating in the $50,000,000 Governments recently purchased as follows:
a. With credit cheap and redundant we do not believe that business recovery will be accelerated by making credit cheaper and more redundant.
b. We find no reason to believe that excessively cheap money will promote or create a bond market, seeing evidence in the recent past to the contrary, and, further, do not consider the promotion or creation of a bond market one of the functions of the Federal Reserve System.
c. We believe that there may come an opportune moment to put money into the market when that action will have a beneficial effect and feel that, if, at such a time, our open market portfolio is excessive, there may be hesitation to increase it.[14]

In July he advanced still another argument:

... to make credit progressively cheaper and more abundant may cause an unfavorable psychological reaction, rather than a favorable one.[15]

At the September meeting of the OMPC, he voted for maintaining the status quo and against further easing. At another meeting in January 1931 Calkins agreed that the bill rate should be kept low but that "over-sloppy conditions in the money market" should be corrected by sales of government securities.

In April he was apprehensive of results, and especially that the System would not reverse quickly enough, but agreed to cooperate in further easing. However, in August he was again opposed to additional purchases, maintaining that they would not do any good, that the Reserve banks should maintain their liquidity, and that an urgent demand for credit from other sources might be embarrassing if the Federal Reserve were "tied up in securities."[16]

BOSTON

The Boston Reserve Bank was a strong and consistent opponent of policies of active ease. In early 1930 Deputy Governor Paddock reported that there was "more clearing to be done" and that his bank favored a policy of marking time and did not yet endorse carrying the easing process any further. In June he and his directors still preferred "to see things go along as they were for a time" since there was no pressure for borrowing in that district and money was available at reasonable rates.

Roy A. Young, who resigned from the Federal Reserve Board to become Governor of the Boston Bank on September 1, 1930, revealed himself as a

[14]Letter to Roy A. Young, June 16, 1930.

[15]Letter to Harrison, July 10, 1930.

[16]Minutes of the OMPC, August 11, 1931.

strong opponent of open-market purchases, with leanings toward the commercial loan theory. Within a few days after assuming his new office, he informed Burgess in New York that he saw no immediate need to purchase securities and that his people in Boston thought New York had at times been too quick to buy.

In April 1931 Young thought it inadvisable for the System to buy more securities in the open market, though he felt that the Reserve banks should stand ready to buy from any member bank needing accommodation in that fashion. Since Boston usually followed the New York discount rate, he said that it would probably follow suit if New York reduced to 1 1/2 percent. In June, he told Burgess that though he did not want to be a wet blanket he did not see what good purpose could be served by security purchases.[17] He was the only member of the Executive Committee of the OMPC to vote against purchases of securities in that month.[18] He did, however, agree to purchases in July. In August he told the OMPC that his directors had participated only reluctantly in the last purchases and were opposed to any more.[19] He voted against further purchases, commenting that he

would rather see the portfolios of the Federal Reserve System composed of bills and discounts, and regretted to see two important functions nullified by operations in government securities.[20]

DALLAS

Governor Talley was yet another opponent of actively expansionary policies. He complained to Case in March 1930:

Everyone wants to keep business jazzed up all the time, and have it run along at boom figures. It seems to me the sounder course to pursue, after having done this for some time, is to catch up and let the public pay some of its debts....[21]

Three months later he believed that open-market purchases had helped demoralize the banking situation.

We do not see that the open-market purchases, either during March or including the later purchases, have changed the business situation but merely tend to further demoralize the banking situation. It is true that there has been an increase in bond purchases but the thought remains that maybe either some of the credit which the system has put out in being absorbed in that direction or that funds which have become redundant from business recession and should be kept liquid pending business revival are being used in that direction and both sources are being used to absorb an overissue of securities instead of savings being used for that purpose. The proceeds of the issues since they have been underwritten are of course already in the market, and my thought is that when there is a business revival the shortage of commercial funds will be felt much

---

[17]Burgess memorandum to Harrison, June 18, 1931.

[18]Minutes of the Executive Committee of the OMPC, June 22, 1931.

[19]Minutes of the OMPC, August 11, 1931.

[20]Minutes of the OMPC, August 11, 1931.

[21]Letter of March 15, 1930.

sooner than would be the case if the situation had been allowed to run its course with not quite so much oar-dipping by the system.[22]

Talley explained later that he and his directors were opposed not to easier money, but only to artificial ease—to rates below natural levels. ". . . Satisfaction of a demand for further capital supplies would tend to increase overproduction."[23] In September he told the OMPC that the period up to the end of the year was not the time for firming but that excess reserves should be absorbed before the System took further action. If the System was not getting enough bills, this was a sign that the market did not want additional money. In October he expressed his hope that New York would not buy government securities too quickly.

> I have about come to the conclusion that except in emergency situations governments are a poor instrument, or I might say not the best instrument, for open market operations, and that bills constitute a very much more satisfactory instrument . . . .
> The bill rate at the present time is too low but it has reached its present levels by reasons of our overpurchase of governments.[24]

In April 1931 Talley favored a reduction of the New York discount rate, primarily because this action might move funds out of New York. In June he conceded that Federal Reserve purchases of securities "might have an important effect in helping banks to maintain their liquidity and so encouraging them to use their funds courageously."[25] Representing the Dallas Bank at a meeting in August, Deputy Governor Gilbert informed the OMPC that he was personally opposed to the purchase of government securities, though not of bills, and that the free-gold position of his bank prevented its participation in security purchases.[26]

CLEVELAND

Governor Fancher of Cleveland sometimes supported the New York position, but not consistently. In January 1930 he thought that the November program had been largely successful and that the existing discount rate was encouraging needed liquidation. However, he felt that further easing and a reduction of the discount rate might be desirable in February and he saw no objection to a slight reduction of bill rates. In June he favored purchases of government securities but was skeptical whether the System could do much to help the bond market. In July he and his directors wanted to facilitate recovery but

. . . it was their opinion that continued purchases of government securities would not

---

[22]Letter to Harrison, June 13, 1930.

[23]Letter to Harrison, July 15, 1930.

[24]Letter to Harrison, October 6, 1930.

[25]Minutes of the Executive Committee of the OMPC, June 22, 1931.

[26]Minutes of the OMPC, August 11, 1931.

contribute substantially to that recovery and that, therefore, they would not then favor further purchases.[27]

By April 1931 Fancher thought easing action should be taken both to encourage business and to discourage gold inflows. In August he reported that his Board of Directors was divided on the issue of open-market policy. He saw nothing that would warrant purchases at the time but believed that the Executive Committee should have power to meet unforeseen developments.

RICHMOND

Governor Seay sometimes supported the New York position, sometimes not. His bank appears to have been one in which the directors took strong positions. In early 1930 he reported that a majority of his directors favored continuing the bank's 5 percent rate and that he and they thought policy should be directed to maintenance of the present trend of ease rather than positive action in either direction. By July he favored more positive action.

I am in favor of the continued purchases of government securities by the Federal Reserve banks, partly because if we do not make these purchases we will be guilty of neglecting the only means by which we can contribute to the recovery of business, and partly because, as I believe, the result cannot be otherwise than favorable, even though it may be only to a limited extent. The pressure of abundant capital funds will inevitably find an outlet.

By January 1931 Seay though bill rates had become too low.

We have discussed the question of bill rates among our officers, and I confess we are unable to see the logic of following the bill rate down to such levels when there is a demand for more bills than come into the market, and when we do not want the bills ourselves and have been thinking of selling Government securities, which I strongly advocate. It seems to us that we contribute to a further sloppiness of the market by reducing our own bill rates, and under existing conditions are unable to see the necessity or advisability of following the rates down to such a level.[28]

He was of the same opinion in February.

We are out of sympathy with the present low rates, partly brought about, as we believe, by the deliberate action of the Federal Reserve System . . . .
We are also out of sympathy with the extremely low rates for bankers' acceptances . . . . This bank, by vote of its directors, has withdrawn from participation in purchase of bankers' acceptances at current rates, and we are not taking any of these bills offered to us from any source at the present time.[29]

In April 1931, when the OMPC was considering further easing actions, Seay still had no confidence that the policy would accomplish much or that recovery was dependent on further ease of credit. Indeed, he felt that such a policy might even be construed as a move in the wrong direction and a policy of desperation. However, since little risk was involved he said he would prob-

---

[27]Letter to Federal Reserve Board, July 23, 1930.

[28]Letter to Kenzel (at New York), January 29, 1931.

[29]Letter to Burgess, February 19, 1931.

ably recommend a 3 percent rate at Richmond if New York reduced to 1 1/2 percent. In August Seay informed the OMPC that his bank had cooperated in the past but as they had

> ... a very small amount of free gold his directors would not be willing to reduce that amount further by participating in purchases.[30]

ST. LOUIS

Governor Martin's position seems to have been similar to that of Governor Seay; their views were somewhat alike and both had directors who took an active interest in policies. Some of Martin's directors appear to have been strongly opposed to easing actions. In early 1930 he opposed reductions of discount rates and other such actions because they might retard the necessary process of liquidation. In March he saw no benefit in purchases of securities.

> ... I cannot see how the situation can be benefited by putting fifty millions of dollars, or, in fact, any other amount, into the general market at this time .... The reason that more money is not being used is because it is not needed, and when there is already sufficient money to meet the expressed needs, it seems to me unwise artificially to add to the amount already sufficient in order to encourage a use which because based on a redundancy of money rather than on actual needs may be hazardous ....
> We would prefer for the moment not to participate in this purchase of Governments but we can be counted on if there is actual need of our doing so.[31]

Deputy Governor Atteberry, writing for the St. Louis Bank, indicated his own and the bank's opposition to fictitious easy money.

> The discussion here develops the idea that excessive efforts in the interest of fictitious easy money may have just the opposite effect from that intended. It has been suggested that such efforts have the psychological effect of increasing the feeling of uncertainty and thus discouraging buying other than necessity demands. I have talked with a number of business men and in almost every instance they are aware that the Federal Reserve banks are exerting unusual efforts to stimulate business by easy money, but the effect is greater cautiousness on the part of business until the turn is evident.[32]

In April 1931, when the OMPC was considering easing measures, Martin observed that because there was no historical precedent it was difficult to predict results but he favored trying the experiment. He said that St. Louis would follow any reduction of bill-buying rates and probably also a reduction of discount rates. In July he was willing for the System to experiment by purchasing more securities.

> I cannot see that the purchase of governments has done any harm and from the standpoint of the country as a whole, as you say, psychologically it may have been of some benefit. Therefore it seems to me worthwhile to continue the experiment, being ready to reverse action just as soon as the first evidence of the wrong effect appears.[33]

---

[30]Minutes of the OMPC, August 11, 1931.

[31]Letter to J. H. Case, March 10, 1930.

[32]Letter to Harrison, July 9, 1930.

[33]Letter to Harrison, July 14, 1931.

In August he told the OMPC that his bank wanted to be as helpful as possible, but because of its free-gold position his directors felt that they had gone as far as they could in participating in credits to foreign central banks and purchases of government securities.[34]

MINNEAPOLIS

Governor Geery of Minneapolis was another opponent of aggressive easing policies. In January 1930 he saw no reason to lower his discount rate because it was already well below commercial rates and banks still had loans they wanted to liquidate. In March he thought easing policies had been carried far enough.

Frankly, I cannot see the desirability of further ease of credit. It seems to me money is getting almost "sloppy.". . .

However, if you decide to go into the market and buy $50,000,000 of Government securities during the next few weeks, we should be glad to take our proportion of them, purely for the sake of earnings, which we need.[35]

In September he agreed reluctantly to purchases of securities if necessary to prevent gold exports and rising seasonal demands for credit from firming interest rates but "with a feeling on our part that there is no immediate need for the purchase."[36] He added later he would prefer to see member banks borrow a little from the Federal Reserve before securities were purchases.

At an OMPC meeting in August 1931 Geery reported that the Executive Committee of his Board of Directors opposed further purchases of government securities, largely because of the bank's free-gold position.

KANSAS CITY

The limited amount of information available from the records permits only a few comments on the thinking and policy attitudes at the Kansas City Bank. Governor Bailey and Deputy Governor Worthington never took the initiative in easing policies, and they usually went along with the majority, which means that they usually opposed policies of active ease.

In August 1931 Deputy Governor Worthington reported to the OMPC that Governor Bailey and a majority of his directors were agreed that easy money had been carried too far and had not accomplished the desired results.[37]

ATLANTA

Governor Black of Atlanta was from the beginning of the depression a supporter of easier monetary policies. He voted for almost every proposed purchase of securities, and his bank participated in all purchases up to the

---

[34]Minutes of the OMPC, August 11, 1931.

[35]Letter to J. H. Case, March 11, 1930.

[36]Telegram to Federal Reserve Board, September 2, 1930.

[37]Minutes of the OMPC, August 11, 1931.

time it became concerned about its free-gold position. In April 1931 he approved an easing program proposed to the OMPC by Harrison and believed it would be at least partially effective. In June he favored the purchase of all or such part of the authorized $100 million of government securities as seemed likely to be beneficial.[38] Later, as a member of the Executive Committee of the OMPC, he voted for purchases up to $50 million.

CONCLUSIONS

With ideas such as those described above so widely prevalent within the System, it is no wonder that the Reserve banks other than New York and Atlanta were unwilling to support positive and aggressive expansionary policies, including prompt and sharp reductions in discount and bill-buying rates and large purchases of government securities. The latter had little chance of gaining majority approval. Suppose that the OMPC, as reconstituted, had been faced at any time during the period with this question: "Shall the System buy a large amount of government securities for the purpose of making conditions in the money market considerably easier than they now are?" The probable vote in the OMPC would have been as follows:

Yes	No	Dependent on circumstances
New York	Boston	Cleveland
Atlanta	Philadelphia	Richmond
	Chicago	St. Louis
	Minneapolis	
	Kansas City	
	Dallas	
	San Francisco	

The proposal would have met no more cordial reception in the Executive Committee of the OMPC. The probable vote of the four continuing members would almost certainly have been:

Yes	No
New York	Boston
	Philadelphia
	Chicago

When Atlanta was the fifth member it would have joined New York; Cleveland's vote was not so predictable.

Proposed purchases of government securities had more chance of approval if their professed purpose was to maintain the status quo in money market conditions—to meet seasonal increases in the demand for credit, to offset the effects of gold outflows, to discourage gold inflows, and so on. Such purchases were believed to have less "artificial" effects.

---

[38]Burgess memorandum to Harrison, June 18, 1931.

VIEWS IN THE FEDERAL RESERVE BOARD

The members of the Board at the beginning of this period were:

Roy A. Young, Governor
Edmund A. Platt, Vice-Governor
Adolph C. Miller
Charles S. Hamlin
George R. James
Edward H. Cunningham
Ex Officio Members:
Andrew W. Mellon, Secretary of the Treasury
J. W. Pole, Comptroller of the Currency

Several changes occurred during the period. As already indicated, Young resigned on September 1, 1930, to become Governor of the Boston Reserve Bank and was succeeded as Governor of the Board by Eugene Meyer on September 16. Platt resigned on September 15, 1930, to enter private banking and was not replaced until 1933. Cunningham, the representative of agriculture, died in November 1930 and his place was filled in May 1931 by Wayland W. Magee, a Nebraska farmer.

The economic thinking and policy attitudes of these men differed widely. Meyer was the only member of the Board during this period who consistently favored a vigorous open-market policy. From the time he assumed office in September 1930 he urged pruchases, sometimes larger purchases than were favored by New York. However, he was usually unable to convince the representatives of the Reserve banks other than New York and Atlanta. His attitudes contrasted sharply with those of his predecessor, Young. Miller's attitude toward open-market policy changed markedly. During the first months of the depression he continued to believe that open-market policy should be deemphasized and used only in case of emergency or great stress. However, by September or October 1930 he had become more sympathetic to the use of this instrument, and in early 1931 he supported larger purchases. In August 1931 he told the OMPC that

he felt, skeptical as he might be toward Open Market Policy as an instrument of the Federal Reserve System, that if there ever had been a justification for its bold, experimental use, even though it might only serve to demonstrate the limits of the availability of such a policy, that situation exists at the present time.[39]

At the other extreme were Cunningham and James, who almost always opposed purchases of government securities. Platt and Hamlin took intermediate positions. They were generally inclined to vote against purchases designed to create further ease in the money markets, though they could sometimes be persuaded to approve. Mellon and Pole were somewhat more inclined to approve, but not always.

Thus the Board tended to be unfriendly to large open-market purchases to increase monetary ease until after mid-September 1930, when Meyer suc-

---

[39]Minutes of the OMPC, August 11, 1931.

ceeded Young and Miller began to shift his position. Such proposals during this earlier period were likely to be disapproved by Young, Miller, Cunningham, James, Hamlin, and probably one or more of the other members. Board support of open-market purchases increased after that time, but the Board was neither unified enough nor strong enough to overcome the opposition of the large majority of the Reserve banks.

In general, the Board's attitudes toward reductions of discount and bill-buying rates were more favorable than their attitudes toward purchases of government securities, especially during the earlier part of the period. However, they generally favored less rapid and smaller reductions than those proposed by New York. Time after time during the first half of 1930, the Board disapproved, delayed, or lessened the extent of the reductions proposed by New York. In such cases, Cunningham and James always voted to disapprove and they were usually joined by Miller and Platt. Young and Hamlin usually voted for approval, often joined by Mellon and Pole—when they were present. Thus the outcome frequently turned on the presence or absence of the *ex officio* members of the Board.

CONCLUSIONS

The economic thinking and policy attitudes of Federal Reserve officials during this period differed widely—perhaps as widely as those of professional economists, bankers, and other businessmen outside the System. They differed on the causes of the depression, on the nature of the adjustments required for recovery, on the responsibilities of the Federal Reserve, and on the effects that would flow from Federal Reserve actions. Under these circumstances it was impossible for the System to agree upon and carry out a unified and ambitious expansionary policy. By August 1931 several of the Reserve banks were citing the deterioration of their free-gold positions as a reason for their opposition to further purchases of securities, but even then this was only one reason among several. Up to this time they opposed larger purchases and lower bill-buying and discount rates not because they lacked sufficient gold reserves or free gold but because the majority believed that more active easing policies would be unhelpful or even harmful.

Among the ideas that most inhibited more active expansionary policies were these: (1) Liquidation was natural and desirable to make necessary adjustments in the economy and pave the way for recovery. (2) Artificial easing measures were not only unhelpful but actually harmful because they delayed necessary liquidation, damaged confidence, tempted banks to buy bonds or otherwise decrease their liquidity, threatened a revival of speculation, and so on. (3) The Federal Reserve, as a System of short-term productive credit, had no responsibility for the bond market. (4) Credit conditions should be judged by the behavior of interest rates on the safest and most liquid types of short-term instruments. (5) The Federal Reserve should adjust the supply of this credit to business demands at "normal" rates of interest; it should avoid or correct "over-sloppy" conditions. (6) Open-market purchases of government securities were the most artificial of all easing actions, but abnormally low bill-buying rates were also to be avoided.

10

Federal Reserve Policies, October 1929 – September 1931

The Federal Reserve took a number of actions to increase the supply and decrease the cost of reserve funds for member banks during the period between the stock-market crash and the time of Britain's departure from the gold standard in September 1931. However, larger amounts of funds were made available from sources not subject to direct control by the Federal Reserve. One major source was the increase in the monetary gold stock, largely reflecting gold imports. (See Table 10-1.) The gold stock actually declined slightly from November 1929 to February 1930, chiefly because of withdrawals of foreign funds and a brief revival of foreign securities issues in the American market. It began to rise in February and continued upward to the end of this period with only a few interruptions. The rise of the gold stock had supplied $128 million of reserve funds by August 1930, $254 million by January 1931, and $607 million by August 1931.

These additions to reserve funds were augmented up to about August 1930 by large inflows of currency from circulation, these reflecting the public's decreased demands for coin and paper money for transactions as payrolls and retail trade declined. The decline in circulation to August 1930 was $335 million. Thus during the period from September 1929 to August 1930 the $128 million increase of the gold stock and the $335 million inflow of currency from circulation contributed $463 million of reserve funds.

After that point, however, surges of bank failures and the growing distrust of banks brought large withdrawals of currency. By August 1931 currency in circulation was actually $136 million above its level of 2 years earlier and $471 million above its low point in August 1930, this despite the continuing fall of economic activity, payrolls, and retail trade. We have no way of knowing precisely how much currency was "hoarded" at this time, but it was probably above $600 million, and perhaps considerably more than this amount. This $471 million rise of currency in circulation between August 1930 and 1931 offset almost all the reserve funds supplied by the $479 million rise of the gold stock.

In short, during the first half of this period bank reserves gained from both gold inflows and return flows of currency, but in the second half currency outflows largely offset the effects of continued gold inflows.

147

TABLE 10-1

Changes in Member Bank Reserves and Selected Related Items
September 1929-August 1931
(monthly averages of daily figures in millions of dollars)
All changes are cumulative from September 1929 levels

| | Federal Reserve Credit | | | | | | |
	Bills dis counted	Bills bought	U.S. Govern- ment securi- ties	All other FRC	Total FRC	Gold stock	Money in circu- lation	Member Bank reserves
1929								
October	− 84	+108	− 11	+10	+ 23	+ 13	− 1	+ 51
November	− 16	+ 67	+150	+ 3	+204	+ 6	+ 34	+186
December	−166	+ 91	+281	+10	+216	− 44	+132	+ 40
1930								
January	−468	+ 85	+320	− 7	− 70	− 85	−159	+ 14
February	−591	+ 56	+315	−26	−246	− 51	−257	− 30
March	−695	+ 17	+375	−29	−332	+ 26	−279	− 5
April	−738	+ 37	+365	−19	−355	+ 75	−293	+ 15
May	−722	− 47	+364	−26	−431	+137	−314	+ 21
June	−718	− 88	+406	−27	−427	+160	−322	+ 57
July	−743	− 75	+418	−24	−424	+164	−328	+ 82
August	−755	− 76	+434	−32	−429	+128	−335	+ 57
September	−780	− 32	+432	−31	−411	+135	−318	+ 62
October	−773	− 44	+437	−27	−407	+152	−310	+ 72
November	−748	− 45	+434	−35	−394	+185	−283	+ 98
December	−631	+ 28	+479	−30	−154	+215	+ 12	+ 80
1931								
January	−716	− 23	+482	−41	−298	+254	−116	+ 98
February	−753	−127	+438	−49	−491	+288	−213	+ 35
March	−793	−106	+439	−46	−506	+314	−221	+ 51
April	−814	− 56	+435	−40	−475	+343	−164	+ 41
May	−806	− 85	+434	−44	−501	+399	−132	+ 52
June	−779	−108	+445	−39	−482	+497	− 61	+ 69
July	−800	−150	+509	−32	−473	+590	+ 25	+ 72
August	−746	− 94	+547	−27	−320	+607	+136	+ 10

Source: Board of Governors of the Federal Reserve System, *Banking and Monetary Statistics,* Washington, D.C., 1943, p. 371. The net effect of changes in all other factors capable of affecting the volume of member bank reserves was very small during this period.

The Federal Reserve also contributed by purchasing government securities; by August 1931 its holding had increased $547 million. About 70 percent of this increase had occurred by March 1930. Thus the total amount of reserve funds contributed by changes in the gold stock, currency in circulation, and Federal Reserve holdings of government securities was $897 million by August 1930 and $1,018 million by August 1931.

Yet the last column of Table 10-1 shows that actual member bank reserves never rose as much as $100 million above their level in September 1929. What happened to the funds contributed by these sources? They were absorbed or offset by decreases of Federal Reserve credit in other forms, chiefly in Federal Reserve holdings of acceptances and loans to member banks. Acceptance holdings declined both because of the decrease in the total amount outstanding and because the Federal Reserve buying rate was not reduced enough. The latter was at times a matter of controversy between the New York Bank, which wanted quicker and larger reductions, and the Board and the other Reserve banks. However, the largest reduction was in Federal Reserve loans to member banks. In effect, member banks used most of the reserve funds supplied from other sources to reduce their borrowings at the Federal Reserve.

Federal Reserve officials interpreted and reacted to these developments in widely different ways. Some viewed the repayment of member bank borrowings with the proceeds from gold imports and return flows of currency as a part of the natural process of liquidation. This, they believed, was sufficient to ease pressures for contraction and to set the stage for recovery. They tended to look on reductions of bank borrowings from the Federal Reserve as practically equivalent to increases in their reserves. Members could, they argued, borrow again if they wished to expand credit in response to legitimate demands for it. Others viewed the matter quite differently, especially as the depression continued. They commented with increasing frequency on the growing unwillingness of member banks to show in their statements borrowings from the Federal Reserve, the greater demands of banks for liquidity, and the unwillingness of banks to assume the risks involved in borrowing and lending. A few arrived at the conclusion that banks could not really be put under pressure to expand until they had been enabled to pay off all their borrowings and to accumulate large excess reserves. However, these were few indeed.

These developments also drew criticisms from abroad, and especially from Britain. The United States, like France, was becoming a great sinkhole for gold. Gold imports were being sterilized or offset by decreases in central bank credit. This was, they maintained, a clear violation of the rules of the international gold standard game and increased deflationary pressures on other countries. Officials at the New York Bank were sensitive to these criticisms and sometimes referred to them in arguing for larger purchases of government securities or for other easing actions.

FEDERAL RESERVE POLICIES, OCTOBER 1929–JULY 1930

When the OMPC met in Washington on January 28, 1930, its first meeting since November 12, it reviewed economic developments and its own policies since the stock-market crash. It had already taken a number of easing actions. Its holdings of government securities had been increased by $341 million. New York's bill-buying rate applicable to maturities up to 120 days had already been reduced in 4 steps from 5 1/8 to 4 percent and its discount rate in 2 steps from 6 to 4 1/2 percent. Six other Reserve banks had reduced their discount rates from 5 to 4 1/2 percent, but 5 kept their rates unchanged at 5 percent. Partly because of these actions but partly also because of currency inflows and reductions in demands for credit, interest rates had declined somewhat.

At the end of their meeting on January 29, members of the OMPC agreed that:

1. The panicky feeling has subsided.
2. A business recession has taken place, the extent or duration of which is not yet possible to determine.
3. Money has been made available to commerce and industry at more reasonable rates.
4. Liquidation is progressing in an orderly fashion.
5. Rediscounts have been reduced to under $450 million.
6. However, there is a large volume of security loans in member banks which they are anxious to get reduced.
7. Liquidation has been slower in country banks than in the city banks.

They disagreed, however, on the policy implications. The New York representative denied that credit was really easy, repeating Harrison's judgment in a letter to the other governors on January 10:

It cannot be said ... that the country has yet the full benefit of freely available credit at reasonable rates. The bond market is somewhat improved but is still restrictive. Mortgage money is difficult to obtain.... In the meantime the evidences of business recession have become constantly clearer.

New York wanted more purchases of securities and reductions of both bill-buying and discount rates. Most of the other members disagreed; they thought money was already easy enough, if not too easy. The outcome was a recommendation by the majority that

no open market operations in government securities are necessary at this time either to halt or to expedite the present trend of credit.[1]

They did agree, however, that money rates should not be allowed to become firmer, either because of the expected seasonal rise of demands for credit or because of reductions in the Federal Reserve bill portfolio. To avoid this, they requested the Board to permit reductions in the minimum bill-buying rates in order to give the Reserve banks more flexibility in their operations. Thus the governors were already divided on policy, and especially on purchases of government securities; the split was to widen in the following months.

The next meeting of the OMPC was held on March 24. Several further easing actions had been taken in the interim. Six Reserve banks had reduced their discount rates to 4 percent and 5 to 4 1/2 percent, all being approved immediately by the Board. New York had reduced its discount rate in 2 steps from 4 1/2 to 3 1/2 percent and its lowest bill-buying rate in 7 steps from 4 to 3 percent. A majority of the Federal Reserve Board felt that the New York Bank was reducing too fast and delayed or limited the size of some proposed reductions. Cunningham and James disapproved most frequently, and they were joined sometimes by Miller and Platt. When New York proposed a 4 percent discount rate on January 30th the Board disapproved it on a tie vote. Those voting against it stated that their votes were based not only on their own judgments but also on the opinions expressed by the governors at the recent meeting of the OMPC. New York renewed its proposal on February 6; this was approved only when Platt shifted his vote after Mellon had commented that the reduction would help business. New York's later proposal of

---

[1] Minutes of OMPC, January 29, 1930.

a 3 1/2 percent discount rate was approved unanimously by the Board, though Cunningham feared that the reduction might harm confidence. The Board also delayed several proposed reductions of bill-buying rates. Partly because of the decline of Federal Reserve acceptance holdings, the Board took the initiative in proposing to New York on March 5 that it buy $25 million of government securities a week for 2 weeks. This was done, but most of the other governors made it clear when they assembled on March 24 that they thought the purchases unnecessary and perhaps harmful. They concluded that

for the present, at least, the Federal Reserve has proceeded far enough in the direction of easy credit as a stimulus to business and that for the time being, unless some unforeseen development occurs, there should be no increase in the government security or bill portfolios.

They favored reduction of the minimum bill-buying rate to 2 1/2 percent but opposed purchases at any rate below 3 percent in the absence of unforeseen developments. The Board approved the OMPC position on security purchases and agreed that bills should not be purchased at a rate below 3 percent. After several refusals, it approved a 2 1/2 percent minimum bill-buying rate on May 1, the same day that it approved a 3 percent discount rate for New York after having disapproved the same rate a week earlier.

When the governors assembled for the meeting of the OMPC on May 21, the stock-market revival had ended and both business activity and commodity prices were continuing to fall. Harrison, recently returned from a trip to Europe, reported that the depression and deflation of prices were becoming worldwide. This, he believed, was due in part to overproduction of some principal commodities, but

... it also appeared to reflect a shortage of working capital, and thus a restriction of purchasing power, in a number of countries, and had been affected by the stringent credit conditions prevailing last year in world money markets which in turn were in part a reflection of the use of funds for speculation centering about the New York security markets but worldwide in its scope. The recovery of world trade appeared in turn to be in no small degree dependent upon the restoration of purchasing power through the medium of foreign borrowings in the New York money market, just as the recovery of domestic trade appeared to be much dependent on the new financing of domestic enterprise in the United States.[2]

Harrison concluded that the necessity of purchasing government securities might become imminent at any time, and an unidentified member of the Board suggested immediate purchases of securities

to remove every possible restraint of business as far as credit was concerned, and particularly as to the desirability of an active bond market.[3]

The governors were not swayed; a majority of them recommended at the close of the meeting:

In the present circumstances it does not appear to the Conference that any affirmative recommendation as to open market operations is advisable just now. But it is the

---

[2]Minutes of the OMPC, May 21-22, 1930.

[3]*Ibid.*

sense of the Conference that if the situation so develops as to require an open market operation by the System the members of the Conference will be prepared to reconvene or else, if a meeting of the whole Conference is not practicable, to act promptly on recommendations of its executive committee.[4]

After Harrison reported this to the New York directors they voted that it would be desirable to purchase up to $25 million of government securities each week for two weeks,

it being felt that such purchases at this time could do no harm and might prove helpful both from the point of view of their direct influence on the bond market and of the psychological benefit which might also arise.[5]

When Harrison polled all the members of the OMPC, seven Reserve banks approved, St. Louis imposed no objection, and Philadelphia, Chicago, Dallas, and San Francisco disapproved. The Executive Committee of the OMPC approved by a three-to-two vote, with Philadelphia and Chicago in the minority. The Board also approved by a four-to-three vote, but only after Platt shifted from "not voting" to "aye." Miller, James, and Cunningham disapproved. Having received the necessary approvals, though by narrow margins, Harrison bought $50 million of securities for the System account between June 4 and June 14.

The New York directors were unanimous in their belief that this action was inadequate and recommended further purchases of $50 million during the next two weeks. Harrison presented this proposal to the Executive Committee of the OMPC on June 23, only to have it turned down by all the other members. Instead, the group approved by a four-to-one vote MacDougal's motion that "no further purchases of government securities be made for [the] System account at this time." It did not, however, accept his proposal to reduce holdings of both government securities and bills.

Rebuffed by the Executive Committee, Harrison wrote to all the Reserve banks on July 3 advocating further purchases. He was again rebuffed, with only Richmond and Atlanta supporting the New York position. No further purchases were made in July.

FEDERAL RESERVE POLICIES, JULY-DECEMBER 1930

Whether adequate or not, Federal Reserve policies from the time of the stock-market crash until late July 1930 had been active. In contrast, Federal Reserve policy was quiescent from July to December 1930. Few actions were taken, and the actions that were taken were aimed at maintaining the status quo, as measured by market rates of interest, rather than at creating greater ease. For example, New York proposed no changes in either its discount or bill-buying rates, though the 5 Reserve banks that had been maintaining 4 percent discount rates did lower them to 3 1/2 percent. A $25 million pur-

[4]*Ibid.*

[5]Minutes of the Board of Directors of the Federal Reserve Bank of New York, May 29, 1930.

chase of government securities in August was supported only as a partial offset to gold exports to France during that month. The emphasis during this period was on preventing a firming of interest rates, not on reducing them.

This policy was stressed at the meeting of the OMPC on September 25. Miller seems to have been the only one present who even suggested the possibility of large purchases to "awaken and make more active the credit structure," and he did not press the point. This time, Harrison agreed with what he believed to be the majority opinion:

the present policy of the System should be to maintain the present easy money position in the principal money centers and that while the System should be prepared to buy or sell Government securities in order to maintain that position, nevertheless there appears to be no reason at the present time either to buy or to sell.[6]

On the other hand, several governors—notably MacDougal, Norris, Calkins, and Young—thought credit conditions were too easy and that the System should consider sales of securities, though not until after seasonal demands had subsided. At the end of the meeting the OMPC recommended that it be authorized to buy or sell up to $100 million of government securities, but that purchases or sales should be made only to maintain the status quo. The Board approved this recommendation on October 2.

The Board understands that the Conference is of the opinion that no change of the existing situation with regard to money rates is desirable—neither firming of rates nor easing of rates; and that, therefore, no operations in the open market are contemplated, except as they may become necessary to counteract factors threatening a disturbance of the status quo with respect to money rates. It is the understanding of the Board that the authority to purchase or sell government securities is to protect the existing level of rates, not to alter it.

The Federal Advisory Council thought that even this policy was perhaps too liberal. It resolved on November 18:

In the opinion of the Federal Advisory Council the present situation will be best served if the natural flow of credit is unhampered by open market operations or changes in the rediscount rates. The seasonal demands during the balance of the year should be met by rediscounting on the part of member banks.[7]

In any event, the only further purchases of government securities before late June 1931 occurred in December to meet banking difficulties in New York, and these securities were sold in January. Thus, between mid-August 1930 and late June 1931 the Federal Reserve bought no further government securities for general policy purposes.

December brought a wave of bank failures in various parts of the country. Most spectacular was the failure in New York City of the Bank of the United States, a bank with 400,000 depositors and the largest bank ever to fail in this country up to that time. This led to runs on several other New York City banks and to net withdrawls of more than $150 million of currency. It was largely to meet this situation that the New York Reserve Bank

---

[6]Minutes of the OMPC, September 25, 1930.

[7]*Annual Report of the Federal Reserve Board,* 1930, p. 228.

reduced its discount rate to 2 percent and its lowest bill-buying rate to 1 3/4 percent and purchased $123 million of government securities. Of these, over $43 million were for its own account. The Executive Committee of the OMPC, meeting on December 20, approved the New York action under the circumstances but debated whether the securities should be sold after the turn of the year. It finally decided that the OMPC should meet in January to consider the whole question.

FEDERAL RESERVE POLICIES, JANUARY-AUGUST 1931

At the OMPC meeting in Washington on January 21, all agreed that the depression was deepening, bond markets were weak, and foreign issues were virtually unsalable in the American market. Yet no one advocated further purchases of government securities; the only question at issue was whether to sell, and if so how many and under what conditions. Governor Meyer of the Federal Reserve Board seems to have been the only one completely opposed to any sales. He believed that return flows of currency and further gold imports should not be offset by security sales because of the very bad banking situation, the growing unwillingness of banks to show borrowings from the Federal Reserve in their published reports, and the probable unfavorable public reaction because Federal Reserve sales of securities would be interpreted as a policy of tightening. Harrison took an intermediate position, stating that

there was no disagreement from the belief that in view of the undue excess of credit prevailing in most of the important markets of the country an opportunity is presented to dispose of some of the securities held in the open market account for the purpose of taking up the excess caused by the return flow of money and credit, the lack of demand for credit and some gold imports.[8]

Some of the governors wanted even larger sales. For example, Calkins wanted to sell perhaps $100-200 million, and McDougal wanted to sell enough to raise interest rates somewhat so that they would not have to be increased as much after business recovery began. The outcome was a compromise recommendation:

It would be desirable to dispose of some of the System's holdings of Government securities as and when opportunity affords itself to do so without disturbance or any undue tightening of the money position.[9]

The Board approved the recommendation after the governors agreed to delete "undue," but Meyer was unhappy. As it turned out, the OMPC sold all the securities purchased in December but no more. Few other policy actions were taken before the next meeting of the OMPC in late April. However, 4 Reserve banks reduced their discount rates by one-half of 1 percent in January, largely

---

[8]Minutes of the OMPC, January 21, 1931.

[9]*Ibid.*

because of the similar reduction at New York on December 24. New York also reduced its lowest bill-buying rate in 3 steps to 1 3/8 percent.

When the Governors' Conference and the OMPC convened in Washington on April 27, 1931, Harrison presented a 9-page memorandum describing gloomy developments and prospects both at home and abroad. At home the depression was deepening and financial institutions deteriorating. Bank failures were widespread, as were currency withdrawals, and the capital of many banks had been impaired by their large losses on loans and securities. Still more would be in trouble if examiners valued their bonds and other assets at current market prices. The bond market was very weak, except for the best issues.

While bonds of the highest grade are selling at or close to their highest prices in recent years practically all other categories of bonds continue to be depressed and without a broad market . . . bonds which are less than prime can hardly be sold. There is no material market for foreign issues.[10]

Developments in most other countries were no more heartening. The depression and deflation of prices continued, several countries were threatened with political instability, and many were injured by losses of gold and other international reserves. Harrison admitted that the last was due in part to the virtual cessation of American foreign lending and to the fact that gold imports had been largely offset or sterilized by decreases in total Federal Reserve credit.

After Harrison had surveyed Federal Reserve policies since the stock-market crash, he concluded that they had merely removed the restrictive pressures imposed in 1928 and 1929 and had not provided a "vigorous stimulant to business or finance." He noted that Federal Reserve holdings of government securities, at $602 million, were at the same level as in August 1930 and only $25 million above the level in June 1930.

Broadly speaking, the open market program of the Federal Reserve System since the stock market crash in the autumn of 1929 consisted of a rapid reversal of the policies which had been designed in 1928 and 1929 to place vigorous pressure upon the money market and the member banks. These policies had involved a decrease of about $450,000,000 in security holdings between December 1927 and October 1929. Between October 1929 and August 1930 the operation was exactly reversed and $450,000,000 of securities were purchased, bringing the total back again to around $600,000,000.

It is fair to say that the open market operations undertaken during this period were not pursued with the idea that thereby any vigorous stimulant might be given to business or finance, but rather with the idea of removing in a period of reaction and depression the pressure which had been placed upon the market in 1928 and 1929, a period of inflation and expansion. In this way the System undertook simply to remove impediments which might otherwise unnecessarily delay a restoration of more normal operations in the money market. In particular it was recognized that the pressure of high money rates and a restricted supply of funds in 1929 had shut off a certain amount of the supply of mortgage and long time capital to various types of borrowers, including foreign borrowers whose purchasing power for our goods was thus seriously curtailed.[11]

Though he had at times been guilty of the practice, Harrison now

---

[10]Minutes of the OMPC, April 27, 1931.

[11]*Ibid.*

pointed to the error of judging general credit conditions by those in the larger centers.

... apart from the relatively easy position of the banks in the larger cities, credit cannot be said to very cheap or very plentiful generally throughout the country. For one reason or another, it has become fairly well bottled up in the larger banks in the larger cities.

He concluded:

... it is clear that the seriousness of the present world situation and the central position of the United States in the whole world picture makes it desirable to tax our ingenuity that the Federal Reserve System may put forth every possible effort within its power towards maintaining a measure of credit stability throughout the world and towards eventual business recovery.[12]

Governor Meyer agreed.

The representatives of the Reserve banks reacted more favorably than at earlier meetings. Most of them were apprehensive but thought that some benefits might be achieved. They seemed to be especially impressed by the arguments relating to the bad banking situation and international gold flows. At the end of the meeting they recommended that the Executive Committee of the OMPC be authorized

if and when it appears to them necessary or advisable, to purchase up to $100 million of government securities ... it was not the intention to purchase government securities immediately but rather to attempt to carry out the policy, first, through bill rates, second, through the reduction of discount rates, and then, if necessary, to resort to the purchase of government securities.[13]

The Board approved on May 7. Reductions of both bill-buying and discount rates followed immediately. New York, which had reduced its lowest bill-buying rate to 1 1/4 percent on April 27, reduced to 1 1/8 percent on May 8 and to 1 percent on May 13. Its later proposal to reduce to three-quarters of 1 percent was never approved by the Board. New York also reduced its discount rate to 1 1/2 percent on May 7. O. M. W. Sprague, then at the Bank of England, wrote to Harrison:

It is an historic event—the lowest rate that has even been established by a central bank in any country. It signifies, I suppose, that we are experiencing the worst depression that has ever been recorded.[14]

Within 2 days, 6 other Reserve banks reduced their rates by one-half of 1 percent and by the end of the month 3 others had followed suit. Only Minneapolis and Atlanta failed to act.

Purchases of government securities were delayed, partly because the OMPC had recommended that purchases not be made immediately but only after reductions in bill-buying and discount rates had been tried. Officials and directors of the New York Bank were skeptical about the usefulness of further purchases, but after mid-June they recommended purchases of $50 million.

---

[12]*Ibid.*

[13]Minutes of the OMPC, April 29, 1931.

[14]Letter of May 8, 1931.

The Executive Committee of the OMPC approved on June 22, though Young disapproved and Norris abstained. Meyer approved but was disappointed that purchases were not to be larger. Another $40 million was purchased in July for the System account, and in early August the New York bank purchased $50 million for its own account as a partial offset to reserve losses resulting from currency withdrawals and sales of bills by the Bank of France to build up its deposits at the Federal Reserve. Thus the effect of purchases in June, July, and August was not further easing but maintenance of the status quo.

When the OMPC convened on August 11 for what proved to be its last meeting before the international financial crisis spread to the United States, conditions both at home and abroad were confused and threatening. Gold was still flowing in, but the crisis was now endangering Britain. France was still letting its holdings of dollar acceptances run off and transferring the proceeds to its deposit account at the Federal Reserve. The decline of domestic business activity, which had been interrupted in the early months of the year, had now resumed. Bank failures were increasing and net currency withdrawals had amounted to $270 million in the last three months. Bond prices, especially prices of lower-grade bonds, were falling. More and more of the Reserve banks had become apprehensive about their free-gold or gold reserve positions. Harrison told the Federal Reserve Board:

> . . . it appears that nothing can be done by the Federal Reserve System to help the situation through the discount rate or through operations in the bill market, the only possible helpful action being the purchase of Government securities in rather large amounts. In this connection, he referred to the free gold of the Federal Reserve banks now amounting to about $750,000,000, which could probably be increased to $1,000,000,000 through the retirement of excess Federal Reserve notes held in the cash of the Federal Reserve banks and branches, and to the distribution of this free gold and the fact that five of the Federal Reserve Banks hold only what might be considered very close to their operating minimums.
>
> He stated that no member of the Conference is in favor of purchasing large amounts of Government securities just at this time, and it is felt that there would be no point in putting large amounts into the market until such time as it should appear that the effect would not be limited to the mere piling up of excess reserves in member banks which would not be employed . . . . The difficulty at the present time, he said, lies in the fact that prime investments have been brought up until they are on a very low yield basis; that secondary bonds consist largely of railroad issues aggregating approximately $7,750,000,000, $5,000,000,000 of which are likely within a short time to become illegal for investment by savings banks, insurance companies and for trust funds due to provisions of law relative to earnings of issuing companies; and that in addition there is pressure on the market due to forced liquidation of bond portfolios of closed banks.
>
> On the other hand, he stated the existing situation is so critical that most of the conference felt that the System should be prepared to act quickly in the event conditions develop to a point where it appears that an operation in Governments might encourage or facilitate recovery.[15]

Harrison moved that the Executive Committee be authorized to purchase up to $300 million of government securities under such conditions. Most of the governors opposed such a large authorization. When Fancher offered an amendment to reduce the authorization to $120 million, only

---

[15]Minutes of the Federal Reserve Board, August 11, 1931.

Harrison and Young voted against it. Harrison did so because he thought purchases would have to be larger to be effective. Young opposed both the amendment and the final motion because he thought that an emergency should be dealt with through bill purchases and that sufficient bills would come to the Federal Reserve at its prevailing buying rate of 1 percent. Several of the governors, in opposing the larger authorization, referred to their inadequate free-gold positions, but they also repeated their earlier reasons for opposition to large purchases—doubts that the purchases would do any good, the desirability of keeping the Reserve banks liquid, and so on.

At least 2 members of the Board, Miller and Meyer, were dissatisfied with the $120 million authorization. It was on this occasion that Miller stated, regarding open-market purchases, that

... if there ever had been a justification for its bold, experimental use, even though it might only serve to demonstrate the limits of the availability of such a policy, that situation exists at the present time.[16]

Meyer was unhappy about the small authorization and angry at the procedures of the OMPC and the attitudes of some of the governors. He complained that some had come with mandates from their directors and that the Board had been given no chance to participate in the discussion until after the OMPC had arrived at its recommendation. To make matters worse, some governors had gone home before the meeting with the Board.

Though the Board approved the OMPC recommendation, no further securities were purchased until December, and then in only very small amounts. In the meantime the entire financial system was to be put under heavy strains resulting from the breakdown of the international gold exchange standard, widespread bank failures, and more currency hoarding. Security purchases under these conditions were considered futile.

CONCLUSIONS

Though by the end of this period an increasing number of the Reserve banks were expressing concern about their free-gold positions, the failure of the Federal Reserve to embark upon a more ambitious easing program, including much larger purchases of government securities, resulted not from any shortage of gold reserves or free gold but from the deliberate choices of Federal Reserve officials. We have already examined the major reasons for these policy decisions. Further comments will be made on only one of these—judgment of the reserve positions of all banks by the reserve positions of the principal banks in the major financial centers. Table 10-2 presents relevant data, comparing reserve positions in mid-1931 with those in mid-1929. By almost every measure, banks in the larger centers fared better. For example, Column 5, expressing borrowings in June 1931 as a precentage of the banks' total reserves at that time, shows that total member bank borrowings had fallen so much that they were equal to only 7.8 percent of their reserves. The

---

16*Ibid.*

TABLE 10-2

Reserve Positions of Member Banks, June 1929 and June 1931
(changes between June 1929 and June 1931 in millions of dollars;
monthly averages of daily figures)

Class of Member Bank	Total reserves (1)	Borrow-ings at Federal Reserve (2)	Unborrowed reserves (1) − (2) (3)	Excess reserves (4)	Borrowings in June 1931 as percentage of total reserves in that month (5)
All members	+$ 90	−$787	+$877	+$87	7.8%
New York Central Reserve City	+ 120	− 170	+ 290	+ 64	0.5
Chicago Central Reserve City	+ 8	− 61	+ 69	+ 2	1.2
Reserve City	+ 19	− 367	+ 386	+ 12	5.4
Country	− 59	− 188	+ 129	+ 8	24.3
Country Banks by Federal Reserve Districts					
Boston	− 3	− 27	+ 24	+ 1	15.6
New York	+ 3	− 34	+ 37	+ 4	20.1
Philadelphia	− 1	− 28	+ 27	+ 1	27.9
Cleveland	− 10	− 19	+ 9	0	20.0
Richmond	− 6	− 20	+ 14	0	62.0
Atlanta	− 5	− 20	+ 15	+ 1	50.0
Chicago	− 12	− 18	+ 6	+ 3	15.4
St. Louis	− 4	− 8	+ 4	+ 1	26.9
Minneapolis	− 4	− 2	− 2	+ 1	14.8
Kansas City	− 4	− 2	− 2	0	32.1
Dallas	− 8	− 1	− 7	− 1	37.9
San Francisco	− 7	− 5	− 2	− 1	20;0

Source: Derived from data in Board of Governors of the Federal Reserve System, *Banking and Monetary Statistics,* Washington, D.C., 1943, pp. 396-399 and 928-939.

figure was one-half of 1 percent for central reserve city banks in New York, 1.2 percent for those in Chicago, and 5.4 percent for reserve city banks. However, for country member banks as a group it was 24.3 percent. In no Federal Reserve district were country bank borrowings less than 14 percent of their reserves, and in 3 districts the figure was 37 percent or more. On these borrowings many banks were paying discount rates far above the New York rate of 1 1/2 percent. For example, discount rates were 3 percent at Richmond and Atlanta, in which districts country banks were borrowing amounts equal to 62 and 50 percent of their reserves, respectively.

Column 1, showing changes in total reserves during the 2 years preceding June 1931, tells a similar story. Country banks lost $59 million of reserves while New York gained $120 million. Chicago and reserve city members also gained. Column 3 indicates that while the unborrowed reserves of all member banks rose $877 million, those of country members in 4 Midwestern and Western Federal Reserve districts actually declined.

Federal Reserve policies during this period were probably not generous enough to remove pressure for liquidation and to create pressure for expansion by banks located in the major financial centers. They were almost certainly inadequate to relieve contractionary pressures on country members and many others.

11

The International Financial Crisis

Foreign monetary and financial developments did not in any way limit the Federal Reserve's freedom of action or impose restrictive pressures on the American monetary system during the period preceding September 21, 1931, the date of Britain's departure from the gold standard. In fact, as already noted, gold imports since September 1929 had amounted to some $640 million. However, Britain's departure from gold brought a sharp reversal. By the end of October the United States had lost $727 million of gold. Small amounts of gold flowed in during November and December, only to be followed by further gold losses of $549 million by mid-June 1932. Net gold losses from mid-September 1931 to mid-June 1931 were $1,107 million. To make matters worse, September and October 1931 brought a surge of bank failures and currency withdrawals, the latter amounting to $393 million. Thus by the end of October 1931, gold outflows and currency withdrawals had drained off nearly $1,120 million of commercial bank reserves and placed the entire banking system under severe contractionary pressures.

Britain's departure from gold was the culmination of an international financial crisis which swept across Central Europe and affected many other countries as well. It was much like a banking crisis within a country; it seemed to come suddenly as creditors lost confidence and rushed to withdraw their funds. However, this action was only the final stage; back of this dramatic finale were institutional weaknesses and a slow but fatal undermining of financial positions as the worldwide depression lowered incomes and asset prices and virtually paralyzed international investment.

THE GOLD EXCHANGE STANDARD

Britain's departure from gold marked the end of the international gold standard which had been reconstructed so laboriously in the preceding six or seven years. As noted earlier, the type of gold standard reestablished in the latter half of the 1920s was largely a mixed gold bullion and gold exchange standard. Central banks and governments held a part of their international reserves in the form of gold and a part in the form of claims against foreign

160

currencies, the latter chiefly against the British pound sterling and the American dollar. These claims were in several forms—deposits, acceptances, short-term government securities, and so on. At the end of 1929 the gold reserves of all central banks and governments amounted to about $10.3 billion, and their foreign exchange holdings were more than $2 billion. Thus, nearly 20 percent of official international reserves were in the form of claims against foreign currencies. For countries other than the United States and Britain, foreign exchange reserves were relatively much more important—amounting to more than $2 billion, or about 35 percent of their gold holdings of $5.7 billion.

The restoration of exchange-rate stability in the late 1920s also increased the international mobility of short-term funds and led to large increases in the stock of private short-term claims against the principal international financial centers, thus adding to the total short-term liabilities of New York, London, and some other centers. For example, at the end of 1929 the total short-term liabilities of the United States to foreign official and private holders were $2,748 million. This was considerably less than the nation's gold stock of nearly $4 billion. Britain was in a far different position; her gold stock was only $710 million while her gross short-term liabilities to foreigners were $2,195 million and her net short-term liabilities to foreigners were $1,340 million. Total international short-term debts at the end of 1930 were estimated at $14 billion.

The gold exchange standards of the 1920s differed in important ways from those employed in the period before World War I. For one thing, they were adopted by much more powerful countries. In the prewar period, the practice of holding official international reserves in the form of claims against foreign currencies was largely confined to colonial areas and to nonindustrialized countries, whose holdings were small, both individually and in the aggregate. Withdrawals of these funds posed little threat to the big international financial centers. However, in the 1920s some of the most financially powerful countries in the world accumulated large claims against foreign currencies. (See Table 11-1.) The Bank of France alone held more than $1 billion of foreign currency claims in mid-1930, mostly against New York and London, and the aggregate holdings of foreign currencies by the central banks of France, Germany, Italy, and Belgium were about $1,485 million. This system was indeed an effective method of economizing gold, as long as the central banks holding foreign exchange continued to consider it at least "as good as gold" and were willing to hold it. However, such large and concentrated holdings were also dangerous. Anything that damaged confidence in the stability of the dollar or the pound in terms of gold could lead central banks to demand gold for their dollar or sterling claims. Moreover, the stability and growth of the gold exchange system was imperiled by a feeling in some quarters that, "First-class countries hold their international reserves in gold; only lower-rank countries hold foreign exchange." Somehow reliance on a foreign currency as an international reserve suggested dependence on the center country, or even colonial status. Such feelings did not bother small countries, but some larger and more sensitive ones, especially France, felt it strongly. Almost from the time that it first began to accumulate large amounts of dollars and sterling in

TABLE 11-1

*Gold and Foreign Exchange Holdings of
Selected Central Banks, May 1929*

	Foreign exchange as percent of total gold and foreign exchange reserves
Central Bank of Chile	87.7
Bank of Greece	84.7
National Bank of Czechoslovakia	59.5
National Bank of Austria	53.6
South African Reserve Bank	49.7
Banca d'Italia	48.9
Sveriges Riksbank	43.9
Bank of Poland	42.2
Bank of France	41.7
National Bank of Copenhagen	35.2
National Bank of Switzerland	34.5
National Bank of Belgium	33.8
Netherlands Bank	26.9
Norges Bank	23.8
National Bank of Roumania	21.4
Reichsbank	14.5
National Bank of Hungary	9.7
Bank of Spain	3.7

Source: Computed from data in C. H. Kisch, "Memorandum on Legal Provisions Governing Reserves of Central Banks" in *The International Gold Problem,* Oxford University Press, London, 1931, pp. 138-140.

1926, the Bank of France was a reluctant holder, clearly hoping to convert them into gold as this became feasible.

Even in the late 1920s there was a tendency toward a "maldistribution of gold," and this continued in the early 1930s. Britain found it difficult to retain gold without inflicting excessive unemployment on her people. France, which had undervalued the franc, continued to gain gold. So did the United States, except in the years when she was lending generously abroad. The international reserves of the rest of the world depended heavily on the state of the American balance of payments. When it was in deficit, the United States supplied the rest of the world with gold and dollar reserves; when it was in surplus the rest of the world lost gold and dollars.

WORLDWIDE DEPRESSION AND THE BREAKDOWN

Whether the gold exchange standard would have survived and functioned acceptably if prosperity had continued is a debatable question. In fact, however, it broke down after nearly two years of depression, and in breaking down added to deflationary pressures. The processes through which it was first weakened and then destroyed were similar to those in the United States preceding the collapse of the banking system—the continuing decline of demands for output reflected in a grinding deflation of employment, real output, money incomes, and asset prices and a paralysis of the investment process. World trade fell even faster than world output and incomes, and international lending virtually stopped. For the latter, there were many related reasons—decreased incentives to borrow and invest, deterioration of the creditworthiness of potential borrowers, and the decline of saving and of willingness to bear risk in the capital-exporting countries. Such sweeping changes inevitably affected balances of international payments and international reserve positions, but the nature and severity of the impact varied greatly from country to country.

Countries relying heavily on exports of agricultural products and other raw materials were hit first and hardest. Their response to the sharp decrease of world demand for their products was much like that of the American farmer; they tended to maintain output, with the consequence that their prices fell sharply. For example, price declines in the year 1929-1930 were 40 percent or more for coffee, rubber, wool, and corn, and between 20 and 30 percent for raw silk, tin, copper, wheat, and sugar. These prices fell even more as the depression deepened. Thus the export earnings of such countries fell sharply; they had far smaller receipts of foreign currencies with which to buy imports and service their debts. Some became unable to meet existing debts, and even more were unable to command confidence that they could service additional loans. Partly because of this, they received almost no new loans and were expected to pay interest and to repay principal on those already outstanding.

Even as early as 1930 several countries whose balance of payments positions depended heavily on exports of raw materials, receipts of foreign loans, or both lost large amounts of their gold and foreign exchange reserves. Some merely adopted restrictive monetary policies, but by mid-1931 a considerable number had abandoned gold, or had imposed limitations on payments to other countries, or both. As shown in Table 11-2, the countries that abandoned gold or imposed control of foreign exchange transactions before September 1931 were mostly those that had relied heavily on exports of raw materials and receipts of foreign loans. During this early period gold flows were largely from countries of these types toward the United States and Western Europe, with most of the gold gravitating to the United States and France.

Decreased flows of dollars from the United States to the rest of the world contributed greatly to these difficulties. (See Table 11-3.) During the late 1920s America's payments for imports of goods and services averaged about $5.5 billion a year. These fell sharply as American incomes decreased. They declined 20 percent by 1930, 43 percent by 1931, and 62 percent by 1932. American net exports of long-term capital funds fell even more sharply. In 1929 they were far smaller than in preceding years, but they continued to fall, except for a brief revival in the spring of 1930. By 1931 the flow had reversed; repayments of loans by foreigners exceeded new long-term loans by the United States. Total United States payments for imports of goods and services and net long-term capital overflows, which had averaged about $6.2 billion in the late 1920s, declined by more than half by 1931 and by more than two-thirds by 1932.

Such were the backgrounds of the international financial crisis of 1931: a huge volume of outstanding international short-term debts aggregating per-

TABLE 11-2

Countries Abandoning Gold Standards or Instituting Control of Foreign Exchanges in 1931 and 1932

Period	Countries abandoning gold standards	Countries instituting control of foreign exchanges
1. Before September 1931	Australia New Zealand Brazil Chile Paraguay Uruguay Venezuela Peru	Canada Austria Hungary Germany
2. September–November 1931	Bolivia United Kingdon Colombia Denmark Egypt India Irish Free State Norway Portugal Sweden Canada Finland	Denmark Greece Hungary Persia Argentina Austria Brazil Bulgaria Czechoslovakia Estonia Finland Latvia Turkey Yugoslavia
3. December 1931–June 1932	Chile Greece Siam Peru	Roumania Persia Paraguay
4. June–December 1932	Union of South Africa	

Source: Compiled from various sources, including Annual Reports of the Bank for International Settlements and World Economic Surveys by the League of Nations. Some countries abandoned gold, then attempted to return to it, and then abandoned again.

haps $14 billion; a virtual cessation of long-term international capital flows; widespread deflation of money incomes and asset prices; and deteriorated creditworthiness. Conditions were ripe for a crisis somewhere.

CRISIS IN EUROPE

The crisis that was to sweep most countries off the gold standard within a few months began in Vienna with the failure of the Credit Anstalt in May 1931. This was the most important bank in Austria, with large loans to depressed Austrian industry and large deposits of foreign funds. The failure shook confidence in all Austrian banks and in the ability of the Austrian government to maintain the gold value of its currency. Foreign creditors rushed to withdraw their short-term funds, and they were probably joined by some Austrians. In the tradition of international central-bank cooperation

TABLE 11-3

*Some Principal United States Payments to the Rest
of the World, 1926-1933 (in millions of dollars)*

	Payments for imports of goods and services	Net long-term capital outflows	Total
1926	5,555	696	6,251
1927	5,383	991	6,374
1928	5,465	798	6,263
1929	5,886	240	6,126
1930	4,416	221	4,637
1931	3,125	-208	2,918
1932	2,067	-251	1,816
1933	2,044	- 70	1,974

Source: U.S. Department of Commerce, *Historical Statistics of the United States,* Washington, D.C., 1960, pp. 562-564.

developed during the 1920s, foreign central banks offered their aid. The Bank for International Settlements, 10 European central banks, and the Federal Reserve provided about $14 million of assistance, of which $1,083,000 was from the Federal Reserve. This amount was far too small to meet the drain, however. Austria did not formally abandon to gold standard, but she imposed strict controls over all gold and foreign exchange transactions—a device that was to be adopted by many others and that would choke international trade and capital movements.

The next victim was Austria's neighbor, Hungary. As withdrawals mounted, the Bank for International Settlements, the Federal Reserve, and several European central banks gave assistance, this time a total of $21 million, of which $2 million came from the Federal Reserve. Again the operation was unsuccessful; in July Hungary imposed strict controls over all transactions in gold and foreign exchange.

The run then spread to Germany, which had a deeply depressed economy, very large short-term debts to other countries, and heavy investments in Austria and Hungary. Withdrawals began in May, accelerated in June, and became ensnarled with questions relating to reparations payments and other international political issues. In response to President Hindenburg's appeal for assistance, President Hoover proposed on June 21 a one-year moratorium on all payments on intergovernmental debts. Most governments agreed within a week but France, unwilling to sacrifice economic claims and political objectives, dragged out the discussion. In the meantime, as one observer put it on July 4,

The position in Germany has worsened because, while folks have been talking and arguing in Paris, the Reichsbank has been bleeding to death.[1]

The French approval on July 6 came too late. The Reichsbank had by this time exhausted a $100 million credit from the Bank for International Settle-

[1]Norman cable to Harrison.

ments and other central banks, including $25 million from the Federal Reserve. Total withdrawals between May and late July approached $1 billion. At this stage the German government clamped tight controls on all international transactions, thus freezing large amounts of foreign funds. These controls were to be retained and made even more restrictive until after the end of World War II.

By this time the crisis was spreading to one of the two great international monetary and financial centers—London. Monetary conditions there had actually improved during the first half of 1931. Britain gained about $125 million of gold during this period, losses to France being more than offset by inflows from other countries. Then the tide turned in mid-July. Exactly why this occurred at that time is not wholly clear, but three developments were relevant. One was publication of the findings of the Macmillan Report, which revealed that London's short-term liabilities to the rest of the world were even larger than had been suspected. Another was the crisis in Austria, Hungary, and Germany, which damaged confidence in the stability of national currencies and froze large amounts of foreign claims. Still another was the large deficit in the British government's budget. The continued fall of employment and incomes in that country not only reduced the government's revenues but also increased greatly its dole payments to the unemployed. Both British and foreign observers viewed the deficit as a symbol and source of financial and monetary weakness.

By July 22 the Bank of England had lost more than $100 million of gold, mostly to France, Holland, Belgium, and Switzerland. To counter withdrawals of funds, it raised its discount rate from 2 1/2 to 3 1/2 percent and a week later to 4 1/2 percent. It also sold some of its dollar holdings to support sterling and arranged with the New York Reserve Bank to buy up to $25 million of sterling. The drain continued. On August 1 the Bank of England announced that it had received credits of $250 million, half from the Bank of France and half from the Federal Reserve. This announcement neither restored confidence in sterling nor stopped withdrawals; almost all of the credit was exhausted by August 21. It was now clear that the problem was too large to be solved by central-bank credits alone. The British government therefore sought to borrow from private bankers in New York and Paris. It found, however, that private bankers would not attempt to float loans for it until its budget was put in order. Since the Labour government was unwilling to do this, Prime Minister MacDonald resigned and formed a National government with the sole mandate of saving the pound. After he announced a program of higher taxation and reduced expenditures he received a loan of $400 million from private sources in New York and Paris on August 28. The announcement slowed withdrawals for a few days, but by mid-month the drain had again accelerated. The end came on Saturday, September 19, 1931. By this time more than $1 billion of funds had been withdrawn from the London market since mid-July. The British government decided over the week-end that it could not keep the pound redeemable in gold, that it should act while it still held some £ 130 million of gold reserves, and that gold payments should be suspended as of Monday, September 21.

The sterling exchange rate in terms of dollars and other gold currencies began to fall immediately. In June it had averaged about $4.86; by September 25 it had fallen to $3.83. It then continued downward, ranging between $3.75 and $3.28 in 1932 and the first 3 months of 1933. Foreign holders of sterling, both private and official, suffered large losses as measured in their own currencies. For example, the Netherlands Bank lost its entire net worth, and the Bank of France, which held about £ 86 million of claims against London, is reputed to have lost about $100 million. Both central banks had to call upon their governments to replenish their capital accounts.

Within a few weeks after Britain's departure from gold, large numbers of other economically important countries had abondoned gold payments, or imposed controls on gold and foreign exchange transactions, or both. (See Table 11-2, above.) These included all members of the British Empire except Canada and the Union of South Africa, three Scandinavian countries, and many more. Still others followed suit in December 1931 and in 1932. By the end of 1932 the only major countries that remained on gold and were permitting relatively free international payments were the United States, France, Belgium, Switzerland, and the Netherlands.

Britain's suspension of gold payments marked the end of the international gold standard. The United States resisted until March 1933 and the continental European gold bloc until 1936, but in the end they all succumbed. A new gold standard system truly international in scope and affording a high degree of freedom of international payments was not to be reestablished until well after World War II.

CRISIS IN THE UNITED STATES

The British suspension brought an immediate surge of withdrawals from the United States. On September 22, gold drains amounted to $116 million, the largest gold loss ever suffered by the United States in a single day. Gold outflows totaled $238 million by September 28 and $727 million by October 28. Then, as noted earlier, there were small net inflows in November and December, followed by another $549 million of gold outflows by mid-June 1932. These reflected largely withdrawals of foreign-owned short-term claims against dollars, though there were also some foreign sales of long-term dollar securities. Outflows of American-owned funds appear to have been small. Net reductions of short-term claims against the United States were $504 million between September 16 and October 28, and $1,346 million between September 16 and July 13, 1932.

Dollar balances were withdrawn by both private foreign holders and foreign central banks and governments. Private holders disposed of their dollar balances in several ways. Some demanded gold directly from the United States. Some sold the dollars to the central banks of their own countries. Others exchanged their dollars for the currencies of other countries that were considered to be in stronger monetary positions—such countries as France, Switzerland, Belgium, and the Netherlands. Even greater were the withdrawals of dollar balances by foreign central banks, and most of these were for the purpose of liquidating the gold exchange standard. Thus the National Bank of Belgium sold all of its foreign exchange, which at the beginning of the period amounted to $116 million, and acquired $131 million of gold. The Netherlands Bank sold $56 million of exchange and increased its gold reserves by $77 million. The Bank of Switzerland reduced its exchange holdings by $91 million and acquired $188 million of gold. The Bank of France, the most powerful of them all, reduced its holdings of dollars from $600 million in August 1931 to only about $100 million in mid-1932.

The most obvious reason for such central-bank decisions to liquidate their dollar balances and their holdings of other foreign currencies, was their fear of losses. After the events in Austria, Hungary, Germany, Britain, and many other countries, every national currency was suspect. The Swiss central bank even withdrew funds from France. Not only in France and Switzerland but elsewhere as well, there were recurrent rumors about the weakness of dollar claims—about the unsound conditions of even the largest New York banks, the dangers inherent in the continuing deficit in the federal budget, a rising sentiment within the Federal Reserve for "inflationary" policies, inflationary proposals in Congress, and the lack of American determination and ability to keep the dollar freely convertible into gold at its existing value.

Though such fears undoubtedly precipitated withdrawals of dollar balances by foreign central banks as well as by private holders, at least one central bank—the Bank of France—was somewhat predisposed to liquidate its foreign exchange holdings, and its attitudes may have influenced others. We have already referred to the reluctance of France to hold large amounts of foreign exchange. This was evident even before the legal stabilization of the franc on June 25, 1928. After that date, officials of the bank took the position that though the law permitted them to hold the foreign exchange already acquired, the intention of the law was not to permit further acquisitions.

> Since June 25, 1928, the Bank has felt that it would not be in accord with the intention of the laws prepared by the Government and passed by the Chambers at the time of the stabilization of the franc, for the Bank to build up its reserves of foreign exchange by direct and systematic purchases in the open market.[2]

Moreover, there was a strong feeling, reinforced by events in 1931, that the bank should liquidate its exchange holdings, provide a gold basis for the franc, and subject the franc and other moneys to the discipline of a true gold standard.

> We deem it out duty, more than ever, to assure for the franc the metallic coverage which is the only basis upon which a money can be supported. We consider the convertibility into gold not as a servitude which has grown out of date, but as a necessary disciplinary requirement. We see in it the only efficient guarantee for security of contracts and for the morality of business transactions.[3]

---

[2]Letter from Robert Lacour-Gayet, an official of the Bank of France, to Emanuel Goldenweiser, Director of the Division of Research and Statistics of the Federal Reserve Board, December 3, 1930.

[3]*Bank of France Report of Operations,* 1931.

In a letter to Harrison in March 1932, Governor Moret stated that he had favored liquidation of the gold exchange standard even before the onset of the 1931 crisis.

The monetary crisis which developed in Europe beginning with the Spring of 1931, and which finally ended in the suspension of the convertibility into gold of the pound sterling, confirmed my conviction that it would be advisable to return everywhere, as soon as possible, to the true gold standard; and that we, ourselves, at the Bank of France ought to furnish an example by liquidating our holdings, which, up to a certain point, might have been considered as indicating the maintenance of a kind of artificial gold exchange standard . . . .

Since motives of principle have caused me to foresee the necessity of a policy of this nature, my decision has only been substantiated by the fall of the pound sterling, which greatly affected French opinion, and which resulted in consequences for the Bank of France of which you are aware. The application of this decision was put into operation under the pressure of circumstances, at a moment which, I must admit, was not favorable; but this application was put into effect without delay and was applied indiscriminately to all the foreign currencies the Bank has in its portfolio.

The reluctance of officials of the Bank of France to continue holding foreign exchange may also have been influenced by their opposition to what they considered to be excessively easy money conditions and low interest rates in London and New York during the period before Britain's departure from gold. They believed that such policies did not promote recovery and only delayed necessary liquidation. An official of the New York Reserve Bank reported after a discussion with Governor Moret and two deputy governors of the Bank of France in August 1931:

During a period of economic depression Moret feels that the Bank of France should keep its rate fairly high to prevent improper use of its credit and to hasten a healthy liquidation and return to prosperity. To maintain a very low rate does, in his opinion, merely put off the evil day of settlement, foster unsound positions and prolong the depression, while when improved conditions appear to be just around the corner and the necessary liquidation has been accomplished his rate should be lowered. During prosperous times, he said, he was in favor of a rather low rate of discount . . . .

I might mention here parenthetically that Lacour-Gayet takes the same line as Governor Moret. In fact, he is even more in favor of higher rates and a deflationary policy. Carriguel is also opposed to such low levels of rates in both Paris and New York.[4]

Moret also opposed rate reductions in New York because these brought pressure on the Bank of France to reduce its rates in order to avoid gold imports, which he did not want. For example, when New York reduced its discount rate to 2 percent in December 1930, Moret reluctantly followed suit, observing that there was nothing in the French domestic situation to justify such action. He was even more unhappy when New York reduced its rate to 1 1/2 percent in the spring of 1931, and did not follow suit. His unhappiness was increased by the fact that the bank's holdings of foreign securities were subject to a French tax equal to one-half of the discount rate of the Bank of France. Thus, when the bank was earning only about three-quarters of 1 percent on its bill holdings in New York and its discount rate was 2 percent, it actually lost money on its investments. For this reason the bank began in

---

[4]Memorandum by Jay Crane, August 28, 1931.

June 1931 to let its bill holdings run off and to transfer the proceeds to its deposit account at the Federal Reserve.

Moret was also convinced that the weakness of sterling and the dollar resulted from excessively easy monetary policies. He cabled Harrison on September 30:

> I take this opportunity to call your attention to the consequence under present circumstances of the very low level of money rates.

Every move of the United States toward easier monetary conditions, and even rumors that such steps were contemplated, lessened confidence that the gold value of the dollar would be maintained.

Officials of the Bank of France were in a difficult position. On the one hand, they sincerely wanted to cooperate with the Federal Reserve to avoid embarrassment to the United States. On the other, they were convinced that the gold exchange standard should be liquidated, they had suffered large losses on their sterling holdings, and they feared a similar experience with their dollars. Political leaders reminded them that the government had been forced to reconstitute the bank's capital because of its losses on sterling and warned against a repetition.

The bank's behavior in late September and October reflected these fears and conflicting desires. It asked to have $50 million of gold earmarked on September 22 and another $45 million during the next two weeks. It also requested the Federal Reserve to send weekly reports on its free-gold position. Moret asked if the United States would give a gold guarantee, but Harrison responded negatively.

> . . . does not the answer to your inquiry resolve itself into this, that each country must determine for itself whether it wants to be on a gold exchange standard or a metallic gold standard and not by indirection to seek all the profit of the former plus the protection of the latter?[5]

In mid-October two deputy governors of the Bank of France conferred at length with officials at the Federal Reserve Bank of New York and the Federal Reserve Board. On October 22 they reported to Premier Pierre Laval, who was conferring with President Hoover, that

> We have time and again been formally assured of the unshakable determination of the United States to remain on the gold standard. Needless to say, we have given the same assurance as concerns the Bank of France . . . . France and the United States must above all make plain their absolute fidelity to the gold standard.[6]

Hoover and Laval gave such an assurance in a joint statement on October 24:

> . . . we are convinced of the importance of monetary stability as an essential factor in the restoration of normal economic life in the world in which the maintenance of the gold standard in France and the United States will serve as a major influence.[7]

---

[5]Harrison cable to Moret, October 2, 1931.

[6]Memorandum of October 22, 1931.

[7]Herbert Hoover, *Memoirs: The Great Depression, 1929-1941*, Macmillan, New York, 1952, p. 96.

French fears may also have been somewhat allayed by restrictive Federal Reserve actions in October. These included increases in the New York discount rate from 1 1/2 to 2 1/2 percent on October 9 and to 3 1/2 percent on October 16, as well as increases in its bill-buying rate in several steps from 1 to 3 1/8 percent. In any case, France took little gold during the period from late October through December. Also, encouraged by higher market rates in New York, it resumed purchases of dollar acceptances and other earning assets. It was rumored that the New York Reserve Bank and the Bank of France had agreed that the former would follow conservative monetary policies and that the latter would cease taking gold from the American market. Harrison denied this categorically.

There was not any such agreement, nor any such bargain. The Bank of France is perfectly free at any time it chooses to withdraw its dollar funds. The Federal Reserve Bank of New York is equally free in its credit and discount rate policies. In fact, there has never been a time in any of my conversations with any central bank when there was any request or even any suggestion that they or we should in any way make a commitment as to any future policy that would in any way destroy or limit our complete freedom of action in our own self interest.[8]

January brought new troubles—more adverse rumors about the dollar and a resumption of gold withdrawals. An article by H. Parker Willis in a Paris newspaper created quite a stir on the continent. It stated that in the United States "Inflation is the order of the day"; the Federal Reserve banks as well as the legislative assemblies seem to have decided to take this road; discount and bill-buying rates are to be lowered; efforts are to be made to broaden the credit base of the Federal Reserve; and credit will be created on the basis of long-term paper.[9] Fears were intensified later when the Federal Reserve began to reduce its bill-buying rate and to purchase government securities. The Bank of France resumed its gold purchases in mid-January, as did the central banks of Belgium and Switzerland. One newspaperman thought these were the reasons:

Mr. Allen of the United Press tells me this morning that one of their men who had called at the Bank of France gives the following reasons for French withdrawals of balances here, though it is not quite clear whether these reasons were the ones given by the Bank of France.
(1) Disappointment at reduction of our acceptance rate, which is interpreted as an abandonment of the agreement made in October,
(2) Concern over the possible inflation which Paris says is advocated by a group in the Federal Reserve System,
(3) Concern that the gold cover for credit in the United States is now only 5% compared with France's 20%,
(4) Bankers point to the federal deficit and lack of information as to the activities of the Reconstruction Finance Corporation.
They indicate that the movement of gold may total as much as $600,000,000.[10]

---

[8]Harrison letter to Meyer, December 18, 1931.

[9]Cable from the Bank of France to the Federal Reserve Bank of New York, January 15, 1932.

[10]Burgess memorandum to Harrison, January 23, 1932.

The American ambassador in London informed Harrison that

In France ... it is generally understood that the withdrawals are to a great extent in-
spired ... by the political demands from members of the French parliament who have
evinced considerable nervousness ever since the large loss experienced with the drop of
sterling.[11]

American gold exports to France in the first two and a half months of
1932 totaled $219 million. There was a brief respite in the latter half of
March and early April, after which gold outflows resumed. By this time adverse rumors in France concerning the dollar were widespread; these were
traceable in large part, though not entirely, to the aggressive easy-money
policy initiated by the Federal Reserve in late February. The Bank of France
was under heavy pressure to liquidate all of its dollar balances.

It must first be clearly understood that the Banque de France is at present faced
with irresistible political pressure gradually to withdraw its balances and gold from
abroad.... This pressure arises from the heavy loss sustained by the Banque de France
in its sterling balances, a loss now taken over by the Government. But the Chambre des
Députés is determined to incur no risk whatsoever of further similar losses, and the
assurances of the Banque as to the American dollar do not satisfy them.[12]

Also, Federal Reserve officials had by this time concluded that the sooner all
these balances were liquidated, the better. Harrison and other Federal Reserve
officials had from the beginning told the French that they were free to ear-
mark or withdraw gold whenever they wished, and in January Harrison told
Senator Glass that the remaining French balances were a continuing source of
irritation and concern. On April 9, Harrison wrote to Moret:

We have felt for some time that it would be desirable rather than hurtful from the point
of view of our position to have the Bank of France gradually repatriate its dollar
balances.

The Bank of France quickly accepted the invitation; it allowed its bill holding
in New York to run off and earmarked about $12.5 million of gold each week
until the end of May. Then on June 1 it both increased its gold earmarking to
$25 million a week and sold dollars in the exchange market. At this time the
Bank of France still held about $165 million in dollar balances. Harrison
feared that the continued outflow of gold week after week, together with
French sales of dollars in exchange markets, would be more injurious to the
position of the dollar than a once-and-for-all liquidation. On June 9, after
conferring with the Federal Reserve Board, he invited Moret to convert immediately all of his remaining $93 million of dollar balances into earmarked
gold. This was done during the next few days, though the Bank of France
retained a working balance of about $10 million. The last of the French
earmarked gold was shipped in July.

This shipment marked the end of American gold losses. In fact, the
nation's gold stock rose nearly $600 million in the latter half of 1932. How-

---

[11]Letter of March 1, 1932.

[12]Thomas W. Lamont cable from Paris to J. P. Morgan & Co. in New York, April
18, 1932.

ever, the drain of both foreign funds and gold had been huge between September 21, 1931 and mid-June 1932. Total short-term liabilities to foreigners fell about $1.3 billion. Of this, more than $500 million was accounted for by the reduction of the dollar balances of the Bank of France; further amounts were withdrawn by the central banks of Belgium, the Netherlands, and Switzerland. The monetary gold stock declined about $1,107 million, with about $891 million going to France, the Netherlands, Switzerland, and Belgium. (See Table 11-4.)

TABLE 11-4

Net Gold Exports from the United States to Selected Countries by Months, September 1931-July 1932 (in millions of dollars)

Month	France	Netherlands	Switzerland	Belgium
1931				
September	24.1	4.2	a	a
October	32.5	35.9	17.6	9.7
November	a	a	0.5	a
December	15.2	9.9	1.3	5.9
1932				
January	83.8	6.3	1.8	¹12.6
February	98.2	8.7	a	17.9
March	37.5	—	a	6.3
April	24.5	18.7	a	0.6
May	63.1	58.5	53.6	19.9
June	111.4	a	62.0	26.3
July	21.5	a	a	a
Total, September–July	511.8	142.6	137.5	99.2

Source: Board of Governors of the Federal Reserve System, *Federal Reserve Bulletin,* 1931-1932.
ᵃ= none or less than $500,000 .

THE FOREIGN EXCHANGES

The international financial crisis of 1931 imposed deflationary pressures on the American economy most directly and dramatically by precipitating large withdrawals of foreign funds and gold. However, it also brought deflationary effects by intensifying restrictions on international trade and payments and by depreciating exchange rates on many foreign currencies.

As stated earlier, many countries responded to actual and threatened losses of gold and foreign exchange by imposing restrictions on international trade and payments. These became widespread and were used increasingly to restrict imports and to limit or prevent capital outflows. The resulting reduction of international trade, including reduced demands for American exports, inevitably tended to reduce employment and income in the United States.

So did the depreciation of foreign currencies in terms of gold and the dollar. Following the widespread departures from gold in 1931, the world tended to be divided into two monetary groups. "The gold group" included the countries that continued to maintain approximately constant gold values for their currencies and relatively free international payments. Its principal members were the United States, France, Belgium, Switzerland, and the

Netherlands. In the "nongold group" were the countries that allowed their currencies to depreciate significantly in terms of gold and the "gold group" currencies. Table 11-5 shows the behavior of the dollar exchange rates on the currencies of 22 of these "nongold" countries. For example, the next-to-last column indicates that by December 1932 the exchange rate on the British pound has fallen 32 percent below its level prior to September 1931 and that many of the other currencies had declined this much or more. Viewed another way, exchange rates on the dollar and other gold currencies had risen 47 percent or more in terms of these nongold currencies.

These widespread and large declines of exchange rates tended to depress the economies of countries in the gold group by increasing their imports, decreasing their exports, and lowering the domestic prices of both their exports and their import-competing goods. This is not to say that the depreciations were completely unjustified and had no beneficial effects. Some currencies, such as the British pound, had been overvalued and should probably have been depreciated earlier. Moreover, several countries took advantage of their new freedom to initiate expansionary policies designed to raise their national incomes and stop price deflation. However, on balance the decline of these exchange rates was so large—the rise of the exchange rate on the dollar in terms of these currencies was so great—as to have a sharply deflationary impact on the American economy.

TABLE 11-5

Indexes of Exchange Rates on Selected Foreign
Currencies in Terms of Dollars
Average in 1929 = 100

	Index of Exchange Rate on Foreign Currency				Index of the exchange rate on the dollar in December 1932
Country	1930 average	1931 average	1932 average	Dec. 1932 average	
United Kingdom	100	93	72	68	147
Australia	95	73	58	54	185
British India	100	93	73	69	145
Egypt	100	93	72	68	147
New Zealand	97	86	66	62	161
Denmark	100	94	71	64	156
Finland	100	95	62	57	175
Norway	100	94	68	63	159
Sweden	100	94	69	67	149
Argentina	88	70	61	62	161
Brazil	91	60	60	65	154
Canada	100	97	89	87	115
Greece	100	100	64	42	238
Japan	107	106	61	45	222
Mexico	98	99	66	66	152
Portugal	100	95	72	68	147
Chile	100	100	66	50	200
China	71	54	52	47	213
Spain	80	65	55	56	179
Straits Settlements	100	94	72	70	143
Uruguay	87	56	48	48	208
Yugoslavia	100	100	93	76	132

Source: Board of Governors of the Federal Reserve System, *Banking and Monetary Statistics*, Washington, D.C., 1943, pp. 662-682.

12

Federal Reserve Responses
to the Crisis

This chapter examines Federal Reserve policies from the time of Britain's departure from the gold standard on September 21, 1931, to late February 1932, when the Federal Reserve began to initiate an easy-money policy. The period witnessed the most rapid contraction of bank credit and the money supply ever experienced in America. For example, the money supply, narrowly defined to include only demand deposits and currency, which had declined $2.7 billion during the 2 years preceding mid-1931, fell $1.7 billion, or 7 percent, in the latter half of the year. The money supply more broadly defined to include also time deposits at commercial banks fell $4.9 billion, or 12 percent, in the last 6 months of 1931, as compared with a decline of $3.6 billion during the 2 preceding years. As would be expected in the face of such a rapid contraction of bank credit, financial markets were demoralized. Short-term interest rates in the open market rose to twice their level in mid-1931, and the prices of even the highest-quality bonds fell sharply. Prices of lower-grade bonds fell much more, and many became virtually unsalable.

All this was closely related to the large reductions of bank reserves, which in turn were related to decreases in the monetary gold stock and drains of currency into circulation. Reserve losses were especially large up to the end of October. As noted earlier, the gold stock decreased $727 million during this period. Bank failures were widespread; 827 banks failed in September and October alone. Largely because of this and the resulting distrust of other banks, currency in circulation rose $393 million. Thus drains on member bank reserves because of gold losses and currency withdrawals amounted to $1,120 million during the period from September 21 to October 28. (See Table 12-1.)

Effects on bank reserves were mixed during the period from the end of October to February 24, 1932. The gold stock actually increased in the last 2 months of 1931 but began to decline again in January. On February 24 it was $666 million below its level in mid-September. Currency withdrawals continued as another 994 banks failed in the November–February period; on February 24 currency in circulation was $505 million above its level in mid-September. Thus drains on bank reserves between mid-September and February 24 because of gold losses and currency withdrawals amounted to $1,171 million.

175

TABLE 12-1

Changes of Member Bank Reserves and Selected Related Items, September 1931–February 1932ᵃ (in millions of dollars)

Changes during week ending:	Reserve Bank Credit Outstanding					Gold stock	Money in circulation	Member Bank Reserve Balances	
	Bills discounted	Bills bought	USG's	All other	Total			Total	Excess (est.)
1931									
September 23	+ 47	+ 25	− 4	− 32	+ 36	− 119	+ 76	− 138	− 117
September 30	+ 23	+ 226	+ 4	+ 10	+ 263	− 156	+ 82	+ 84	+ 73
October 7	+ 135	+ 112	+ 4	+ 17	+ 261	− 99	+ 185	− 87	− 30
October 14	+ 160	+ 149	− 11	− 11	+ 286	− 218	+ 42	− 54	− 24
October 21	+ 70	+ 39	0	+ 4	+ 113	− 87	+ 32	+ 53	+ 61
October 28	+ 19	− 44	0	− 2	− 27	− 48	− 24	− 47	− 30
November 4	− 12	− 83	+ 1	− 8	− 102	− 23	+ 64	− 107	− 93
November 11	− 21	− 45	+ 1	+ 22	− 45	+ 23	− 26	− 23	0
November 18	− 22	− 63	0	− 7	− 92	+ 35	− 46	+ 25	+ 17
November 25	+ 24	− 54	0	− 1	− 31	+ 24	+ 6	+ 7	+ 5
December 2	+ 32	− 57	− 10	− 1	− 36	+ 37	+ 32	− 44	+ 40
December 9	+ 7	+ 34	0	+ 2	+ 25	+ 12	− 2	+ 13	+ 39
December 16	− 27	+ 82	+ 189	+ 14	+ 94	+ 20	+ 69	+ 82	+ 56
December 23	+ 213	+ 50	− 148	+ 17	+ 32	+ 18	+ 155	− 167	+ 85
December 30	+ 113	+ 70	+ 45	− 32	+ 196	+ 7	− 101	+ 322	+ 304
1932									
January 6	− 206	− 52	− 37	+ 13	− 281	0	+ 29	− 287	− 277
January 13	0	− 61	− 14	− 11	− 87	− 1	+ 42	− 42	− 15
January 20	+ 1	− 26	+ 1	− 2	− 27	− 6	+ 6	− 22	+ 1
January 27	+ 19	+ 6	+ 1	+ 9	+ 12	− 25	− 24	− 27	+ 14
February 3	+ 17	+ 13	+ 3	+ 3	+ 31	− 20	+ 42	− 8	+ 22
February 10	− 36	− 23	+ 8	− 1	+ 31	+ 3	+ 6	+ 32	+ 21
February 17	+ 27	− 13	− 1	+ 2	+ 2	− 34	− 16	+ 1	+ 8
February 24	− 11	− 13	0	− 22	− 47	− 19	+ 16	− 26	+ 16
Change, September 16–October 28	+ 454	+ 507	− 15	− 14	+ 932	− 727	+ 393	− 189	− 67
Change, September 16–December 30	+ 761	+ 109	+ 61	− 8	+ 923	− 558	+ 544	− 95	+ 136
Change, September 16–February 24	+ 572	− 85	− 1	− 31	+ 455	− 666	+ 505	− 540	− 176

ᵃThis table does not show changes in the following related items: Treasury currency outstanding, Treasury cash holdings and deposits at the Federal Reserve, nonmember deposits, and other Federal Reserve accounts.

Source: Board of Governors of the Federal Reserve System, *Banking and Monetary Statistics*, Washington, D.C., 1943, p. 386.

FEDERAL RESERVE POLICIES,
SEPTEMBER 21-END OF OCTOBER 1931

The Federal Reserve response to the domestic and international drain on commercial bank reserves during late September and October conformed to the classic rule for dealing with crises: Lend freely but at high interest rates. The System bought no government securities to meet the drain, but it did lend freely to member banks and it bought bills freely, both from the Bank of France and other foreign central banks that were liquidating their dollar holdings and from others. However, it raised both its bill-buying and discount rates. The lowest bill-buying rate was raised from 1 to 1 1/4 percent on September 25; 3 more increases brought it to 3 1/8 percent by October 16. New York raised its discount rate from 1 1/2 to 2 1/2 percent on October 9 and to 3 1/2 percent on October 16. By early November discount rates were at 3 1/2 percent at all the Reserve banks except Richmond and Dallas, which had established 4 percent rates.

The first increase of the discount rate, that at New York on October 9, came only after the drain had been under way for more than two weeks. This delay reflected differences of judgment concerning the desirability of rate increases. At first, the directors and officers of the New York Bank were opposed to an increase, both because of its restrictive domestic effects and because they feared that it would be construed as a sign of weakness and would stimulate, rather than inhibit, foreign withdrawals of funds. Governor Meyer had other views. He told Harrison that the Board had expected New York to propose an increase after its directors' meeting on October 1 and would have approved such a proposal. In his view, a rate increase would be considered not as a sign of weakness but as a sign of strength and of determination to maintain the gold value of the dollar. When rates were increased the purpose was almost certainly to inhibit the outflow of foreign funds rather than to deal with domestic currency withdrawals. Increases of discount and bill-buying rates could inhibit gold outflows in two ways—by giving foreign holders a higher yield on their holdings of dollar claims and by creating greater confidence abroad that the gold value of the dollar would be defended. Federal Reserve officials may have placed special emphasis on the second effect in view of the adverse rumors about the dollar that were circulating abroad, the patent uneasiness of the French and other foreigners who had suffered losses on their holdings of sterling, and the extreme antipathy of the French to "excessively" easy credit conditions. The suspension of gold withdrawals during November and December might not have occurred if the Federal Reserve had not raised its discount and bill-buying rates and if, instead, it had purchased large amounts of government securities to offset the drains of gold and currency. In retrospect, however, it can be argued that the damage to the American economy might have been less if the French and other foreign holdings of dollar balances had been liquidated more quickly.

When the Executive Committee of the OMPC met on October 26, its first meeting since the beginning of the crisis, Harrison surveyed the dreary situation—the continuing gold withdrawals, numerous bank failures, currency hoarding, rapid credit liquidation, falling bond prices, and rising interest rates.

Neither he nor any other member thought that purchases of securities would serve any useful purpose under the circumstances. McDougal thought that November maturities should be allowed to run off unless conditions changed, but the outcome was a decision to neither buy nor sell.

FEDERAL RESERVE POLICIES, NOVEMBER 1931-FEBRUARY 24, 1932

At the meeting of the OMPC in Washington on November 30 its members were unanimously of the opinion that the outlook was still too uncertain to permit the formulation of a long-range policy, that the meeting should concern itself only with policies for the remainder of the year, and that another meeting should be held in January to consider policies for the longer run. All opposed an immediate purchase of government securities, but a majority noted that some purchases might be necessary around mid-December because of heavy maturities at that time of bills held by the Federal Reserve, a seasonal increase of currency in circulation, and a large Treasury financing operation. The purpose of any such purchases would be not to ease credit but to prevent a further firming of interest rates. The outcome was the following recommendation, which was later approved by the Federal Reserve Board:

... While the Conference was of the opinion that there is no occasion for any immediate purchase of Government securities, nevertheless they voted that in view of all circumstances and in order to be prepared if and when occasion arises, the Executive Committee be authorized in its discretion to buy up to $200,000,000 of Government securities before the end of the year. It was the sense of the Conference that the Committee should also be authorized in their discretion to sell any securities so bought after the turn of the year if conditions then permit. The Conference felt there should be another meeting of the Conference early in January to consider the System's general operations and policies in the light of conditions as they then exist.[1]

The System purchased about $230 million of government securities in December, but it had sold over $200 million by mid-January.

The two-day meeting of the OMPC on January 11-12 brought no immediate purchases of government securities, but it did lead to the formulation of an overall program to deal with the credit situation. The members of the OMPC and the Board agreed that something effective should be done to halt the rapid deflation of credit and the decline of bond prices.

... not only have new issues or refunding issues become impossible, but the credit of various borrowers including various municipalities has become impaired so that bank credit has become unavailable to many. This situation has been reflected in the discontinuance of many business projects, further decline in business activity and commodity prices. This situation is not curing itself but it tends to grow progressively worse unless positive steps are taken to change the trend.[2]

They believed, however, that under the circumstances open-market purchases

---

[1]Minutes of the Federal Reserve Board, December 1, 1931.

[2]Preliminary memorandum for the OMPC meeting of January 11-12, 1932.

alone could not succeed; a broader program was required to deal with a number of serious problems. One of these was the deep depreciation of bond prices. The price declines that had already occurred not only made new issues virtually impossible but had also impaired the capital of many banks and other financial institutions. A study of member banks in the New York district in December 1931 revealed conditions that were widely prevalent elsewhere.

The average bank in the second Federal Reserve District has a bond account which is from two to four times as large as the total capital funds of the bank, and there are more than 150 banks in the district whose bond accounts are considerably more than four times their total capital funds, that is capital, surplus, and undivided profits. Therefore, the decline in bond prices which has taken place since the spring of the year, amounting on the standard indexes to from 20 to 25 percent, has resulted in a great many cases in depreciation in the market value of bond holdings equal to or in excess of the total capital funds of the bank. The severe declines in bond prices since the middle of September in particular have brought serious depreciation . . . .

If the banks of this district were all examined today and their bonds revalued at today's market prices it may be estimated conservatively that close to 300 of them would show losses, largely on bond account, equal to or nearly equal to their total capital funds, and that probably 150 to 200 more banks would show some capital impairment. In other words, more than half of the member banks in this district have depreciation on their bond accounts at present market prices sufficient to cause capital impairment. While the banks have some losses from other causes their principal difficulty lies in bond depreciation . . . .

It appears inevitable that large numbers of additional banks will be closed unless supervisory authorities adopt a less rigid procedure in dealing with bond depreciation. If banks continue to be closed by reason of bond depreciation, the situation must inevitably become steadily worse. Each bank that closes causes further withdrawals of deposits from nearby banks, necessitating the further sale of bonds, and thus putting still more pressure on the bond market. Pressure is already being exerted by reason of the sale of bonds held by closed banks.[3]

Harrison and others at the meeting were especially worried about the status of railroad bonds, of which more than $7 billion were outstanding. Because of the poor earnings positions of the railroads and actual or threatened defaults, many of these bonds had already depreciated sharply, and there was a danger that they would become ineligible for purchase by insurance companies, savings banks, and trust funds, in which case the market would become completely demoralized. The consensus was that the problem could be solved only if the wages of railroad employees were reduced in order to improve the earnings of the railroads. Wage cuts of 10 percent occurred on February 1, 1932.

Several other measures were advocated at this meeting to deal with the depreciation of bonds and other bank assets. (1) The first was adoption of less rigid methods of valuing bonds in bank examinations. In September the Comptroller of the Currency had ruled that national banks would not be required to charge off depreciation in the four highest classes of bonds, but that they should charge off 25 percent of the depreciation on all other bonds not in default and total depreciation on bonds in default. These rules were

---

[3]Memorandum at the Federal Reserve Bank of New York dated December 8, 1931.

applied to national banks in all cases in which the total depreciation had not impaired capital, and even in some cases in which capital was impaired. It was now proposed that the Comptroller's rule should be applied to all national banks, including those with impaired capital, and that state supervisory authorities should follow similar rules. (2) The second measure was formation of a bond pool to support bond prices. The OMPC proposed that some of the larger commercial banks, perhaps aided by other types of financial institutions, should purchase bonds at strategic times to cushion price declines and perhaps even to raise prices. (3) The final proposal was the establishment of a large government-sponsored financial institution to lend to member banks on types of collateral not eligible for loans from the Federal Reserve and to lend to institutions without access to the Federal Reserve. Almost from the time he became Governor of the Federal Reserve Board in September 1930, Eugene Meyer had urged President Hoover to establish an institution similar to the old War Finance Corporation which Meyer had headed during World War I, but Hoover demurred. Finally, in October 1931, Hoover agreed to ask bankers to form a private corporation for the purpose and promised to request the Congress to create a federally sponsored Reconstruction Finance Corporation when it convened in January. The National Credit Corporation, established in October with $500 million of private capital, proved to be quite timorous and inadequate, as Meyer had predicted. Congress was considering the Reconstruction Finance Corporation bill when the OMPC met on January 11, and President Hoover approved the bill on January 22. As originally constituted, the RFC had $500 million of capital and authority to borrow $1.5 billion. To expedite its operations, the Reserve banks supplied it with both facilities and personnel.

The OMPC also discussed the financial problems of the Treasury, which were exacerbated by the deteriorated condition of the bond market, widespread disapproval of federal deficits, and fears of more to come. Secretary of the Treasury Ogden L. Mills did not conceal his worries from the OMPC and the Board.

He indicated that the Treasury felt that the problem to be dealt with was much larger than merely financing the Treasury but was rather one of preserving government credit and of restoring a normal functioning of credit machinery.

The Treasury faces a problem of raising about one and a half billion dollars additional money between now and June 30 to meet current expenditures and the requirements of the Reconstruction Finance Corporation, the farm loan banks, and the proposed home loan banks. The effects of increasing the national debt during the past year had not been inflationary as might have been expected but rather the reverse. Funds appear to have been withdrawn from other necessary uses to finance Treasury requirements. We suffered the evils of an unbalanced budget without any of its advantages.

If the Treasury and the Federal Reserve banks do not now work in close harmony it will not be possible to obtain the one and a half billion dollars required except by very sharp increases in interest rates, which would in turn result in severe depreciation in government and other securities and further impair the credit of the Government, which must be restored. We now have to deal with an emergency only comparable with the emergency of war and are justified in returning to war techniques in the sale of government securities.

. . . June 30 next must be a deadline beyond which the national debt will not be increased. The inclination of banks to subscribe would be increased by reductions of Federal reserve discount rates to give some differential between those rates and the rates on government securities. If banks can be induced to borrow and buy the net effect must be an expansion of credit. This could not fairly be called an inflation of credit in view of the recent unprecedented deflation which has occurred.

Mr. Mills felt that, in the interest of maintaining the credit of the government, maintaining the value of securities, strengthening the credit structure, and reversing deflationary trends, the Treasury was justified in asking cooperation in the use of methods used in the last great crisis of the country. Any danger such a program might involve can be avoided if it is a temporary expedient to terminate definitely at the end of the fiscal year. He said this termination would be supported firmly and definitely by the Executive and he had reason to hope by Congress.[4]

Harrison observed that

whatever action was taken would be taken not simply for the benefit of the government but as part of a broad general program to combat deflation.[5]

He also stated that the broad general program should include these parts:

(1) Passage of RFC bill.

(2) Organized support of the bond market predicted upon railroad wage cuts.

(3) Federal Reserve and member bank cooperation with the Treasury program.

(4) Buying bills when possible.

(5) Reduction in discount rates.

(6) Buying of Governments, if necessary, facilitated by an alleviation of the free gold position.

He believed that the System's hands should not be tied on any of the last four points . . . .[6]

Most of the governors favored reducing discount rates in order to encourage banks to borrow, if necessary, to buy government securities and agreed to recommend rate reductions to their directors. The only question was whether to reduce their ordinary discount rates or to establish preferentially lower rates for loans collateraled by government securities. Harrison preferred the former. In fact, however, the only reductions in January were at Richmond and Dallas, which lowered their rates from 4 to 3 1/2 percent, and the only reduction in February came on the 26th when New York lowered its rate from 3 1/2 to 3 percent. Reductions of bill-buying rates came more quickly. The lowest rate was reduced from 3 to 2 3/4 percent on January 12 and to 2 5/8 percent on February 26. These reductions were not large enough to prevent a continuing decrease of Federal Reserve bill holdings. No government securities were purchases until after February 24, and most of the governors made it clear that they were opposed to purchases before legislation had been enacted to ease their "free-gold" positions. This was achieved with the passage of the Glass-Steagall Act on February 27.

---

[4]Minutes of the OMPC, January 11-12, 1932.

[5]*Ibid.*

[6]*Ibid.*

THE "FREE-GOLD" QUESTION

How much was Federal Reserve policy in 1931 and early 1932 affected by a shortage of free gold? Was there in truth a shortage of free gold which could not be alleviated under existing laws? Was the shortage of free gold, real or only alleged, the reason, or a major reason, for the failure of the Federal Reserve to embark upon a more ambitious policy of open-market purchases in 1931 and the first two months of 1932? Was the United States on the verge of being forced off the gold standard because of a shortage of free gold in this period? These questions have been widely and hotly debated. Perhaps we shall not be able to present definitive answers, but we can throw some light on the issues.

As a first step, it is necessary to distinguish between the reserve requirements and the collateral requirements applicable to the Federal Reserve banks. The Federal Reserve Act provided that each Reserve bank should hold gold reserves equal to at least 40 percent of its outstanding Federal Reserve notes, and reserves in the form of gold or lawful money equal to at least 35 percent of its deposit liabilities. Thus the average reserve requirement against Federal Reserve notes and deposits was between 35 and 40 percent. Table 12-2 shows that the Reserve banks suffered no shortage of reserves during the period under discussion. In fact, their reserves in excess of legal requirements averaged more than $1.8 billion during the first 9 months of 1931 and never fell below $1.2 billion until June 1932, and their actual reserve ratios never fell below 60 percent during this period.

However, the Federal Reserve Act also required that all Federal Reserve notes outstanding—those issued by the Federal Reserve agent who was the Board representative at each Reserve bank—should be backed 100 percent by collateral, and the only assets legally acceptable as collateral were gold and "eligible paper." The latter included only acceptances and paper discounted by member banks; it excluded government securities. Gold held as reserves against Federal Reserve notes also counted as collateral, but gold held as collateral behind Federal Reserve notes could not be counted as reserves against Federal Reserve deposits. When a Reserve bank had eligible paper equal to at least 60 percent of its outstanding Federal Reserve notes the amount of its free gold was equal to its excess reserves. However, to the extent that its holdings of eligible paper fell below 60 percent of its outstanding Federal Reserve notes, it had to use more gold as collateral, thereby reducing its free gold below the amount of its excess reserves. Thus the free-gold problem of the Reserve banks, as contrasted with any reserve problem they might have, reflected an inadequacy of their holdings of eligible paper to use as collateral for their Federal Reserve notes.

The scarcity of free gold did not limit the ability of the Federal Reserve to meet gold withdrawals or to issue currency when these drains were met by increased member bank borrowings or by Federal Reserve purchases of bills. In such cases, the drains provided the Reserve banks with more eligible paper to use as collateral.

President Hoover was wrong when he stated in a campaign speech on October 4, 1932 that at one point the United States was within two weeks of

TABLE 12-2

The Reserve Positions of Federal Reserve Banks, 1931-1932
(monthly average of daily figures)

	Excess over legal requirements (in millions)	Actual reserve percentage
1931		
January	$1,704	79.0%
February	1,811	83.4
March	1,838	84.0
April	1,848	83.5
May	1,896	84.4
June	1,959	84.3
July	2,008	84.3
August	1,970	81.4
September	1,848	77.5
October	1,214	62.6
November	1,221	63.1
December	1,322	65.2
1932		
January	1,373	66.5
February	1,384	67.4
March	1,457	69.7
April	1,472	69.3
May	1,306	64.8
June	989	58.4
July	915	56.3
August	1,016	58.2
September	1,123	60.0
October	1,219	61.5
November	1,277	62.4
December	1,309	62.5

Source: Board of Governors of the Federal Reserve System, *Banking and Monetary Statistics,* Washington, D.C., 1943, p. 348.

being forced off the gold standard. After referring to gold withdrawals and domestic hoarding of currency and gold, he concluded:

These drains had at one moment reduced the amount of gold to a point where the Secretary of the Treasury informed me that unless we could put into effect a remedy, we could not hold to the gold standard but two weeks longer because of inability to meet the demands of foreigners and our own citizens for gold.[7]

He wrote later:

On February 7, 1932, Secretary Mills informed me that the gold situation had become critical, and that there was immediate danger of not being able to meet foreign withdrawals and "earmarking" which were then going on at the rate of $100,000,000 a week. He was greatly alarmed that we were within two or three weeks of being forced off the gold standard by inability to meet these gold demands.[8]

Federal Reserve officials had no such fears. They knew that the excess

---

[7]William Starr Myers (ed.), *The State Papers and Other Public Writings of Herbert Hoover,* Doubleday, New York, 1934, Vol. II, p. 302.

[8]*The Memoirs of Herbert Hoover: The Great Depression, 1929-1941,* Macmillan, New York, 1952, pp. 115-116.

reserves of the Reserve banks were about $1.4 billion, that their free gold was about $400 million, and that gold losses would increase the Reserve banks' holdings of eligible paper to the extent that member bank borrowings and Federal Reserve bill holdings rose. On January 19, 1932, an official of the New York Reserve Bank estimated the effects on the Reserve banks' reserve and free-gold positions on the assumptions that the Bank of France withdrew all of its remaining $600 million of dollar balances, that the Federal Reserve took over the acceptances and government securities sold by the Bank of France, and that member banks increased their borrowings to meet the remainder of the gold drain. He concluded that free gold would still amount to about $400 million, and that the excess reserves of the Reserve banks would total approximately $785 million.[9] Thus a scarcity of free gold could not limit the ability of the Federal Reserve to meet gold drains, but it could limit the Federal Reserve's ability to purchase government securities, which were not acceptable as collateral for Federal Reserve notes. Free gold would be reduced to the extent that gold losses were offset by Federal Reserve purchases of government securities, rather than by member bank borrowings and sales of bills to the Federal Reserve. Also, purchases of government securities for other purposes would reduce free gold to the extent that the purchases reduced member bank borrowings or Federal Reserve bill holdings. Thus the real restraint imposed by a scarcity of free gold, if there was such a scarcity, was on the ability of the Federal Reserve to acquire government securities.

This brings us back to a question raised earlier: "Was there in truth a shortage of free gold which could not be alleviated under existing laws?" Table 12-3 shows the actual amounts of free gold, with collateral required against all Federal Reserve notes issued by the Federal Reserve agents, including both those in circulation and those held by the Reserve banks themselves. Free gold could have been increased by about $300 million by reducing to a minimum the amounts of Federal Reserve notes held in the Reserve

TABLE 12-3

The Free Gold of the Federal Reserve System, 1931-1932
(end-of-month figures, in millions of dollars)

	Free gold
1931	
July	747
August	656
September	578
October	606
November	571
December	357
1932	
January	469
February	397

Source: Henry Hilgard Villard, "The Federal Reserve System's Monetary Policy in 1931 and 1932," *Journal of Political Economy*, December 1937, p. 734.

---

[9]Burgess memorandum to Harrison.

banks. On several occasions Federal Reserve officials discussed practical methods of doing this: by keeping their holdings of Federal Reserve notes to a minimum at all times, by returning their note holdings to the Federal Reserve agent before the close of business each day, by appointing assistant Federal Reserve agents at each branch office to issue and retire notes, and so on.

Milton Friedman and Anna J. Schwartz have suggested two other methods that the Federal Reserve could have used to increase its free gold. (1) "Bills could have been purchased instead of government securities, since they were eligible as collateral for Federal Reserve notes."[10] The Federal Reserve certainly failed to exploit this useful device. Its bill holdings did rise $551 million during the month following the onset of the crisis on September 21, reaching a peak of $769 million on October 21. From that point they declined almost continuously, falling $693 million by the end of February, when their total was only $76 million. Thus on this date the Federal Reserve was holding for its own account only 8 percent of the $919 million of dollar acceptances outstanding but it was also holding $312 million, or 34 percent of all outstanding acceptances, for the accounts of its foreign correspondents. This left $532 million, or 58 percent of the total, in private hands. By lowering its bill-buying rate sharply relative to market rates, the Federal Reserve could almost certainly have increased its bill holdings and it might have induced additional issues of bills.

Friedman and Schwartz also suggest that (2) "Member banks could have been encouraged to increase their discounts."[11] They believe that this would have been facilitated if the Federal Reserve had lowered its discount rates enough to make it profitable for member banks to carry government securities, or if preferentially lower discount rates had been applied to loans collateraled by government securities. This method might indeed have induced some increase in member bank borrowings and thus have increased free gold. However, I am skeptical that it would have been successful under the circumstances. For one thing, member banks in general must have been quite reluctant to show borrowings on their balance sheets because they might be construed as a sign of weakness. Times were hardly propitious for a Federal Reserve campaign to convince banks that the tradition against continuous borrowing had been suspended. Also, the willingness of banks to assume the risks involved in holding government securities, and especially longer-term issues, must have been lowered greatly by the sharp decline of bond prices during the preceding months. Few would have been enticed by a margin between the yield on governments and the discount rate to assume the risks involved in large additional borrowings.

The conclusion remains, however, that the Federal Reserve did not exploit the legal means available to it to increase its free reserves by reducing the amounts of Federal Reserve notes held by the Reserve banks themselves,

---

[10]*A Monetary History of the United States, 1867-1960*, Princeton University Press, Princeton, 1963, pp. 404-405.

[11]*Ibid.*, pp. 405-406.

by reducing its bill-buying rates relative to market rates, and by reducing its discount rates, either by flat reductions or by the establishment of preferential rates relative to yields on government securities and other interest-yielding assets.

This brings us back to another question that was raised earlier: "Was the shortage of free gold, real or only alleged, the reason, or a major reason, for the failure of the Federal Reserve to embark upon a more ambitious policy of open-market purchases in 1931 and the first two months of 1931? Friedman and Schwartz answer with an emphatic "no."

The conclusion seems inescapable that a shortage of free gold did not in fact seriously limit the alternatives open to the System. The amount was at all times ample to support large open market purchases. A shortage was an additional reason, at most, for measures adopted primarily on other grounds. The removal of the problem did not of itself lead to a change of policy. The problem of free gold was largely an ex post justification for policies followed, not an ex ante reason for them.[12]

I concur in general with these conclusions, though with reservations. A shortage of free gold was certainly not the only reason for the failure of the Federal Reserve to make large purchases in the open market during this period. There were also the many reasons, examined in earlier pages, that led a majority of Federal Reserve officials to oppose ambitious easy-money policies even before the autumn of 1931, when there was clearly no shortage of free gold. With the upsurge of bank failures at that time and the onset of gold withdrawals, Federal Reserve officials found still other reasons for not engaging in large open-market purchases: the paramount importance of defending the gold value of the dollar; a belief that under the circumstances open-market purchases would not be effective and should be postponed until conditions were more favorable; and the accompanying contention that purchases should be undertaken only as a part of a broader program which would require time for development. If Federal Reserve officials had thought differently on these issues they would have been more disposed to use available methods of increasing their free gold and to assume the risks involved in large purchases.

However, I believe that Friedman and Schwartz go too far in stating that "The problem of free gold was largely an ex post justification for policies followed, not an ex ante reason for them." Whether or not they should have been, directors and officers of several of the Reserve banks were deeply concerned about their free-gold positions and stated this concern several times in the latter part of 1931 and early 1932. Moreover, a number of the Reserve banks declined to participate in purchases of securities, citing their shortage of free gold as the reason. Among these were the Reserve banks of Kansas City, Dallas, St. Louis, Minneapolis, Richmond, San Francisco, Chicago, Boston, and Atlanta. Meyer and Harrison knew that a marked improvement in free-gold positions was a necessary prerequisite to getting the assent of the governors to large open-market purchases.

One reason for this situation was the highly uneven distribution of free

---

[12]*Ibid.*, p. 406.

TABLE 12-4

Excess Reserves and Free Gold of the Federal Reserve Banks,
October 31, 1931 and February 15, 1932 (in millions of dollars)

Federal Reserve district	October 31, 1931		February 15, 1932	
	Excess reserves	Free gold	Excess reserves	Free gold
Boston	40	21	98	9
New York	466	437	488	266
Philadelphia	99	34	84	31
Cleveland	88	27	116	33
Richmond	18	12	44	12
Atlanta	9	10	43	7
Chicago	204	44	545	30
St. Louis	15	15	45	11
Minneapolis	18	10	28	2
Kansas City	6	21	53	16
Dallas	6	11	20	4
San Francisco	4	21	69	22
Total	972	663	1,392	444

Source: Data for October 31 from Board of Governors of the Federal Reserve System, *Federal Reserve Bulletin,* November 1931, p. 648. Data for February 15 from a memorandum at the Federal Reserve Bank of New York.

gold among the Reserve banks. For example, Table 12-4 shows that on October 31, when total free gold was $663 million, 66 percent of it was at New York, and 72 percent was at New York and Chicago. On February 15, when free gold totaled $444 million, 60 percent was concentrated in New York and 7 percent in Chicago. Free gold at 4 of the Reserve banks was less than $10 million. Excess reserves were also distributed quite unevenly, with large concentrations in New York and Chicago. Methods for dealing with the unequal distributions were, of course, available. (1) The Board could require the Reserve banks with the largest excess reserves or free gold to lend to those with less ample supplies, transferring gold in exchange. (2) New security purchases could be allocated to the Reserve banks with the largest amounts of free gold. This was done to a limited extent in 1931 and more in 1932. (3) Bills could be transferred to the Reserve banks most in need of free gold in exchange for government securities. The extent to which this could be done was limited in late 1931 and early 1932 by the System's small holdings of bills. (4) Government securities could be traded for gold by the Reserve banks most in need of free gold or reserves. This was also done to some extent.

However, these methods were exploited only partially. For this there appear to have been several reasons. One was that the Reserve banks opposed to large purchases were not inclined to favor measures that would make such purchases possible. Another was the reluctance of some Reserve banks to relinquish control over the size and composition of their earning assets. Still another was the deterioration of Reserve bank earnings. (See Table 12-5.) In 1929, when their earning assets were large and average interest yields were relatively high, all the Reserve banks enjoyed net earnings comfortably in excess of their dividend requirements. However, this situation changed as both the volume of their earning assets and average interest rates fell. By 1931

TABLE 12-5

Federal Reserve Bank Net Earnings in Excess of Dividend Requirements,
1929-1931 (in thousands of dollars)

Federal Reserve Bank	1929	1930	1931
Boston	+ 2,132	− 452	− 849
New York	+ 8,719	+ 575	−2,360
Philadelphia	+ 2,864	+ 100	− 121
Cleveland	+ 2,795	− 169	− 858
Richmond	+ 974	− 382	− 497
Atlanta	+ 1,107	0	− 313
Chicago	+ 4,254	− 157	− 561
St. Louis	+ 567	− 315	− 351
Minneapolis	+ 611	+ 9	− 135
Kansas City	+ 757	− 460	−4 439
Dallas	+ 504	+ 10	− 143
San Francisco	+ 1,536	−1,039	− 432
Total	+26,819	−2,280	−7,057

Source: Board of Governors of the Federal Reserve System, *Annual Reports,*
Washington, D.C., 1929-1931.

none of the Reserve banks had sufficient earnings to meet its dividend requirements, and all were drawing on surplus for this purpose. Under these conditions, some of the Reserve banks were reluctant to part with earning assets to
improve their free-gold or reserve positions.

By January both Meyer and Harrison were convinced that the Federal
Reserve Act should be amended for two purposes—to increase the free gold of
the Reserve banks and to enable the banks to lend to members on a wider
range of assets. They knew that getting such legislation would be difficult
because no banking bill could be enacted without the approval of Senator
Glass, who would be strongly inclined to oppose both measures. Glass was still
devoted to the commercial loan theory as it applied to both collateral for
Federal Reserve notes and eligibility for discount at the Federal Reserve.
Eugene Meyer later wrote of him,

> He wanted to make the existing Federal Reserve Act conform more rigidly to the
> unrealistic theories he had learned from Professor H. Parker Willis, while I wanted as I
> had for years, to make the Act abandon those theories and become liberalized in accord
> with facts and needs . . . . The evil he worried about was inflation. He saw inflation in
> everything.[13]

Meyer and Harrison believed that the most they could expect to get were
temporary powers.

On January 4 Harrison met with a small group of Chicago and New
York bankers to discuss broader Federal Reserve lending powers, methods of
increasing free gold, and possible approaches to Senator Glass. Harrison outlined three possible devices for increasing free gold: to remove all collateral
requirements and make Federal Reserve notes general claims against Federal
Reserve assets; to make the notes a government currency with a lien on
Federal Reserve assets; or to allow government securities to be counted as

---

[13]Eugene Meyer papers.

collateral. At this stage Harrison favored either of the first two measures. He visited Glass during the next week and several more times in late January and early February. Glass was also visited by Meyer, Burgess, and Russell Leffingwell, but he still refused to sponsor the amendments. Secretary Mills then arranged for Meyer, Harrison, and General Dawes to call on President Hoover on February 8 to ask him to intercede. Hoover did so, inviting to breakfast the next morning the Republican and Democratic congressional leaders and the ranking members of the Senate Committee on Banking and Currency.[14] It was at this meeting that Glass agreed to sponsor what became the Glass-Steagall Act on February 27. However, he did so reluctantly, and both then and at the congressional hearings made no secret of his dislike for the new provisions. Meyer later commented:

> A funny thing about this act is that though its purpose was to avoid imminent disaster, the economy being by now in a state of collapse, the objection was raised that it would be inflationary. This was as if a doctor with a dying patient on his hands should refrain from giving him proper treatment for fear if he got well he might do something foolish. Senator Glass had this fear and was zealous to prune back the "inflationary" possibilities of the measure.[15]

The Glass-Steagall Act included three principal provisions, the last two of which were scheduled to expire automatically a year later, though they were later extended. (1) Federal Reserve banks were authorized, with the consent of at least five members of the Federal Reserve Board, to lend to groups of five or more member banks. Meyer and Harrison predicted that this provision would not be useful, and no loans were made under it in 1932. (2) Also subject to the consent of at least five members of the Board, the Reserve banks were empowered to lend to members on assets not otherwise eligible for discount. However, this paper was ineligible for use as collateral for Federal Reserve notes and was subject to a discount rate at least one-half of 1 percent higher than the highest regular discount rate in effect at the lending Reserve bank. (3) Subject to rules and regulations by the Federal Reserve Board, the Reserve banks were authorized to use government securities as collateral for Federal Reserve notes.

Even after the Glass-Steagall Act became effective on February 27, the Board was reluctant to allow the Reserve banks to pledge government securities as collateral for Federal Reserve notes. It delayed approval until May 2, and the first government securities were pledged on May 5. This delay probably increased the difficulty of securing the governors' agreement to earlier and larger purchases. The reasons for the Board's reluctance and delay are unclear. One was probably a fear that quick and large pledges of government securities as collateral would increase the already widespread charges abroad, especially in France, that the United States was embarking on "inflationary" policies. Another was probably their knowledge of Senator Glass' basic opposition to such actions. They may well have assured the Senator that the powers would be used as sparingly as possible.

---

[14]*The Memoirs of Herbert Hoover, The Great Depression, 1929-1941,* Macmillan, New York, 1952, p. 117.

[15]Meyer papers.

In any case, the Board's grant of permission on May 2 to pledge government securities as collateral was on a very limited basis. In effect, it set an overall quota of $400 million of free gold for the Reserve banks as a whole, this being made up of individual quotas for the various Reserve banks. These quotas are shown in Table 12-6. Several Reserve bank officials, mostly those of Reserve banks with branches, complained that their quotas were too "tight" to permit smooth and efficient operations. New York relinquished $10 million of its quota to help San Francisco. Some of the Reserve banks might have felt more secure and willing to acquiesce in open-market purchases if their free-gold quotas had been larger.

TABLE 12-6

*Free-Gold Quotas Established for the Federal
Reserve Banks on May 2, 1932 (in millions of dollars)*

Federal Reserve Bank	Amount
Boston	25
New York	110
Philadelphia	25
Cleveland	35
Richmond	15
Atlanta	30
Chicago	65
St. Louis	15
Minneapolis	10
Kansas City	20
Dallas	10
San Francisco	40
Total	400

Source: Minutes of the Federal Reserve Board, May 2, 1932.

Let us now return to Federal Reserve policies in February 1932. The situation in the middle of that month was well described by Burgess in a letter to Harrison.

Most of the points of our January program have now been achieved: rail wages have been reduced, the administration had made a definite commitment on balancing the budget, the Reconstruction Finance Corporation is in operation, and the bond pool has been operating—though feebly. Everybody else has done the task assigned to him, but the Reserve System has not as yet done its part. There was a very good reason for not doing so, and that was the limited amount of our free gold in the face of European gold withdrawals. The new legislation removes that impediment, and I should think places a considerable obligation upon us to go forward with the program which was our part of the general plan.[16]

Burgess advocated that the Executive Committee of the OMPC be asked to approve purchases under the January authorization by the OMPC to purchase up to $200 million and that another meeting of the OMPC be held with a week.

---

[16]Burgess letter from Washington to Harrison, February 16, 1932.

Even before the Executive Committee can meet some action seems desirable, and I should think that we should explore, first, the possibility of buying a block of bills as we did once before; second, reducing our buying rate, and third, reducing the discount rate. At any rate, I am clear that some sort of action is important before the new movement gets "cold."

I have discussed these questions with Goldenweiser, who is in general agreement, and, I find, has been thinking in terms of a security purchase of half a billion dollars as a necessary step in relieving member bank indebtedness. I am not yet prepared to go quite that far, but I am clear we ought to begin.

In discussing the matter with the other Governors, it may be noted that considerable security purchases are now justified to offset gold exports if for no other reason, a step which is now possible under the new legislation.[17]

However, no significant policy actions were taken until after the next meeting of the OMPC on February 24-25.

---

[17]*Ibid.*

13

The Easy-Money Policy of 1932

The period from February 24 through the end of 1932, which is the subject of this chapter, divides naturally into two subperiods. The first, from February 24 through June, witnessed the liquidation of the large remaining foreign balances in the United States and gold losses of $430 million. It also brought more than $1 billion of purchases of government securities, the largest ever made by the Federal Reserve System up to that time. The lowest bill-buying rate was decreased in 3 steps from 2 3/4 to 1 percent. New York and Chicago lowered their discount rates from 3 1/2 to 2 1/2 percent, but the other Reserve banks kept their rates unchanged at 3 1/2 percent. Developments during the second half of the year were quite different. Gold flows reversed, increasing the nation's gold stock by $585 million, and the Federal Reserve took no further significant policy actions. There was not a single change of either bill-buying or discount rates, and open-market operations were almost negligible in amount.

FEDERAL RESERVE POLICIES, FEBRUARY 24-JUNE 30, 1932

When the OMPC convened in Washington on February 24, the economy was still under the strong deflationary pressures which had followed September 21. Economic activity and prices were still falling. Member bank reserves had decreased $540 million during this period, while bank borrowings at the Federal Reserve rose $572 million. Bank credit and the money supply were still declining. Short-term interest rates, though down slightly from their peaks, were still nearly double their levels in mid-September 1931. Bond markets were demoralized. The Bank of France was earmarking gold at a rate of $12.5 million a week, and Harrison informed the governors that gold losses would continue and probably become more rapid. The Glass-Steagall Act had not yet been approved by Congress, but Meyer predicted favorable action within the next few days.

After discussing some implications of the new legislation, including both their broadened powers to lend and the use of government securities as collateral for Federal Reserve notes, the governors turned to open-market policy.

192

Harrison explained that no action had been taken under the authorization given the Executive Committee on January 12 to purchase up to $200 million of government securities,

... partly because various elements in the domestic program had developed more slowly than had been anticipated, partly because of gold withdrawals to Europe, and partly because of the limited amount of free gold held by the System .... The important reason for considering action at this time was the continued rapid deflation of bank credit which was a seriously depressing influence on the whole business structure and the price level.[1]

He therefore proposed that the Executive Committee be authorized to purchase up to $250 million of government securities at a rate of approximately $25 million a week. This proposal met a mixed reception. Young and McDougal flatly opposed it, the latter commenting that on general principles he preferred to see the banks borrowing to secure funds. Norris commented that he would approve if he thought all troubles were behind, but he feared more. Several governors questioned the effectiveness of purchases and whether funds put out in this way would relieve the country banks most heavily in debt instead of remaining in the principal financial centers. Meyer and Harrison replied that purchases alone might not do the job, but that they would be effective in conjunction with the overall program adopted in January. They would offset currency hoarding and gold outflows and relieve banks of deflationary pressure. Moreover, by borrowing in the principal financial markets and spending the money throughout the country, through the RFC and otherwise, the Treasury would distribute funds widely. Miller observed that there had never been a safer time to operate boldly and that he would approve even larger purchases than those being discussed. Seay, who in January had opposed purchases, now thought that "the time has come to lay down a barrage all along the line."

   The outcome was that the OMPC approved the recommendation, with Young and McDougal dissenting, but with this proviso:

... It is understood that purchases under this program shall be made after a meeting of the Executive Committee called for the purpose of considering such purchases and that the program shall be subject to review by the Conference at any time on call of the Conference or the Federal Reserve Board.[2]

The Executive Committee approved, with Young and McDougal dissenting again, adding its own condition that purchases should begin only after passage of the Glass-Steagall Act. From that time until the next meeting of the OMPC on April 12, System purchases averaged approximately $25 million a week. (See Table 13-1.) Because of its more favorable free-gold position, New York took a major part of these purchases.

   Before the OMPC meeting on April 12, at least the members of the Federal Reserve Board and the directors and officers of the New York Bank had become convinced that larger and more rapid purchases were required. On

---

[1]Minutes of the OMPC, February 24-25, 1932.

[2]Minutes of the Board of Directors of the Federal Reserve Bank of New York, February 25, 1932.

TABLE 13-1

Changes in Member Bank Reserves and Selected Related Items, March–August 1932

Change during week ending	Reserve Bank Credit Outstanding					Gold stock	Money in circulation	Member Bank Reserve Balances	
	Bills discounted	Bills bought	USG's	All other	Total			Total	Excess (est.)
March 2	− 7	− 17	+ 19	0	− 5	0	− 10	+ 24	+ 25
March 9	− 80	+ 22	+ 25	+ 2	− 31	+ 12	− 38	+ 8	+ 17
March 16	− 87	− 32	+ 57	− 2	− 64	+ 12	− 23	+ 9	+ 11
March 23	+ 5	− 24	− 7	− 10	− 37	+ 7	− 42	+ 8	+ 26
March 30	− 33	− 16	+ 37	− 1	− 10	+ 7	− 41	0	− 3
April 6	+ 2	− 8	+ 13	+ 5	+ 12	+ 8	+ 19	+ 31	+ 29
April 13	+ 6	− 6	+ 100	− 1	+ 87	− 16	− 35	+ 69	+ 65
April 20	− 64	− 3	+ 93	− 11	+ 14	− 3	+ 2	+ 32	− 47
April 27	− 33	− 3	+ 113	+ 8	+ 85	− 9	− 27	+ 135	+ 131
May 4	− 26	+ 1	+ 96	+ 5	+ 74	− 24	+ 51	+ 33	+ 30
May 11	− 35	− 2	+ 98	− 3	+ 60	− 30	+ 18	+ 3	− 8
May 18	− 6	− 2	+ 81	− 3	+ 69	− 39	+ 18	+ 48	+ 50
May 25	+ 6	− 3	+ 59	− 3	+ 60	− 68	+ 38	+ 22	+ 23
June 1	+ 24	− 3	+ 50	+ 4	+ 74	− 100	+ 56	+ 11	+ 84
June 8	+ 7	+ 1	+ 70	+ 1	+ 74	− 128	+ 15	+ 13	+ 9
June 15	− 6	+ 30	+ 47	0	+ 72	− 70	+ 15	+ 11	− 5
June 22	− 8	− 12	+ 38	0	+ 18	+ 8	+ 38	+ 35	− 25
June 29	− 18	+ 10	+ 71	− 5	+ 58	+ 3	+ 144	+ 32	− 29
July 6	+ 30	+ 13	0	+ 19	+ 62	+ 2	+ 126	+ 71	+ 58
July 13	+ 16	− 15	+ 20	− 12	+ 9	+ 10	− 61	+ 52	+ 54
July 20	+ 22	− 10	+ 15	− 6	+ 21	+ 20	+ 21	+ 21	+ 31
July 27	− 13	− 12	+ 5	+ 4	− 16	+ 9	+ 45	+ 36	+ 35
August 3	− 38	+ 1	+ 5	+ 2	− 34	+ 26	+ 38	+ 60	+ 69
August 10	− 35	− 2	+ 5	+ 1	− 31	+ 18	+ 21	+ 50	+ 54
August 17	− 9	+ 3	0	− 1	− 13	+ 41	− 1	+ 18	+ 10
August 24	− 16	− 1	0	− 6	− 23	+ 18	− 22	+ 62	+ 60
August 31	+ 6	− 2	0	+ 4	+ 10	+ 24	+ 8	+ 4	+ 7

Source: Board of Governors of the Federal Reserve System, *Banking and Monetary Statistics,* Washington, D.C., 1943, p. 386.

April 4 the Executive Committee of the New York Board of Directors expressed the opinion that the System should purchase up to $50 million a week. Then on April 7 the New York directors voted to purchase during that statement week $50 million for the bank's own account in addition to the $25 million for the System account. The Board disapproved, but only because it did not wish to jeopardize agreement at the OMPC meeting scheduled for April 12. Several developments seem to have brought this new feeling of urgency. Perhaps one was the desire to prepare against larger gold withdrawals. It was on April 9 that Harrison, after conferring with the Board, wrote to Moret that "... it would be helpful rather than hurtful from the point of view of our position to have the Bank of France gradually repatriate its dollar balances." Congressional pressures also played a role. At the opening of the OMPC meeting on April 12, Meyer

called attention, merely as a matter of information, to the fact that a resolution had been offered in the Senate asking the Federal Reserve Board to state its program for dealing with the situation and to indicate any legislation necessary. Consideraton of this resolution had been postponed. He stated that the Federal Reserve Board felt that the Reserve System could now undertake to do more toward aiding in the recovery than it had yet done, and that he believed the time had come when the System might be expected to use its powers more fully in an effort to stop the credit decline.[3]

Also highly influential were the "inflationary" bills before the Congress. One was the so-called "Goldsborough Bill," which proposed:

Sec. 1. The Federal Reserve Board and the Federal Reserve banks are hereby authorized and directed to take all available steps to raise the present deflated wholesale commodity level of prices as speedily as possible to the level existing before the present deflation, and afterwards to use all available means to maintain such wholesale commodity level of prices ....
Sec. 3. If, in carrying out the purpose of section 1, the gold reserve is deemed by the Federal Reserve Board to be too near to the prescribed minimum, the board is authorized to raise the official price of gold if the other methods already authorized appear inadequate; if, on the other hand, the gold reserve ratio is deemed to be too high the Federal Reserve Board is authorized to lower the official price of gold if the other methods authorized appear inadequate.[4]

Another bill, introduced by Senator Thomas, would have authorized the Reserve banks to issue Federal Reserve bank notes based on a special issue of 2 percent government bonds to supply money for a soldiers' bonus.[5] Representative Patman proposed a little later that a soldiers' bonus be financed by an issue of government fiat money.[6] Such proposals, which created fears

---

[3]Minutes of the OMPC, April 12, 1932.

[4]Hearings before the Subcommittee of the Committee on Banking and Currency, House of Representatives, on H.R. 10517 (For Increasing and Stabilizing the Price Level of Commodities, and for Other Purposes), 72nd Congress, 1st Session (March 1932), p. 1.

[5]Senate Bill 3874, 72nd Congress, 1st Session (March 1, 1932), pp. 4989-4990.

[6]H.R. 7726, 72nd Congress, 1st Session (June 16, 1932), pp. 13140-13141. Patman's bill also provided that the Treasury should deliver an equal value of bonds to the Federal Reserve banks, which the latter would sell as and when directed by the Federal Reserve Board.

abroad, also frightened Federal Reserve officials. The latter unanimously opposed them as "inflationary," and at least some officials thought they might be headed off by more liberal Federal Reserve actions. Senator Thomas was said to have told Harrison that he might not press for congressional action if the System would proceed more vigorously.[7]

It was under such conditions that the OMPC met with the Board on April 12. Miller told the group

that a critical point had been reached in the credit situation, that nearly every other reasonable expedient had been tried and exhausted, but that the full force of Federal Reserve action had not yet been exerted and he believed the time had come to use the resources of the System courageously.[8]

Hamlin agreed with Miller and with Meyer's earlier remarks. Magee added that a rise of agricultural prices was necessary. Secretary Mills called for action, saying that

he believed a great duty now rested on the Federal Reserve System; that Congress and the administration had done all they could in developing remedial action, and yet deterioration was taking place steadily. For a great central banking system to stand by with a 70 percent gold reserve without taking active steps in such a situation was almost inconceivable and almost unforgivable. The resources of the System should be put to work on a scale commensurate with the existing emergency.[9]

Harrison stated that the "only practical program was a dramatic purchase of government securities"; that member banks would cooperate in bringing about a credit expansion, partly because they were so deeply concerned about their depreciated bond accounts. The soldiers' bonus and the state of the federal budget remained as sources of uncertainty, he felt, but the Federal Reserve should not wait until these issues were settled.

Some of the governors were skeptical. Calkins asked whether purchases would lead to large withdrawals of foreign funds; Harrison replied that some funds would be withdrawn, but not enough to be embarrassing. McDougal wondered

whether the Federal Reserve System could retain confidence of the public after inaugurating a policy of this sort, which was in some measure inflationary, particularly since it involved use of government securities as collateral for Federal Reserve notes.[10]

Young was skeptical whether the program would do any good, and cited the 1931 experience as an indication of the futility of purchases. He was unswayed by Meyer's reply that the 1931 program had been negated by the German collapse and Britain's departure from gold and that conditions were now more favorable. In the end, Young was the only governor to vote against the recommendation of the Conference that

---

[7]Milton Friedman and Anna J. Schwartz, *A Monetary History of the United States, 1869-1943*, Princeton University Press, Princeton, N.J., 1963, p. 385.

[8]Minutes of the OMPC, April 12, 1932.

[9]*Ibid.*

[10]*Ibid.*

... the executive committee be authorized to purchase up to $500,000,000 of government securities in addition to the unexpired authority granted at the meeting of the Open Market Policy Conference on February 24, and that those purchases, at least in the initial weeks, should be at a rate as rapid as may be practicable and if possible should amount to $100,000,000 in the current statement week.[11]

The recommendation was put into effect immediately. Within 5 weeks, by May 11, Federal Reserve holdings had increased $500 million. It was decided that New York, whose free gold reserve was large, should absorb at least the first week's purchases, that the next week's purchases would be spread among the Reserve banks in accordance with their free-gold positions, and that beginning with the third and fourth weeks the Board would act promptly on requests to pledge government securities as collateral for Federal Reserve notes. As stated earlier, the Board gave permission for the latter procedure, effective May 5. With this action it again became feasible to allocate securities among the Reserve banks on the "usual allotment ratios based upon each bank's expenses and dividends to System totals" rather than on the basis of free-gold holdings.[12]

Largely because of these Federal Reserve purchases ($500 million of government securities during the 5 weeks ending on May 11), member banks were able to reduce their borrowings at the Federal Reserve by $164 million, to increase their actual reserves by $202 million and to raise their excess reserves from $110 million to $281 million.

At its meeting on May 17 the OMPC voted, with Young and McDougal dissenting,

to authorize the Executive Committee of the OMPC to continue the purchase of Government securities for System account as may seem advisable from week to week but not to exceed an aggregate of $500,000,000 without another meeting of the Open Market Policy Conference.

This recommendation lacked the sense of urgency and affirmative action that had characterized the April 12 recommendation. It gave no mandate to purchase "at a rate as rapid as may be practicable." Instead, it left decisions as to the rate and amounts of purchases within the $500 million limit to the Executive Committee, on which Young, Norris, and McDougal could constitute a majority. The result was a tapering off of purchases. The System did purchase $80 million during the first week, and a total of $416 million during the 6 weeks ending June 29. However, these purchases were insufficient to offset the $612 million drain on member bank reserves resulting from a $394 million decrease of the gold stock and a $218 million increase of currency in circulation. Member bank reserves decreased $110 million. June 29 marked the end of large Federal Reserve purchases; only $50 million were purchased during the remainder of the year, all of these during July and August.

The tapering off and discontinuance of purchases reflected in large part a return of the majority of the governors, including a majority on the Executive Committee of the OMPC, to their former positions relative to open-mar-

---

[11]*Ibid.*

[12]Burgess telegram to all Reserve banks, May 5, 1932.

ket purchases. Young and McDougal had voted against the May 17 authorization, and Norris was usually unsympathetic. Now they pointed to two new developments to support their positions. One was the rise of member bank excess reserves above $200 million and at times above $300 million. Never before had member banks held such large excess reserves for any extended period. These governors thought that the volume was certainly adequate, if not excessive. Another development was the difficulty of acquiring short-term government securities, which led to the purchase of some longer-term bonds. Several of the governors opposed such purchases because of the risk involved, the alleged resulting decrease of the liquidity of the Reserve banks, and the possibility that such bonds could not be sold fast enough when the Federal Reserve wished to reverse its policy. Such fears were premature, to say the least. At their peak in 1932, bonds constituted only $438 million of the Federal Reserve's total holdings of $1,851 million of government securities. Surely, their holdings of more than $1 billion of Treasury bills and certificates maturing within a year were at least adequate to meet any probable need for sales.[13]

Burgess encountered differences of opinion when he telephoned the members of the Executive Committee of the OMPC on May 21 to propose purchases of $50-60 million of government securities during the following week. Black approved immediately. The others agreed that it was wise for the Federal Reserve statement to show some purchases each week, but McDougal thought that they should be very moderate. Norris said that member bank reserve positions should be the guide; he felt it might be well to maintain excess reserves of about $300 million:

There was no object in going beyond that and piling up excess reserves indefinitely.[14]

Young agreed with Norris, adding his view that purchases should be kept as small as possible to make the authority last. They approved purchases of $70 million during the week ending June 8, largely because of gold losses of $100 million during the preceding week and $128 million that week. However, when Burgess called them on June 9, proposing purchases of $50-60 million, he found that the governors had returned to form. Black agreed, but Young, Norris, and McDougal voted for purchases as small as possible. Burgess commented that he had carried them as far as possible by phone and that a meeting of the Executive Committee was now required.[15]

At a meeting held in New York on June 16, with Meyer and Magee of the Board present, the Executive Committee approved these proposals:

1. That until further notice sufficient purchases of government securities should be made to keep excess reserves of member banks at a figure between $250,000,000 and $300,000,000.
2. That the system should continue to show an increase from week to week in

---

[13]Board of Governors of the Federal Reserve System, *Banking and Monetary Statistics*, Washington, D.C., 1943, p. 343.

[14]Burgess memorandum at the Federal Reserve Bank of New York, May 21, 1932.

[15]Burgess memorandum at the Federal Reserve Bank of New York, June 9, 1932.

total holdings of government securities in order to avoid the creation of a feeling that the policy of the system had been changed, but that such increases should be in amounts as small as might be, to preserve these excess reserves, and take care of special conditions arising from week to week.[16]

Though the vote was unanimous, Young noted that he voted affirmatively only to carry out the OMPC decision, not as a representative of his own district opinion. Norris later indicated that the same applied to himself and McDougal.

> You noted the fact that Governor Young's vote was controlled by the determined policy of the Committee rather than as a representation of his own District opinion. Governor McDougal's own view has been consistently against the purchase of governments, and I have "gone along," as I have stated at previous meetings, rather against my own judgment and in deference to the majority opinion. This being the position of the majority of the Committee, I think it is not quite fully reflected in your preliminary draft.[17]

Purchases during the 2 weeks between June 15 and June 29 amounted to $109 million. However, about $42 million of these were made by the Chicago Reserve Bank for its own account to cope with acute banking difficulties and currency withdrawals in that city. Moreover, total purchases in this period were not sufficient of offset currency drains or to prevent excess member bank reserves from falling to $220 million.

In the meantime, Harrison wrote to Meyer on June 23,

> There is increasing difficulty in securing participation in purchases by other Federal Reserve banks.

Boston, Richmond, Kansas City, Dallas, and San Francisco were not participating in purchases during that week; Chicago was hesitant to participate further; Atlanta would not participate in purchases during the coming week; and Martin was having trouble persuading the Executive Committee of his directors to participate while the reserve ratio of the St. Louis Bank was below those at Chicago and Kansas City. Some said their decisions were based on their inadequate reserve positions. This is hardly credible. The reserve ratio for the Reserve banks as a group was then over 58 percent; Richmond's ratio was the lowest at 48.2 percent; at all the other Reserve banks it was above 50 percent.[18]

FEDERAL RESERVE POLICIES, JULY-DECEMBER 1932

As mentioned earlier, the Federal Reserve took few policy actions during this period. There were no changes in discount or bill-buying rates and purchases of government securities totaled only $50 million. The principal factors which enabled member banks to reduce their borrowings from the

---

[16]Minutes of the Executive Committee of the OMPC, June 16, 1932.

[17]Norris letter to Burgess, May 21, 1932.

[18]*Federal Reserve Bulletin*, July 1932, p. 460. The data refer to June 30, 1932.

Federal Reserve by $203 million and to increase their reserves by $448 million during the period from June 29 to December 27 were a $585 million increase in the gold stock and a $146 million increase in Treasury currency outstanding. The latter reflected largely an increase in national bank notes made possible by legislation in July which extended the issue privilege to additional types of Treasury bonds.[19] This legislation was neither requested nor approved by President Hoover or Federal Reserve officials, but the President signed the bill because he wanted the Federal Home Loan Bank Act, to which this provision was attached as a rider.

When the OMPC opened its meeting in Washington on July 14, Meyer, Harrison, and others reviewed recent developments and prospective problems. The RFC was now making many loans to banks and others. Banking and industrial committees had been established in all the Federal Reserve districts, as Secretary Mills had requested in mid-May. These committees were composed of bankers and businessmen, and their principal purposes were to ascertain the extent to which private credit needs were or were not being met, to find out why credit needs were not being met when this was the case, and to arrange for credit when possible. The banking and industrial committees worked closely with both the Reserve banks and the RFC. The governors also discussed operating procedures and problems that they would face if a bill introduced by Glass and still before the Congress should be enacted. This was a bill to authorize the Reserve banks to lend directly, or to participate in loans to, individuals and corporations. It became law on July 21.[20]

Meyer expressed his view that open-market purchases, together with the other measures taken, had been highly useful. In their absence, the large gold losses and currency withdrawals might have had disastrous results, but the purchases not only offset these drains but also enabled members to reduce their borrowings and to accumulate excess reserves, now amounting to about $150 million. He hoped the purchases would continue. Harrison agreed.

He expressed the opinion that, with the removal of the obstacles which have heretofore existed, the System is in the best position it has been during the last few years to test the theory of open market purchases and that he did not believe the policy should be reversed, but should be continued to a point where the excess reserves of the member banks of the System would amount to $250,000,000, the goal originally set. The program, as he saw it, included three major steps; first, concerted action looking toward the discontinuance of bank failures and the restoration of confidence, both of the public and of bankers; second, the continued purchase of Governments by the System with a view to maintaining excess reserves of member banks at around $250,000,000; and, third, more effective action toward commercial credit expansion through the banking and industrial committees which have been organized in the various districts....[21]

---

[19]*Annual Report of the Federal Reserve Board,* 1932, p. 23. This provision was included in the Federal Home Loan Bank Act approved on July 22, 1932. It extended the circulation privilege for 3 years to all Treasury bonds bearing interest not in excess of 3 3/8 percent and made an additional $3 billion of bonds eligible as a basis for national bank notes. However, the limiting provision was that limiting a national bank's note issue to the amount of its paid-in capital.

[20]*Annual Report of the Federal Reserve Board,* 1932, p. 20.

[21]Minutes of the OMPC, July 14, 1932.

Again the reactions of the governors were mixed. McDougal probably repeated the views he had written to Harrison on July 9:

> We are of the opinion that no additional purchases should be made by the System merely for the purpose of increasing the amount of member bank excess reserves. While purchases by the System for the purpose of offsetting gold exports were probably justified, we believe that the additional purchases made were much too large and have resulted in creating abnormally low rates for short-term U.S. Government securities . . . .
> While the passage of the Glass-Steagall Act permitted Federal Reserve banks to pledge Government securities to secure Federal Reserve note issue was necessary for the purpose of meeting export demands for gold, we feel that the further pledge of such securities to create additional member bank reserves is dangerous and if indulged in much farther may raise the question as to the integrity of our Federal Reserve note issue.
> For the reasons stated above, it is our opinion that the System should not increase its purchases of U.S. Government securities and that this bank should not increase the amount of its participation in these purchases.

Some thought the target level of excess reserves should be $150 million rather than $250 million. Also,

> The governors of a number of banks pointed out that with their reserve percentages not far from 50 percent their directors were reluctant to participate much further in open market purchases, particularly unless the operations were a united System undertaking. A number suggested the desirability of a redistribution of government securities to bring about a leveling up in reserve percentages.[22]

However, the governors were unable to agree on a new formula for allocating securities. Meyer warned that there was a tendency in Congress to centralize the System and

> that the open market program offered a test of the capacity of the System to function effectively in its present form.[23]

At the end of its meeting the OMPC recommended

> That the executive committee be authorized to buy Government securities to the extent necessary to maintain excess reserves of member banks at approximately 200 million dollars, total purchases to be limited to the amount previously authorized by the OMPC which is 207 million dollars. For the guidance of the executive committee it was the sense of the Conference that except in unusual or unforeseen circumstances purchases should not exceed 15 million dollars a week, but for the next four weeks should be not less than 5 million dollars a week.

Young, McDougal, and Seay voted against the resolution. Others probably would have joined them except for a fear that a sudden cessation of purchases would bring adverse public reactions and aid the "inflationists" in Congress.

In fact, actual purchases were equal to only the minimum amounts included in the recommendation: $15 million the first week and then $5 million a week for 3 weeks. On August 13, New York recommended to the other members of the Executive Committee of the OMPC that purchases be discontinued

---

[22]*Ibid.*

[23]*Ibid.*

in view of the fact that the program for purchases at a minimum rate of $5,000,000 for four weeks was terminated, and that gold gains and other causes were keeping member excess reserves well in excess of $200,000,000.[24]

This time there was unanimous agreement. No further purchases were made between August 10 and the end of the year. However, continued gold inflows enabled member banks to reduce their borrowings somewhat and to accumulate more than $400 million of excess reserves by the end of September and over $500 million by the end of the year.

The preliminary memorandum presented to the OMPC at its meeting on November 14 pointed to a number of favorable developments since the last meeting on July 14. There was some evidence of a more than seasonal expansion of business activity: gold continued to flow in; the rate of bank failures had decreased, and some currency was returning to the banks; total excess reserves of member banks now exceeded $450 million, and some of these were spreading to smaller centers; liquidation of bank credit seemed to have been checked, and there had been some expansion after excess reserves reached substantial levels. Under such circumstances, none of the governors favored purchases. The only question was whether the System should sell securities, and if so, when and how many. Seay and McDougal voted to allow some of the December maturities to run off, but all the other governors agreed that no sales should be made during the remainder of the year and that another meeting should be held early in January to determine policy in light of conditions at that time.

The "inflationary" sentiment in Congress was a major subject of discussion at the OMPC meeting on January 4. Senator Thomas was asserting that "the shortage of real money in actual circulation is directly responsible for the major part of the present depression," and was urging that the dollar be "cheapened" by decreasing its gold value, by increasing the quantity of money, or both.[25] Senator Borah proposed a reduction in the gold value of the dollar to aid farmers; Senator Bankhead urged a greater monetary role for silver to raise its value; and Senator Wheeler favored remonetization of silver.[26] There were also proposals to issue fiat money and to direct the Federal Reserve to use its powers over credit to raise commodity prices.[27] The governors and members of the Board feared that open-market sales of securities would aid the "inflationists." For example, Meyer

referred to the agitation, especially in Congress, for the adoption of inflationary measures and pointed out that under conditions like these the System must of necessity give due consideration to such factors in reaching a determination as to future policy.[28]

Secretary Mills also

---

[24]Burgess memorandum to Harrison, August 13, 1932.

[25]*The New York Times,* December 4, 1932, p. 1.

[26]*The New York Times,* January 4, 1933, p. 1. See also issue for January 5, p. 29.

[27]*The New York Times,* January 24, 1933, p. 5.

[28]Minutes of the OMPC, January 4, 1933.

reviewed the proposals for inflation which were being made to the Congress and suggested that any slackening in Federal Reserve open market policy might provide an excuse for an unsound inflation bill.[29]

Black

saw no economic reasons for letting maturities run off, and he was greatly impressed by the dangers of unsound inflationary proposals and believed they could only be combatted by the continuance of the present policy of the Federal Reserve System.[30]

Calkins was impressed by neither the political argument nor the power of the System to deal with the "inflationists."

No one at the meeting favored further purchases at that time and no one was opposed in principle to some sales, especially not in view of the expected seasonal return flow of currency. The questions at issue were how many securities to sell and how sales might be made with a minimum of adverse reactions. Meyer observed that

what is most required is assurance as to the continuance of pressure of excess reserves.[31]

Miller agreed and

suggested that the precise amount of excess reserves maintained was an incidental detail, but that the important question was one of policy and direction of movement, and that there might be harm in stopping excess reserves from accumulating.[32]

Harrison

further suggested that any reduction in security holdings should in any event not exceed the return flow of currency, and that the System should not attempt to offset gold imports since that might be interpreted as constituting a policy of sterilization of gold.[33]

Some of the governors favored larger sales. For example, several suggested that all January maturities be allowed to run off, and Seay proposed sales of not less than $200 million.

The resolution finally adopted authorized the Executive Committee

(a) To reduce the System's holdings of short term Treasury bills in order to offset such amount of the return flow of currency as may seem desirable, provided such action does not result in any substantial reductions in existing excess reserves, and

(b) If necessary, to purchase Government securities in sufficient amounts to prevent member bank excess reserves falling below the present general level.

It was informally understood that the resolution should be interpreted as follows:

(a) Treasury bills up to $125 million be allowed to run off in January to the extent that there is a return flow of currency, but not to bring excess reserves below $500 million.

---

[29] *Ibid.*

[30] *Ibid.*

[31] *Ibid.*

[32] *Ibid.*

[33] *Ibid.*

(b) When the resolution refers to present level of excess reserves it means approximately $500 million.

(c) When the resolution refers to the return flow of currency it means the return flow from the December peak just before Christmas.

(d) There would be another meeting of the Conference before any increase in the System holdings of government securities above $1,851,000,000.[34]

Though the resolution was approved unanimously, Seay, McDougal, and Young voted for it only because it was a "step in the right direction" and said that they preferred larger sales and a smaller volume of excess reserves. Meyer congratulated the OMPC on the form of its resolution, stating that its specification in terms of the volume of excess reserves provided "a more scientific basis of action" than did stipulating amounts of securities to be bought or sold.

Between January 4 and the end of the month, the Federal Reserve sold $87 million of government securities, and member bank excess reserves ranged between $573 million and $627 million. However, February brought developments that not only ended Federal Reserve sales but also led to the collapse of the entire commercial banking system. This is the story of the next chapter.

1932 IN PERSPECTIVE

Were the improvements in the reserve positions of member banks between February 24 and the end of 1932 sufficient to relieve the banks of pressure to contract credit and put them under pressures to expand, perhaps even to restore the credit liquidated during the period before February 24? Were the Federal Reserve purchases prior to mid-1932 sufficient to do this? If not, were the further improvements during the second half of the year, largely owing to gold imports, adequate for the purpose? If one looks only at the improvement of reserve positions during this period as a whole he is inclined to answer in the affirmative. (See Table 13-2.) However, one becomes more skeptical on looking at the absolute reserve positions of member banks and comparing these with the reserve positions of the banks before the onset of the financial crisis in September 1931.

Consider first developments between February 24 and June 29, when Federal Reserve purchases virtually ended. (See Columns 2, 3, and 5 of Table 13-2.) As noted earlier, the Federal Reserve contributed $1,060 million during this period by purchasing government securities. About $500 million of these funds were absorbed by the $69 million decrease of Federal Reserve bill holdings and the $430 million decrease of the gold stock. Member banks decreased their borrowings at the Federal Reserve by $365 million and added $156 million ot their reserve balances. Yet at mid-year, when the Federal Reserve terminated its purchases, members still owed the Reserve banks $470 million, while their excess reserves were only $220 million. Thus, their net free reserves were negative by $250 million.

---

[34]*Ibid.*

TABLE 13-2

Member Bank Reserves and Selected Related Items 1931-1932

Federal reserve bank credit	Sept. 16, 1931 (1)	Feb. 24, 1932 (2)	June 29, 1932 (3)	Dec. 28, 1932 (4)	Changes			
					Feb. 24, 1932– June 29, 1932 (5)	June 29, 1932– Dec. 28, 1932 (6)	Feb. 24, 1932– Dec. 28, 1932 (7)	Sept. 16, 1931– Dec. 28, 1932 (8)
Reserve bank credit outstanding								
Bills discounted	263	835	470	267	− 365	− 203	− 568	+ 4
Bills bought	218	133	64	33	− 69	− 31	− 100	− 185
U.S. government securities	742	741	1,801	1,851	+1,060	+ 50	+1,110	+1,109
All Other	56	25	11	17	+ 14	+ 6	− 8	− 39
Total	1,279	1,734	2,346	2,168	+ 612	−178	+ 434	+ 889
Gold Stock	4,729	4,063	3,633	4,218	− 430	+585	+ 155	− 511
Treasury currency outstanding	2,023	2,054	2,057	2,203	+ 3	+146	+ 149	+ 180
Money in circulation	4,801	5,306	5,362	5,400	+ 56	+ 38	+ 94	+ 599
Other items—Total[a]	812	669	640	708	− 29	+ 68	+ 39	− 104
Member bank reserve balances								
Total	2,418	1,878	2,034	2,482	+ 156	+448	+ 604	+ 64
Excess (estimated)	203	27	220	554	+ 193	+334	+ 527	+ 351
Addenda								
Unborrowed reserves	2,155	1,043	1,564	2,215	+ 521	+651	+1,172	+ 60
Net free reserves	− 60	− 808	− 250	287	+ 558	+537	+1,095	+ 347

[a]This includes Treasury cash holdings, Treasury deposits with Federal Reserve banks, nonmember deposits, and other Federal Reserve Accounts.

Source: Board of Governors of the Federal Reserve System, *Banking and Monetary Statistics*, Washington, D.C., 1943, pp. 386-387.

Member bank reserve positions in mid-1932 appear even less expansionary when one compares them with the reserve positions prevailing in mid-September 1931 and remembers that these earlier positions were insufficient to arrest contraction and induce expansion. (See Columns 1 and 3 of Table 13-2.) From mid-September 1931 to mid-1932, member bank borrowings had risen $207 million while total reserves had fallen by $384 million. Thus their unborrowed reserves had decreased by $591 million. Also, their net free reserves were negative by $250 million in mid-1932 as compared with a negative figure of only $60 million in mid-September 1931. One thing is clear: Federal Reserve purchases prior to mid-1932 were insufficient to offset the deterioration of bank reserve positions that had occurred since the onset of the financial crisis.

Member bank reserve positions, however measured, improved markedly during the second half of 1932, thanks largely to $585 million of gold imports and a $146 million increase in national bank notes. Member banks paid off $203 million of their borrowings at the Federal Reserve and increased their reserve balances $448 million, thus increasing their unborrowed reserves by $651 million. By the end of the year their excess reserves had risen to $554 million and their net free reserves were positive by $287 million. Yet there is reason to doubt that the banks as a whole felt under pressure to expand at this time. For one thing, their net free reserves became positive for the first time only in October, and in the last 3 months of the year averaged only about 10 percent of total member bank reserves. It is doubtful that this amount of net free reserves over such a short period would exert much expansionary pressure on a banking system which had been through such trying ordeals and feared more. Moreover, it is worth noting that even at the end of 1932 member bank borrowings were still $4 million larger than they had been in mid-September 1931, and their reserves were only $64 million larger.

Whether or not the banking system as a whole was under pressure to contract further or to expand at the end of 1932, the various classes of banks

TABLE 13-3

Reserve Positions of Member Banks by Classes, December 1932
(monthly averages of daily figures, in millions of dollars)

	All member banks	Central reserve city banks	Reserve city banks	Country banks
Total reserves	2,435	1,369	625	440
Borrowings at Federal Reserve	281	0	63	218
Excess reserves	526	446	44	36
Unborrowed reserves	2,154	1,369	562	222
Net free reserves	+ 245	+ 446	− 19	−182

Source: Board of Governors of the Federal Reserve System, *Banking and Monetary Statistics,* Washington, D.C., 1943, pp. 396-399.

were in widely differing reserve positions. As shown in Table 13-3, member banks as a group had $526 million of excess reserves and were borrowing $281 million in December; thus their net free reserves were positive by $245 million. However, central reserve city banks in New York and Chicago were

TABLE 13-4

Changes in Member Bank Reserve Positions, January 1932–December 1932
(in millions of dollars)

Class of Member Bank	Total reserves (1)	Total reserves plus balances at other domestic banks (2)	Borrowings at the Federal Reserve (3)	Excess reserves (4)	Unborrowed reserves (5)	Net free reserves (6)
All member banks	+456	+1,203	−536	+491	+992	+1,027
Central reserve city banks	+502	+ 684	− 52	+440	+554	+ 492
Reserve city banks	+ 1	+ 486	−311	+ 45	+484	+ 356
Country banks—Total	− 48	+ 32	−173	+ 7	+125	+ 180
Country banks by Federal Reserve district						
Boston	− 4	+ 34	− 24	+ 1	+ 20	+ 25
New York	− 9	+ 20	− 58	+ 1	+ 49	+ 59
Phildelphia	− 5	+ 3	− 19	0	+ 14	+ 19
Cleveland	− 5	− 3	− 11	+ 1	+ 16	+ 11
Richmond	− 1	+ 11	− 17	0	+ 7	+ 18
Atlanta	− 3	0	− 10	+ 2	+ 10	+ 10
Chicago	− 7	− 15	− 17	+ 1	+ 10	+ 19
St. Louis	− 1	+ 3	− 11	+ 2	− 7	+ 12
Minneapolis	− 2	− 6	+ 5	− 1	+ 2	− 3
Kansas City	− 4	− 4	− 2	+ 1	+ 5	+ 1
Dallas	− 1	+ 7	− 6	+ 1	− 4	+ 7
San Francsico	− 5	− 17	− 1	+ 1		0

Source: Computed from various tables in Board of Governors of the Federal Reserve System, *Banking and Monetary Statistics*, Washington, D.C., 1943. All data are monthly averages of daily figures except that balances held at other domestic banks relate to year-end figures.

completely out of debt to the Federal Reserve and held $446 million of excess reserves. In contrast, both reserve city and country members as groups were in negative net free reserve positions. Country banks' excess reserves amounted to only $36 million, and their borrowings, at $218 million, were equal to nearly 50 percent of their total reserves. On these borrowings the banks outside the New York and Chicago districts were paying a discount rate of 3 1/2 percent. In some degree these figures do not portray accurately the relative "potential reserve positions" of the various classes of banks because they take no account of balances held with other banks, at least some of which could be used to repay borrowings or to increase balances at the Federal Reserve. At the end of 1932 these balances held at other domestic banks were $409 million for central reserve city banks, $1,243 million for reserve city banks, and $766 million for country banks. Even after these figures are taken into account, however, it seems likely that many banks, and especially country banks, still felt under pressure to contract rather than expand.

The discussion above related to absolute reserve positions in December 1932. Table 13-4 shows that the improvement in reserve positions between January and December was shared quite unevenly among the various classes of banks. Column 1 indicates that while total member bank reserves rose $456 million, reserves of central reserve city banks rose $502 million, reserves of reserve city banks remained virtually constant, and reserves of country members actually declined $48 million. Country members in every Federal Reserve district suffered net reserve losses. The picture is altered somewhat when changes in balances at other banks, as well as in total reserves, are taken into account, as is done in Column 2. However, the sum of these two balances rose only $32 million for country members while it increased $486 million for reserve city members and $684 million for central reserve city members. Changes in the other measures of reserve positions are also worth noting. (See Table 13-4.)

Why New York and Chicago failed to reduce their discount rates below 2 1/2 percent and the other Reserve banks failed to go below 3 1/2 percent remains a mystery. Perhaps they felt that under the circumstances rate reductions would do no good, a conclusion of doubtful validity in view of the number of banks, and especially of country banks, that continued to be in debt. However, if this was a mistake it was minor as compared with the System's failure to buy many more securities sooner in order to saturate banks with reserves in excess of legal requirements and even in excess of the amounts that banks hungry for liquidity would want to hold.

The decline of bank loans and investments was not reversed or even stopped. However, the rate of decrease was reduced from 9 percent in the first half of 1932 to 3 percent in the second half.

14

The Banking Collapse

Up to March 1933, the Federal Reserve had achieved at least one of the purposes for which the System had been established: It had prevented credit stringencies and financial crises from developing into panics. It had done this at the end of the inflation in the spring of 1920, at the time of the stock-market crash in October 1929, and during the international crisis beginning in September 1931. However, it failed to prevent the collapse of the entire banking system at the beginning of March 1933.

Even as late as the beginning of December 1932, the collapse appeared unlikely. In fact, the banking situation seemed to be improving at that time. Bank failures in 1932 numbered 1,453, considerably fewer than the 2,293 in 1931, and 561 of these had occurred in January and February and another 283 in June and July. Since that time failures had averaged less than 100 a month. Prices of bonds, especially those of the highest grades, had improved somewhat and short-term interest rates had fallen. One important reason for these developments was undoubtedly the improvement of bank reserve positions resulting from Federal Reserve purchases of government securities, from the large gold imports during the latter half of the year, and from some net return of currency to the banks. The RFC was also an important contributor. (See Table 14-1.) During 1932 it authorized loans of $950 million to 5,582 banks and trust companies and actually disbursed $851 million. Of the total authorization, $56 million went to aid the reorganization or liquidation of 535 closed banks. Banks also benefited indirectly from RFC loans to other types of financial institutions and to others, as these borrowers were relieved of pressure to sell their bonds and other assets in the market and were enabled to pay off some of their borrowings from banks. Borrowings from the RFC might have been larger and more helpful if that agency had not been forced to disclose the names of its borrowers.

However, the commercial banking system was basically in a very weak and vulnerable condition. For one thing, the statistics on bank failures understate the extent to which banks failed to meet their liabilities fully and punctually. Various measures short of bank closings were used as early as 1931 and even more extensively in 1932 to prevent or limit deposit withdrawals. One was "depositors' agreements," under which depositors agreed to defer with-

TABLE 14-1

Loans by the Reconstruction Finance Corporation,
February 2-December 31, 1932 (in millions of dollars)

Loans to	Amounts authorized	Amounts advanced	Amounts repaid	Outstanding on Dec. 31
Banks and trust companies	950	851	256	595
Building and loan associations	100	94	10	84
Insurance companies	83	68	6	62
Mortgage loan companies	94	88	11	77
Credit unions	0.5	a	a	0.4
Federal land banks	29	19	a	19
Joint-stock land banks	6	3	a	2
Agricultural credit corporations	4	3	1	2
Regional agricultural credit corporations	7	5	a	5
Livestock credit corporations	13	12	4	8
Railroads (including receivers)	337	284	12	272
Total, Sec. 5 of the Resconstruction	1,624	1,428	300	1,128
Finance Corporation Act	1,624	1,428	300	1,128
Self-liquidating projects	147	16	a	16
Financing of agricultural commodities and livestock	55	1	a	1
Amounts made available for relief and work relief	113	80	a	80
Total, Emergency Relief and Construction Act of 1932	314	97	a	97
Grand Total	1,938	1,525	300	1,225

aLess than $500,000

Source: Board of Governors of the Federal Reserve System, *Federal Reserve Bulletin,* February 1933, p. 66.

drawals of varying percentages of their deposits over periods ranging up to five years. Another was reorganization of banks through waiver or surrender of a part of the depositors' claims. In some cases depositors made outright contributions; more commonly assets were placed in a trust account with the hope that they could be liquidated later.[1] In some cases in which the law permitted it, individual banks or groups of banks limited the percentages of deposits that could be withdrawn. A number of municipalities declared city-wide bank holidays, and at the beginning of November Nevada declared a state-wide bank holiday. There can be no doubt that in the absence of such measures bank closings would have been more numerous in 1932. In January and February 1933 a number of additional states enacted laws permitting such measures and in effect authorizing banking moratoria.

Moreover, the capital of many banks had been seriously impaired and even wiped out by the decline in the value of bank assets. The Comptroller of the Currency and other bank supervisory authorities might avoid closing banks by appraising their assets at "intrinsic values" considerably above their current market prices, but this device provided no basic solution. Though prices of the

---

[1]Board of Governors of the Federal Reserve System, *Federal Reserve Bulletin,* December 1937, p. 1206.

highest-grade bonds rose somewhat in the latter part of 1932, the bond accounts of most banks remained seriously depreciated. In December the average prices of corporate bonds were about 30 percent below their levels in September 1929 and in mid-1931.[2] Many other banks assets for which there were no published price quotations could have been sold, if at all, only at great discounts from their face values. The farm mortgage situation was still deteriorating, with legal or *de facto* moratoria spreading widely. Millions of mortgages on urban homes were delinquent on interest or principal or both, and millions of business firms were in no position to pay their debts. The gravity of this situation was recognized at a meeting of Federal Reserve officials in mid-November 1932. They conceded the importance of liquidating closed banks and of making funds available to depositors, but concluded that "the solvency and health of *existing* institutions is of paramount importance."[3] The availability of loans to banks had been increased by the establishment of the RFC and the broadening of Federal Reserve lending powers, but many banks required new capital, which no government agency was then authorized to supply. Moreover, some banks lacked good collateral for borrowing. An official of the New York Reserve Bank told his directors in December that

with due allowance for bond depreciation and bad and doubtful loans, many banks have reached the point where they are pledging, as security for loans, practically all of their available collateral, and stated that, in some cases, if further loans were to be made by this bank they would have to be on a less well secured basis than had been our general practice.[4]

Thus the banking system entered 1933 with both liquidity and solvency problems. In this respect the banking situation prior to the panic of 1933 differed from those preceding many of the crises and panics of the 19th and early 20th centuries. These earlier crises and panics had come at the end of a period of prosperity or early in a recession, when most of the debtors to the banks were creditworthy, and bank assets had not yet depreciated significantly. Some banks might have impaired their capital, but in general the banks' problem was only one of inadequate liquidity. In this sense the banks were "basically sound." In 1933, by contrast, the banks faced an acute liquidity problem and great numbers of them were "basically unsound." Depositors had ample reason to lose confidence in them.

The political situation in the first months of 1933 made it virtually impossible to develop a governmental program to deal with the banking crisis. This was the interregnum between Roosevelt's election in November and his inauguration in March. Hoover would have found it difficult to exercise effec-

[2]*Standard Statistics Base Book*, January 1932, pp. 128-132, and *Statistical Bulletin*, April 1934, pp. 16-19. This source indicates that in December 1932 the average market price of a $100 bond was $63.20 for 20 industrial bonds, $61.20 for 20 railroad bonds, $82.20 for 20 public utility bonds, and $68.30 for the 60 bonds combined.

[3]Minutes of the Federal Reserve Board, December 5, 1932. This was the conclusion of a conference of Federal Reserve agents held in Washington on November 16.

[4]Minutes of the Board of Directors of the Federal Reserve Bank of New York, December 29, 1932.

tive leadership even if he had tried harder to do so. He had been defeated by a landslide; he faced a Democratic majority in the House of Representatives and a Republican majority of only one in the Senate. Moreover the Congress itself would adjourn within a few weeks, and many of the incumbent Congressmen had been defeated. Hoover felt that he should take no important action without the concurrence of the incoming President, but Roosevelt took the position that while Hoover was President he should act on his own responsibility. Neither on this nor on other important issues could the two men cooperate effectively. The result was inaction.

Widespread discussion about the possibility of "inflationary" policies under the incoming administration added to the growing confusion and uneasiness. Both within and outside Congress there were many proposals for monetary expansion: to "do something for silver" by remonetizing it, by large government purchases, and by accepting it in payment of war debts; to issue scrip at local, state, or national levels; to issue fiat money; to decrease the gold value of the dollar; to direct the Federal Reserve to raise commodity prices; and so on. There were also many proposals to increase federal expenditures. Senator Thomas even called upon Wall Street to demand inflation, claiming that only that group "can give this order and set in motion the machinery which will pull us out of the mire."[5] Senator Borah created quite a stir both at home and abroad when he asserted that it would be impossible to balance the federal budget under existing conditions.[6] Such proposals, which were widely reported and discussed, did not go unchallenged. Bankers, businessmen, editors, and many others leaped into the fray, demanding that all these dangerous and unsound inflationary schemes be rejected and that the budget be balanced at all costs. Hoover was convinced that the current deterioration of economic and banking conditions resulted solely from such proposals and joined others in calling upon Roosevelt to disavow them and set fears at rest. He did this first in a letter to Roosevelt on February 17. Later, in a letter to Senator Simeon Fess on February 21, he stated:

In the interest of every man, woman and child, the President-elect has, during the past week, been urged by the saner leaders of his own party, such as Senator Glass and others, by myself and by Democratic bankers and economists whom he had called on for advice, to stop the conflagration before it becomes uncontrollable, by announcing firmly and at once that (a) the budget will be balanced even if it means increased taxation; (b) new projects will be so restricted that government bond issues will not in any way endanger the stability of government finances; (c) there will be no inflation or tampering with the currency; to which some have added that as the Democratic party is coming in with an overwhelming majority in both houses, there can be no excuse for abandonment of Constitutional process.[7]

---

[5]*The New York Times,* February 7, 1933, p. 27.

[6]*The New York Times,* January 24, 1933, p. 27.

[7]William Starr Myers and Walter H. Newton, *The Hoover Administration: A Documented Narrative,* Scribners, New York, 1936, pp. 353-354. The Hoover letter to Roosevelt on February 17 appears on pp. 338-340.

On that same day Senator Fess publicly called upon Roosevelt to disavow any intention of "tampering with sound money."[8]

Replying to Hoover's letter of February 17, Roosevelt made it clear that he disagreed with the President's diagnosis of the causes of the worsening banking situation.

I am equally concerned with you in regard to the gravity of the present banking situation—but my thought is that it is so very deap-seated that the fire is bound to spread in spite of anything that is done by way of mere statements. The real trouble is that on present values very few financial institutions anywhere in the country are actually able to pay off their deposits in full, and the knowledge of this fact is widely held. Bankers with the narrower viewpoint have urged me to make a general statement, but even they seriously doubt if it would have a definite effect.

I had hoped to have Senator Glass' acceptance of the Treasury post—but he had definitely said no this afternoon—I am asking Mr. Woodin tomorrow—if he accepts I propose to announce it tommorrow together with Senator Hull for the State Department. These announcements may have some effect on the banking situation, but frankly I doubt if anything short of a fairly general withdrawal of deposits can be prevented now . . . .[9]

Roosevelt adamantly refused to make any public statement on the situation or on his intentions, and his very refusal tended to confirm fears.

Thus distrust of the dollar was added to distrust of the banks. Such was the general background of the banking panic of 1933. Let us now look at some of the events leading up to it.

DEVELOPMENT OF THE PANIC

The rate of bank failures began to rise again in the latter part of December 1932. Failures in that month were 161, followed by 236 in January. These included some large banks; deposits in banks that failed during these 2 months totaled over $200 million. Currency outside banks declined less than seasonally during the first two week in January and then began to rise contraseasonally. Several cities declared local bank holidays or authorized local banks to limit withdrawals, and on January 20 Iowa authorized banks in that state to restrict withdrawals. Gold imports, which had been almost continuous since mid-1932, ceased in mid-January; gold exports then began, though they maintained a low rate until late February. (See Table 14-2.)

The first statewide holiday, aside from that declared in Nevada at the end of October, came in Louisana on February 4, when the Governor declared a one-day holiday to give one of the largest banks in New Orleans time to complete arrangements for an RFC loan. Not wishing to reveal the real reason for his action, he first thought of declaring a holiday in honor of the great pirate, Jean Lafitte, but finally settled on celebrating the anniversary of

---

[8]*The New York Times*, February 22, 1933.

[9]Myers and Newton, *op. cit.,* p. 345. When this letter was written is unclear. It was delivered to Hoover on March 1, but in a covering note Roosevelt stated that it had been written a week earlier but was not sent because a secretary had assumed that it was only a draft of a letter.

TABLE 14-2

Changes in Member Bank Reserves and Selected Related Items,
January–March 1933 (in millions of dollars)

Changes during week ending:	Reserve Bank Credit Outstanding					Gold stock	Money in circulation	Other factors	Member Bank Reserve Balances	
	Bills discounted	Bills bought	USG's	All other	Total				Total	Excess (est.)
Jan. 4	− 16	0	0	+12	− 5	+ 19	− 17	− 2	+ 32	+ 28
Jan. 11	− 3	− 1	− 39	−16	− 57	+ 25	− 81	−12	+ 60	+ 45
Jan. 18	+ 1	0	− 34	− 4	− 38	+ 17	+ 13	− 5	− 29	− 18
Jan. 25	+ 16	− 1	− 15	− 2	− 3	− 10	+ 9	+13	− 32	− 36
Feb. 1	+ 4	0	+ 1	0	+ 3	− 8	+ 41	+29	− 75	− 74
Feb. 8	− 16	0	+ 20	+10	+ 15	− 13	+ 53	−32	− 19	+ 2
Feb. 15	+ 33	0	+ 25	− 7	+ 51	− 24	+ 149	+63	−183	−161
Feb. 22	+ 41	+149	+ 25	0	+ 215	− 51	+ 134	− 1	+ 35	+ 61
Mar. 1	+ 385	+204	+ 2	− 6	+ 585	−117	+ 731	−32	−233	−129
Mar. 8	+ 702	+ 33	+ 45	−72	+ 708	−100	+ 819	+52	−262	−143
Change during:										
January	+ 39	− 2	− 92	−14	− 68	+ 40	− 30	+65	− 63	− 69
February	+ 308	+301	+103	+ 2	+ 717	−173	+ 900	−51	+305	−190
Change:										
Jan. 18–Mar. 1	+ 463	+352	+ 58	− 5	+ 868	−223	+1,117	+35	−507	−337
Jan. 18–Mar. 8	+1,165	+385	+103	−77	+1,576	−323	+1,936	+87	−769	−480

Source: Board of Governors of the Federal Reserve System, *Banking and Monetary Statistics*, Washington, D.C., 1943, p. 387.

America's severance of diplomatic relations with Germany.[10] Acute banking difficulties in Detroit led the Governor of Michigan to proclaim, on February 14, an eight-day statewide banking holiday, later extended into March. Troubles now spread like wildfire. Though the Michigan holiday stopped withdrawals in that state, it created problems elsewhere. Currency hoarding rose, funds were withdrawn from banks in other states to send to Michigan or to meet payments that would otherwise have been met from deposits in Michigan banks, deposits were shifted from weaker to stronger banks, and bankers drew down their interbank deposits. New York City banks alone lost $520 million of interbank deposits in the following two weeks, bringing their total losses since February 1 to $757 million.

Largely because of banking troubles in Baltimore, the Governor of Maryland declared a statewide holiday on February 25. About the same time Indiana, Arkansas, and Ohio authorized restrictions on withdrawals, and still more states enacted laws permitting restriction on withdrawals or readjusting the liabilities of banks without establishing receiverships. It was on this date, February 25, that the Congress by joint resolution authorized the Comptroller of the Currency to exercise with respect to national banks the same powers given to state officials with respect to state-chartered banks. By this time withdrawals were restricted in many states that had not yet declared holidays, and restrictions spread rapidly during the following days. Bank holidays were declared on March 1 by Alabama, Kentucky, Tennessee, and Nevada, on March 2 by six more states, and on March 3 by seven more.

In the meantime, Washington viewed the situation with growing concern but took no action to stop the closings, to restrict withdrawals, or to close the banks. Hoover wrote to the Federal Reserve Board on February 22, stating in part,

I should like to be advised by the Board as to whether the Board considers that the situation is one that has reached a public danger and whether the Board considers any measures should be undertaken at this juncture and especially what, if any, further authority should be obtained.[11]

The Board's reply on February 25 was unhelpful. Essentially, it stated only that the Board was keeping in close touch with the situation, that it approved the powers given to the Comptroller of the Currency by the joint congressional resolution, and that

at the moment the Board does not desire to make any specific proposals for additional measures or authority but it will continue to give all aspects of the situation its most careful attention.[12]

Hoover wrote to the Board again on February 28.

Since my letter of a few days ago the banking situation had obviously become one of even greater gravity. I naturally wish to be properly advised as to such measures as can

---

[10]*The New York Times*, February 12, 1933, p. E1.

[11]Myers and Newton, *op. cit.*, p. 355.

[12]*Ibid.*, p. 357.

be taken to prevent the hardships to millions of people which are now going on. Although the Board is not the technical adviser of the President, yet it appears to me that in the larger sense it should be prepared to advise me as to the measures necessary for the protection of the banking and currency system in times of emergency. I would, therefore, be glad to know whether the Board considers it desirable:

    (a) To establish some form of Federal guarantee of banking deposits; or

    (b) To establish clearing house systems in the affected areas; or

    (c) To allow the situation to drift along under the sporadic State and community solutions now in progress.[13]

In its reply on March 2 the Board opposed federal guarantee of bank deposits, as it had done when a bill for this purpose was before the Congress in the spring of 1932. It also stated that the issuance of clearing-house certificates or other substitutes for cash was a matter for banks in the various communities to decide and that the Federal Reserve, the Finance Department of the United States Chamber of Commerce, and others were providing interested communities with information concerning mechanics and procedures. In effect, the Board provided no answer to Hoover's third question. It replied:

All sorts of proposals and possibilities for dealing with the general situation with which we are confronted have been and are being canvassed and discussed, but so far no additional measures or authority have developed in concrete form, which at the moment, the Board feels it would be justified in urging.[14]

This letter was apparently written early in the day of March 2. A rapid deterioration of the situation during the day goaded the Board into action. Late in the day a member of the Board called upon the President to tell him that the Board was holding a special meeting at 8 o'clock that evening and that it would like to know whether the President, under the authority of the Trading with the Enemy Act which became law during World War I, would declare a general banking holiday to run for at least 36 hours until Roosevelt's inauguration. Hoover replied that evening, saying that he would like the Board's advice as to the use of his authority under the Trading with the Enemy Act "for the purpose of limiting the use of coin and currency to necessary purposes."[15] At their meeting that evening, members of the Board agreed unanimously that such a proclamation would be inadequate and that the President should declare a national banking holiday to become effective the next morning, Friday, March 3, and to extend through Monday, March 6. However, no action was taken. Whether or not the Trading with the Enemy Act provided an adequate legal basis for such a proclamation became a moot question. The Board's counsel said it did, but Hoover and his aides were doubtful and feared serious consequences if a proclamation were issued and later declared to be illegal. Hoover refused to act without Roosevelt's explicit approval, which was not forthcoming.

    Friday, March 3 brought more confusion and frustration. Further attempts during the day to obtain agreement between Hoover and Roosevelt

---

[13]*Ibid.*, p. 359.

[14]*Ibid.*, p. 363.

[15]*Ibid.*, p. 364.

proved futile. The Board met almost all day and far into the night. At the same time, the governors of New York, Illinois, and several other states were considering statewide holidays. In New York, and apparently also in some other states, bankers were unwilling to take the onus of asking the Governor to act, though they would not oppose a holiday declared by the Governor on his own initiative.

Meyer wrote to Hoover just after midnight, urging the declaration of a national holiday to become effective that morning, March 4. Hoover still refused to act without Roosevelt's concurrence, which the latter still refused to give. Hoover partisans claim that Roosevelt opposed such a proclamation; Roosevelt partisans claim that he did not oppose it but merely took the position that the matter was still Hoover's responsibility. When informed in the small hours of the morning that no action would be taken in Washington, Governor Lehman of New York declared a statewide banking holiday. Similar actions were taken in Illinois, Massachusetts, New Jersey, and Pennsylvania. Thus on the morning of Roosevelt's inauguration the banking collapse was almost complete; virtually every bank in the country was closed or operating only under restrictions. One of the first official acts of the new President was to issue an executive order proclaiming a national bank holiday to become effective on Monday, March 6, and to extend through Thursday, March 9. This order prohibited not only currency withdrawals, but also other banking transactions and all dealings in gold, silver, and foreign exchange. The banking system, including the Federal Reserve banks, was inoperative and the gold standard suspended, at least temporarily.

The drain on the monetary and banking system during the crisis had been huge, especially during the last two weeks before the collapse. (See Table 14-2, above.) Between mid-January and the collapse, currency in circulation rose $1,936 million and the nation's gold stock fell $323 million.[16] These items drained off $2,259 million of member bank reserves, an amount only $286 million less than the total amount of member bank reserves in mid-January. Domestic withdrawals during February included only $92 million in gold coin and $58 million in gold certificates, but such withdrawals became somewhat more rapid during the first 3 days of March. The reserves of the Federal Reserve banks fell about $700 million. Only 150 banks failed during February. However, failures would undoubtedly have been much more numerous and both domestic and foreign withdrawals very much larger in the absence of bank holidays and other restrictions on withdrawals.

FEDERAL RESERVE POLICIES IN THE CRISIS

At its meeting on January 4 the OMPC had authorized its Executive Committee to sell government securities in order to offset the return flow of currency if this would not reduce member bank excess reserves below $500

---

[16]These data relate to changes between January 18 and March 8. Since the entire banking system was closed from March 4 through March 9, it is assumed that the data for March 8 are approximately the same as they were on the eve of the collapse.

million. It was also authorized to buy securities as required to maintain this level of excess reserves, but it was forbidden to raise total System holdings above the prevailing level of $1,851 million without another meeting of the Conference. Acting under these instructions, the Executive Committee sold $88 million during the next 3 weeks. At the end of this period, on January 25, member banks excess reserves stood at $573 million. Then, primarily because of currency drains and gold losses, they began to decline, slowly at first and then more rapidly. Under these circumstances the Executive Committee discontinued its sales and actually bought $45 million during the 2 weeks ending February 15. Member bank excess reserves were down to $340 million on this date.

The Detroit banking crisis and the Michigan bank holiday on February 14 brought a rapid worsening of the situation. Currency in circulation rose $134 million during the week ending February 22, following an increase of $149 million during the preceding week, and the gold stock declined $51 million. There were also very large shifts of deposits within the banking system. Weekly reporting member banks in New York City alone lost $242 million of interbank deposits during this week and another $278 million in the following week. The Executive Committee purchased $25 million of government securities during the week ending February 22. This raised total system holdings to $1,834 million, only $17 million below the total authorized by the OMPC at its meeting on January 4.

The directors of the New York Bank met on February 16 to consider what might be done in the face of the deteriorating situation. Harrison told them that it would be "difficult if not impossible to hold a meeting of the System Open-Market Policy Conference at this time."[17] He probably meant both that the governors would be unwilling to leave their banks under the circumstances and that they would refuse to authorize further purchases. On the latter, at least, he was probably right. He knew that Young had voted against the purchases being made that week; that McDougal also voted against these purchases, stating that his directors refused to participate; that Calkins was also opposed; and that several of the other governors were becoming concerned about the reserve positions of their banks. The 62.6 reserve percentage on February 22 for the Reserve banks as a group would not appear to justify concern. However, reserve percentages varied widely among the Reserve banks. For example, at the end of January they ranged from 78.7 percent at Chicago and 75.9 percent at Boston to 48.3 percent at Dallas and 51.6 percent at Minneapolis. These could, of course, be adjusted by transfers of other assets among the Reserve banks or by rediscounting by some Reserve banks for others. However, some governors were reluctant to cooperate, as we shall see later.

The outcome of the New York meeting on February 16 was a decision to meet the situation at least in part through bill purchases. New York proposed, and the Board approved immediately, a reduction of the lowest bill-buying rate from 1 to one-half of 1 percent. This action, together with

---

[17]Minutes of the Board of Directors of the Federal Reserve Bank of New York, February 16, 1933.

mounting pressures on the market, brought large increases in the System's bill holdings. These rose from only $31 million in mid-February to $180 million on February 22, to $384 million on March 1, and to $417 million by the time the banking system collapsed. The last offerings to the Federal Reserve came despite increases of its bill-buying rate to 1 percent on February 27, to 1 1/2 percent on March 1, to 2 percent on March 2, and to 3 1/4 percent on March 3. After February 22 there were no further purchases of government securities until after March 1, when New York purchased $45 million for its own account.

By March 1 the situation was becoming desperate. Since mid-January member banks had lost $507 million, or about 20 percent of their reserves, despite the fact that they had increased their borrowings at the Federal Reserve by $463 million. Drains on New York City banks were especially heavy, largely because of gold exports, losses of interbank and other deposits, and currency withdrawals. In January these banks had about $300 million of excess reserves and were out of debt to the Federal Reserve; now most of them had lost their excess reserves and were borrowing heavily. Such drains and shifts also created reserve problems for the Reserve banks. Since early February these banks as a group had lost about $400 million of reserves. These losses, together with the large increase in Federal Reserve notes, lowered their reserve percentage from about 67 to 54.6. (See Table 14-3.) There were also large shifts of reserves among the Reserve banks. New York was the heaviest loser. Reserve banks that did not at this time participate in the System's purchases of bills because of their reserve positions included not only New York but also Philadelphia, Cleveland, Richmond, Atlanta, Kansas City, and Dallas. By the end of February, New York was drawing reserve funds from the other Reserve banks. On February 28, March 1, and March 2, New York sold at least $155 million of bills and government securities to the other Reserve banks, of which $10 million were sold to Boston and $145

TABLE 14-3

The Reserve Positions of the Federal Reserve Banks,
January–March 1933 (amounts in millions)

Date	Deposits (1)	Federal Reserve notes in circulation (2)	Total deposits plus Federal Reserve notes (3)	Total reserves (4)	Reserve percentage (4) ÷ (3) (5)
January 4	$2,587	$2,738	$5,325	$3,436	64.5%
January 11	2,644	2,687	5,331	3,509	65.8
January 18	2,608	2,697	5,305	3,522	66.4
January 25	2,587	2,706	5,293	3,547	67.0
February 1	2,540	2,730	5,270	3,535	67.1
February 8	2,500	2,773	5,273	3,522	66.8
February 15	2,376	2,891	5,267	3,461	65.7
February 22	2,399	3,000	5,399	3,378	62.6
March 1	2,157	3,580	5,737	3,134	54.6
March 8	1,951	4,215	6,166	2,857	46.3

Source: Board of Governors of the Federal Reserve System, *Annual Report of the Federal Reserve Board,* Washington, D.C., 1933, p. 97.

million to Chicago. The latter took these only reluctantly, and refused the next day to take any more.

New York and Chicago raised their discount rates from 2 1/2 to 3 1/2 percent on March 2. Officials could hardly have expected that such rate increases would, under the circumstances, have any appreciable effect on either the domestic or the foreign drain. They probably raised rates because this was the traditional thing for a central bank to do when it was concerned about its reserve position, or to adjust official rates to the rapidly rising market rates, or for both reasons.

March 3 was a frantic day at the Federal Reserve Bank of New York as well as in Washington. Its directors convened for a special meeting at 4 o'clock that afternoon and adjourned only at 2:40 the next morning. Harrison had nothing but bad news for them. The dollar was now under heavy selling pressure in exchange markets, and especially in Paris. There was an arrangement under which the Guaranty Trust Company of New York supported the dollar in Paris. Now, however, this bank found itself the only large buyer in that market and was no longer willing to carry the burden alone. It had asked the advice of the New York Reserve Bank on the possibility of forming a syndicate of New York banks to carry out a supporting operation. Harrison commented that failure to maintain the market for dollars would result in a severe depreciation of the dollar exchange rate and "would affect adversely our continued adherence to the gold standard."[18] However, he

said that this request presented an awkward situation because, while it would be undesirable for us to form such a syndicate of banks, to refuse to do so is almost the equivalent of saying that the dollar is no longer to be supported in Paris and almost means announcing we may go off the gold standard tomorrow morning.[19]

In the end, the Guaranty Trust was told it should sound out other New York City banks on the syndicate idea. It did so, but they refused to participate.

The reserve position of the New York Reserve Bank on the afternoon of March 3 was deplorable. Its actual reserve percentage was only 24, and it needed about $250 million from the other Reserve banks to meet its reserve requirements. Chicago definitely refused to purchase more bills and government securities from the New York Bank's account, and the Federal Reserve Board was not yet willing to bring pressure on it to make such purchases or to order it to rediscount for New York. Harrison informed his directors that he had told both Meyer and Secretary Mills that it was imperative that they take at least one of the three following steps that night:

    a. Declaration of a national holiday for Saturday, March 4 and Monday, March 6.
    b. Suspension of specie payments.
    c. Suspension of Federal Reserve reserve requirements.[20]

He believed that the last action should not be taken without one of the other

---

[18]Minutes of the Board of Directors of the Federal Reserve Bank of New York, March 3, 1933.

[19]*Ibid.*

[20]*Ibid.*

two, because it alone could not prevent large losses of gold and withdrawals of currency from the banks. The directors then adopted a resolution requesting the Federal Reserve Board to urge the President to declare a nationwide bank holiday for Saturday, March 4 and Monday, March 6. This was telephoned immediately to Meyer and Secretary Mills. The Board would probably have arrived at the same decision without this advice.

Though the New York directors learned of it only during their meeting, the Board had already suspended reserve requirements for all the Reserve banks for a period of 30 days. When their meeting was over the directors still did not know whether a national holiday would be declared. Harrison then went to a meeting with Governor Lehman and learned that the federal government would not act. The governors of New York and several other states did. The result was in effect a nationwide holiday on a state-by-state basis.

The winds of crisis that had developed slowly during the first half of February had gained velocity after the Michigan difficulties and became a hurricane in the first 3 days of March. A total of $1,886 million of currency was withdrawn from the banks between February 1 and March 4. (See Table 14-4.) Of this amount, $202 million was withdrawn in the first half of

TABLE 14-4

Changes of Currency in Circulation and the Monetary Gold Stock Between February 1 and March 4, 1933 (in millions of dollars)

Change during period	Currency in circulation	Monetary gold stock
February 1-15	+ 202	− 37
February 15-28	+ 691	−131
February 28-March 4	+ 993	−137
Total change, February 1-March 4	+1,886	−305

Source: Computed from data in Board of Governors of the Federal Reserve System, *Banking and Monetary Statistics,* Washington, D.C., 1943, pp. 376 and 387. This table assumes that the published data for March 8 also reflect conditions on March 4.

February and $691 million in the latter half. Withdrawals during the first 3 days of March were equal to all those during the preceding 4 weeks. Much the same was true of decreases in the nation's gold stock. Total losses in this period were $305 million. Of these, $37 million came in the first half of February, $131 million in the second half, and $137 million in the first 3 days of March. Thus by March 3 the banking system was doomed; it would have to close either through official holidays or sheer inability to meet withdrawals.

CONCLUSION

On reviewing events during the five weeks preceding the banking collapse, one is not inclined to award medals for outstanding performance to many officials in either the federal government or the Federal Reserve. Hoover deserves none for imaginative leadership or courageous action in the face of crisis. Roosevelt merits none for cooperation and helpfulness. The Federal Reserve Board deserves none for effective leadership within the System, or for devising effective methods or programs, or for its attitude toward a federal guarantee of bank deposits, or for responding helpfully to the President's requests for advice. Most of the governors of the Reserve banks merit none because of their opposition to purchases of government securities, and at least one is disqualified by the reluctance of his bank to make its resources available at the point of greatest need within the System.

Yet before pronouncing final harsh judgments, one should think of alternatives and consider at least two difficult questions: "Given the conditions that had developed by January 1933, could the panic have been averted?" "Even if the closing of the banking system could have been averted, would it have been in the long-run national interest to do so?"

The answer to the first question turns in part on one's diagnosis of the causes of the banking collapse and gold withdrawals. Hoover was surely wrong in contending that the banks were basically sound and that all difficulties stemmed from current "inflationary" proposals, rumors that Roosevelt intended to "tinker with the currency" and to tolerate budget deficits, and Roosevelt's refusal to issue reassuring statements. As already noted, great numbers of banks were "fundamentally unsound," in the sense that their net worth would have been wiped out or at least seriously impaired if their bonds and other earning assets have been valued at the prices they would have commanded in the market. Yet the question remains whether or not the panic resulted in part from "fears of inflation."

Here a distinction must be made between "fear of banks"—fear that the banks would be unable to meet their obligations in some sort of currency—and "fear of the dollar"—fear that the dollar would depreciate in terms of gold, or its purchasing power, or both. Logically it would seem that "fear of inflation" should not itself lead to withdrawals of currency other than gold coin or gold certificates from the banks or induce depositors to shift funds from one bank to another. If the banks were expected to pay depositors promptly and in full, deposits would depreciate no more than other nongold moneys in terms of gold or purchasing power. However, it is not clear that most depositors were thinking "logically" at that time. Irrational fears of budget deficits and "inflation" were widespread in conservative circles, and many may have come to the conclusion that such policies would weaken the banking system. In any case, it is interesting to note that by far the larger part of currency withdrawals from the banks was in forms other than gold coins and gold certificates. For example, while total currency withdrawals during February amounted to $893 million, gold coin in circulation rose only $92 million and gold certificates only $48 million.[21] There were, however, large withdrawals of gold coin and gold certificates during the first 3 days of March. These data suggest that, at least until the late stages of the panic, the problem was primarily "fear of the banks" rather than "fear of the dollar." Moreover, some part of the gold withdrawals probably reflected "fear of the

---

[21]Board of Governors of the Federal Reserve System, *Banking and Monetary Statistics*, Washington, D.C., 1943, p. 412.

banks." Gold withdrawals had occured during banking panics in the past, even when there was no talk of "inflationary" policies. Americans who decided to withdraw currency from banks could at little or no extra cost take it in the form of gold coin or gold certificates. It is also probably true that some foreigners withdrew their funds because they feared that deposits in American banks would be lost or frozen and that investments here would depreciate in terms of dollars. It should be remembered in this connection that both stock and bond prices fell sharply in this period.

What would have been the effects if Roosevelt had stated strongly and unequivocally that he would indeed balance the budget, maintain the gold value of the dollar, and veto "inflationary" measures? For reasons already given, I believe that such a statement would not have stopped, or even have decreased significantly, either currency withdrawals from the banks or shifts of deposits within the banking system. It would probably have reduced somewhat gold exports and domestic withdrawals of gold coins and gold certificates, but it would not have stopped them. For one thing, as already indicated, at least some of these drains resulted from "fear of the banks." Moreover, such reassuring statements might not have been credible, especially in view of the nation's experience with the repeated reassuring statements of the outgoing administration. In view of the mounting pressures for some sort of expansionary financial measures both in and outside the Congress, some probably doubted that Roosevelt could have stopped such measures even if he wished to do so. It is even possible that such a statement, issued under crisis conditions, would have generated more fears than it allayed.

Because of such difficulties of diagnosis it is virtually impossible either to say with certainty whether, given the conditions that had been generated by the end of January, a banking collapse could have been averted, or to state the minimun ingredients of an effective program for this purpose. I am inclined to believe that the banks could have been kept open, with or without reassuring statements by Roosevelt, if the Federal Reserve had used all its powers to this end, buying very large amounts of government securities, purchasing bills freely at low interest rates, and lending freely even on questionable bank assets at low discount rates. However, this is conjecture.

This leads to the second question, no easier to answer: "Given conditions as they had developed by February 1933, would it have been in the nation's long-run interest to avert a closing of the banking system?" This, in turn, raises other questions. "What are the costs and benefits to be compared?" "How much different would the monetary and banking policies of the incoming administration have been if the banks had not been closed?" "Does one approve or disapprove of the different policies that would have resulted if the banks had remained open?" These questions are so conjectural, and their answers turn so much on analysis and evaluation of both the policies actually followed by the Roosevelt administration and the ones that would otherwise have been followed, that I offer no measured judgments. I do, however, offer the opinion that by February 1933 the banking system had deteriorated so badly that it could not perform the banking functions necessary to economic recovery. It could not command the confidence of depositors, and it would not assume the risks involved in supplying the amounts of money and both the amounts and types of bank credit required to finance the increases of demand needed for a recovery of production and employment. Merely to avoid bank closings was not enough; both the banks and the attitudes toward them required rehabilitation. If the banking collapse was necessary to clear the way for this process it was worth its great cost. In any case, the greater tragedy was not that the federal government and the Federal Reserve failed in 1933 to prevent the banking collapse; it was that they failed earlier to prevent the deterioration of monetary and economic conditions that made such a collapse possible, if not inevitable.

15

Eligible Assets and the
Availability of Credit

The following pages deal with two separate but related subjects relevant to the behavior of money and credit and the effects of Federal Reserve policies in the early 1930s. The first relates to the Federal Reserve Act's narrow definition of member bank assets eligible as bases for borrowing at the Federal Reserve. As we have seen, these eligible assets included, before February 1932, only United States government securities and "eligible paper" of types conforming to a version of the commercial loan theory. The law prohibited the Reserve banks from lending to a member on its other assets, even though they might be both sound and liquid—on its securities other than those of the federal government, on its mortgages and other real estate loans, on its loans collateraled by securities, or on any other loan except those conforming to the commercial loan theory. Some have claimed that this narrow definition denied member banks adequate borrowing power, was responsible for the closing of many banks, and brought pressure on banks to reduce their loans and investments rather than expand them. Others have denied that this was in practice a significant limitation, contending that at all times members held eligible assets far in excess of their borrowings, and that their failure to borrow more was attributable to their unwillingness to borrow, or to the unwillingness of the Federal Reserve to lend even on eligible assets, or both.

The other major subject of this chapter is the availability of commercial bank credit during this period. To what extent was the reduction of bank credit and the money supply attributable to a decreased willingness of banks to supply credit and to what extent to decreased demands for credit? Some have emphasized the former, others the latter.

ELIGIBILITY REQUIREMENTS

The significance of the narrow definition of eligible assets depends in part on the availability to the banks of reserves and liquidity from sources other than loans by the Federal Reserve and the terms on which those funds would be made available. It is therefore relevant that during the period before February 1932 there existed only one other set of federally sponsored institutions to lend to or rediscount for banks and other private financial institutions—the 12 Federal Intermediate Credit banks. These lent only on restricted types of medium-term agricultural paper, of which some banks held none at all and many others only small amounts. Legislation in 1932 broadened markedly the availability of loan funds from federally sponsored institutions. We have already seen that in February 1932, more than two years after the onset of the depression, the Reconstruction Finance Corporation began to operate. It stood ready to lend to both member and nonmember banks, as well as to certain other institutions, on sound assets of every kind. Also, the Glass-Steagall Act, which became law during that month, provided for Federal Reserve loans to groups of member banks and permitted the Reserve banks to lend to members on any acceptable assets.

These actions undoubtedly increased the availability of funds to banks, prevented some bank failures, and lessened pressures for contraction. Yet they were not perfect substitutes for more liberal eligibility requirements, under which the Federal Reserve would as a matter of course lend on a much broader range of bank assets. Borrowing from the RFC carried two disadvantages. For one thing, it was not a "matter of course" and suggested that the borrower was in trouble, something which a banker might be reluctant to admit even to himself. Also, there was the danger of adverse public reaction when the RFC published the names of borrowers. The provision for Federal Reserve loans to groups of member banks proved to be useless, largely because members were unwilling to share risks. Granting permission to the Federal Reserve to lend on all acceptable assets was useful, but these loans carried two disadvantages: They were subject to discount rates at least one-half of 1 percent above the ordinary discount rates, and they were not a "matter of course." In any case, these alternatives became available only after the depression had been under way for more than two years.

The significance of eligibility requirements also depends in part on the volume of Federal Reserve funds made available through other channels, and the terms on which they are supplied. I have already indicated my judgment that the major error of the Federal Reserve was its failure to purchase in the open market during the early part of the depression such large amounts of bills and government securities as to relieve almost all banks of the necessity of borrowing and to supply them with reserves much in excess of their legal requirements and also in excess of the amounts they wished to hold for liquidity purposes. The failure of the Federal Reserve to make such large purchases increased the insignificance of eligibility requirements.

Most Federal Reserve officials took the position that existing eligibility requirements were satisfactory and that member banks had an adequte supply of eligible assets, especially in the early part of the depression. For example, in December 1930 the Senate Banking and Currency Committee sent a questionnaire to all the Federal Reserve banks requesting, in part,

state the changes, if any, that you would suggest be made (1) in the provisions of the Federal Reserve Act relative to the type of paper eligible for rediscount, (2) in the rulings and regulations of the Federal Reserve Board relative to the interpretation of these provisions.[1]

Eight of the Reserve banks recommended no change at all. One of the others, Chicago, stated:

We believe that there should be no departure from the principle of eligibility and the basis of issuance of Federal Reserve notes as embodied in the Federal Reserve Act, excepting in cases of extreme emergency, and then only as a temporary measure.[2]

It did suggest, however, some lengthening of maturity to include paper otherwise eligible and a bit more scope to lend in case of emergency, but it asserted that such paper should not serve as collateral for Federal Reserve notes. Dallas favored liberalization only to include longer maturities of paper otherwise eligible and certain types of landlord's obligations. Both Philadelphia and Richmond favored some liberalization in case of emergency, but insisted that such paper should not serve as collateral for Federal Reserve notes.

Both at this time and later, most Federal Reserve officials contended that member banks had an adequate supply of eligible assets and that these were fairly well distributed among the banks.[3] On both conceptual and empirical grounds I question the validity of such statements. What was the criterion of the "adequacy" of the supply of eligible assets? At least three criteria of adequacy are meaningful, but they may yield quite different answers. (1) The first criterion is adequacy to prevent the closing of a bank. This criterion might be met while that bank or others remained under pressure to contract credit. For example, suppose a bank loses deposits and reserves because of currency withdrawals or gold outflows. If it meets the drain by borrowing at the Federal Reserve, it reduces its remaining supply of eligible assets. If it views its remaining eligible assets as a part of its liquidity to meet future needs, as it probably will, it will consider itself less liquid than it would be if eligible assets were defined more broadly. Thus it will be under more pressure to contract. (2) The second possible criterion is adequacy to remove pressures on banks to sell investments or reduce loans. To accomplish this would require a broader definition of eligible assets and also favorable Federal Reserve methods of valuing these assets for loan purposes, favorable Federal Reserve attitudes toward lending, and low discount rates. (3) The third is adequacy to bring pressure on banks to expand their loans and investments. This, if achievable, would require even more liberal policies by the Federal Reserve.

I believe that many member banks lacked sufficient eligible assets to meet even the first test of adequacy, to say nothing of the more exacting second and third. Let us look at some relevant facts. Table 15-1 shows total

---

[1]Senate Banking and Currency Committee, Hearings on S. Res. 71, 71st Congress, 3rd Session, 1931, p. 701. (See also pp. 702-708.)

[2]*Ibid.*, p. 707.

[3]See, for example, *The Federal Reserve Bulletin*, March 1932, p. 142. Friedman and Schwartz also say that, "at all times there was ample eligible paper in the portfolios of member banks." *A Monetary History of the United States, 1869-1960*, Princeton University Press, Princeton, 1963, p. 405.

TABLE 15-1

Eligible Assets and Member Bank Borrowings from the
Federal Reserve, 1929-1932 (in millions of dollars)

Date	U. S. government securities	Eligible paper	Total eligible assets	Member Bank borrowings at the Federal Reserve
December 31, 1929	3,217	4,397	7,614	646
June 30, 1930	3,412	3,905	7,317	274
December 31, 1930	3,485	3,538	7,023	248
June 30, 1931	4,707	3,198	7,905	147
December 31, 1931	4,694	2,593	7,267	623
June 20, 1932	4,979	2,428	7,408	441
December 31, 1932	5,763	2,246	8,009	235

Source: Board of Governors of the Federal Reserve System, *Annual Report of the Federal Reserve Board,* Washington, D.C., 1933, p. 169. These figures exclude government securities pledged against national bank note circulation.

member bank holdings of eligible assets on selected dates. Members did indeed hold eligible assets far in excess of their actual borrowings. On no date were their borrowings at the Federal Reserve as much as 10 percent of their eligible assets. However, the picture is modified somewhat when one examines the distribution of these assets among the member banks and compares the amount of these assets not with actual borrowings at the Federal Reserve but with the total loans and investments of member banks. The ratio of eligible assets to total loans and investments is a rough measure of the ratio of eligible assets to deposit liabilities, but since deposits typically exceed loans and investments this ratio overstates the ratio of eligible assets to deposits. Table 15-2 portrays the situation at the end of 1929. The highly uneven distribution of eligible assets among the banks is evident. Member banks as a group held

TABLE 15-2

Member Bank Holdings of Eligible Assets as Percentages of
Total Loans and Investments, by Class of Bank, December 31, 1929

Classification by ratio of eligible assets to loans and investments	Percentages of Member Banks in Each Category			
	All members	Central reserve city members	Reserve city members	Country members
0.0	1.2	2.7	0.7	1.2
Less than 5	7.8	4.1	5.0	8.0
5 to 9.9	12.7	8.2	11.6	12.8
10 to 19.9	24.2	31.5	33.4	23.6
20 to 29.9	17.9	34.2	24.0	17.4
30 to 39.9	14.3	12.3	14.4	14.3
40 to 49.9	9.9	4.1	7.2	10.1
50 to 59.9	6.2	2.7	2.2	6.4
60 to 79.9	5.0	–	1.3	5.2
80 and over	0.8	–	0.2	0.8
Total	100.0	100.0	100.0	100.0

Source: Board of Governors of the Federal Reserve System, *Federal Reserve Bulletin,* July 1930, p. 408.

eligible assets equal to 21 percent of their total loans and investments. Yet 1.2 percent of all member banks held no eligible assets at all; 9 percent held eligible assets equal to less then 5 percent of their loans and investments; and 21.7 percent had eligible assets equal to less than 10 percent of their loans and investments. For banks in these categories, withdrawals of even a small fraction of their deposits would force them to deplete their eligible assets if they borrowed at the Federal Reserve to meet the drain. Even smaller deposit withdrawals could reduce their remaining holdings of eligible assets to such low levels as to make them feel illiquid and under pressure to liquidate. The other columns in Table 15-2 indicate the situation in the various classes of member banks. Note that the percentage of eligible assets to total loans and investments was below 5 percent at 9.2 percent of the country members, and below 10 percent at 22 percent of these banks.

Table 15-3 portrays the situations of member banks in the various Federal Reserve districts. Here again one is struck by the highly uneven distribution of eligible assets. For example, the percentages of members holding eligible assets equal to less than 10 percent of their total loans and investments ranged from 46.9 in the Philadelphia district and 46.5 in the Cleveland district to 2.4 in the Dallas district and 1.1 in the Kansas City district.

These statistics related to the situation at the end of 1929. Unfortunately, we have no comparable data for later dates. However, there is no reason to believe that the distribution of eligible assets became less uneven as the depression continued, and there is some reason to believe that it became more uneven. For example, between the end of 1929 and the end of 1931 the supply of eligible assets at all member banks decreased 4.6 percent. Those at central reserve city and reserve city members increased 1.9 percent, while those at country members fell 17.7 percent. By the end of 1932 country bank holdings of eligible assets had fallen nearly 27 percent. (See Table 15-4.) The experiences of individual banks within these broad categories undoubtedly differed greatly.

These data alone lead one to conclude that the public statements of Federal Reserve officials exaggerated both the evenness of distribution and the adequacy of eligible assets. Other evidence tends to support this conclusion. For example, if banks had adequate supplies of eligible assets on which to borrow from the Federal Reserve, how are we to explain the surge of bank borrowing from the RFC when it was established in 1932? From the time it opened for business until the end of the year, 5,582 banks and trust companies applied for and received from the RFC loans aggregating $950 million. It is true that some $56 million was lent to 535 closed banks not eligible for loans from the Federal Reserve, and that some unknown amount of the loans was to nonmember banks that possessed sound assets acceptable to the RFC, but many of these loans were to member banks. If eligible assets had been defined much more broadly some of these banks would probably have borrowed from the Federal Reserve earlier.

Further evidence of the probable usefulness of a broader definition of eligible assets, in this case a definition broad enough to permit loans on home mortgages, was given by more than 5,000 banks in answer to a questionnaire in January 1932. This questionnaire was sent out by the Department of Com-

TABLE 15-3

Member Bank Holdings of Eligible Assets, Cumulative Percentages of
Total Loans and Investments, by Federal Reserve District, December 31, 1929
(Cumulative percentages of member banks in each district)

Classification by ratio of eligible assets to loans and investments	All districts	Boston	New York	Phila-delphia	Cleve-land	Rich-mond	At-lanta	Chi-cago	St. Louis	Minne-apolis	Kansas City	Dallas	San Francisco
0.0	1.2	0.7	1.3	3.3	2.8	2.3	2.9	0.7	0.7	0.4	0.0	0.5	0.3
Less than 5	9.0	14.9	15.8	20.7	21.8	9.1	2.1	4.5	8.6	2.9	0.1	0.9	6.6
Less than 10	21.7	41.3	37.6	46.9	46.5	21.6	6.5	13.8	21.4	9.1	1.1	2.4	14.5
Less than 20	45.9	79.2	71.2	77.6	76.6	50.4	25.7	41.6	47.5	28.0	7.7	9.8	43.2
Less than 30	63.9	92.8	89.5	91.0	89.4	70.4	46.7	64.0	70.8	49.3	24.6	21.4	63.6
Less than 40	78.2	98.0	96.0	97.6	97.1	85.2	68.2	78.6	83.9	70.0	50.6	37.9	82.2
Less than 50	88.1	99.3	98.9	99.0	99.1	93.8	83.2	89.4	91.8	85.4	71.9	57.1	93.6
Less than 60	94.3	100.0	99.6	99.5	99.6	97.1	91.6	96.1	96.1	93.9	87.6	73.9	98.2
Less than 80	99.2	—	100.0	100.0	100.0	99.4	98.8	99.6	99.3	99.7	98.9	95.4	99.8
80 and above	0.8	—	—	—	—	0.6	1.2	0.4	0.7	0.3	1.1	4.6	0.2
Total	100.0	100.0	100.0	100.0	100.0	100.0	100.0	100.0	100.0	100.01	100.01	100.0	100.0

Source: Board of Governors of the Federal Reserve System, *Federal Reserve Bulletin,* July 1930, p. 410.

TABLE 15-4

Indexes of Member Bank Holdings of Eligible Assets,
1929-1932 (December 1929 = 100)

Date	Eligible assets of all Member Banks	Eligible assets of central reserve city and reserve city members	Eligible assets of country members
Dec. 31, 1929	100.0	100.0	100.0
June 30, 1930	96.1	96.3	95.8
Dec. 31, 1930	92.2	95.3	85.9
June 30, 1931	103.8	112.2	86.6
Dec. 31, 1931	95.4	101.9	82.3
June 30, 1932	97.3	106.4	78.6
Dec. 31, 1932	105.2	120.8	73.3

Source: Board of Governors of the Federal Reserve System, *Annual Report of the Federal Reserve Board,* Washington, D.C., 1933, p. 169.

merce in connection with a proposal to establish a system of federally sponsored institutions to discount home mortgages.[4] Following are some of the questions and the answers by national and state banks.

1. Would the facilities provided by the proposed home loan discount banks for borrowing on your home mortgages add desirable flexibility and security to the conduct of your institution?

> Yes   4,048
> No   1,270

2. Would operation of the discount banks increase the amount of credit now available for legitimate use in your community?

> Yes   4,594
> No   1,508

3. Is there a demonstrable need for actual home construction, either new houses or remodeling work, that could be undertaken in your community if credit facilities were widened at the present time?

> Yes   2,998
> No   3,253

4. Would the facilities afforded by the proposed discount banks help to relieve the dangers of foreclosures on urban homes and farms?

> Yes   4,394
> No   1,299

In answer to another question, a clear majority of the responding bankers agreed that such discount facilities, if available in the preceding period, would have prevented many bank failures and mortgage foreclosures.

'At the hearings on the Glass-Steagall Bill in February 1932, Governor Meyer testified that

---

[4]Senate Committee on Banking and Currency, Hearings on S. 2959 (Creation of a System of Federal Home Loan Banks), 72nd Congress, 1st Session (January 1932), pp. 650-652.

Some banks, particularly in certain locations, either because of unsatisfactory business conditions, or through unusual withdrawals of deposits, have reached the point where their remaining paper, although good, is ineligible for rediscount . . . . The benefits will not be confined to banks that avail themselves of the privilege. The question what is going to happen to a bank when it sees its supply of paper which is eligible for rediscount reduced in order to meet withdrawals will cease to be the threatening factor which causes other banks to curtail their loans and to worry about their own condition. This will be a confidence-inspiring factor . . . . In a period of declining deposits the banks hold their liquid assets for the purpose of meeting declines in deposits, and hesitate to borrow on them.[5]

Emanuel Goldenweiser, head of the Division of Reserch and Statistics of the Federal Reserve Board, stated at the same hearings that in September 1931 there were less then 100 banks that held no eligible paper, but he admitted that "there were three months of extreme liquidation that followed."[6]
Representative Stevenson of South Carolina retorted that

There are that many in my state now, if I am to take what they say, and I have only 131 left, and there are fully 100 of them out of liquid paper—that is what they say.[7]

After studying experience in the Richmond district during this period, George W. McKinney, Jr., concluded:

Many banks exhausted their supply of eligible collateral and thus were unable to borrow more from the Federal Reserve System. Banks were forced to close their doors because of a lack of liquidity, even though they had plenty of perfectly sound assets on their books. Many of the banks liquidated during the 1930's ultimately paid out 100 cents on the dollar in spite of the adverse conditions under which their assets were liquidated.

Deterioration in the quality of much eligible paper offered led the Federal Reserve banks to take action which intensified this situation. During the early years of the depression all of the Federal Reserve banks except San Francisco were requiring substantial amounts of excess collateral. Although the excess collateral did not have to be in the form of eligible paper, it nevertheless tied up assets which might well have been used as collateral to other borrowings, or which could have been sold to help meet the clamoring demands of the member banks' depositors.[8]

The conclusion seems inescapable that the narrow definition of eligible assets, symbolizing a persistence of commercial loan ideas, contributed to bank closings and to liquidation of credit by banks that succeeded in remaining open. Also, as we shall see later, some banks refused to make loans that were ineligible as a basis for borrowing at the Reserve banks. This is not to say that an inadequate supply of eligible assets was solely responsible for the failure of banks to borrow more to maintain or expand their loans and investments. Also relevant were the unwillingness of some banks to show borrow-

---

[5]House Banking and Currency Committee, Hearings on H.R. 9203 (Liberalizing the Credit Facilities of the Federal Reserve System), 72nd Congress, 1st Session (February 12, 1932), pp. 3 and 15.

[6]*Ibid.*, p. 24.

[7]*Ibid.*

[8]*The Federal Reserve Discount Window: Administration in the Fifth District,* Rutgers University Press, New Brunswick, N.J., 1960, p. 18.

ings on their balance sheets or to assume the risks of borrowing and lending; the tendency of some, but not all, Reserve banks to be overly conservative in valuing eligible assets and in determing their acceptability; and the failure of some of the Reserve banks to make larger reductions in their discount rates.

One wonders how different the monetary history of this period would have been if member banks had been permitted to borrow on all types of assets, and if the Federal Reserve had lent freely up to their full value and at low discount rates. The results would surely have been better, even if these actions would not have been good substitutes for larger purchases in the open market.

AVAILABILITY OF BANK CREDIT

To what extent were the reductions in the money supply and the quantity of bank credit outstanding, and also the reduction of spending for output, attributable to a decrease in the availability of bank credit, and to what extent were they due to decreased demands for credit? It is easy, and valid as far as it goes, to reply that both played their roles. Demand functions for credit, including bank credit, undoubtedly decreased as the profitability of business investment declined. Supply functions of bank credit also decreased, if for no other reasons than the rise of estimated risks and the decreasing willingness of banks to bear risk. These answers are not very revealing, but one encounters serious difficulties in trying to unravel cause-and-effect relationships. For one thing, the total demand function for credit and the total supply function of credit are not independently determined. A shift of one function is likely to shift the other. For example, suppose there is a decrease of the credit supply function, which tends to raise interest rates or otherwise make more onerous the terms on which credit can be secured. This may decrease spending, both directly and through multiplier and other repercussive effects, lower the marginal efficiency of investment, and thus reduce both the investment demand function and the demand for credit. On the other hand, a decrease of investment demand may itself lower spendings for output, real output, and prices both directly and indirectly, thus increasing the risks of lending and reducing the supply functions of credit. These functions undoubtedly interacted in complex ways during the depression. The following pages will have little more to say about these interactions or about the decreased demand functions for credit. They will assume that the latter occurred and played an important role in the decline, and will concentrate on the availability of bank credit.

Contemporary and later discussions of the availability of bank credit, its adequacy or inadequacy, and its role in the depression, suffered from ambiguities and lack of precise and uniform definitions. For example, the very term "availability" raises the questions: "How much?" "For whom?" "For what purposes?" "At what interest rates, and on what other terms?" There was not even agreement on what should be included as "bank credit." Some thought the banks should be responsible for nothing except commercial loans, others thought they should also make other short-term loans, while still others thought they should take some share of mortgages and bonds. Most of the studies during the period related to the availability of loans to bank customers, rather than to total bank credit, including bank holdings of bonds and other longer-term assets. The terms "adequacy" and "inadequacy" were not defined precisely. Sometimes "adequacy" related only to the supply of credit relative to the demands of customers whose credit ratings remained high; in other cases it was related to demands of all customers who could be expected to repay eventually, though perhaps not in a short period. Only rarely was the "adequacy" of supply related to the needs of the economy at high levels of activity rather than to depressed customers' demands with economic activity at a low level.

Another obstacle to analysis of the availability of credit and its role in the depression is a scarcity of information about its behavior, especially during the earlier months of the depression. Most of the available studies pertain to 1932 and later periods. Yet there is reason to believe that inadequacy of the supply of bank credit relative to current demands played less of a role in depressing business activity during the earlier phases than it did later. I see no reason to dispute the general conclusions reached in a study by the National Industrial Conference Board:

During 1930, this shrinkage of commercial loans no more than reflected business recession. During 1931 and the first half of 1932, it unquestionably represented pressure by banks on customers for repayment of loans and refusals by banks to grant new loans.[9]

This statement relates only to commercial loans. It should be added, therefore, that even in the early part of the period banks did not give strong support to bonds and mortgages, and in the latter part they attempted to liquidate some other assets as well as commercial loans.

All the evidence indicates that bank refusals to lend, or restrictions on amount lent, occurred widely, at least after 1930. This is supported by the findings of the National Industrial Conference Board in a study made in the late summer of 1932. Questionnaires were sent to about 9,000 industrial firms located in various sections of the country. They yielded 3,438 usuable returns. Of these firms, 1,322 had had no recent experience with banks, while 2,116 were dependent in some degree on bank credit. Of the latter, 1,650 had encountered no difficulty in obtaining credit, but 466, or 22 percent of those dependent on banks, had experienced credit refusal or restriction.[10] The rate of refusal was much larger for smaller firms.

By no means all of these refusals or restrictions of credit were based on the financial condition of the applicant. The reasons given for such denials are listed below:[11]

Total number of stated reasons   638

Reasons based upon the condition of the concern applying for credit or

---

[9]*The Availability of Bank Credit*, National Industrial Conference Board, New York, 1932, p. 32.

[10]*Ibid.*, p. 62.

[11]*Ibid.*, pp. 112-113.

having credit restricted 220
Reasons based on the conditions of the bank 145
Reasons based upon the policy of the bank · 273

Only about a third of the total reasons given related to the condition of the applicant. Most prominent among these were: "current earnings position unsatisfactory," "financial statement generally unsatisfactory," "unstable market conditions in the applicant concern's industry, making loans too risky," "applicant already borrowed up to credit limit," and "ratio of current assets to current liabilities unsatisfactory."

Most prominent among the reasons based upon the condition of the bank were "inadequate cash reserves through losses in deposits or otherwise"—this alone accounted for more than half of all reasons given in this category; among others were "banking condition generally unliquid, with rearrangement of assets to improve liquidity," and "bank loans already extended to the legal limit." Appearing most frequently among the reasons based upon the policy of the bank were "no loans granted on plant and equipment or real estate," "loans not made because of disapproval of the bank examiner," "no loans granted except on collateral listed on the New York Stock Exchange," "no loans granted on accounts receivable," "money probably required for a long time," "loans not made because customer was too new at the bank for purposes of credit extension," and "loan not made because bank would be compelled to borrow from its Federal Reserve Bank, which was against its policy."

The above suggests some of the reasons, singly or in combination, for bank refusals or restrictions of loans. We shall later explore these further and examine the types of loans and investments most often refused or restricted.

Table 15-5 presents some facts about the behavior of the various types of member bank loans and investments during the three years following 1929.

Total bank loans and investments fell 28 percent during this period as a whole. Three types of earning assets rose—U.S. government securities, obligations of state and local governments, and short-term open-market private paper. In general, these were the safest and most liquid types of earning assets. All other types of loans declined, as did bank holdings of foreign securities and corporate bonds. Movements within this longer period were diverse. During the first half of the period, extending to mid-1931, total bank loans and investments declined 11 percent. This decrease reflected declines of bank loans to other banks, loans on securities, and "other loans," which include commercial loans. During the second half of this period, the only earning assets to increase were U.S. government securities and state and local obligations. All others, including corporate bonds, declined.

How are these great differences in behavior to be explained? At least some part, perhaps even a large part, of the very large decreases of loans on securities and of "other loans," and perhaps of loans to banks, was probably due to decreases of demand for bank loans of these types, though for reasons to be given later I am confident that this is not the sole explanation. In any case, "decreased demands for bank credit" cannot explain the behavior of open-market assets. Banks need not depend on the volume of new issues of these assets to increase their holdings; they can increase them by bidding some

TABLE 15-5

Indexes of Member Bank Loans and Investments by Type, 1929–1932
(December 31, 1929 = 100)

Type of loan or investment	Dec. 31, 1929	June 30, 1930	Dec. 31, 1930	June 30, 1931	Dec. 31, 1931	June 30, 1932	Dec. 31, 1932
Total loans and investments	100	94	92	89	81	74	72
Increased assets							
U.S. government obligations	100	105	107	138	138	145	169
State and local government obligations	100	101	122	122	112	117	126
Open-market private paper	100	129	127	152	76	113	124
Decreased assets							
Other domestic securities	100	110	114	113	100	94	90
Real estate loans	100	99	101	101	95	91	90
Foreign securities	100	110	114	102	86	76	72
Loans to banks	100	75	88	64	111	80	62
Loans on securities	100	103	93	82	67	55	51
Other loans	100	90	85	78	71	60	52

Source: Board of Governors of the Federal Reserve System, *Banking and Monetary Statistics*, Washington, D.C., 1943, pp. 74, 76, 77.

of the existing stocks away from other investors. For example, outside the commercial banking system there were large stocks of foreign securities, mortgages, and corporate and other private domestic bonds which the banks could have bought. Yet they decreased their holdings of these assets while they made net purchases of open-market private paper and of obligations of federal, state, and local governments. My view is that the differential behavior of the various types of bank assets reflects in large part attempts by banks to readjust their portfolio positions ot protect their liquidity and solvency. Shifts in the composition of bank assets were not to take advantage of more favorable differentials in quoted market yields. In general, shifts were in the opposite direction. Banks bought assets whose quoted yields were falling relative to the quoted yields on the assets they were selling or avoiding.

After studying developments in the Chicago Federal Reserve district, Charles O. Hardy and Jacob Viner concluded that during the depression many bankers became unwilling to make types of loans that they had welcomed during the preceding period.[12] Though their study was made in August 1934, their principal findings are almost certainly valid for at least the months immediately preceding the 1933 banking crisis. They found that banks had become much less willing to make working capital loans.

By far the most important issue which arises in connection with the availability of bank credit in the seventh Federal Reserve district has to do with the so-called "working-capital" or "slow" loans. In accepted banking theory in Great Britain and the United States, it has always been taught that banks should make only self-liquidating loans, that is, that they should advance funds to manufacturers only if they were to be used to buy raw materials or meet payrolls, or to produce goods already sold, the proceeds of the sale being used to retire the loan; or to finance seasonal operations like cold storage or the merchandising of agricultural products; or to enable retailers to carry inventories through a seasonal peak.

In practice, however, at least in America, banks have never confined themselves, either in the distant or in the recent past, to this type of loan. To a considerable extent they have financed the purchase of equipment and even buildings, knowing that the money could not be repaid out of turnover, but only very slowly amortized out of profit. To a still larger extent they have pursued a similar policy with regard to the permanent working capital of the business, by which is meant the minimum investment in inventory, accounts receivable, and miscellaneous supplies which is never liquidated so long as the business goes well, as distinguished from the seasonal or other temporary peak load which is actually liquidated from time to time . . . .

The most striking difference between the present situation and that which prevailed for many years prior to the advent of the present depression is the disfavor into which these working capital loans, nominally short-time, but really long-run, have fallen. This disfavor is evident in the attitudes both of bank examiners and of bankers. Many examiners have been pressing the banks to secure drastic curtailments of loans classified as "slow," pretty much regardless of the quality of security, and this attitude seems to have the approval even of many bankers . . . .

The situation is made worse by the fact that some, though apparently not very many bankers have the idea that in order to qualify as a good commercial loan, not only must the transaction be a self-liquidating one, but the liquidation must occur within some arbitrary time limit . . . .

This wave of righteousness among the banks and the bank examiners accounts for

---

[12]*Report on the Availability of Bank Credit in the Seventh Federal Reserve District*, U.S. Government Printing Office, Washington, D.C., 1935.

a very large proportion of the current discontent over the unavailability of bank credit. Of the cases which we have investigated and tabulated, 65.2 per cent are applications for capital loans, and only 23.5 per cent are for commerical or self-liquidating loans.[13]

Some banks were not only refusing to make new loans of these types but were still pressing for liquidation of old ones.

Hardy and Viner also found that many banks which had lent on real estate before the depression now looked upon such loans with disfavor and even refused to make any at all.[14] They concluded that bank examination policies were partly, but by no means wholly, responsible for these shifts of policy.

Another finding was that more than 20 percent of loans refused were apparently "good."[15] A study of the credit experiences of a large number of small business firms in August 1934 by the Bureau of the Census supported the conclusions both that large numbers encountered difficulty in securing bank credit and that some of these applicants had satisfactory credit ratings.[16] For example, of the 6,158 concerns covered in the survey, 71 percent were classified as borrowers of capital and 29 percent as nonborrowers or as concerns with no credit experience. Of the 4,387 borrowing concerns, 45 percent reported credit difficulties.[17] This percentage was larger for the smaller firms. Judging by the usual financial ratios and ratings by Dun and Bradstreet, at least 20 percent of these were creditworthy.[18] The National Industrial Conference Board study of conditions in 1932 found ratings for only 61 percent of the concerns reporting credit refusals or restrictions, but of those for which ratings were available, 20 percent were rated fair or limited, about 30 percent were rated good, and 50 percent were rated high.[19]

Though such statistics are hardly reliable enough to support quantitative conclusions, they do suggest strongly that by no means all of those who suffered refusal or restriction of credit lacked creditworthiness.

Studies by or for the banking and industrial committees established in all the Federal Reserve districts are another source of information concerning the availability of bank credit in the summer and autumn of 1932. Unfortunately many of these studies are no longer available and some of those that remain are difficult to interpret. However, the few that I have seen lend support to these qualitative conclusions: (1) In many communities mortgage money was virtually unavailable from commercial banks and other lenders. In some cases this was true even though the property was completely unencumbered. (2) Banks and other financial institutions that had suffered withdrawals

[13]*Ibid.*, pp. 13-14. This report contains a number of enlightening reports from field investigators.

[14]*Ibid.*, pp. 14-15.

[15]*Ibid.*, p. 51.

[16]U.S. Department of Commerce, *Survey of Reports of Credit and Capital Difficulties,* U.S. Government Printing Office, Washington, D.C., 1935.

[17]*Ibid.*, p. 2.

[18]*Ibid.*, p. 3.

[19]*Op. cit.*, p. 97.

were restricting both the amounts and types of loans that they would make. Some of these banks, and others as well, would make loans of types eligible as a basis for borrowing at the Federal Reserve, but not other types. (3) Because of their desire for liquidity, many banks refused to make term or working-capital loans which were sound but which could not be repaid quickly. (4) Many customers of failed banks suffered from the unavailability of bank credit. Other banks, concerned about their own position or their old customers, were unable or unwilling to lend to customers of closed banks. (5) There were many unsatisfied demands for loans by both business firms and individuals for such purposes as payment of taxes, payment of interest on mortgages and other debts, consolidation of debts, meeting living expenses, and so on.

CONCLUSIONS

Commercial bankers were roundly denounced, both at the time and later, for refusing or restricting loans to their customers. In a sense the indictment is too narrow; banks also contributed to the decline by restricting purchases and even by liquidating bonds and some other types of open-market assets. While many bankers failed to exhibit great courage and fortitude, little is to be gained by heaping blame on individual bankers. Most of them behaved as might have been expected under the circumstances; each tried to survive. Each knew that his liquidity and solvency were impaired, that his depositors might withdraw currency or shift their funds to other banks, that the credit-worthiness of most applicants for loans had deteriorated, and that many of the loans being requested would prove to be illiquid in the short run, no matter how sound they might be over a longer period. Common prudence dictated that each banker should husband the liquidity and solvency of his own bank, even if the pursuit of such policies by large numbers of banks would serve to wreck the banking system and the economy.

Whatever one may think of the conduct of bankers during the period, primary responsibility must lie with those makers of public policy who allowed a situation to develop in which individual bankers found it necessary or to their advantage to liquidate credit rather than expand it. Among these are Federal Reserve officials, who failed to flood the banking system with liquidity by purchasing large amounts of securities, who failed to press for a broadening of eligible assets before the depression had been under way for more than two years, who failed to relax standards of bank examination sufficiently, and who opposed federal insurance of bank deposits. Also included are the President and those members of Congress who allowed the narrow definition of eligible assets to continue so long, who failed to enact deposit insurance, who delayed so long the establishment of additional federally sponsored institutions to lend to banks and other financial institutions and even then favored very conservative lending policies by these institutions, and who in general did so little to arrest the depression.

Monetary Policies under the New Deal

III

16

The Political and Economic Environment

When Roosevelt assumed the presidency on March 4, 1933, the economic and financial system was in shambles. Real GNP was more than 30 percent below its level in 1929 and even further below its current capacity levels. More than 13 million workers, or more than a quarter of the labor force, were totally unemployed, and millions more had only part-time jobs. Most of these were receiving no relief, or at best only inadequate amounts. Average prices of output and assets had fallen at least 25 percent. National money income had declined more than 45 percent. The entire debt structure was disrupted. Defaults and delinquencies were widespread on almost every major type of debt except that of the federal government—on debts of state and local governments, business firms, homeowners, and farmers. Many farmers were organizing debtors' strikes, and an increasing number of states were imposing mortgage moratoria. Virtually all commercial banks were closed, and most other types of financial intermediaries were practically paralyzed. Things were little brighter in the international sphere. The international gold standard had been swept away, and no satisfactory substitute had yet been developed. Exchange rates were fluctuating erratically. International capital movements had come to a standstill. International trade in goods and services had fallen to a very low level, not only because of the drastic decline of world incomes but also because of rising official restrictions, such as increased tariffs, quantitative limitations, and exchange controls.

Clearly, something had to be done. Roosevelt was in a strong position to act vigorously if he wished to do so. He had won by a landslide, polling 22,800,000 votes to Hoover's 15,800,000, and commanding 472 electoral votes to Hoover's 59. Aside from the 3 traditionally Republican New England states—Maine, New Hampshire, and Vermont—Hoover won only Connecticut, Pennsylvania, and Delaware. The House of Representatives included 310 Democrats and 117 Republicans, while the Senate comprised 60 Democrats and 35 Republicans. Roosevelt would be in a powerful position if he could command enough support in these large Democratic majorities. He found that this was no recalcitrant Congress; many of its members wanted to move faster and further than he did. They reflected the changed attitudes of the public. There were, of course, dissenters from this view; a minority thought that even

Hoover's policies had been too active, and some did not want any major departures from the policies of the preceding years. However, the general mood was, "We want change, and we want action; do something!" The grinding forces of deflation which had disrupted the economy and inflicted widespread hardships had also altered old attitudes, weakened inhibitions against government intervention, and opened the way to a variety and extent of government action which would have been generally disapproved a few years earlier.

These conditions, combined with Roosevelt's penchant for bold and experimental actions, virtually assured that the new administration would play a much more active role and extend its activities into many sectors of the economy. This change was accompanied, almost inevitably, by a decline in the relative role of the Federal Reserve, whose prestige was then at a low ebb. During the preceding years, the government itself had assumed almost no role in monetary policy and had taken few other measures to promote economic recovery. The Federal Reserve had held the center of the stage, almost without competition. Now the roles were almost reversed. The Federal Reserve and its policies did not become insignificant, but they were overshadowed as the government seized the initiative and took bold and far-reaching actions in the monetary area and many others. For example, the government ended the convertibility of the dollar into gold and then aggressively lowered its value in terms of gold and foreign currencies. At the end of January 1934, it adopted a new gold standard, under which the gold value of the dollar was decreased nearly 41 percent and the official price of gold was increased about 69 percent. By this process, the Treasury reaped a gold profit of $2.8 billion, which it could use at its discretion to increase the monetary base. A veritable "golden avalanche," primarily from abroad but also from domestic sources, added huge amounts to the monetary base. These were supplemented by large Treasury purchases of silver for monetary purposes. Changes in the volume of bank reserves emanating from these sources generally dwarfed changes resulting from Federal Reserve actions.

The government also took many other actions which should be included under "monetary policy" if that term is construed broadly to include measures bearing directly upon the supply, availability, and cost of credit. Only a few of the most important of these will be mentioned here. (1) It provided loans and other funds, both directly and indirectly, to banks and other financial intermediaries. The RFC, which had been established in February 1932, was provided with large additional resources and urged to provide financial assistance on more generous terms. It supplied large amounts of funds directly to banks and other financial intermediaries, both by lending to them and by purchasing equity claims against them, the latter improving their net worth positions. It also supplied funds indirectly to these institutions by lending to other types of borrowers, such as state and local governments, railroads, and other business firms. The federal home loan banks, which accelerated their operations, and the Home Owners' Loan Corporation, which was established to rehabilitate mortgages on urban residential real estate, also supplied very large amounts of funds directly and indirectly to banks, savings and loan associations, insurance companies, and other holders of home mortgages. Similar functions were performed by the federal land banks and the newly established Federal Farm Mortgage Corporation, which purchased a great many farm mortgages. Through these processes, large amounts of the private debts in the portfolios of financial intermediaries were replaced or supplemented with government securities or securities guaranteed by the government. In effect, the government sold direct claims against itself, or its agencies issued securities carrying a government guarantee and used the proceeds to buy up, or to lend upon, claims against private debtors.

(2) The government increased the safety and attractiveness of claims against major types of privately owned financial intermediaries. Thus, the Federal Deposit Insurance Corporation was established to insure the first $5,000 of each deposit account in most of the nation's commercial banks. The Federal Savings and Loan Insurance Corporation was created to serve a similar function for most of the savings and loan associations. (3) Insurance for certain types of private debts was provided. The Federal Housing Administration was created to insure amortized mortgages on homes. The newly created Commodity Credit Corporation lent to farmers on commodities and guaranteed such loans by private lenders. (4) The government itself created many new types of financial institutions and authorized federal charters for others. Among those in the field of agricultural credit were a central bank for cooperatives and 12 regional banks for cooperatives, and 12 production credit corporations and many production credit associations. Those in the area of housing credit included federal savings and loan associations and the Federal National Mortgage Association.

Thus we find that the relative role of the Federal Reserve in monetary policy declined even if we construe "monetary policy" very narrowly to include only regulation of the behavior of the sizes of the monetary base and the money supply. Its relative decline was even greater if we construe monetary policy more broadly to include all actions which affect directly and significantly such questions as the liquidity of banks and other financial intermediaries and the supply, availability, and cost of credit. It is for this reason that we shall devote much attention to policies other than those of the Federal Reserve.

To provide a background for our discussion of monetary policies in this period, it will be useful to examine briefly some of the principal economic and financial developments between early 1933, when the depression reached its nadir, and the end of 1941.

THE COURSE OF ECONOMIC RECOVERY

The recovery was disappointingly slow, spasmodic, and incomplete. Not until 1937 did total output, measured by GNP at constant prices, rise to the levels achieved in 1929. (See Table 16-1.) It fell below that level again during the sharp but brief recession of 1937-1938, and then resumed its rise. The rate of recovery increased after the nation embarked upon a rearmament program in the spring of 1940 and thereafter accelerated its expenditures for military purposes.

TABLE 16-1

Real GNP and Unemployment, 1929–1941

Year	GNP at constant 1929 prices (in billions of dollars) (1)	Index of (1) 1929 = 100 (2)	Potential GNP at constant 1929 prices (in billions of dollars) (3)	Actual GNP as percent of potential GNP (4)	Unemployment	
					Number of unemployed (in millions) (5)	Unemployed as percent of the labor force (6)
1929	$104.4	100	$104.4	100%	1.6	3.2%
1930	94.4	90	107.5	88	4.3	8.7
1931	87.8	84	110.7	79	8.0	15.9
1932	74.8	72	114.0	66	12.1	23.6
1933	72.7	70	117.4	62	12.8	24.9
1934	79.5	76	120.9	66	11.3	21.7
1935	87.8	84	124.5	71	10.6	20.1
1936	99.5	95	128.2	78	9.0	16.9
1937	105.3	101	132.0	80	7.7	14.3
1938	100.5	96	136.0	74	10.4	19.0
1939	108.7	104	140.1	78	9.5	17.2
1940	118.1	113	144.3	82	8.1	14.6
1941	136.4	137	148.6	92	5.6	9.9

Sources: Actual GNP computed from data in various tables in U.S. Department of Commerce, U.S. Income and Output, Washington, D.C., 1958. Unemployment data from U.S. Department of Commerce, Historical Statistics of the United States, Washington, D.C., 1960, p. 70.

However, actual real output remained below "capacity" or "potential" levels throughout the period, especially during the years prior to 1941. The productive potential of the economy rose throughout the depression. The labor force increased by 6.7 million between 1929 and 1941, and technology continued to advance. The stock of capital would have grown rapidly if the nation's real income had been high enough to permit a high rate of real saving. It is reasonable to assume that the productive potential increased at a compound annual rate of at least 3 percent after 1929. An average growth rate of at least 3 percent had been achieved during earlier decades and was achieved again after the end of the depression. Column 3 of Table 16-1 shows "potential GNP" for each year on the assumption of a 3 percent compound annual growth rate from the level actually realized in 1929. A comparison of actual and potential GNP reveals that output remained far below potential levels throughout the period, especially before 1941. Output averaged 24 percent below its potential during the years 1934-1940, inclusive. Even in 1941 it was still 8 percent below its potential.

The unemployment data tell much the same story. In no year prior to 1941 did the number of the totally unemployed average below 7.7 million or the average unemployment rate decline below 14.3 percent. The unemployment rate averaged nearly 18 percent during the years 1934-1940, inclusive. Even in 1941 it was 9.9 percent. In addition, part-time unemployment remained widespread almost until the end of the period.

As indicated in Table 16-2, the major components of GNP, all measured in real terms, behaved in quite different ways. Total government purchases of goods and services actually declined in 1933 but rose in each of the following years except 1937. The sharp rise in 1941 reflects the acceleration of the rearmament program. Personal consumption, which had fallen 19 percent from 1929 to 1933, rose thereafter; after 1936 it was at or above its level in 1929. Gross private domestic investment behaved far worse. In no year prior to 1941 did it come close to its 1929 level. Residential construction, which normally accounts for a large fraction of total private investment, never recovered fully during this period. During most of these years it was deeply depressed. The same was true of nonresidential construction. Purchases of new producers' durable goods performed a bit better, but they rose above their 1929 level only in 1941. The failure of the New Deal to induce an adequate revival of private investment is the key to its failure to achieve a self-sustaining and complete recovery of output and employment.

Since the above data for real GNP are annual aggregates, they cannot show movements within years. To indicate intrayear movements of output we shall use the Federal Reserve index of industrial production, which is available on a monthly basis. (See Figure 2.) It should be remembered, however, that this measure of real output is much less comprehensive than GNP and that it moves more quickly and widely.

In March 1933, industrial production was only 47 percent of its level during the summer of 1929. It then rose sharply into July, only to suffer a relapse that lasted until January 1934. During this period it lost nearly half of the gains achieved between March and July 1933. A new recovery began in February 1934 and continued into the spring of 1937, at which time indus-

TABLE 16-2

Index of GNP and Its Major Components at Constant Prices, 1932-1941
1929 = 100

| Year | Total GNP (1) | Government purchases of goods and services (2) | Personal consumption (3) | Gross Private Domestic Investment | | | |
				Total GPDI (4)	Residential construction (5)	Non residential construction (6)	Producers' durable equipment (7)
1929	100	100	100	100	100	100	100
1932	72	111	82	12	26	31	30
1933	70	106	81	13	20	29	34
1934	76	121	85	23	28	35	44
1935	84	123	90	45	39	43	60
1936	95	145	99	59	49	60	82
1937	101	141	103	74	54	71	94
1938	96	154	100	42	55	52	64
1939	104	160	106	61	79	58	75
1940	113	165	112	82	89	71	96
1941	137	256	119	103	94	84	113

Source: Computed from data in The National Income and Product Accounts of the United States, 1929-1965, principally p. 4, U.S. Department of Commerce. One component of gross private domestic investment—change in business inventories—is not shown. This item was negative in the years 1932-1934 and in 1938, and positive but small in relation to total private investment in the other years.

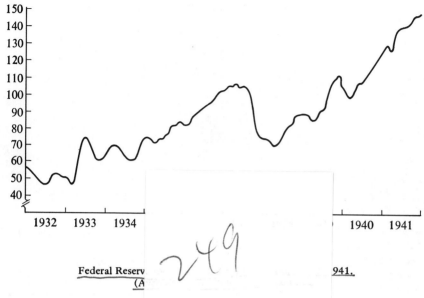

trial production was 5 per   ut still far below
its potential levels.

Then came what is best described as "a sharp recession within a depression." This lasted from the spring of 1937 to June 1938. Industrial production fell by a third, and at its low point was 30 percent below its level in mid-1929. Real GNP in 1938 was 5 percent below that in the preceding year and 26 percent below its potential. The average unemployment rate jumped to 19 percent and part-time unemployment increased.

Though the 1937-1938 recession was sharp, painful, and discouraging, it was mercifully short. A new recovery began in the late spring of 1938, continued until the economy came to be affected by the new world war, and then accelerated. In 1939, the last full year before the economy was influenced significantly by the war, real GNP was 4 percent above its level in 1929 but 22 percent below its potential. The number of unemployed averaged 9.5 million, and the unemployment rate was 17.2 percent. While the labor force increased by 6 million between 1929 and 1939, the number actually employed decreased by 1.8 million.

Though World War II broke out in September 1939, its expansionary effects on the American economy began to be significant only in 1940. Then they were of two major types: increased demands for American exports and increased demands for output by the federal government to implement an expanding national defense program. Belligerent countries that were later to become America's allies demanded more American exports to help meet their civilian and war needs, and nonbelligerents turned increasingly to American exports as supplies from belligerent countries decreased. U.S. exports had averaged below $4.4 billion in the years immediately preceding 1940; in 1941 they were $1.5 billion higher.

Far greater was the increase of federal expenditures for output to be

TABLE 16-3

U.S. Exports and Federal Purchases of Goods
and Services, 1936-1941 (in millions of dollars at current prices)

| | | Federal Purchases of Goods and Services | | |
Year	U.S. exports	Total	National defense	Other
1936	3,539	4,935	—	—
1937	4,553	4,664	—	—
1938	4,336	5,409	—	—
1939	4,432	5,105	1,249	3,856
1940	5,355	6,015	2,214	3,801
1941	5,925	16,882	13,750	3,132

Source: The National Income and Product Accounts of the United States, 1929-1965, p. 2.

used in the expanding national defense program. Total federal expenditures for goods and services ranged below $5.4 billion in the years immediately preceding 1940. In 1941 they were $16.9 billion, of which expenditures for national defense were nearly $13.8 billion. Thus the government was spending for national defense alone about two and a half times as much as it had spent for all purposes in the years immediately preceding 1940. This combination of increased demands for American exports and rising government purchases of goods and services for defense purposes raised output much closer to full employment levels. They did so by increasing directly both demands for output and private incomes, through multiplier effects on consumption expenditures, and through raising actual and prospective sales and profits enough to revive private investment spending. However, even in 1941 output was still at least 8 percent below its potential, and the unemployment rate averaged nearly 10 percent.

Not until the nation had been in the war for well over a year did Americans come to realize how far below its potential the economy had been operating in the prewar period. It is very difficult to compare meaningfully wartime and peacetime rates of real output, and there is reason to believe that the estimates of wartime output have an upward bias. However, if one takes the official estimates at face value, real GNP in 1944, the peak year of the war effort, was more than 75 percent above its levels in 1929 and in 1939.

PRICE LEVELS AND NATIONAL MONEY INCOME

One major objective of the Roosevelt administration was to raise prices to their pre-depression levels. It sought to do this in two quite different ways: by increasing aggregate demands for output through monetary and fiscal policies, and by raising individual prices through production controls, price supports, or agreements. These devices were employed in the New Deal agricultural program, for example, and the National Recovery Administration used them in its attempts to increase industrial prices. However, all these measures together were only partially successful; prices remained below their 1929 levels throughout the period, and especially before 1941. For instance, in 1939 the major price indexes were below their 1929 levels by these amounts: the GNP price deflator by 16 percent, the wholesale price index by 19 percent, and the consumer price index also by 19 percent.

Reflecting both the lag in the recovery of real output and the limited rise of prices of output, GNP at current prices remained below its 1929 level until 1941. (See Table 16-4.)

TABLE 16-4

Price Levels and GNP at Current Prices
(GNP in billions of dollars)

Year	GNP at current prices	Index of GNP at current prices 1929 = 100	Price Indexes, 1929 = 100		
			GNP price deflator	Wholesale prices	Consumer prices
1929	$104.4	100	100	100	100
1930	90.4	87	96	90	97
1931	75.8	73	87	76	88
1932	58.0	56	78	68	79[
1933	55.6	53	77	69	75
1934	65.1	62	82	78	78
1935	72.2	69	83	84	80
1936	82.5	79	83	85	81
1937	90.4	87	86	90	73
1938	84.7	81	85	82	82
1939	90.5	87	84	81	81
1940	99.7	96	85	82	81
1941	125.4	119	92	91	86

FISCAL POLICIES

Fiscal policies affect monetary policies in many ways—through their influence on the nature and magnitude of the tasks faced by the monetary authorities, through their effects on the government's financing needs, through their effects on the supply of earning assets to financial institutions and others, and so on. We shall therefore review briefly the nature of fiscal policies in the years 1933-1939, devoting primary attention to the tax and expenditure policies of the federal government, but also noting the general nature of the fiscal actions of state and local governments.

Many myths still surround Roosevelt's fiscal policies: that even in the early years of his administration, Roosevelt was much influenced by Keynes; that the prime purpose of his fiscal actions was to increase aggregate demands for output; that the timing and magnitudes of his tax and expenditures actions were specifically designed to raise aggregate demands for output to full employment levels; and that the net effects of these policies were consistently and strongly expansionary.

In fact, however, Roosevelt's policies were not influenced by the new Keynesian type of analysis before the late 1930s, if at all. Roosevelt had formulated no definite fiscal policies before becoming President. At no time during his administrations did he advocate or adopt a set of fiscal policies directed specifically at, and adapted to, the objective of increasing aggregate demands for output to the levels required for complete recovery. For this, his attitudes toward budget deficits and increases in the national debt provide at least partial explanations. As already mentioned, he excoriated Hoover repeatedly during the 1932 campaign for his budget deficits and the consequent threat to the government's credit, and he promised to put the government's financial house in order. Of course, he did not balance the budget; there were deficits during every year he was in office. Yet there is no reason to doubt that in 1932 and later years he was sincerely concerned about the deficits, that he felt constrained to limit their size, and that he incurred the deficits he did primarily because he valued so highly the benefits of the programs for which expenditures were increased.

It is significant that tax rates were never decreased under Roosevelt; in fact, they were increased well before the end of the depression. Moreover, expenditure increases were undertaken primarily because of benefits to the recipients, such as the unemployed and farmers. There were, of course, references to their general contributions to incomes and purchasing power and to indirect benefits to other sectors. However, expenditure increases were primarily oriented toward specific programs, and on the whole were inadequate to raise aggregate demand to full employment levels.

The data in Table 16-5 are adequate to support only limited conclusions.[1] However, they can be used in a valid way to cast doubt on any

TABLE 16-5

Government Expenditures and Deficits on Income and Product Account, Calendar Years, 1929-1941 (in billions of dollars at current prices)

	Expenditures			Surplus or Deficit (−) on Income and Product Account		
Year	Federal	State and local	Total	Federal	State and local	Total
1929	2.6	7.8	10.4	1.2	−0.2	1.0
1930	2.8	8.4	11.2	0.3	−0.6	−0.3
1931	4.2	8.5	12.7	−2.1	−0.8	−2.9
1932	3.2	7.6	10.8	−1.5	−0.3	−1.8
1933	4.0	7.2	11.2	−1.3	−0.1	−1.4
1934	6.4	8.1	14.5	−2.9	+0.5	−2.4
1935	6.5	8.6	15.1	−2.6	+0.5	−2.1
1936	8.7	8.1	16.8	−3.6	+0.5	−3.1
1937	7.4	8.4	15.8	−0.4	+0.7	+0.3
1938	8.6	9.0	17.6	−2.1	+0.4	−1.7
1939	8.9	9.6	18.5	−2.2	0	−2.2
1940	10.0	9.3	19.3	−1.3	+0.6	−0.7
1941	20.5	9.1	29.6	−5.0	+1.3	−3.8

Source: The National Income and Product Accounts of the United States, 1929-1941, pp. 52 and 54. Because of rounding, items may not add to totals shown.

[1] Some of their shortcomings for analytical purposes are these: (1) They do not distinguish between purchases of goods and services and transfer payments. (2) All values are at current prices, and thus do not indicate precisely the behavior of "real" expenditures and deficits. (3) The implied changes in receipts include both those emanating from changes in national income and those resulting from changed tax rates.

contention that the net effects of both the tax and expenditure policies of all levels of government combined, or of the federal government alone, were consistently and strongly expansionary. On balance, the fiscal policies of state and local governments were less expansionary after 1933 than they had been in earlier years. Though these units did increase their expenditures, their tax receipts rose even more, so that deficits in 1933 and earlier years were replaced by tax surpluses in every year but one after 1933. A part of the increase in state and local revenues resulted automatically from the rise of business activity and incomes. However, there were also extensive increases in effective tax rates, and especially state and local sales taxes, during the period.

Federal expenditures did rise in each year after 1932, except in 1937, and thus contributed somewhat to aggregate demand. However, the increases were quite small as compared with the large gap between actual and potential output. Moreover, the expansionary effects of the rise of federal expenditures were at least partially offset by the higher effective tax rates in effect during this period as compared with those during the years before 1933. It will be remembered that the Revenue Act of 1932 came into full effect in 1933 and remained in force during the remainder of this period. As E. Cary Brown has described that Act:

> ... The Federal Revenue Act of 1932 virtually doubled full-employment tax yields and essentially set the tax structure for the entire period up to the second world war ....
>
> The Revenue Act of 1932 pushed up rates virtually across the board, but notably on the lower and middle-income groups. The scope of the act was clearly the equivalent of major wartime enactments. Personal income tax exemptions were slashed, the normal tax as well as surtax rates were sharply raised, and the earned-income credit equal to 25 per cent of taxes on low incomes were repealed. Less drastic changes were made in the corporate income tax, but its rate was raised slightly and a $3,000 exemption eliminated. Estate tax rates were pushed up, exemptions sharply reduced, and a gift tax was provided. Congress toyed with a manufacturers sales tax, but finally rejected it in favor of a broad new list of excise taxes and substantially higher rates for the old ones.[2]

There were also further tax increases, even before the expansion of the defense program in 1940. For example, corporate tax rates were raised gradually to 19 percent, and new payroll taxes were imposed to finance the new social security program enacted in 1936. Yields of the latter had risen to nearly $1.9 billion by 1939.

E. Cary Brown has attempted to measure the "net contribution" of government fiscal operations to aggregate demand during the years 1929-1939.[3] He defines and measures the "net contribution" for any year as the net shift of aggregate demand by government taxes and expenditures, this being stated as a percentage of that year's full employment level of real GNP. For example, a positive figure of 1 percent indicates that fiscal policy shifted aggregate demand upward by an amount equal to 1 percent of that year's full employment level of GNP. He then poses two major questions:

---

[2]"Fiscal Policies in the Thirties: A Reappraisal," *American Economic Review*, December 1956, pp. 868-869.

[3]*Op. cit.*, pp. 857-879.

1. How did the net contributions of fiscal policies in the various years, 1930-1939, compare with that in 1929?
2. How did these contributions during the years 1933-1939 compare with those during the years immediately preceding the New Deal?

To answer these questions involves difficult technical problems and many assumptions, but his findings seem generally valid. Some of the most important of these are summarized in Table 16-6.

TABLE 16-6

*E. C. Brown Estimates of Net Shift of Demand as Percent of
Full Employment Level of GNP in Constant Dollars*

Year	All governments	Federal	State and local
1929	1.4	−0.4	1.8
1930	1.9	0.0	2.0
1931	3.6	1.7	1.8
1932	1.8	1.0	0.9
1933	0.5	0.5	0.1
1934	1.5	2.0	−0.4
1935	1.6	1.9	−0.3
1936	2.6	2.5	0.2
1937	0.2	0.1	0.1
1938	1.2	1.2	0.0
1939	2.0	1.4	0.5

Source: E. Cary Brown, "Fiscal Policies in the Thirties: A Reappraisal, *American Economic Review*, December, 1956. The above data appear as Column 14 in a table on p. 865.

The answer for state and local fiscal operations is clear-cut. In 1929, when these governments as a group were running deficits to finance public works programs, their net contribution was 1.8 percent. It remained at or slightly above this level in 1930 and 1931, fell sharply in 1932, and was even lower during the remainder of the period. It was slightly negative in 1934 and 1935, and zero in 1938.

Net contributions of federal fiscal actions behaved more erratically. In 1929, when the federal budget was in surplus by nearly $1.2 billion, the net contribution was slightly negative. It became zero in 1930, and was positive in all the following years, but by small and varying amounts. A major part of the 1.7 percent net contribution in 1931 was accounted for by the payment of a soldiers' bonus, which Hoover disliked, and the 2.5 percent contribution in 1936 was largely attributable to a soldier's bonus of $1.7 billion, which Roosevelt disliked. In the other years after 1933, net contributions ranged below 2 percent, being in most years considerably below that figure. We shall see later that the sharp drop from 2.5 percent in 1936 to 0.1 percent in 1937 undoubtedly helped precipitate the recession of 1937-1938. One is led to agree with Brown that,

Fiscal policy, then, seems to have been an unsuccessful recovery device in the thirties—not because it did not work, but because it was not tried. [4]

[4]*Op. cit.,* pp. 863 and 866.

In any case, monetary policies were not assisted by fiscal policies whose net effects were consistently and strongly expansionary. Of course, fiscal policies could have been worse, and would have been if Roosevelt had really tried to achieve an annually balanced budget, raising effective tax rates and decreasing expenditures to the extent necessary to achieve this goal.

These deficits, together with issues to finance federally sponsored financial agencies or to make loans to private borrowers, brought large increases in the federal debt. At the end of March 1933, the sum of the Treasury's direct interest-bearing obligations plus securities bearing its full guarantee was $21.4 billion. This climbed to $47.1 billion by the end of 1939, and to $63.8 billion by the end of 1941. We shall find that a major part of the increases of the money supply and of bank credit during the period reflected bank purchases of these securities.

MONETARY AND FINANCIAL DEVELOPMENTS

Though we shall later analyze them in much more detail, it will be useful to sketch briefly at this point some of the major monetary and financial developments between March 1933 and the end of 1941. Of basic importance were the huge additions to the monetary base and improvements in the reserve position of the banking system.

Two developments account for most of the improvement in the reserve position of the banking system during the remainder of 1933—return flows of currency to the banks and Federal Reserve purchases of government securities. Currency in circulation declined nearly $2 billion between March 8 and the end of August. Also, the Federal Reserve increased its holdings of government securities by $595 million between mid-May and mid-November. Largely because of receipts of funds from these sources, member banks were enabled, before the end of 1933, to reduce their debts to the Federal Reserve to less than $120 million and to raise their excess reserves above $700 million.

Further improvements in the reserve positions of banks and further additions to the monetary base came from quite different sources after the end of 1933. The Federal Reserve made only very small further contributions, and there was some drain of currency into circulation as national income rose. By far the greatest contributor was "the golden avalanche." (See Table 16-7.) The monetary gold stock, which had averaged below $4 billion in 1932, averaged almost $9.1 billion in 1935, nearly $16.1 billion in 1939, and $22.5 billion in 1941. Further funds, almost $1 billion, were supplied by increases in outstanding Treasury currency; these resulted largely from Treasury purchases of silver for monetary purposes. These huge increases enabled banks to retire virtually all their borrowings at the Federal Reserve and to increase greatly both their total and their excess reserves. Member bank borrowings never exceeded $25 million after July 1934, and they were lower most of the time. Their total reserves, which averaged $2.3 billion in 1933, averaged $5 billion in 1935, $10.4 billion in 1939, and $13.4 billion in 1941. Their excess reserves rose above $1.5 billion in 1934 and were above this level in every succeeding year except 1937. (See Table 16-7.)

TABLE 16-7

Member Bank Reserves and Some Related Items, 1932-1941
(annual averages of daily figures, in millions of dollars)

	Total Federal Reserve credit	Monetary gold stock	Treasury currency outstanding	Total Member Bank reserves	Borrowings from the Federal Reserve	Excess reserves
1932	2,077	3,952	2,096	2,114	521	256
1933	2,429	4,059	2,271	2,343	283	528
1934	2,502	7,512	2,381	3,676	36	1,564
1935	2,475	9,059	2,478	5,001	7	2,469
1936	2,481	10,578	2,503	5,989	6	2,512
1937	2,554	12,162	2,567	6,830	14	1,220
1938	2,600	13,250	2,711	7,935	9	2,522
1939	2,628	16,085	2,879	10,352	5	4,392
1940	2,487	19,865	3,018	13,249	4	6,326
1941	2,293	22,546	3,156	13,404	5	5,324

Source: Board of Governors of the Federal Reserve System, *Banking and Monetary Statistics,* Washington, D.C., 1943, p. 368.

The money supply, after reaching its low point in early 1933, increased almost continuously thereafter, although with a lull during the 1937-1938 recession. For example, the average money supply in 1939 was 72 percent above its 1933 level and 27 percent above its level in 1929. (See Table 16-8.) It grew even more rapidly in 1940 and 1941.

The income velocity of money never recovered from the low levels reached in 1932 and 1933 and remained far below its levels in 1929 and 1930. In fact, it hovered around its 1932-1933 levels during the years 1934-1938 and then decreased slightly. Whether because of the low levels of

TABLE 16-8

The Money Supply and GNP at Current Prices, 1929-1941
(annual averages, amounts in billions of dollars)

	The money supply (demand deposits plus currency)	GNP at current prices	Income velocity of money (2) ÷ (1)
1929	$26.4	$103.1	3.91
1930	25.5	90.4	3.55
1931	23.6	75.8	3.21
1932	20.6	58.0	2.82
1933	19.5	55.6	2.85
1934	21.5	65.1	3.03
1935	25.5	72.2	2.83
1936	29.2	82.5	2.83
1937	30.3	90.4	2.98
1938	30.0	84.7	2.82
1939	33.6	90.5	2.69
1940	39.0	99.7	2.56
1941	45.9	124.5	2.71

Sources: GNP data from *The National Income and Product Accounts of the United States, 1929-1965,* p. 2. Money supply data computed from monthly data in Friedman and Schwartz, *A Monetary History of the United States, 1869-1960,* Princeton University Press, Princeton, 1963, pp. 712-716.

TABLE 16-9

Commercial Bank Loans and Investments, 1932-1941
(data as of June 30, in billions of dollars)

	1932	1933	1934	1935	1936	1937	1938	1939	1940	1941
Total loans and investments	36.3	30.6	32.8	34.7	38.7	39.6	37.2	39.4	41.2	47.6
Total loans	22.0	16.5	15.7	15.0	15.6	17.4	16.1	16.4	17.4	20.3
On real estate	5.0	4.2	3.7	3.5	3.5	3.7	3.9	4.1	4.4	4.7
Collateral	7.3	5.4	5.3	4.7	4.7	4.9	3.8	a	a	a
All other	9.8	6.9	6.8	6.8	7.4	8.9	8.5	a	a	a
Total investments	14.3	14.1	17.1	19.7	23.1	22.1	21.1	23.0	23.8	27.3
U.S. government obligations	6.3	7.5	10.3	12.8	15.3	14.6	14.1	15.7	16.6	20.1
Obligations of state and local governments	2.3	2.3	2.4	2.7	2.9	2.8	2.8	3.3	3.6	3.7
Other securities	5.7	4.3	4.4	4.3	4.9	4.8	4.3	4.0	3.6	3.5

aData on collateral and all other loans for 1939-1941 are not available on a basis comparable to those for preceding years.

Source: Board of Governors of the Federal Reserve System, *All Bank Statistics*, Washington, D.C., 1959, pp. 34-35.

TABLE 16-10

Interest Rates and Yields on Selected Types of Debt Instruments, 1933–1941
(annual averages, percent per annum)

Type of Instrument	1933	1934	1935	1936	1937	1938	1939	1940	1941
Short-term									
3-month Treasury bills (dealer quotation)		0.28	0.17	0.17	0.28	0.07	0.05	0.04	0.13
4-6-month prime commercial paper	1.73	1.02	0.76	0.75	0.94	0.81	0.59	0.56	0.54
90-day prime bankers' acceptances	0.63	0.25	0.13	0.16	0.43	0.44	0.44	0.44	0.44
Rates charged by commercial banks in principal cities									
Total, 19 cities	4.27	3.45	2.93	2.68	2.59	2.53	2.78	2.63	2.54
New York City	3.43	2.45	1.76	1.72	1.73	1.69	2.07	2.04	1.97
7 Northern and Eastern cities	4.46	3.71	3.39	3.04	2.88	2.75	2.87	2.56	2.55
11 Southern and Western cities	5.04	4.32	3.76	3.40	3.25	3.26	3.51	3.38	3.19
Long-term									
U.S. government bonds	3.31	3.12	2.79	2.65	2.68	2.56	2.36	2.21	1.95
High-grade municipal bonds	4.71	4.03	3.41	3.07	3.10	2.91	2.76	2.50	2.10
Corporate bonds									
High-grade-total	4.38	3.93	3.46	3.19	3.27	3.12	2.92	2.77	2.67
Moody's ratings									
Aaa	4.49	4.00	3.60	3.24	3.26	3.19	3.01	2.84	2.77
A	6.09	5.08	4.55	4.02	4.01	4.22	3.89	3.57	3.30
Baa	7.76	6.32	5.75	4.77	5.03	5.80	4.96	4.75	4.33

Sources: Various tables in Board of Governors of the Federal Reserve System, *Banking and Monetary Statistics,* Washington, D.C., 1943.

interest rates or for other reasons, the public demanded to hold unusually large money balances relative to its rate of spending for output.

Though banks failed to expand to the limits permitted by their reserves, total bank credit did increase. From their low point in June 1933, total loans and investments of all commercial banks increased 54.6 percent by June 1940 and 55.6 percent by June 1941. (See Table 16-9.) It is significant that nearly 86 percent of the total increase up to June 1940 was accounted for by the increase of bank holdings of U.S. government securities and most of the remainder by increased holdings of obligations of state and local governments. Bank holdings of "other securities"—mostly corporate bonds—rose slightly until mid-1936 and thereafter fell below their level in June 1933. Total bank loans rose very little before 1940. In fact, they remained below their level in mid-1933 in all of these years except 1937.

Why did banks fail to expand significantly their holdings of private debts and confine their increases largely to holdings of government obligations? This is difficult to explain fully. One factor was undoubtedly their exchange of private debt for federal debt in the process of rehabilitating farm and home mortgages and some other types of private debts. Inadequacy of private demands may also help to explain the failure of bank loans to increase, but it does not explain the decline of bank holdings of corporate bonds after mid-1936. There is strong evidence, as we shall see later, that a major factor was the banks' continuing desire for high levels of safety and liquidity and their aversion to risk. Thus the falling levels of interest rates during the period are not a reliable index of the availability of bank credit to most private borrowers.

As might be expected in view of the incompleteness of the economic recovery and the high and rising amounts of excess reserves in the banking system, the period after June 1933 was one of low and generally declining interest rates. The decline was especially great for the safest and most liquid types of short-term, open-market paper. (See Table 16-10.) In fact, the yield on short-term Treasury bills virtually disappeared during the latter part of the period. Most other interest rates also declined, although not as much.

17

Financial Rehabilitation

With virtually all the nation's banks closed or severely restricted in their operations under state-proclaimed holidays, the entire financial system was paralyzed when Roosevelt became President. Additional currency was unavailable, checks could not be cleared or collected, other financial intermediaries could not operate, the securities exchanges had to remain closed, and foreign exchange operations were at a standstill. It was clear, therefore, that one of the first of the many tasks facing the new administration was to reopen the banks, or at least a large majority of them, and to guard against a new round of currency and gold withdrawals. However, to accomplish this goal would require time.

REOPENING THE BANKS

On March 6, Roosevelt invoked the Trading with the Enemy Act, which had been enacted in 1917, and issued an executive order proclaiming a nationwide bank holiday to extend through Thursday, March 9. At the same time, he called a special session of Congress to convene on March 9. In the interim, no bank was to pay out any coin, bullion, or currency or to transact any other business whatsoever without permission by the Secretary of the Treasury. The Secretary permitted only very limited banking operations during this period.

At its first meeting on March 9, Congress passed the Emergency Banking Bill presented to it that morning by the President, and Roosevelt signed it the same day. The Act confirmed actions taken under executive order and gave the President full power to control the banks for the protection of depositors; to open banks found to be in sound condition; to put on a sound basis banks found to require reorganization; and to control foreign exchange transactions, gold and currency movements, and all banking transactions.

The Act also carried three other important provisions: (1) It provided that the Comptroller of the Currency might be appointed as Conservator of National Banks, much as banking officials in many states had been empowered to act as conservators of state-chartered banks. As Conservator, he could reorganize a national bank, without declaring it bankrupt and putting it into receivership, by arranging for deposit claims to be readjusted and for the RFC to subscribe to preferred stock to be issued by the bank. (2) It authorized the Reserve banks to issue Federal Reserve bank notes, which would be collateraled by government securities and subject to no reserve requirements. Thus any increase in demands for currency could be met without recourse to clearing-house certificates or other cash substitutes, which were being considered in many cities. In fact, however, it was not necessary to issue any Federal Reserve bank notes. (3) It authorized the Reserve banks to lend on a wider range of assets under unusual conditions.

Armed with this legislation, the President extended the bank holiday indefinitely and announced plans for reopening "sound" banks. An executive order issued on March 10 empowered the Secretary of the Treasury to license banks found to be in satisfactory condition, permitting them to conduct their usual banking business, but stipulating that they should pay out no gold or gold certificates and supply no currency for hoarding. In determining which banks should, and which should not, be adjudged to be in "satisfactory condition," officials faced difficult policy problems, in addition to the sheer work of making such judgments in a short period of time. To allow very weak banks to open would invite a new round of bank failures and bank runs. However, there were strong pressures to reopen as many banks as possible. These pressures emanated from the desire to make banking facilities generally available, from bankers who feared adverse effects on their banks if they were not declared "sound," and from state banking officials who wanted favorable treatment of their banks. In the end, "satisfactory condition" appears to have been interpreted quite generously.

The Secretary announced on Saturday, March 11 that reopening dates would be Monday, March 13 for the Federal Reserve banks and for sound commercial banks located in the 12 Federal Reserve bank cities, March 14 for sound banks in about 250 other cities with recognized clearing houses, and March 15 for sound banks located elsewhere. Other banks would be licensed to reopen as they were found to be in, or were put into, satisfactory condition. President Roosevelt, in a radio address on Sunday, March 12, assured the nation that the reopened banks would be able to meet every legitimate call and that the government was determined not to have "another epidemic of bank failures."

The reopenings proceeded on schedule. It appears that by the end of the week about 75 percent of all member banks had been reopened without restrictions. On April 12, the first date after the banking crash for which comprehensive data are available, unrestricted licenses had been granted to members accounting for 90 percent of the total resources of all member banks. State authorities had licensed about 7,400 nonmember banks, or 71 percent of the total number of such banks. However, about $4 billion of deposits were still tied up in some 4,200 member and nonmember banks that had been operating prior to the banking crash but were not yet licensed or freed from restrictions on their operations.[1] Fortunately, the reopening of

---

[1]*Annual Report of the Federal Reserve Board, 1933*, pp. 14 and 22-24.

banks was not followed by a resumption of currency withdrawals. In fact, net inflows of currency to the banks amounted to $1.25 billion by the end of March and to $2 billion by the end of August.

PROBLEMS OF FINANCIAL REHABILITATION

Thus, the reopening of large majority of the banks accounting for an even larger proportion of total bank assets and deposits had been achieved quickly and with relative ease. A much more complex and difficult problem remained—that of rehabilitating the banks and other parts of the financial system and of restoring them to something like normal working order. Though both the difficulty of the problem and the time that would be required to solve it were underestimated at the time, it was clear that financial rehabilitation was a prerequisite to recovery.

This broad and complex problem had many parts: (1) There was the problem of financial intermediaries which were either closed or operating under restrictions on withdrawals, or lending operations, or both. These included not only the banks that had closed since the beginning of 1933 but also banks that had closed earlier and other types of distressed intermediaries, such as building and loan associations, mortgage companies, and joint-stock land banks. Large amounts of deposits and other financial claims against these institutions were frozen and unavailable for use; attempts to liquidate their assets were depressing the prices of securities, real estate, and other assets; and they could not perform their normal functions of gathering savings and lending.

(2) There was the problem of the liquidity and solvency of the institutions that had been reopened. Though they had been adjudged to be in "satisfactory condition," this was in many cases an overly generous rating. In fact, great numbers of them were laden with illiquid assets and would have been insolvent if their assets had been valued at prevailing market prices. The serious depreciation in the values of their bond holdings was evident from the published market prices of bonds. Fortunately, there were no such published prices for mortgages and most other types of bank loans, but it was clear that banks would suffer large losses on many of these holdings if they tried to liquidate them. While these conditions continued there was an ever-present danger that new runs on the intermediaries would develop, or at least that the institutions would be unable to attract new flows of funds. Moreover, they could hardly be expected to assume even normal risks while they remained so illiquid and at best only slightly solvent.

(3) There were the problems of ultimate debtors, such as business firms, farmers, homeowners, and some state and local governments. We noted earlier the widespread defaults and delinquencies and the rising tide of mortgage moratoria in early 1933. Millions of debtors were clearly unable to meet their obligations fully and promptly under existing conditions, and many would be unable to survive until money incomes had again been raised to full employment levels. Their plight contributed to the distress of financial intermediaries, robbed the debtors of their creditworthiness, and made them unwilling to

assume the risks of new investment. Thus there was a "financial deadlock"; debtors could meet their obligations fully only when something like full employment had been achieved, but the latter could occur only after the financial system had been restored to working order.

Solution of these complex problems was made even more difficult by conflicting interests and objectives. For example, it was clear that someone would have to take losses in terms of dollars because so many debtors could not and would not meet their obligations fully and promptly. But who should suffer the losses? The federal government and its credit agencies could have absorbed them, scaling down claims against debtors but paying creditors in full. In fact, it did assume risk and suffer some losses as it supplied huge amounts of loans and some equity capital. However, it was not willing to assume all losses, especially as such an act would be construed as a handout to banks and other creditors.

Debt claims were readjusted in many ways—by postponing payment dates, reducing interest charges, or scaling down principal values, or by combinations of these devices. Thus, deposits and other financial claims against banks and other intermediaries were scaled down, placed in restricted accounts, or exchanged for equity claims. In similar ways but on a much wider scale, debts of farmers, homeowners, business firms, and local governments were readjusted. Under the circumstances, creditors were not in a strong position to resist such adjustments, and their position was further weakened by the government's insistence in many cases on readjustment of debt claims as a prerequisite for government loans. It was weakened too by sweeping changes in the bankruptcy laws and in other laws governing debt contracts, which made it more difficult, and in some cases impossible, for creditors to enforce fulfillment of contracts.

Though readjustment of debt claims occurred on a broad scale, it had serious disadvantages as a rehabilitation device, primarily because an action that benefitted debtors was likely to harm creditors and to have undesirable side effects. For example, scaling down of deposits and other claims against intermediaries did serve to restore the solvency and liquidity of these institutions, but it also reduced the wealth and spending power of depositors and jeopardized the future ability of these institutions to attract funds. Similarly, scaling down of debt claims against farmers, homeowners, and business firms helped these debtors but injured their creditors, including financial intermediaries. Thus debt readjustment alone could not rehabilitate the financial system.

GOVERNMENT FINANCIAL AID

By lending and by purchasing equity claims, the federal government and its agencies supplied huge amounts of funds to aid the process of financial rehabilitation. In this, the Federal Reserve played only a minor role. Its loans to banks fell below $100 million by early 1934 and thereafter remained well below this level. The Reserve banks were empowered to lend directly to business firms after mid-1934, but their total outstanding loans of this type never rose above $35 million. Most of the government funds were disbursed through the RFC, the federal land banks and the Federal Farm Mortgage Corporation, and the Homeowners' Loan Corporation. The processing of applications and disbursing of funds proved to be more time-consuming than was anticipated. In general, the process began about mid-1933, gained momentum until about the end of 1934, slowed down in 1935, and was largely completed by early 1936.

The RFC, which had been established in February 1932, was greatly enlarged in both resources and scope of operations and converted into the government's largest general-purpose institution. Among its many activities, it helped three classes of banks: closed banks, those that were not in bankruptcy but that remained unlicensed to reopen or were operating under restrictions, and banks that were licensed and unrestricted but needed improvements in their liquidity, or solvency, or both. By March 4, 1933 the RFC had already lent nearly $80 million to liquidators of closed banks. (See Table 17-1.) These operations were speeded up, especially after the creation in October 1933 of a Deposit Liquidation Board, whose purpose was to expedite the process. From that time through the end of 1933, the RFC authorized 776 loans, aggregating more than $300 million, to liquidators of closed banks. Between March 4, 1933 and late October, 1937 loan disbursements of this type amounted to more than $875 million. These served the multiple purpose of making funds available to depositors more quickly, of enabling liquidators to realize more on bank assets by disposing of them in an orderly manner, and of lessening downward pressures on the market prices of bank assets.

TABLE 17-1

Assistance by the Reconstruction Finance Corporation to Private Financial Institutions, February 2, 1932-October 23, 1937
(disbursements in millions of dollars)

	February 2, 1932-March 3, 1933	March 4, 1933-October 23, 1937
Loans to		
Banks and trust companies	951.4	186.3
Building and loan associations	101.5	13.2
Insurance companies	80.5	9.2
Credit unions	0.5	0.2
Mortgage loan companies	90.7	199.4
Liquidators of closed banks	79.6	875.2
Liquidators of building and loan associations	—	2.3
Federal land banks	18.8	368.4
Regional agricultural credit corporations	41.4	131.8
Joint-stock land banks	4.9	13.1
Livestock credit corporations	11.9	0.7
Agricultural credit corporations	3.6	2.0
Purchases of preferred stock and loans on such stock in		
Banks and trust companies		1,084.1
Insurance companies		34.3

Source: The Public Papers and Addresses of Franklin D. Roosevelt, Random House, New York, 1938, Vol. 2, pp. 403-404.

The RFC also made further loans to the other two classes of banks—both those licensed and unrestricted and those unlicensed or restricted. However, loans to these banks and trust companies were only about one-fifth as large in the period following March 4 as they had been in the preceding period. A major reason for this was that banks were receiving large inflows of funds from other sources: inflows of currency from circulation, large gold inflows, funds resulting from loans by the Federal Farm Mortgage Corporation and the Home Owners' Loan Corporation, and funds resulting from RFC loans to borrowers other than banks, such as the railroads, holders of farm commodities, and local governmental units.

However, the smaller volume of RFC loans to banks after March 1933 also resulted in part from the adoption of a new method of helping banks—that of supplying funds and increasing bank solvency by subscribing to preferred stock or other equity claims against banks. Such RFC purchases had exceeded $1 billion by October 1937. This fact was closely related to the creation of a new system for insuring bank deposits. The administration had seriously considered establishing at least a temporary deposit insurance program to become effective in March 1933 for banks licensed to reopen. However, it finally decided that such a program might fail if it admitted banks that were not in really sound condition, and that the introduction of such a program should be deferred until necessary preparations had been made.

The Banking Act of 1933, approved on June 16, established the Federal Deposit Insurance Corporation (the FDIC) and provided for two insurance plans—a temporary plan to become effective January 1, 1934 and a permanent plan to succeed it. Of the capital stock of the FDIC, $150 million was subscribed by the Treasury, $139 million by the Federal Reserve banks, and $37 million by participating banks. All licensed member banks were required to join the FDIC; nonmember banks were permitted to do so if they wished and could meet entrance requirements. Most elected to join. The plan initially provided for insurance of the first $2,500 of each deposit account; this was soon raised to $5,000.

Both federal and state banking authorities worked feverishly during the latter part of 1933 preparing the way for deposit insurance. One huge task was to examine nearly 9,000 nonmember banks which had applied for membership, to evaluate their positions, and to determine what financial assistance they needed to qualify for insurance. The RFC supplied most of this assistance; it was in this period that the RFC made most of its purchases of equity claims against banks.

The RFC also supplied large amounts of funds directly to nonbank financial intermediaries. For example, its contributions between March 4, 1933 and late October 1937 were $199.4 million to mortgage loan companies, $13.2 million to building and loan associations, $43.5 million to insurance companies, $368.4 million to the federal land banks, and $146.7 million to other lenders to farmers. (See Table 17-1.)

The federal government and its agencies also supplied large amounts of funds in the process of rehabilitating farm debt. While farmers were demanding that their debt payments be postponed and their debt burdens reduced, their creditors were not in an enviable position. This was true not only of private lenders, such as commercial banks and insurance companies, but also of farm credit institutions established earlier under the auspices of the federal government. For example, all the joint-stock land banks, which had been established under federal charters after 1916 and were privately owned, were highly illiquid, and most of them were insolvent. All were placed in liquidation in 1933. Even the 12 federal land banks, also authorized in 1916, were immobilized. Most of their loans had been made through a large number of national farm loan associations, each of which was, in effect, a cooperative group of farmers. Now most of these associations were unable to meet their obligations to their land banks.

The federal government employed two principal methods, in addition to its efforts to raise farm incomes, to rehabilitate farm debts. One was to stave off foreclosures, postpone debt payments, and scale down debts. The other was to provide large amounts of credit. To expedite these activities, all federal programs in the field of agricultural credit were, in March 1933, concentrated in a new agency—the Farm Credit Administration (the FCA).

An act approved in March 1933 amended the bankruptcy laws to provide for "agricultural compositions and extensions." Acting under this power, the FCA sponsored the formation of debt adjustment committees to encourage debtors and creditors to reach agreements and to avoid foreclosures. Such committees were established in 2,700 counties in 44 states. Though scale-downs were not involved in all the agreements, it appears that total scale-downs of farm debts amounted to about $200 million. Many creditors were under strong pressure to compromise their claims in order to qualify for federal refinancing.[2]

The two principal suppliers of federal funds to rehabilitate farm debt were the federal land banks and the Land Bank Commissioner. The government supplied additional capital to the former, and the latter secured most of his funds from a government subscription of $200 million and from the issue of fully guaranteed bonds by a new institution, the Federal Farm Mortgage Corporation (the FFMC). The federal land banks lent up to 50 percent of the value of farm land plus 20 percent of permanent improvements, and the Land Bank Commissioner supplied additional funds. Both followed generous appraisal practices, evaluating properites not at their current market prices but at "normal appraised value" or "prudent investment value." Both also reduced interest rates.

Huge amounts of farm mortgages were purchased by these institutions. Between May 1933 and June 30, 1936, they advanced about $2.1 billion in mortgage loans. Of this amount, $1,460 million was used to refinance farm mortgages, $60 million to pay taxes, $290 million to pay short-term debts, and nearly $90 million to buy land and to redeem land that had been foreclosed. Holders of farm mortgages were major recipients of the proceeds of these loans. About $295 million went to life insurance companies, $344 mil-

---

[2]The Frazier-Lemke Act of June 1934 provided, in effect, a five-year moratorium on farm foreclosures. This was declared unconstitutional in 1935. It was followed by a second act in 1935, which was held to be constitutional. However, only a few cases were handled under these acts.

lion to commercial banks, and $683 million to others in exchange for re-
financed mortgages.[3] By the end of 1936, nearly 40 percent of all farm
mortgages were held by agencies under the FCA.

Still more funds were supplied by the federal government and its
agencies in the process of rehabilitating home mortgages. The state of debts
on urban residential reas estate was quite similar to that of farm debts.
Owners of great numbers of mortgaged homes were in distress; so were investors in these mortgages, and especially building and loan associations, mortgage companies, insurance companies, and commercial banks.

Here again, the government used two principal methods to ameliorate the
debt situation. One was to postpone maturities and scale down debts. The
other was to supply huge amounts of credit. Some credit had already been
supplied for this purpose prior to March 1933. For example, the RFC had
lent over $100 million to building and loan associations, nearly $81 million to
insurance companies, and nearly $91 million to mortgage loan companies. The
12 federal home loan banks, which had been authorized on July 22, 1932,
were of little help prior to 1933, partly because of the time required for their
organization and partly because of technical defects in the enabling law. However, by the end of 1933 they had lent over $88 million to holders of home
mortgages. Between March 4, 1933 and late October 1937, the RFC lent
another $199 million to mortgage loan companies. (See Table 17-1, above.)
However, most of the burden of refinancing home mortgages was borne by a
new institution authorized by an act of June 13, 1933—the Home Owners'
Loan Corporation (the HOLC).

The HOLC derived its funds from two sources—from a $200 million
capital subscription by the government and from issues of bonds carrying a
full government guarantee. It lent to three types of borrowers: (1) those who
had been in involuntary default on the date of the passage of the Act;
(2) those who had lost their homes through foreclosure, forced sale, or surrender since January 1, 1930; and (3) those who, while holding property free
and clear, were unable to secure from other sources funds to pay past-due
taxes or assessments or to provide necessary repairs.

Applications began to pour in even before the HOLC opened for business. From its inception in mid-1933 to its termination of lending in June
1936, the HOLC made 1,018,000 loans, aggregating $1,093 million. One out
of every 5 mortgaged dwellings had received refinancing aid. The HOLC took
over mortgages amounting to $768 million from building and loan associa-
tions, $500 million from closed commercial banks, $746 million from other
commercial banks, $167 million from savings banks, and $1,007 million from
individual lenders, mortgage companies, and others.[4]

Though large numbers of business firms were delinquent or in default on
their debts and many more had suffered serious deterioration of their credit-

---

[3]The Twentieth Century Fund, *Debts and Recovery, 1929 to 1937*, The Fund,
New York, 1938, p. 148.

[4]*Annual Report of the Federal Home Loan Bank Board for the Year Ending June
30, 1937*, p. 29.

worthiness, the federal government provided for them no specific program comparable to those for farm and home debts. However, some assistance was provided. For one thing, an amendment to the Bankruptcy Act in June 1934 made it possible for corporations to reorganize without going into receivership, doing so by scaling down debts, exchanging debts for equity claims, rearranging maturities, and so on. Those provisions were used in a large number of cases. The railroads, which remained in desperate financial condition, received another $211 million in loans from the RFC after March 4, 1933. In March 1934, Roosevelt asked Congress to establish 12 credit banks for industry to provide working capital for established small - and medium-sized firms that were unable to secure such longer-term funds from other sources. Congress did not comply; instead, it authorized the Federal Reserve banks and the RFC to participate in such loans with private lenders or to make such loans themselves if the loans were sound and if credit was not obtainable on a reasonable basis from the usual sources. Between mid-1934 and the end of November, 1937, thse agencies approved about 4,800 loans aggregating $323 million. However, they rejected more applications than they approved, primarily because the loans were ineligible under the conditions imposed by the Act or could not meet the test of soundness.[5] These loans would undoubtedly have been much larger if the standards of "soundness" applied to them had been as lenient as those applied to mortgages granted by the FFMC and the HOLC.

Though some funds for financial rehabilitation were supplied by other government credit agencies which will not be discussed here, the great bulk of them came from the RFC, the federal land banks and the Federal Farm Mortgage Corporation, and the Home Owners' Loan Corporation. It is impossible to estimate accurately how many of the funds issued by these agencies after March 1933 flowed directly or indirectly to commercial banks, but the total was huge. From the data above, we can identify the following flows to commercial banks, including both closed and operating banks:

From the RFC:	
Loans	$1061.5 million
Stock subscriptions	1084.1 million
From refinancing farm debt	344.0 million
From refinancing home debt	1246.0 million
Total	$3735.6 million

Further large amounts initially disbursed to other borrowers must have flowed indirectly to commercial banks. In addition, there were very large flows of funds, directly and indirectly, from government credit agencies to nonbank financial intermediaries.

Table 17-2 shows that by the end of 1935 holdings of loans and preferred stock by government corporations and credit agencies had grown to the huge sum of $9.4 billion. Most of these were in three categories: loans to and preferred stock in financial institutions, loans on urban homes, and loans to

---

[5]*The Public Papers and Addresses of Franklin D. Roosevelt*, Random House, New York, 1938, Vol. 3, pp. 152-155.

farmers. It is significant that loans to all other types of business firms, except the railroads, were so small. This was one of the great gaps in the program for financial rehabilitation.

TABLE 17-2

Holdings of Loans and Preferred Stock by U.S. Government Corporations and Credit Agencies, December 31, 1935 (in millions of dollars)

Loans to financial institutions	678
Preferred stock	1,018
Loans to railroads	572
Home and housing mortgage loans	2,903
Farm mortgage loans	2,867
Other agricultural loans	750
Other loans	615
Total	9,402

Source: Board of Governors of the Federal Reserve System, *Banking and Monetary Statistics,* Washington, D.C., 1943, p. 517. The government credit institutions included are the Reconstruction Finance Corporation, the federal land banks, the federal intermediate credit banks, the Federal Farm Mortgage Corporation, the Production Credit Corporation, the Commodity Credit Corporation, the federal home loan banks, and the Home Owners' Loan Corporation. Claims of these agencies against each other are excluded.

OTHER FINANCIAL MEASURES

In addition to supplying huge amounts of funds to aid financial rehabilitation, the federal government took a number of other actions bearing directly upon the structure of the financial system and on financial flows. A few of the most important of these will be mentioned briefly.

One device was to provide insurance of claims against two major types of financial intermediaries for the multiple purposes of protecting depositors, of reducing the probability of withdrawals, and of restoring a flow of funds to these institutions. We have already mentioned the FDIC, which came into operation at the beginning of 1934 and insured the first $5,000 of each deposit account at most commercial banks. To provide similar insurance for its members, the Federal Savings and Loan Insurance Corporation (the FSLIC) was established in June 1934. All federal savings and loan associations were required to join and state-chartered associations were permitted to do so if they wished and could qualify.

Another device was to provide insurance for certain types of private debts. The Federal Housing Administration (the FHA) was created in June 1934 to insure long-term amortized mortgages on homes. The Commodity Credit Corporation, established in October 1933, lent upon, and guaranteed private loans on, selected farm products. Its primary purpose was to provide price supports for these products, but in the process it extended and guaranteed large amounts of credit.

The government also established, or authorized federal charters for, several new types of financial institutions, mostly in the fields of agricultural and housing credit. A central bank for cooperatives and 12 regional banks for cooperatives were established to provide long-term funds to agricultural cooperatives. Twelve production credit corporations, each with its cluster of production credit associations, were created to provide short- and medium-term loans to farmers. The latter, managed by farmers, secured most of their funds from the government and from loans by the federal intermediate credit banks.

To provide additional facilities for housing credit, the HOLC Act of June 1933 authorized federal charters for savings and loan associations; these could be established either *de novo* or by conversion of state-chartered associations. The HOLC was empowered to buy shares in these institutions in areas in which such facilities were inadequate.

REHABILITATION OR REFORM?

At least three other new laws in the financial field should be mentioned. (1) First is the Banking Act of 1933. The most relevant innovations in this law were its divorce of investment banking from commercial banks, its prohibition of interest on demand deposits and provision for ceilings on rates paid on time and savings deposits, and its provision for more restrictive control of bank loans on security collateral. (2) Second is the Securities Act of 1933, often referred to as the "Truth-in-Securities Act." The purpose of this Act was to regulate new issues of securities. In effect, it provided that new securities could be offered publicly only after registration with the government, that the issuer and the underwriter should provide full and truthful information, and that violators would be subject to both civil and criminal penalities. (3) Last is the Securities Exchange Act of 1934, which provided regulation of trading on the national securities exchanges. This Act prohibited various types of manipulation and trading abuses on the exchanges and required companies whose securities were traded on the exchanges to provide full and accurate financial data. Violators were subject to both civil and criminal penalties.

All of these laws were highly controversial. Even some who admitted that financial reform was appropriate complained that these actions were unnecessarily stringent, restrictive, and severe. Also debated was whether these reforms promoted or obstructed financial rehabilitation and economic recovery. Roosevelt insisted that these reforms were essential to recovery because the financial system could again function satisfactorily only when the public's confidence in the integrity of financial institutions and practices had been restored. However, many others, including at least a few Federal Reserve officials, believed that they obstructed recovery. Several changes were levied against the Securities Act: (1) It increased the costs and risks of new flotations, especially those of small firms. Costs of providing the required data and of preparing registration statements were high before lawyers and business officials became familiar with requirements. (2) The civil and criminal penalties to be imposed on violators, together with fears that the Act would be administered in an unfriendly spirit, made officers of issuing companies and of underwriters reluctant to assume risks. Similar charges were directed to the penalty provisions of the Securities Exchange Act.

The Banking Act of 1933 was generally supposed to have been designed to remedy serious banking abuses that had become evident in the preceding period, especially those arising out of the activities of commercial banks in investment banking and trading in securities. Such abuses had occurred, and reaction against them provided support for this legislation. Yet Eugene Meyer was correct in his observations that the Act bore the imprint of Senator Glass' devotion to the commercial loan theory and his conviction that commercial banks should avoid any connection with investment securities.[6] He and others believed that this Act obstructed, or threatened to obstruct, recovery in at least three ways: (1) The requirement that commercial banks refrain from engaging in investment banking activities, either directly or through affiliates, tended to decrease the availability of underwriting facilities at the very time that the economy needed all the investment that could be induced. (2) The prohibition of interest on demand deposits led to withdrawals of some correspondent bank deposits from financial centers, and thus derived the central correspondents of funds that they would probably have utilized more effectively than would the banks that withdrew them. (3) The provision for more restrictive control of bank loans on security collateral indicated official opposition to this type of loan. Meyer and others believed that the types of loans made by banks should be broadened, not narrowed. However, the Board did little or nothing to enforce this provision.

It is impossible to estimate the extent to which the reform measures obstructed recovery. They almost certainly did so to some extent by increasing costs and uncertainties, though it is difficult to believe that these were a major obstacle to recovery. However, their negative effects may have been greater in terms of the broader problems of misunderstanding and mistrust between Roosevelt and large sectors of the business and financial community.

CONCLUSIONS

The measures taken by the government to rehabilitate the financial system were indeed numerous and sweeping. They included readjustments of debt contracts; refinancing of huge amounts of farm and home debts; loans to banks and other financial intermediaries; purchases of equity claims against intermediaries; loans to railroads; smaller loans to other types of business firms; insurance of claims against banks and savings and loan associations; insurance of housing mortgages and loans on selected farm products; and establishment of several new types of financial institutions. There can be little doubt that these measures, taken as a whole, helped to improve the financial situation. Yet these measures, together with massive increases of bank reserves and with all the government's other economic policies, failed to achieve full recovery of financial flows and of the saving-investment process. As noted earlier, all major types of private investment—residential construction, other construction, and purchases of producers' durable equipment—remained in the doldrums. Some of the reasons for this failure will be assessed later.

---

[6]In his papers, Meyer make frequent reference to this theme.

18

Gold and Silver Policies

The executive order of March 6, 1933 proclaiming a four-day nation-wide bank holiday not only froze domestic banking transactions but also prohibited foreign exchange operations and exports of gold and gold certificates. As it turned out, this was a preliminary step to almost revolutionary changes in relationships between the dollar and gold and silver. Free redeemability of the dollar into gold was never restored. As restrictions on dealings in foreign exchange were removed, the dollar was allowed to depreciate in terms of both gold and foreign currencies until September. Then the government embarked upon a deliberate and aggressive program to drive up the dollar price of gold, and thus to depreciate the dollar in terms of both gold and foreign currencies. These actions culminated in the adoption of the Gold Reserve Act of 1934, which decreased the gold value of the dollar by nearly 40 percent and put the nation on a limited gold bullion standard. The government also monetized unprecedented amounts of silver.

There is no reason to believe that Roosevelt had decided upon such policies when he assumed office, or even within three or four weeks after that date. If he had, he did not inform Federal Reserve officials or even high-ranking members of his Treasury Department.[1] They expected that free dealing in gold would be restored as soon as the crisis was safely past. These policies evolved step by step in response to strong pressures, both within and outside the government, to raise commodity prices, especially the prices of farm products. We have already noted that there was strong sentiment for "inflation" in the old Congress during the first two months of 1933. Many types of proposals were offered: to decrease the gold value of the dollar, to monetize silver, to order the Federal Reserve to raise prices to the levels of 1926, to order the Federal Reserve to purchase large amounts of government securities, to issue fiat money, and so on. The new Congress was, if anything, more "inflationary" than the old one and more insistent that something be done

---

[1]For example, Secretary of the Treasury William Woodin denied that the United States was abandoning the gold standard; he stated, "We are definitely on the gold standard. Gold merely cannot be obtained for a few days." *The New York Times*, March 6, 1933, p. 1.

quickly. It appeared likely that Congress would enact expansionary monetary legislation mandatory on the President. However, the outcome was a bill giving Roosevelt broad and sweeping discretionary powers over money.

THE THOMAS AMENDMENT

This legislation, named for its sponsor, Senator Elmer Thomas of Oklahoma, was included as Title III of the Agricultural Adjustment Act, which was signed by the President on May 12. Under this Act, the President himself, or the Secretary of the Treasury acting under presidential direction, was empowered to:

1. Enter into agreements with the Federal Reserve Board and the Federal Reserve banks for the latter to acquire directly from the Treasury and to hold up to $3 billion of government securities in addition to those already in their portfolios. If such purchases should require a suspension of reserve requirements by a Reserve bank, the bank would not be subject to either the penalities on its deficiency of reserves or the automatic increases of its discount rate prescribed in the Federal Reserve Act. Though the Federal Reserve was not legally obligated to buy, it was unlikely, under the circumstances, to refuse a formal, or even an informal, request to do so.
2. Issue United States notes (greenbacks) in amounts not to exceed $3 billion. These were to be legal tender for all debts.
3. Fix the gold value of the dollar by proclamation, with the limitation that it should not be reduced more than 50 percent.
4. Fix the silver value of the dollar and provide for the unlimited coinage of gold and silver at fixed ratios. The President could reestablish bimetallism in this country alone, or he could enter into agreements with other countries to establish international bimetallism.
5. Accept silver at a price not to exceed 50 cents an ounce in payment of debts by foreign governments, the total accepted from this source not to exceed $200 million. Any silver acquired in this way was to be coined into silver dollars or held as backing for silver certificates.

Though Roosevelt received these sweeping powers on May 12, he did not rush to use them. He never used his power to issue greenbacks. He did not invoke his power to sell government securities directly to the Federal Reserve, but the very existence of this power increased the willingness of the Federal Reserve to purchase securities in the open market and to assist Treasury financing. Very little silver was monetized before December 1933, and its large-scale monetization began only after mid-1934. In the meantime, however, many steps had been taken to reduce and eliminate the convertibility of the dollar in gold and to permit, and then to force, a decrease of the value of the dollar in terms of gold and foreign currencies.

THE ROAD TO DEVALUATION

The first steps toward a reduction of the gold value of the dollar were actions to end the convertibility of the dollar into gold at a fixed value, both domestically and internationally. As already noted, both the Federal Reserve and other banks were forbidden to pay out gold either domestically or to other countries during the bank holiday. This prohibition was continued after the end of the holiday. On March 8, the Federal Reserve Board requested the Reserve banks to prepare lists showing the names of persons who had recently withdrawn gold or gold certificates and had not redeposited them by March 13, and to give publicity to the request. The deadline was later extended. This thinly veiled threat was superseded on April 5 by an executive order which prohibited hoarding of gold coin, gold bullion, and gold certificates and required holders to turn in amounts in excess of $100 on or before May 1. Even the $100 exemption was eliminated in December. Thus, the domestic convertibility of the dollar into gold was virtually ended.

In the meantime, the international convertibility of the dollar into gold had also been terminated. After March 10, no one was permitted to export gold coin, gold bullion, or gold certificates without authorization by the Secretary of the Treasury. The latter permitted exports of gold previously earmarked for foreign governments and central banks and for the Bank for International Settlements, but granted licenses for other exports only with increasing reluctance. He did permit about $9.6 million of gold exports to Holland and France during the period April 13-17 to cushion the decline of the dollar in terms of the currencies of those countries. However, on April 18, when the exchange rate on the dollar had fallen further, he refused to license gold exports. By this time Roosevelt had definitely decided that he wanted the dollar to depreciate in terms of gold and foreign currencies. At a press conference on May 19 he told assembled reporters:

> If I were going to write a story, I would write it along the lines of the decision that was actually taken last Saturday, but which really goes into effect today, by which the government will not allow the exporting of gold, except earmarked gold for foreign governments of course, and balances in commercial exchange . . . .
> The whole problems before us is to raise commodity prices. For the last year, the dollar has been shooting up and we decided to quit competition. The general effect will be an increase in commodity prices . . . . Let the dollar take care of itself by protecting it against foreign currencies, and letting it seek its own natural level instead of trying artificially to support it.[2]

This decision was effected in an executive order issued on May 20. Virtually no gold exports were permitted from that time through the end of August.

Thus the exchange rate on the dollar was free to "float" in exchange markets from early March through the end of August, 1933. The government did not buy or sell gold or foreign exchange to influence the behavior of exchange rates. However, rates were undoubtedly influenced by various government actions and statements suggesting that the dollar might be devalued.

---

[2]*The Public Papers and Addresses of Franklin D. Roosevelt*, Random House, New York, 1938, Vol. 2, pp. 137-138.

One such action was a congressional resolution on June 5 outlawing "gold clauses" in all private and government obligations, both past and future. These clauses typically obligated the debtor to pay interest and principal in "gold dollars of their present weight and fineness, or their dollar equivalent." To raise the price of gold while these clauses remained in force would have been infeasible, for every increase in the dollar price of gold would have increased proportionally the dollar obligations of debtors. Another action that strongly influenced expectations was the President's veto, in July, of a proposal that the gold value of the dollar be stabilized. This will be discussed later.

The dollar fell sharply in terms of most other major currencies during this period of floating exchange rates. Exchange rates on the other remaining gold-bloc currencies—those of Belgium, Switzerland, and the Netherlands—move approximately in proportion to the rate on the French franc, and exchange rates on several other floating currencies moved approximately in proportion to the rate on the British pound. Table 18-1 shows that between January and May the dollar price of the French franc rose 18 percent and that of the British pound 17 percent. In July, the franc had risen 40 percent and the pound 38 percent since the beginning of the year. In other words, the dollar had declined 29 percent in terms of gold and gold currencies and 28 percent in terms of sterling. These were indeed large changes in such a short period.

TABLE 18-1

Selected Exchange Rates, 1933-1934
(averages of daily rates)

	French franc (in cents per franc)	British pound (in cents per pound)	Index of exchange rates Jan. 1933 = 100	
			Franc	Pound
1933				
January	3.90	336.1	100	100
February	3.92	342.2	101	102
March	3.94	343.3	101	102
April	4.10	357.9	105	106
May	4.59	393.2	118	117
June	4.80	413.6	123	123
July	5.46	465.0	140	138
August	5.37	450.3	138	134
September	5.77	466.5	148	139
October	5.82	466.8	149	139
November	6.27	515.0	161	153
December	6.12	511.6	157	152
1934				
January	6.21	504.9	159	151
February	6.46	503.3	166	150
March	6.58	509.4	169	152
April	6.61	515.3	169	153
May	6.61	510.6	169	152
June	6.60	504.8	169	152
July	6.59	504.1	169	150

Source: Board of Governors of the Federal Reserve System, *Banking and Monetary Statistics*, Washington, D.C., 1943, pp. 670 and 681.

However, by the end of August, and even more within the next few weeks, there arose a feeling within the government, and to some extent outside, that the policy of allowing exchange rates and the price of gold to float was inadequate and should be supplemented or replaced by more positive policies. A major reason for this change was the relapse of recovery. The sharp rise of business activity and prices that had begun in March ended suddenly in July, giving way to abrupt declines. Moreover, foreign exchange rates and the price of gold ceased rising in late July and actually fell slightly in August. Some feared that the exchange rate on the dollar might rise markedly because of such factors as a return flow of the capital funds that had been exported in the preceding period or overt actions by other countries to reduce the values of their currencies in terms of gold and the dollar. Roosevelt therefore decided to take more positive actions to depress the dollar in terms of gold and foreign monies.

The first step was in connection with the establishment of a market for newly mined domestic gold. An executive order on August 29 permitted producers to sell gold abroad by consigning it to the Secretary of the Treasury, who would pay for it at the highest price available in any foreign market. This program continued through October 24, on which date the price of gold was $29.80 an ounce, or 44 percent above the old mint price of $20.67.

This program was superseded on October 25 by a new arrangement under which the RFC aggressively purchased gold at advancing prices. In his fourth fireside chat on October 22, Roosevelt assured the nation that he was determined to raise commodity prices further and added:

> . . . I am going to establish a Government market for gold in the United States. Therefore, under the clearly defined authority of existing law, I am authorizing the Reconstruction Finance Corporation to buy gold newly mined in the United States at prices to be determined from time to time after consultation with the Secretary of the Treasury and the President. Whenever necessary to the end in view, we shall also buy or sell gold in the world market.
>
> My aim in taking this step is to establish and maintain continuous control.
>
> This is a policy and not an expedient!
>
> It is not to be used merely to offset a temporary fall in prices. We are thus continuing to move toward a managed currency.[3]

The RFC paid for gold by issuing its own 90-day debentures. Its intitial purchase price was above the dollar price of gold in London and other centers, and the price was raised daily, almost without interruption, until the middle of November. It was raised five more times during the latter half of November, but only twice more between the first of December and the date on which the dollar was formally devalued, January 31, 1934. Thus the price of gold was increased from $29.80 an ounce on October 28 to $34.45 in mid-January. The latter price was 67 percent above the old mint price. These actions were accompanied by large increases of exchange rates on most foreign currencies. For example, Table 18-1 shows that in January 1934, as compared with levels of a year earlier, the exchange rate on the French franc had risen

---

[3]*The Public Papers and Addresses of Franklin D. Roosevelt, op. cit.*, Vol. 2, pp. 426-427.

59 percent and that on the British pound 51 percent. The dollar had depreciated 37 percent in terms of the franc and 33 percent in terms of sterling. At more than $5, the pound was considerably above its old gold parity of $4.8665.

The major purpose of Roosevelt's policy of depreciating the dollar in terms of gold and foreign currencies was clearly to raise commodity prices, and especially prices of agricultural products. What is not so clear is how he expected his actions in this field to operate upon prices. Such actions could affect domestic prices through three main channels. (1) A depreciation of the dollar exchange rate would have direct effects on the dollar prices of internationally traded goods. To the degree that American actions did not depress the prices of goods in terms of foreign currencies, a decline of the exchange rate on the dollar would raise the dollar prices of American exports and also those of American imports, thus permitting prices of import-competing goods to rise. However, there was no reason to expect that these price increases would spread to purely domestic goods and services. (2) These actions would affect expectations concerning the future course of prices. To the extent that they created expectations of future price increases, they might induce anticipatory buying. (3) They would also affect the volume of bank reserves and the money supply. It is important to note that gold purchases and increases in the price of gold did not add to bank reserves or bring pressure for an expansion of the money supply prior to the end of January 1934. The monetary gold stock was not revalued, and the dollar value of the gold stock remained virtually constant from April 1933 through January 1934. Gold purchased by the RFC was paid for not with claims that would expand bank reserves or the money supply but with interest-bearing RFC debentures. In effect, the purchased gold was "sterilized." Expansionary monetary effects began only after the end of January 1934 when the gold stock was revalued, the Treasury began to spend some of its gold profits, and gold imports began. However, it will be useful to review some other events in 1933 before analyzing the Gold Reserve Act.

THE LONDON ECONOMIC CONFERENCE, JUNE 1933

This conference grew out of resolutions adopted at the Lausanne Conference in July 1932. It was originally expected to be held in late 1932 or January 1933 but was postponed to June, apparently to permit the new U.S. administration to participate. The main items on the agenda were these:

a. Financial questions
   Monetary and credit policy
   Exchange difficulties
   The level of prices
   The movement of capital
b. Economic questions
   Tariff policy
   Prohibitions and restrictions of importation and exportation

Quotas and other barriers to trade
Producers' agreements[4]

The question of war debts was not on the agenda, but the participants recognized that it would inevitably come up and would be an obstacle to success.

It was apparent long before the conference convened that it would be very difficult, if not impossible, to arrive at meaningful agreements on monetary and exchange-rate policies. All participating nations wanted "stabilization," but they differed widely on the appropriate definition of the term and on priorities. For example, to the French "stabilization" meant stability of each nation's currency in terms of gold. They felt that each nation should adopt a gold value for its monetary unit—preferably its old gold value—and then take all steps necessary to defend that value, even if this policy required domestic deflation. The British and various members of the British Empire held quite different views. At the end of a conference in Ottawa in July 1932, they had agreed that the ultimate aim should be restoration of a satisfactory international standard, but that this was both undesirable and impossible before certain conditions had been achieved:

1. A rise of the general level of commodity prices in the various countries to a height more in keeping with the level of costs, including the burden of debt and other fixed and semi-fixed charges . . . .
2. Adjustment of political, economic, and financial factors which caused the breakdown and which, if not adjusted, would do so again.
3. International cooperation to avoid, so far as possible, wide fluctuations in the purchasing power of the standard of value.[5]

In the meantime, they concluded, the most appropriate policies were to assure an ample supply of money at low rates, to secure international cooperative actions to bring about a worldwide rise of wholesale prices, to stabilize exchange rates among countries regulating their currencies in relation to sterling, and to avoid wide day-to-day fluctuations between sterling and gold. To reconcile such widely diverse views as those of the British and the French would have been virtually impossible even if the Americans had not precipitated a breakdown of the conference.

Events at a preparatory conference of experts held in Geneva in November 1932 foreshadowed difficulties that would face the London Conference. John H. Williams reported after attending the Geneva Conference:

The British began the discussions with the question, "How can prices be raised?" The other delegates immediately responded by asking, "When would sterling be stabilized?" because they felt that price increases were impossible until sterling exchange was more stable. The British delegates avoided this question and indicated that sterling could not be stabilized until there was some increase in prices or at least until debts were settled, but they would not discuss the matter at any length.

When the other delegates found that the English were not ready with any program they proposed immediate adjournment and the conference only lasted about ten days, the entire last week being spent largely in a discussion of adjournment.

---

[4]This section draws heavily on records at the Federal Reserve Bank of New York.

[5]*Report of Committee on Monetary and Financial Questions,* Imperial Economic Conference, Ottawa, 1932.

Williams came back with the impression that the stabilization of sterling exchange was a focus of attention, and that it was generally believed that stabilization was the first step towards economic or price improvement. He also got the impression that stabilization of sterling was quite out of the question until the debts had been dealt with.

There was also a great deal of discussion of the German position, and the consensus of view appeared to be that the relaxation of various restrictions in Germany was dependent upon

(1) The stabilization of sterling, and
(2) Some more permanent disposition of the Standstill Agreement.[6]

The American delegations to the London Conference were from the beginning confused and confusing. Though Roosevelt agreed to send delegates, he was unhappy that the conference was to be held before he had time to decide upon policies. He gave the delegates no clearly defined instructions, and the delegates often did not know who was empowered to speak for them. To make matters worse, there were in effect two delegations—one to a conference of representatives of national governments and one to a conference of central bankers. The governmental representatives were to make policies, and the central bankers were to provide expert advice and to work out technical details—a distinction difficult to maintain in practice.

There appears to have been rather general agreement that fluctuations of exchange rates during the conference would lead to jockeying for bargaining positions and would complicate negotiations. At the end of May 1933, the French government sent a message to Roosevelt indicating its judgment that some steps toward stabilization should be taken promptly and inviting him to send representatives to London for the purpose. Roosevelt accepted immediately, sending O.M.W. Sprague to represent the government and George L. Harrison to represent the Federal Reserve Bank of New York. Harrison was accompanied by Jay Crane, a Deputy Governor of the New York Bank. It was clearly understood that any agreement would require Roosevelt's approval, and that Harrison would consult Eugene R. Black, then Governor of the Federal Reserve Board, before making commitments for the Federal Reserve.

Sprague, Harrison, and Crane sailed for London on June 2, and on June 10 began a series of meetings with representatives of the British and French governments and central banks. The French wanted an immediate and permanent stabilization of currencies in terms of gold. The British would agree to no more than a temporary and tentative stabilization and would commit only a very limited amount of gold and other resources to the purpose. The Americans, especially Sprague, were in general agreement with the British position. During the next few days the delegates evolved plans for a temporary stabilization of the three currencies at approximately the existing level of exchange rates. The rate on the pound was about $4. Crane cabled from London to Burgess on June 16:

1. Bank of England has cabled to you text of proposed arrangement.

6Memorandum from W. Randolph Burgess to George L. Harrison, November 23, 1932. John H. Williams was economist for the Federal Reserve Bank of New York and professor of economics at Harvard. He and E. E. Day, an economist at Cornell, attended the Geneva Conference at Roosevelt's request.

2. Representatives of three Treasuries agreed this afternoon to propose a mean rate of 4 dollars for the pound. The Bank of England suggest a mean rate for gold of 123 shillings for five ounces which they say gives a mean rate between the franc and the pound of 85.79 with upper and lower limit of 87.09 and 84.54.

3. The two mean exchange rates above give us a mean rate on the franc of 4.662 and upper and lower limits of 4.731 and 4.593. The spread is figured at 3 percent in each case.

4. The foregoing limits would make possible a 6 percent fluctuation in the dollar-sterling rate or from 3.88 to 4.12 since the dollar and the pound can vary 3 percent each against the gold franc.

5. Maximum amount proposed is 3,000,000 ounces which is all Bank of England would agree to although we think this is on the small side. We could do nothing however as Sprague favors small amount.

6. Sprague is reporting figures to Washington.

In the meantime, and especially on June 14 and 15, there had been widespread rumors of an agreement in London to stabilize the dollar-pound rate at about £1 = $4. Though Secretary Woodin denied this, the rumors were followed by a drop of both commodity and stock prices. At least one group reacted quickly and adversely. The Committee for the Nation telegraphed to Roosevelt on June 16:

> The price of commodities and securities throughout the United States fell today in response to news of the mistaken policy being pursued by the American delegation in London. The pound has already depreciated 31 percent. The dollar must be cut, according to our calculations, 43 per cent to restore our price level. Thus seems that if the English pound were held stationary at its present gold equivalent it would have to go to $5.70. Every attempt to stabilize in the ratio of $4.00 to a pound must raise grave doubts as to early restoration of American price level .... Instead of stabilizing, the United States should act to depress the dollar by selling it abroad .... Our 10 per cent of foreign trade and international finance must be subordinated to our domestic price level which controls the relations of all Americans to each other.[7]

It was on this same day, though not necessarily because of the telegram or other adverse public reactions, that Dean Acheson, Undersecretary of the Treasury, cabled to Harrison, "The President and the Secretary agree that you should come home on the Bremen on Sunday." The first interpretation of this curt message was that it indicated anger at Harrison. However, Burgess explained the next day, in a telephone call from Washington to the New York Reserve Bank, that the message was not as abrupt as it sounded; the President and Secretary wanted Harrison to return and explain the proposals because Sprague's explanations were inadequate.

> Two points seem to be in the minds of the people at Washington, Mr. Burgess said—first, that currency stabilization is a bargaining weapon which should be retained for use at the Economic Conference and second, that even temporary stabilization would be a severe shock to domestic business and price recovery. In any event, it appears clear, Mr. Burgess said, that no affirmative action will be taken by the Government on currency stabilization before Governor Harrison's return, and, we hope, no negative action.[8]

---

[7]Signers of the telegram were Lessing Rosenwald, Frederick H. Frazier, Vincent Bendix, J. H. Rand, Jr., and F. H. Sexauer.

[8]Allan Sproul memorandum, written on June 17, 1933 at the Federal Reserve Bank of New York.

Harrison proceeded to Washington immediately after his return to the United States on June 23 for a series of discussions with the President, the Secretary of the Treasury, and others. Roosevelt's decision is now history; in a sharply worded wireless to the London Conference on July 3 he flatly rejected proposals for stabilization of exchange rates.

I would regard it as a catastrophe amounting to a world tragedy if the great Conference of Nations, called to bring about a more real and permanent financial stability and a greater prosperity to the masses of all Nations, should, in advance of any serious effort to consider these broader problems, allow itself to be diverted by the proposal of a purely artificial and temporary experiment affecting the monetary exchange of a few Nations only . . . .

The sound internal economic system of a Nation is a greater factor in its well being than the price of its currency in changing terms of the currencies of other Nations . . . . Let me be frank in saying that the United States seeks the kind of dollar which a generation hence will have the same purchasing and debt-paying power as the dollar value we hope to attain in the near future. That objective means more to the good of other Nations than a fixed ratio for a month or two in terms of the pound or the franc.[9]

It is doubtful that the Conference would have achieved much even if Roosevelt had been more cooperative, but his message virtually assured its failure. It dragged on for a few more weeks but achieved no meaningful agreements on exchange-rate behavior, cooperation to raise levels of commodity prices, reductions of trade barriers, or revival of international lending. Many internationalists must have shared the dismay of officials at the Bank for International Settlements:

They have witnessed the high hopes aroused on every continent by the convocation of the London Monetary and Economic Conference, which was to find joint solutions for financial ills and economic difficulties and to prepare the way for a reconstituted international monetary system—hopes which were dashed to the ground when this vast assembly met and promptly discovered that it was either in disaccord on fundamentals (especially as regards early currency stabilization) or, if in agreement on some fundamentals (for example on the economic side), in disharmony as to the ways and means of reaching the agreed objectives . . . .

In international financial and monetary relations the twelve months have been a series of retrograde movements—more moratoria, more transfer impediments, more artificial clearings, more gold hoarding than during any year on record, more conversion of foreign balances and their repatriation into the home currency, or in gold, by private and central banks, an almost complete cessation of new long-term lending abroad and a further limitation or reduction of the volume of short-term credits.[10]

Jockeying for position with respect to exchange rates continued after Roosevelt's message to the conference. For example, Harrison was called to Washington to meet with Governor Black on July 11 to discuss a proposal that the New York Bank might export a certain amount of gold to London to be sold there for sterling, and use the proceeds to purchase dollars when and if necessary to prevent the exchange rate on the pound from rising above its former mint parity of $4.8665. Black apparently approved, and the New York

---

[9]*The Public Papers and Addresses of Franklin D. Roosevelt, op. cit.*, Vol. 2, pp. 264-265.

[10]*Annual Report of the Bank for International Settlements*, 1933/34, p. 5.

Bank, in cooperation with the Bank of England, used at least $1,300,000 of gold for this purpose before the end of July.[11] However, in early August, Governor Black and Dean Acheson told Jay Crane at New York that the President was not disposed to approve licenses for further transactions in gold under the cooperation agreement with the Bank of England.[12] Then, on September 19, Secretary Woodin informed the New York Bank that the President was concerned that some action might be taken to prevent the pound from rising above $4.86.

The Secretary said that he merely wanted to make certain that nothing would be done to keep stërling down because he felt that it would be helpful to have the pound go to, say $5. He added that it would strengthen Roosevelt's hand tremendously in dealing with the inflationists.[13]

Though Roosevelt had vetoed even a temporary *de facto* stabilization agreement when the exchange rate was around £1 = $4, he became quite receptive to a formal agreement when the pound had risen above $5.10, and he even took the initiative in making such a proposal to the British, using Henry Morgenthau, Jr., his new Secretary of the Treasury, and Governor Harrison as intermediaries. On November 27, following a visit with the President at Warm Springs, Morgenthau requested Harrison to ask Montagu Norman whether he thought the British government would be willing to join the U.S. government in a *de jure* stabilization of their currencies. Harrison telephoned Norman on November 28, and later reported to the President:

On December 1, Governor Norman advised me on the telephone that he had discussed the matter with Sir Frederic Leith-Ross of the British Treasury, and that he (Governor Norman) was quite certain that the British Government would not now be willing to consider *de jure* stabilization of the pound in terms of gold in the near future whether by their own action alone or jointly with the United States Government, nor would they be willing to give any commitment as to a minimum rate of stabilization in the future. Governor Norman went on to say, however, that they would be glad to consider an arrangement for *de facto* stabilization of the dollar-sterling exchange rate for a temporary period through the use of an agreed amount of gold. He asked me to ascertain, if possible, whether Washington would be interested now in considering such an arrangement.[14]

No such temporary and limited agreement was reached, perhaps because Roosevelt was by then nearing a decision to fix a new gold value for the dollar without an international agreement.

---

[11]Minutes of the Board of Directors of the Federal Reserve Bank of New York, July 13 and 20, 1933.

[12]*Ibid.*, August 3, 1938.

[13]Memorandum from Jay Crane to George Harrison, September 19, 1933.

[14]Harrison letter to Roosevelt, December 12, 1933. For an account of this episode from the British point of view see Henry Clay, *Lord Norman,* Macmillan, London, 1957, pp. 405-408.

FEDERAL RESERVE POLICIES, MARCH 1933-JANUARY 1934

The reserve positions of member banks began to improve almost immediately after the reopening of banks in mid-March. (See Table 18-2.) At first,

TABLE 18-2

Reserve Positions of All Member Banks, January 1933-February 1934
(monthly averages of daily figures, in millions of dollars)

	Total reserves	Unborrowed reserves	Borrowings at the Federal Reserve	Excess reserves	Net free reserves
1933					
January	2,516	2,262	254	584	330
February	2,291	1,985	306	417	111
March	1,847	966	881	n.a.[a]	n.a.[a]
April	2,040	1,717	323	379	56
May	2,069	1,816	253	319	66
June	2,160	1,976	184	363	179
July	2,221	2,100	113	436	323
August	2,331	2,215	116	565	449
September	2,451	2,348	103	675	572
October	2,557	2,466	91	758	667
November	2,559	2,469	90	794	704
December	2,588	2,493	95	766	671
1934					
January	2,740	2,655	85	866	781
February	2,799	2,745	54	891	837

[a]n.a. = not available

Source: Board of Governors of the Federal Reserve System, *Banking and Monetary Statistics,* Washington, D.C., 1943, pp. 396-397.

the improvement resulted largely from return flows of currency to the banks, which amounted to nearly $1.2 billion by the end of March and to nearly $2 billion by the end of July. The Federal Reserve also supplied reserve funds through its purchases of $595 million of government securities between mid-May and mid-November. Thus by October member banks were enabled to reduce their borrowings at the Federal Reserve below $100 million and to accumulate more then $700 million of excess reserves. The Federal Reserve also reduced its bill-buying rates and its discount rates. The minimum bill-buying rate, which had been increased to 3 1/2 percent during the crisis, was reduced in 5 steps, reaching one-half of 1 percent on October 20, at which level it remained through 1941. The discount rate at the end of the banking crisis was 3 1/2 percent at all the Reserve banks. New York reduced its rate to 3 percent on April 7; 2 more reductions brought it down to 2 percent by October 20. Rate policy was less active at the other Reserve banks. Discount rates at the end of the year were 3 1/2 percent at 5 Reserve banks, 3 percent at 1 bank, 2 1/2 percent at 5 other banks, and 2 percent at New York.

The nature, timing, and magnitude of Federal Reserve policy actions, and especially of its open-market operations, during this period were strongly influenced by the advent of the new administration and by the numerous proposals for "inflation." Most Federal Reserve officials had been fearful of the inflationary sentiment in Congress in late 1932 and early 1933 before Roosevelt came into office. They became even more apprehensive after the new Congress convened, and especially after the Thomas Amendment was introduced in Congress on March 10, and they hoped that somehow the legislation could be defeated. After the bill became law on May 12, they hoped that Roosevelt could be persuaded not to use his discretionary powers. Even some of those who continued to believe that large open-market purchases would serve no useful purpose were persuaded by the argument that a more cooperative and expansionary "voluntary" policy by the Federal Reserve might help head off the adoption of even more objectionable policies, such as sales of securities directly from the Treasury to the Federal Reserve, issues of greenbacks, abandonment of the gold standard and devaluation of the dollar, or monetization of silver.

On April 22 the Open-Market Policy Conference held its first meeting since January 4. The Governors' Conference had met on the preceding day. Three principal topics were discussed: the Treasury's heavy financing needs; the pending Thomas Amendment, and especially the section that would give the President power to direct the Secretary of the Treasury to arrange with the Federal Reserve banks for purchases of up to $3 billion of securities directly from the Treasury; and the maturity distribution of government securities in the System's portfolio.

With respect to the Thomas Amendment, the governors concluded:

> As drafted, this provision of the law is not obligatory so far as the Federal Reserve banks are concerned. But the conference was generally in agreement that during the period of the emergency it would be advisable for the Federal Reserve banks, so far as possible and consistent with their own position and requirements, to cooperate with the Treasury with a view to facilitating any necessary issues of government securities or to support the market for government securities in order to make such public issues possible. The majority of the conference, however, did not feel that at the present time it would be advisable for the Federal Reserve banks to purchase government securities solely for the purpose of increasing member bank reserves.[15]

The OMPC adopted two important resolutions at the conclusion of the meeting:

> ... while as a general principle the average maturity of Government securities held in the System account should be kept as short as possible, nevertheless, in the present emergency and especially in view of the need of full cooperation with the Treasury in meeting its fiscal problems, the Executive Committee should be authorized, from time to time, to shift maturities in the System account if conditions in the market or requirements of the Treasury appear to make that advisable.
> ... subject to the approval of the Federal Reserve Board the executive committee be authorized to arrange with the Secretary of the Treasury from time to time to purchase up to one billion dollars of government securities to meet Treasury requirements.[16]

Note that the Executive Committee was authorized to purchase securities only to meet Treasury requirements." Harrison and at least one member of the Federal Reserve Board were unhappy about this restriction. However, one member

---

[15]Minutes of the OMPC, April 22, 1933.

[16]*Ibid.*

of the conference, Governor Seay of the Richmond Bank, thought that it would be better to abstain from purchases in the open market and to force the Treasury to take responsibility for selling directly to the Reserve banks. On May 8 he wrote to Burgess,

... if circumstances require us to purchase any large amount of government securities, we should buy them directly from the Treasury, and thus force the Tresaury, in effect, to make us its direct instrumentality of expansion, or inflation, which of course is the purpose of the Act, and thus make the Treasury responsible for what might follow.

He elaborated in another letter to Burgess on May 16.

I do not think there is any point to the suggestion or argument of preserving the independence of the Federal Reserve Banks, or System, when it comes to buying three billions of securities, or even one billion, in addition to what we already have. I am quite positive that the conference, or the majority of the conference, if not confronted with the inflation bill and if it did not have to choose between methods of inflation, would vote against the purchase of such an extraordinary amount. I do not call that preserving the independence of the Federal Reserve System . . . .

We are very firm here in desiring to have a policy determined in this case by the Federal Reserve Board for the System.

The Board delayed until May 12 its approval of the OMPC recommendations of April 22, and in its approval omitted the phrase "to meet Treasury requirements." Thus, the Board was willing to give the Executive Committee broader discretion as to to purpose of purchases than had been granted by the OMPC. At a meeting in Washington on May 23, the Executive Committee decided that Harrison should telegraph the other governors, asking their consent to remove the restrictive phrase. A majority, but only a small majority, of the governors consented. A few were strongly opposed. For example, Governor Hamilton of Kansas City replied:

Our estimate of sentiment of Conference was that large majority of members was opposed to an open market policy such as was followed last year and we believe the proposed amendment is equivalent to a return to last year's policy and is contrary to spirit of resolution adopted.

Governor Seay remained opposed, for several reasons:

I do not approve amendment of the conference resolution as suggested, nor do I approve purchases in open market as heretofore made, believing it would be futile now as it was before, nor do I approve adding further to system holdings of governments except at the behest of the Treasury and in direct furtherance of Treasury plans. I agree with Glass that we should not be clogged up with Government bonds, and I think that any action of that kind should be at the direct request or suggestion of the Treasury in conformity with the inflation act.

Governor Calkins of San Francisco cautiously requested more information, commenting that purchases to meet Treasury requirements were all right, but "We are indisposed to embark once more upon a program the futility of which we think has been demonstrated."[17]

Federal Reserve purchases of securities began immediately after the May 23 meeting, initially at a rate of $25 million a week. Governor Black would

---

[17]Files of the OMPC, May 1933.

have preferred larger purchases, but concurred with the decision on the understanding that purchases would be stepped up promptly if the need developed. Table 18-3 shows the pattern of purchases. Average weekly purchases ranged above $20 million through July 5, declined to about $11 million through August 16, rose to about $35 million through mid-October, and then tapered off quickly. No purchases were made after mid-November. In fact, total Federal Reserve holdings of government securities remained virtually unchanged at $2,432 million from that time through the end of March 1937—a period of more than 40 months. There were, however, numerous shifts in the maturity composition of the portfolio during this period, primarily to promote "orderly conditions" in the government securities market.

At its meeting on June 10 the Executive Committee of the OMPC considered reducing its rate of purchases but decided that this would be unwise. Governor Black urged that purchases proceed at a rate of $25 million a week, so as to avoid the risk "of appearing to stop the policy." Governor Young of Boston, ordinarily no advocate of open-market purchases, said that purchases ought to stay above $20 million, "or else we will be open to the accusation of stopping our program and would arouse the inflationists to hostility." Acheson reported that Secretary Woodin suggested purchases up to half of the amount in the preceding week. In fact, purchases were not reduced until after July 5; then they averaged $11 million a week until mid-August.

In the meantime, on July 20, the open-market authority had been reorganized in accordance with the Banking Act of 1933, which had become law in June. The old System Open-Market Policy Conference was superseded by a Federal Open-Market Committee (FOMC), which was composed of a representative from each of the 12 Reserve banks.[18] The FOMC voted to set up an Executive Committee composed of the representative of the New York Reserve Bank as chairman and representatives of the Boston, Philadelphia, Cleveland, and Chicago Reserve banks. This change in formal organization brought no immediate change in policy.

By mid-August, when the relapse of recovery and declines of commodity prices were clearly evident, both Federal Reserve and government officials agreed that the rate of Federal Reserve purchases should be increased. At a meeting of the Executive Committee of the New York Board of Directors on August 21,

> Harrison reported on the conference held on August 17-18 by the committee formed to study the monetary policy under the chairmanship of Treasury Secretary Woodin. This committee believed that large open market operations would be advisable .... Woodin and Black stated that they thought it desirable for the Federal Reserve to purchase $25 million this week. They pointed out that due to the decline of prices, particularly agricultural prices, and some hesitation in business, considerable sentiment was arising in support of the issuance of U.S. notes under Title 3 of the Farm Relief Act approved May 12. It was held it would aid greatly in avoiding this danger if it were clear that the Federal Reserve system was using its open market powers vigorously. The directors thereupon voted to raise their purchases from $25 to $50 million.

---

[18]*Annual Report of the Federal Reserve Board,* 1933, p. 44.

TABLE 18-3

Federal Reserve Holdings of U.S. Government Securities,
May-November 1933 (Wednesday figures in millions of dollars)

1933	Total holdings	Net purchases during week ending
May 17	1,837	0
May 24	1,862	25
May 31	1,890	28
June 7	1,912	22
June 14	1,932	20
June 21	1,955	23
June 28	1,975	20
July 5	1,995	20
July 12	2,007	12
July 19	2,017	10
July 26	2,028	11
August 2	2,038	10
August 9	2,048	10
August 16	2,059	11
August 23	2,094	35
August 30	2,129	35
September 6	2,166	37
September 13	2,203	37
September 20	2,238	34
September 27	2,274	36
October 4	2,309	35
October 11	2,344	35
October 18	2,375	31
October 25	2,400	25
November 1	2,420	10
November 8	2,430	10
November 15	2,432	2
Total purchases, May 17-November 15		595

Source: Board of Governors of the Federal Reserve System, *Banking and Monetary Statistics*, Washington, D.C., 1943, p. 387.

Purchases averaged $35 million a week between mid-August and mid-October. Governor Calkins' reaction could not have been predicted on the basis of his earlier positions. On August 25 he wrote to Harrison:

I am of the opinion that open market purchases for the past week might better have been $50,000,000, instead of $35,000,000, and that purchases for the next and several succeeding periods should be in considerable amounts, say $50,000,000, or even $100,000,000 per week.

As you recall, I was consistently and persistently of the opinion that putting more money into a market already gorged when nothing else was being done was a futile process, and I think that the correctness of the view was amply confirmed. It is, however, one thing to try to create an effect by such means in the absence of any other effort and quite another thing to add that pressure to other efforts put forth for the same purpose.

An effort is now being made to create purchasing power, raise prices, increase employment, and revive courage, and with those things under way, it is my view that the Federal Reserve System should do its full part, even at the risk of subsequently having to realize that its efforts were ineffective. In other words, we are not in a position to see the best course and follow it, but probably are in a position to elect one of several traditionally unorthodox expedients.

Harrison, other members of the Executive Committee of the FOMC, and probably other Federal Reserve officials as well, became increasingly apprehensive as purchases continued, especially in view of the fact that a major purpose had become that of "minimizing the risk of drastic methods of currency inflation." On September 21, Harrison read to the Executive Committee parts of a memorandum of his conversation with Governor Black on September 16:

> As I see the picture, I said, we now have, largely through open market operations and a return flow of currency, created approximately $700,000,000 of excess reserves and a very easy money market position. Certainly from the point of view of the credit and banking situation there would appear to be no need for any further purchases of Government securities. Our operations to date, together with other factors, have resulted in placing the banks of the country as a whole in a position to make a very substantial expansion of bank credit as soon as there is a demand for it by borrowers entitled to have it on the basis of good credit risk. Consequently, further purchases of government securities in the open market must be justified by factors outside the immediate banking and credit picture or, to put it differently, outside those matters specifically and immediately within the jurisdiction of the Federal reserve banks, as central banks.
>
> For some weeks now, under the authority granted by the Open Market Committee with the approval of the Federal Reserve Board in May, the Executive Committee has been making weekly purchases partly because of the need for creating an easy banking position but in latter weeks largely because we have been informed by Governor Black, Secretary Woodin, Mr. Acheson, Mr. Sprague, and others from Washington, that this is an important and advisable way for the Federal Reserve banks to cooperate with the Government's program of recovery and an especially weighty factor in minimizing the risk of drastic methods of currency inflation, such as greenbacks. I explained to Governor Black, however, that I had some hesitation in recommending a continuance of open market operations for these reasons alone, unless I was definitely sure that his views as to the needs for these purchases represented the views of the Federal Reserve Board as a whole. In other words, there being no clear cut need from the banking and credit position, I wanted to be sure that the Federal Reserve Board considers that a continuance of open market purchases are advisable or necessary as a contribution to the Governmental program of recovery and also as a substantial means of minimizing the risk of greenbacks.
>
> Governor Black said he understood my position perfectly; that he agreed with it entirely; that I was quite right in assuming that the Federal Reserve Board, as well as he, felt that it was advisable to continue open market purchases at about the present rate.

The other members agreed fully with Harrison and voted to continue purchases at an unchanged rate. Similar views were expressed at the FOMC meeting on October 10-12. The Executive Committee was authorized to continue purchases, but members of the FOMC doubted that the policy would be effective in the absence of a broader program, including at least these elements: (1) rehabilitation of banks and institution of deposit insurance; (2) rehabilitation of borrowers, whose net worth and liquidity had been so badly impaired; (3) modification of liabilities under the Securities Act of 1933, which hindered recovery of securities flotations; and (4) termination of threats of currency inflation, which were undermining confidence in the dollar, inducing capital exports, and hindering recovery of bond prices.

On Saturday, October 21, the President's Monetary Committee recommended that positive actions be taken to depress the value of the dollar in terms of gold and foreign currencies. As a member of that committee, Harrison refused to sign that part of the report recommending that the "Federal Reserve banks be authorized to sell dollars in the foreign exchange markets with a view to depressing the dollar until the quotation in terms of the pound sterling should reach $4.86."[19] The New York Reserve Bank was designated as agent for the RFC in buying gold and selling dollars. Officers and directors of that bank debated whether they could ethically implement a policy which they considered to be wholly unsound. However, they agreed to do so on the understanding that they were acting solely as fiscal agent for the Treasury, and that the latter took full responsibility for decisions and actions.

Members of the Executive Committee must have been gloomy when they met on October 25, for the President had announced three days earlier his decision to raise the dollar price of gold. Their first inclination was to stop security purchases immediately. However, they feared the probable depressing effect on bond markets if they terminated purchases "at a time when the bond market was already adversely affected by recent developments." They therefore decided to taper off gradually. They purchased $10 million in each of the 2 following weeks, $2 million in the third week, and then stopped. In fact, the Federal Reserve took no further significant policy actions until long after the Gold Reserve Act had been approved at the end of January 1934.

THE GOLD RESERVE ACT OF 1934

By December 1933 the government was moving toward a new and stable gold value for the dollar. As already noted, the RFC aggressively drove up the price of gold between October 24 and the end of November, the price per ounce rising from $29.80 to $33.93, for an increase of $4.13. Further increases were only 9 cents in December and 39 cents in January, bringing the price to $34.45.[20] During December, Roosevelt considered the possibility of proclaiming a new gold standard under executive order, relying on the broad powers delegated to him by the Thomas Amendment. The Federal Reserve was informed that it would be required to surrender to the Treasury, at the old price, all of its holdings of gold and gold certificates. Thus, the Treasury would reap the profits resulting from an increase in the dollar price of gold. Federal Reserve officials were perturbed and engaged legal counsel to advise them whether such a requirement would be legal. A few officials may have thought that the Federal Reserve had some ethical claim to any gold profits. However, they were more concerned about two other questions: (1) their official responsibility for protecting the legal rights of the Reserve banks; and (2) the resulting effects on the location of power to regulate money and credit. The Federal Reserve would retain power if it owned the gold profits. However, if the gold profits accrued to the Treasury, the latter would acquire power to influence the behavior of bank reserves by controlling the rate at which it spent the profits. In the end, Roosevelt decided to request new legislation rather than to take action on the basis of existing laws.

---

[19]Minutes of the Board of Directors of the Federal Reserve Bank of New York, October 26, 1933.

[20]*Annual Report of the Secretary of the Treasury for the Fiscal Year Ending June 30, 1934*, p. 205.

On January 15 the President asked Congress for legislation "to organize a sound and adequate currency system."

> Permit me once more to stress two principles. Our national currency must be maintained as a sound currency which, insofar as possible, will have a fairly constant standard of purchasing power and be adequate for the purposes of daily use and the establishment of credit.
>
> The other principle is the inherent right of Government to issue currency and to be the sole custodian and owner of the base or reserve of precious metals underlying that currency. With this goes the prerogative of Government to determine from time to time the extent and nature of the metallic reserve . . . .[21]

More specifically, he requested these powers:

1. To terminate the circulation of gold and gold certificates, to vest in the government title to all monetary gold within its boundaries, and to keep that gold in the form of bullion rather than coin.
2. To require the Federal Reserve banks to surrender their holdings of gold and gold certificates in exchange for gold certificates of a type which only the Reserve banks would be permitted to hold. Payment would be at the old official price; any profits resulting from revaluation to accrue to the Government.
3. To empower the President to fix a gold value for the dollar, with the limitation that this should not be less than 50 per cent nor more than 60 per cent of the old gold value of 23.22 grains. Thus the President could set the gold value of the dollar anywhere within the range of 11.66 and 13.93 grains of fine gold. In other words, he could fix the price of an ounce of gold within the range of $34.45 and $41.34. The prevailing price of gold at that time was $34.45.
4. To empower the Secretary of the Treasury to buy and sell gold at home and abroad and to deal in foreign exchange as such. "As a part of this power, . . . out of the profits of any devaluation, there should be set up a fund of two billion dollars for such purchases and sales of gold, foreign exchange, and Government securities as the regulation of the currency, the maintenance of the credit of the Government and the general welfare of the United States may require."[22]

Note that the powers granted to the Secretary were very broad and at least potentially competitive with those of the Federal Reserve.

The Gold Reserve Act of 1934, passed by Congress on January 30, gave Roosevelt all the powers he had asked for. In a presidential proclamation the next day, he made the Act effective and fixed a new gold weight for the dollar. This was 13.71 grains of fine gold, representing a decrease of 40.96 percent. The new price per ounce was $35, representing an increase of 69.33 percent above the old official level of $20.67. Thus the Treasury reaped a profit of $14.33 on each ounce of its holdings of monetary gold, for a total of $2,805 million. Though the dollar price of gold was not fixed, at least temporarily, the new system did not include a firm commitment to buy and sell gold freely and without restrictions or to refrain from further changes in the official price. For one thing, Roosevelt retained the power to fix and change the price between $34.45 and $41.34 an ounce, and he specifically

---

[21]*The Public Papers and Addresses of Franklin D. Roosevelt, op. cit.,* Vol. 3, p. 44.

[22]*Ibid.,* p. 43.

stated that, "... I reserve the right by virtue of the authority vested in me to alter or modify this Proclamation as the interest of the United States may seem to require."[23] Moreover, gold might be sold, bought, or held only in accordance with the rules and regulations prescribed by the Secretary of the Treasury, who was also empowered to deal in gold and foreign exchange. The Secretary quickly decided to buy all gold offered, except that which had been illegally held, at the official price of $35 less a quarter of 1 percent handling charge. Thus he prevented any rise of the dollar in terms of gold and of gold currencies. However, he delayed announcement of an official sale price and indicated that he might limit sales. The dollar could, of course, depreciate further in terms of gold and gold currencies to the extent that the Treasury's sale price for gold was increased or to the extent that gold was not supplied to meet demands. In fact, he did sell gold at a price of $35 plus a quarter of 1 percent handling charge, but only to meet demands for export—which proved to be almost negligible—and domestic demands for artistic, industrial, and scientific purposes.

Why did Roosevelt select $35 as the price of gold? One rumor has it that he lightheartedly observed that "$35 seems like a nice round number." The story is probably true. However, he had what he considered to be good substantive reasons for wanting the price in that vicinity. He certainly did not want a price below the prevailing level of $34.45, for that would mean a rise of the exchange rate on the dollar in terms of gold currencies and probably also in terms of sterling. He might have liked a higher price for gold, and thus an even lower exchange rate on the dollar, but such a price would have created problems. For one thing, further depreciation of the dollar would increase the probability that countries injured by the rise of exchange rates on their currencies would retaliate by devaluing their own currencies, by imposing restrictions on American exports, or by other means. Moreover, a larger decrease in the gold value of the dollar would evoke increased dissent at home. Even some of those who favored a decrease thought that a 40 percent reduction was too large. For example, O.M.W. Sprague told a congressional committee:

I do not think anyone can dispute the proposition that the revaluation of the dollar to 60 percent is establishing a value that is far below its equilibrium value at the present time.[24]

The ensuing avalanche of gold imports suggests that Sprague's judgment was correct. These will be dealt with in the next chapter.

SILVER POLICIES

The monetization of large amounts of silver in 1934 and the following years did not result from any initiative taken by Roosevelt or other members

---

[23]*Ibid.,* p. 70.

[24]Hearings on H.R. 6976 (Gold Reserve Act of 1934) before the House Committee on Coinage, Weights, and Measures, 73rd Congress, 2nd Session (January 15, 1934), p. 4.

of his administration. In fact, the President cooperated only reluctantly. Time after time he fought off mandatory silver legislation, and he used his permissive powers to purchase largely to maintain his support in Congress and to gain congressional support for other legislation. The pressure to "do something for silver" emanated from a strong coalition in Congress reflecting opposition to the preceding deflation, lingering loyalties to bimetallism, and the interests of silver producers. Among the strongest leaders in the movement were Senators William E. Borah of Idaho, Carl Hayden of Arizona, Burton Wheeler of Montana, and Key Pittman of Nevada.[25]

As already noted, the Thomas Amendment gave the President broad permissive powers to monetize silver; he was authorized to accept limited amounts of silver in payment of war debts, to provide for the unlimited coinage of silver, and to establish a bimetallic standard in the United States alone or in agreement with other countries. Roosevelt used none of these powers before December 21, 1933. However, he had taken one action that was to increase pressures on him to purchase silver; he had appointed Senator Key Pittman as a delegate to the London Economic Conference.

Pittman's principal contribution to the conference was to promote the "London Silver Agreement," which placed a far heavier burden on the United States than on the other signatories. The agreement was in two principal parts. (1) Large holders of silver—such as China, India, and Spain—agreed to sales quotas for a four-year period. In general, however, the quotas were large enough to permit these countries to sell as much silver as they would have sold in the absence of the agreement. (2) Silver-producing countries—the United States, Mexico, Canada, Peru, and Australia—agreed to consume certain quotas each year for four years. The purchase quota of the United States was by far the largest—nearly 70 percent of the total. (See Table 18-4.) This country's obligation to purchase was equal to 98.5 percent of its silver production in 1932; for no other country was this percentage above 17.4.

Most silverites in Congress considered the measures included in the London Silver Agreement to be quite inadequate. They would at most raise the price of newly mined domestic silver, they did not provide for adequate additions to the monetary base, they did not give adequate price support for accumulated silver stocks, and they did not provide for the establishment of bimetallism. Agitation to do something more for silver gained support as commodity prices fell after July 1933. It was under such conditions and pressures that Roosevelt, on December 21, ratified the London Silver Agreement and directed the Secretary of the Treasury to purchase all newly mined domestic silver at a price of 64.5 cents an ounce. The price was a disappointment to many silverites, who had hoped to recieve the full coinage value, or $1.29 an ounce.

This action failed to quiet the silverites. In fact, agitation rose during the early months of 1934. At some times more than 40 silverite bills were in

[25] For an account of the political processes involved, see A. S. Everest, *Morgenthau, the New Deal and Silver*, Kings Crown Press, New York, 1950. For an excellent brief discussion of American silver policy, see G. Griffith Johnson, *The Treasury and Monetary Policy, 1932-1938*, Harvard University Press, Cambridge, Mass., pp. 161-200.

TABLE 18-4

Purchase Allotments under the
London Silver Agreement

	Ounces	Percent of five-country total	Percent of purchase obligation to silver production in 1932
United States	24,421,410	69.78%	98.5%
Mexico	7,159,108	20.45	13.3
Canada	1,671,802	4.78	10.1
Peru	1,095,325	3.13	17.4
Australia	652,355	1.86	10.0
Total	35,000,000	100.00	

Source: A. S. Everest, *Morgenthau, the New Deal and Silver*, Kings Crown Press, New York, 1950, p. 29.

the legislative mill, and many of them carried mandatory provisions. Roosevelt compromised again; on May 22 he sent to Congress a message which led to the passage of the Silver Purchase Act of 1934, approved on June 19. This Act left intact the purchase program for newly mined domestic silver and added these provisions:

1. It stated that the ultimate objective of policy was to achieve and maintain a situation in which three-quarters of the total monetary stocks of gold and silver would be in the form of gold and one-quarter in the form of silver.

2. It authorized and directed the Secretary of the Treasury to purchase silver at home and abroad until the monetary value of the silver stock was equal to one-third of the value of the monetary gold stock, or until the market price of silver rose to the level of its monetary value ($1.29 an ounce). However, the rates, times, and conditions of purchase were left to the discretion of the Secretary of the Treasury.

3. To reduce profits of speculators in silver, it provided that no more than 50 cents an ounce should be paid for silver located in the United States on May 1, 1934, and that profits from dealing in silver should be taxed at a 50 percent rate. On August 9 Roosevelt nationalized domestic stocks of silver at a price of 50 cents an ounce.

Secretary Morgenthau purchased silver far too slowly to please many silverites, monetary stocks of silver never came close to equaling one-third of the nation's mounting stocks of monetary gold, and market prices of silver remained considerably below $1.29 an ounce. Nevertheless, purchases were very large, as is shown in Table 18-5. More than 2.6 billion ounces of silver were purchased during the years 1934-1942, inclusive. Of the total amount purchased, 19 percent was newly mined domestic silver, 4 percent was the silver nationalized under Roosevelt's order of August 9, 1934, and 77 percent was foreign silver. The total cost of these purchases was more than $1.4 billion. This represented approximately the amount added by silver purchases to the American reserve base of high-powered money, for the Treasury issued silver coins and silver certificates only in amounts sufficient to cover the purchase cost of silver. The silver profit or seigniorage was held unused in

TABLE 18-5

Silver Production in the United States and Silver Purchase by the Government, 1934-1942[29] (in millions)

Year	Silver production in the U.S. (ounces)	Silver Acquired by U.S. Government							
		Newly Mined Domestic Silver		Nationalized Silver		Foreign Silver		Total Acquisitions	
		(ounces)	(dollars)	(ounces)	(dollars)	(ounces)	(dollars)	(ounces)	(dollars)
1934	32.5	21.8	14.1	110.6	55.3	172.5	86.5	304.9	155.9
1935	45.6	38.0	27.3	2.0	1.0	494.5	318.2	543.1	346.5
1936	63.4	61.1	47.3	0.4	0.2	271.9	150.3	333.4	197.8
1937	71.3	70.6	54.6	—	—	241.5	108.7	312.1	163.3
1938	61.7	61.6	42.4	—	—	355.4	156.9	417.1	199.3
1939	63.9	60.7	40.1	—	—	282.8	120.5	343.5	160.6
1940	67.0	68.3	48.5	—	—	139.8	50.9	208.1	99.4
1941	71.1	70.5	50.1	—	—	72.6	27.1	143.1	77.2
1942	55.9	47.9	34.0	—	—	14.3	6.0	62.2	40.0
Total	532.4	500.5	358.4	113.0	56.5	2045.3	1025.1	2658.5	1440.0

[29]Source: Treasury Bulletins.

Treasury vaults. Note that the largest purchases were made during the years 1934-1939.

We have already remarked that American gold policies increased sharply dollar exchange rates on gold-standard currencies, the British pound sterling, and many other currencies. The American silver-purchase policies, and the attendant rise of silver prices in terms of dollars, virtually wrecked the monetary systems of China and of a few other countries that were still on silver standards. Many proponents of the American silver policies argued that these policies would actually help "the teeming millions in the Orient" by increasing their purchasing power in world markets. Exchange rates on silver-standard currencies had fallen sharply during the early years of the depression as the price of silver declined. For example, the exchange rate on the Chinese yuan averaged about 42 cents in 1929; it was less than 22 cents in 1932 and about 20 cents in the first 3 months of 1933. This depreciation of silver currencies, the silverites maintained, was injurious to the economies of those countries. In fact, however, it helped to promote their exports and to shield them against deflationary pressures from other areas. As the price of silver was driven up, exchange rates on these currencies rose. For example, the Chinese yuan was above 40 cents by mid-1935. This decreased markedly the ability of silver-standard countries to export without drastic reductions in their domestic prices. Deflationary pressures were intensified as some of their silver money was melted and exported. In the end, most countries abandoned silver standards and adopted inconvertible standards or tied their currencies to the dollar or the British pound. Thus, a long-run effect of American silver policy was to reduce still further the use of silver abroad for monetary purposes.

Whatever may have been their domestic expansionary effects, American gold and silver policies, and their accompanying effects on exchange rates, tended to intensify deflationary pressures on many other countries.

19

Federal Reserve and Treasury Policies, 1934–1937

This chapter covers the major monetary policies of the Federal Reserve and the Treasury during the period between the end of January 1934, when the Gold Reserve Act became effective, and the autumn of 1937, when the recession of 1937-1938 came to be recognized.

Member bank reserves grew hugely during this period. In January 1934 they averaged about $2.7 billion; they had reached $4 billion by the end of the year, $5.7 billion at the end of 1935, and $6.7 billion at the end of 1936. (See Table 19-1.) They remained at or above this level during 1937. Excess reserves of member banks also grew markedly. At $866 million in January 1934, they were at their highest level in Federal Reserve history. They rose to $1.7 billion by the end of the year and about $3 billion at the end of 1935, and then fluctuated around this level through July 1936. The decrease in August and September of that year reflected the first increase of member bank reserve requirements, but excess reserves averaged above $2 billion from that time through February 1937. The subsequent decline of excess reserves in the spring of that year reflected the second increase of member bank reserve requirements, half of the increase becoming effective in March and the other half in May.

Federal Reserve credit made virtually no net contribution to the increase of total member bank reserves during this period. We have already noted that Federal Reserve holdings of government securities remained at $2,432 million from mid-November 1933 through March 1937. Net purchases in April 1937 amounted to only $96 million. In the meantime, Federal Reserve loans to banks had fallen to very low levels, as had the System's holdings of acceptances. Thus total Federal Reserve credit remained approximately constant. Most of the increase in bank reserves came from two sources: Treasury purchases of silver, and increases in the value of the monetary gold stock. The latter, in turn, resulted from the $2,805 million upward revaluation of the monetary gold stock at the beginning of February 1934 and from subsequent additions to the gold stock.

TABLE 19-1

Member Bank Reserves, January 1934-August 1937
(monthly averages of daily figures, in millions of dollars)

	Total reserves	Borrowings at the Federal Reserve	Excess reserves
1934			
January	2,740	85	866
February	2,799	54	891
March	3,345	41	1,375
April	3,582	31	1,541
May	3,695	26	1,623
June	3,790	22	1,685
July	3,920	18	1,789
August	4,045	16	1,884
September	3,947	18	1,754
October	3,964	11	1,731
November	4,100	10	1,834
December	4,037	10	1,748
1935			
January	4,355	8	2,035
February	4,601	6	2,237
March	4,452	6	2,065
April	4,436	6	2,026
May	4,778	7	2,297
June	4,979	7	2,438
July	4,970	7	2,385
August	5,232	7	2,636
September	5,243	10	2,628
October	5,469	8	2,820
November	5,757	7	3,061
December	5,716	6	2,983
1936			
January	5,780	6	3,033
February	5,808	7	3,038
March	5,420	6	2,653
April	5,300	5	2,510
May	5,638	5	2,800
June	5,484	6	2,593
July	5,861	3	2,907
August	6,181	6	2,458
September	6,345	7	1,852
October	6,594	6	2,043
November	6,785	6	2,219
December	6,665	7	2,046
1937			
January	6,716	3	2,093
February	6,747	3	2,152
March	6,704	6	1,371
April	6,824	10	1,552
May	6,932	16	927
June	6,878	15	876
July	6,845	13	876
August	6,701	17	750
September	6,854	24	900
October	6,954	22	1,043
November	6,919	19	1,104
December	6,879	16	1,071

Source: Board of Governors of the Federal Reserve System, *Banking and Monetary Statistics*, Washington, D.C., 1943, pp. 396-397.

THE GOLDEN AVALANCHE

The nation's monetary gold stock rose from $4,036 million at the end of 1933 to $12,760 million at the end of 1937, an increase of $8,724 million. (See Table 19-2.) Of this increase, about 32 percent resulted from the revaluation of the gold stock at the beginning of February 1934, about 5 percent from domestic gold production, and more than 63 percent from gold imports. The total increase of the gold stock from the end of 1933 to the end of 1941 was $18,701 million, of which net gold imports accounted for $16,850 million, or 90 percent. This was truly a golden avalanche.

TABLE 19-2

Monetary Gold Stock of the United States, 1933-1941
(in millions of dollars)

End of	Monetary value of the gold stock	Increase during the year	Increase from re-valuation of gold stock	Domestic gold production	Net gold imports
1933	4,036	–	–	–	–
1934	8,238	4,202	2,805	93	1,134
1935	10,125	1,887	–	111	1,739
1936	11,258	1,132	–	132	1,117
1937	12,760	1,502	–	144	1,586
1938	14,512	1,751	–	149	1,974
1939	17,644	3,132	–	162	3,574
1940	21,995	4,351	–	170	4,744
1941	22,737	742	–	170	982
Addenda:					
December 1933– December 1937		8,724	2,805	480	5,576
December 1933– December 1941		18,701	2,805	1,131	16,850

Sources: Board of Governors of the Federal Reserve System, *Banking and Monetary Statistics,* Washington, D.C., 1943, pp. 522-525 and 536-542. The figures in the last three columns do not add to the total increase shown in Column 2 because of the omission of melted domestic gold scrap and gold uses for domestic nonmonetary purposes.

Such huge gold imports by the United States would have been almost impossible in the absence of a large increase in the world rate of gold production. (See Table 19-3.) The physical output of gold rose in the early 1930's, even before the price of gold was increased. This was primarily because of rising unemployment in other sectors of the economies of the gold-producing countries and falling costs of production. Gold output rose even more rapidly as prices of gold were increased and costs of production lagged behind. Even in physical terms, the rate of gold output in the latter part of the 1930s was double its average level in the 1923-1929 period. The dollar value of gold output, reflecting both the increase of physical output and the increase in the price of gold, rose even more. In the latter years of the 1930s it was more than three times its level in the 1920s. Yet America's gold imports exceeded the world's total gold production during the years following 1933. For example, gold imports by the United States during the years 1934-1937 inclusive amounted to $5,578 million, while total gold production was only $4,390

TABLE 19-3
World Gold Production

Period	Production in millions of fine ounces	Index of physical gold production (average 1923-1929 = 100)	Value in millions of dollars ($20.67 an ounce, 1933 and earlier; $35 an ounce 1934 and later)	Index of value (average 1923-1929 = 100)
1923-1929	18.8	100	$ 388.6	100
Annual average				
1930	20.9	111	432.1	111
1931	22.3	119	460.7	119
1932	24.1	128	498.2	128
1933	25.4	135	525.1	135
1934	27.4	146	958.0	247
1935	30.0	160	1,050.0	270
1936	32.9	175	1,152.6	296
1937	35.1	187	1,229.1	316
1938	37.1	201	1,319.6	340
1939	39.5	210	1,383.7	356
1940	41.1	219	1,437.3	370
1941	36.2	193	1,265.6	326

Addenda:
Total, 1934-1937, inclusive $4,389.7
Total, 1934-1941, inclusive $9,795.9

Source: Board of Governors of the Federal Reserve System, Banking and Monetary Statistics, Washington, D.C., 1943, p. 542.

million. And American gold imports during the years 1934–1941 inclusive were $16,850 million while the value of gold production was only $9,796 million. America was indeed a sinkhole of gold.

As a first step toward explaining these gold imports, it will be useful to examine the balance of payments of the United States during these years. Table 19-4 shows that the United States enjoyed net receipts on account of trade in goods and services during every year, but that these were equal to only a small fraction of gold imports. For example, the monetary gold stock increased $5,724 million during the years 1934–1937 inclusive, while the aggregate balance on account of goods and services was only $1,141. The balance on account of goods and services minus net unilateral transfers to foreigners aggregated only $344 million for the period. Far more important in explaining gold imports were the huge net inflows of capital funds, both long-term and short-term. These aggregated $4,022 million during the 4 years 1934–1937. Of these net inflows, $1,934 million were long-term capital funds. Some of these represented repatriation of American funds from abroad; others reflected purchases by foreigners of long-term claims against American entities. Net inflows of short-term capital funds aggregated $2,087 million. Some of these were American short-term funds repatriated from abroad; many more were foreign funds seeking asylum in the United States. Table 19-4 shows that large net inflows of capital funds continued until 1941. Thus the role of the United States in international capital flows was reversed. In the 1920s the United States was a large net exporter of capital; now it was a large net importer of both long-term and short-term funds.

Conventional specie-flow analysis might lead one to expect that gold flows far smaller than those that actually occurred would have restored equilibrium in balances of payments and terminated gold flows—that contractionary monetary effects in gold-losing countries and expansionary monetary effects in the United States would have raised the latter's imports of goods and services relative to her exports and would have induced an outflow of capital funds. However, neither governments nor their economies responded in the ways assumed by the specie-flow theory of the equilibration process. A basic difficulty was that even the huge gold inflows did not induce a sufficient increase of the levels of national income and prices in the United States to raise her imports of goods and services relative to her exports. However, there were other obstacles to the process of equilibrating through balances on goods and services account. Many gold-losing countries did not respond by permitting monetary contraction to occur. Exchange rates were in many cases allowed to fluctuate, and adjustments in trade were hindered by exchange controls, tariffs, and quantitative restrictions.

One might have expected that even if the large gold flows did not restore equilibrium in balances of payments through their effects on trade in goods and services, they would at least have terminated capital flows to the United States and induced capital outflows by lowering interest rates in the United States relative to those in other countries. We have already seen that American interest rates, and especially those on highly liquid and safe assets, did fall to very low levels during this period. However, this fall of interest rates neither stopped capital inflows nor induced net outflows. For this failure

TABLE 19-4

Balance of Payments of the United States, 1934-1941 (in millions of dollars)[a]

	1934	1935	1936	1937	1938	1939	1940	1941
(1) *Balance of goods and services*	601	128	115	297	1,291	1,066	1,719	2,410
(2) *Unilateral transfers*	- 172	- 182	- 208	- 235	- 182	- 178	- 210	-1,136
(3) *(1)-(2)*	429	54	93	62	1,109	888	1,509	1,274
(4) *Capital movement—Total (net)*	425	1,512	1,208	877	441	1,498	1,457	-1,031
Government, long- and short-term	- 5	1	3	2	- 9	- 14	- 51	- 391
Private and foreign Direct and long-term	200	436	777	521	97	27	- 22	- 261
Short-term	230	1,075	428	354	353	1,485	1,530	379
(5) *Errors and omissions*	412	364	157	425	249	788	1,277	476
(6) *Changes in monetary gold stock*[b]	-1,266	-1,822	-1,272	-1,364	-1,799	-3,174	-4,243	- 719

aNo sign indicates receipts. (−) indicates payments.
b(−) denotes increase.
Source: Bureau of the Census, *Historical Statistics of the United States, Colonial Times to 1957,* Washington, D.C., 1960, p. 564.

there were several reasons, aside from the fact that interest rates also fell in many other countries. For one thing, the generally low interest rates in the United States were by no means an accurate indicator of the availability of American funds to foreign borrowers. Total flotations of foreign securities in the American market during the 8 years 1934-1941 were only $203 million. Major reasons for this were the large losses incurred earlier on American loans to foreigners; the passion of financial intermediaries for liquidity and safety; fear that foreign borrowers would be unable to pay, either because of their own lack of creditworthiness or because of balance-of-payments difficulties in their countries or official restrictions on foreign payments; and mounting fears of economic, political, and military disturbances abroad. Also, a large part of the American funds that were repatriated and of foreign funds that flowed to the United States came not to benefit from higher interest rates but to find a haven of relative safety and liquidity. In effect, they were refugee funds. In 1938 and the following years they fled from Europe primarily because of increasing dangers of political and military conflict. Prior to that time, however, they came to the United States primarily because of fears that exchange rates on other currencies might fall in terms of dollars or, to put it another way, because of hopes that the dollar might rise in terms of foreign currencies. These hopes and fears were closely related to the devaluation of the gold value of the dollar in early 1934.

Table 19-5 lists some of the major events that strongly influenced international capital flows, both to and from the United States. Those occurring after the end of 1937, most of which related to military conflicts and fears of war, will be discussed later. We shall concentrate here on those occurring before the end of 1937.

We have already noted that as a result of the American gold purchases in 1933 and the stabilization of the dollar at the end of January 1934, the dollar price of gold was increased about 69 percent above its old official level, and that this was accompanied by sharp increases in the dollar exchange rates on other major currencies. After these actions, the dollar was the strongest major currency in exchange markets. There was, of course, some possibility that Roosevelt would further decrease the value of the dollar in terms of gold and perhaps of other currencies. In fact, rumors that the United States might devalue the dollar further as a recovery measure led to outflows of funds in late 1937 and early 1938. On balance, however, the dollar was much more likely to rise than to fall. It was generally believed that the dollar was undervalued relative to the other major currencies, and that other currencies, especially those of the gold-bloc countries, would have to be devalued sooner or later. Such predictions proved correct. The increased exchange rates on gold-bloc currencies exerted strong deflationary pressures, leading to mounting unemployment, widening labor disputes, and sharp political controversies in those countries. These were accompanied by withdrawals of funds.

Belgium was the first of the gold-bloc countries to succumb. In the spring of 1935 she devalued her currency about 25 percent and then maintained the new gold value until overrun by the Germans in the spring of 1940. Her action further weakened confidence in the other gold-bloc currencies and accentuated withdrawals of funds from gold-standard countries. However,

TABLE 19-5

*Some Events Affecting Capital Flows from
and to the United States, 1934-1941*

Date of period	Nature of the event	Some effects
January 31, 1934	U.S. adoption of new gold value for dollar; widely believed to undervalue dollar in exchange markets.	Repatriation of American funds and inflow of foreign funds encouraged.
February 1935	Gold-clause cases before before the U.S. Supreme Court; some chance that abrogation will be held illegal.	Encouragement of flow of funds to U.S.
Spring of 1935	Economic and political distrubances in gold-bloc countries. Belgium devalues.	Outflows of funds from other gold-bloc countries, many to U.S.
September 1935	Italian-Ethiopian hostilities imminent; fears that Britain may become involved.	Substantial transfers of funds to U.S.
August-October 1936	Economic and political disturbances in France, leading to devaluations in remaining gold-bloc countries.	Large flows of funds to U.S.
Spring of 1937	Widespread rumors that U.S. and perhaps a few other countries will lower official price of gold.	Flows of funds to the U.S.
October 1937-early 1938	Rumors that dollar will be devalued again as a recovery measure.	Large outflows from the U.S.
August-September 1938	First Czechoslovak crisis; fears of war.	Large flows to the U.S.
March 1939	Second Czechoslovak crisis; Germany occupies Bohemia and Moravia.	Flows of funds to the U.S.
August-September 1939	Outbreak of World War II.	Large flows of funds to the U.S.
Spring of 1940	Germany invades Denmark, Norway, and the Low Countries.	Flows of funds to the U.S.

those countries doggedly continued to defend the gold values of their currencies despite the worsening of their economies and recurrent political crises. Not until the autumn of 1936 did France decide that the economic and political costs of defending the gold value of the franc were too high. This decision was reflected in a tripartite agreement on September 25 among the governments of France, Britain, and the United States. This "agreement" was only temporary and had little substantive content. It was limited largely to statements that these nations "look to measures to promote world prosperity"; that in its policy toward international monetary relations each country must "take into full account the requirements of internal prosperity"; that the French government recognized the need to propose to France's parliament "the readjustment of its currency"; and that none should try to obtain an "unreasonable competititve exchange advantage." The agreement did, however, make it politically feasible for the French to devalue. Under the new law, the French franc was to be kept within a range of 66 to 75 percent of its previous gold parity. The other gold-bloc countries quickly followed suit. The devaluation of the Swiss franc was similar to that of the French franc. The Netherlands did not establish a new gold value for the guilder, but the exchange rate on the latter was maintained at about 80 percent of its former parity.[1] Thus by late 1936 no currency in the world was freely convertible into gold at its gold value in 1929. France and several other countries had paid high prices, both economically and politically, in defending the gold values of their currencies as long as they did in the face of devaluations by others.

MONETARY AND BANKING LEGISLATION

Before examining other aspects of Treasury and Federal Reserve policies during this period, it will be useful to review some legislative changes relevant to the power and organization of the Federal Reserve. As noted earlier, an act in June 1934 authorized the Reserve banks to lend directly, and to participate in private loans, to established commercial and industrial firms if these applicants were in sound condition but were unable to secure credit from normal sources at reasonable rates. Federal Reserve officials devoted much attention to this program in 1934 and 1935, setting up industrial advisory committees in every Federal Reserve district to help originate such loans, to judge their quality, and to give publicity to their availability. A total of 8,534 applications had been received by the end of 1937, for a total of $351 million. Of these applications, 2,406 were approved for a total of $151 million. However, total advances outstanding at any one time never exceeded $30.5 million.[2]

In the Securities Exchange Act of 1934, the Federal Reserve Board was given, for the first time, legal power to impose margin requirements for loans on securities. The first regulation under this power was issued on October 1 of that year. Margin requirements were increased twice during 1936 and once in 1937 as stock prices rose, and then lowered in November 1937 after the onset of the recession.[3]

The Banking Act of 1935, approved by Roosevelt on August 23, brought many changes, of which only the most important will be noted here. It provided a permanent program for insurance of bank deposits to supersede

---

[1]*Annual Report of the Board of Governors of the Federal Reserve System*, 1936, pp. 6-7.

[2]Board of Governors of the Federal Reserve System, *Banking and Monetary Statistics*, Washington, D.C., 1943, p. 345.

[3]*Ibid.*, p. 504.

the temporary plan which had been administered by the FDIC since the beginning of 1934. It also clarified and extended somewhat the power of the Federal Reserve Board to prescribe different ceilings on interest rates paid on different classes of time and savings deposits, providing that the Board "shall prescribe different rates for such payment on time and savings deposits having different maturities, or subject to different conditions respecting withdrawal or repayment, or subject to different conditions by reason of different locations, or according to the varying discount rates of member banks in the several Federal Reserve districts."[4] Ceiling rates were the same for all classes of time and savings deposits prior to the end of 1935. They were 3 percent from November 1, 1933, to January 31, 1935, and 2 1/2 percent during the remainder of that year. A new regulation issued at the beginning of 1936 maintained the 2 1/2 percent ceiling for savings deposits, postal savings deposits, and time deposits with maturities of 6 months or more, but provided ceilings of 2 percent on time deposits with maturities of 90 to 180 days and 1 percent on time deposits with maturities of less than 90 days. No further changes were made until after 1941.

A change that was to have important consequences within a year increased the discretionary power of the Federal Reserve Board to change member bank reserve requirements. The Banking Act of 1933 had provided that the Board might change these requirements only if at least five of its members, with the approval of the President, found that "an emergency exists by reason of credit expansion." The new Act permitted the Board to make such changes by an affirmative vote of at least four of its members "in order to prevent injurious credit expansion or contraction." However, requirements were not to be set below the levels in effect prior to the passage of the Act nor at more than double those levels. The first increase occurred in mid-1936 and the second in the spring of 1937.

A major purpose of the Banking Act of 1935 was to clarify the distribution of power within the Federal Reserve System, to achieve a greater degree of centralization of powers over policy-making, and, as a corollary, to lessen the influence of the Reserve banks. This was done in several ways. (1) The old Federal Reserve Board, which had been composed of six members appointed by the President plus the Secretary of the Treasury and the Comptroller of the Currency as *ex officio* members, was abolished and was succeeded by a new Board of Governors of the Federal Reserve System. Now every member of the Board was a governor! The new Board was composed of seven governors appointed by the President with the advice and consent of the Senate; neither the Secretary of the Treasury nor the Comptroller was included on it. Salaries were increased from $12,000 to $15,000 a year, and terms were extended from 12 to 14 years, with the limitation that no member was eligible for reappointment after having served a full 14-year term. Terms of the initial appointees were staggered, so that one expired every two years.

The establishment of the new Board of Governors on February 1, 1936 brought large changes in personnel, for only two members of the old Board

---

[4]*Annual Report of the Board of Governors of the Federal Reserve System*, 1935, pp. 59-60.

were appointed to the new one—M. S. Szymczak, who had been appointed in 1933, and Marriner S. Eccles, who had been appointed in 1934. The latter had been Governor of the old Board and was appointed chairman of the new one. Those who were not carried over were Adolph C. Miller, Charles S. Hamlin, J. J. Thomas, and George R. James. New appointees were Joseph A. Broderick from the New York Federal Reserve district, John K. McKee from the Cleveland district, Ronald Ransom from the Atlanta district, Ralph W. Morrison from the Dallas district, and Chester C. Davis from the St. Louis district. In general, the new Board was younger and more vigorous than the old, and Eccles, who was able, ambitious, and a strong believer in centralization, insisted upon enhancing the power and prestige of the Board even if he met opposition from the Reserve banks.

(2) The Federal Open-Market Committee was reorganized and its powers enhanced. The old FOMC had been composed of representatives of the 12 Reserve banks. The new one was composed of the 7 members of the Board of Governors and 5 representatives of the Reserve banks. The law also strengthened the FOMC by providing that no Reserve bank should engage in open-market operations, or decline to engage in such operations, except in accordance with the direction of, and regulations adopted by, the committee. The FOMC was reorganized in March 1936, and almost immediately began to limit the power of the Reserve banks to engage in open-market operations for their own accounts. For one thing, it ordered the Reserve banks to surrender to the committee all their holdings of government securities, including those in their pension funds. Also, it was impressed upon members of the committee who were representatives of Reserve banks that their powers derived from the Banking Act of 1935, that as committee members they were not representatives of their boards of directors, and that they should not discuss open-market policies with their directors.

(3) The power of the Board over discount rates was clarified and increased. The Federal Reserve Act had previously provided that Federal Reserve banks might from time to time establish discount rates, subject to the review and determination of the Board. This left open the question of whether the Board had the legal power to order a Reserve bank to change an existing rate. This ambiguity was removed, somewhat clumsily, by an amendment adding the phrase, "and each such bank shall establish such rates every 14 days, or oftener if deemed necessary by the Board."

(4) Several changes were made in governing arrangements at the various Reserve banks. The titles of the top officers were changed from "Governor" and "Deputy Governor" to "President" and "Vice-President," a move clearly meant to imply a lowering of their status relative to that of the governors on the new Board. The presidents and first vice-presidents were appointed for five-year terms, and both their initial appointments and their reappointments by their boards of directors were subject to approval by the Board of Governors. In general, the Board increased its surveillance over appointments and reappointments of not only the presidents and first vice-presidents but also of other official and professional personnel at the Reserve banks.

Thus various provisions of the Banking Act of 1935 served to centralize power within the System and to enhance the power and prestige of the Board.

That this shift had important policy effects during the remaining years of the 1930s is doubtful. It would have been more important if further vigorous expansionary actions by the Federal Reserve had been called for.

FEDERAL RESERVE AND TREASURY MONETARY POLICIES, FEBRUARY 1934-AUTUMN 1937

During this period of continuing gold inflows and mounting reserves in the banking system, three major issues relating to monetary policy claimed much of the attention of Federal Reserve and Treasury officials: (1) the Treasury's use of its newly acquired powers to influence monetary and credit conditions; (2) facilitation of Treasury finance and maintenance of "orderly conditions" in markets for Treasury securities; and (3) the "inflationary potential" represented by the large and increasing volume of excess reserves in the banking system.

We noted earlier that the Treasury reaped a profit of $2,805 million from the revaluation of gold at the end of January 1934, and that Roosevelt's executive order provided for the use of $2 billion of these profits to establish an Exchange Stabilization Fund and gave to the Secretary of the Treasury broad powers to use these funds "for such purchases of gold, foreign exchange, and Government securities as the regulation of the currency, the maintenance of the credit of the Government and the general welfare of the United States may require." These profits accrued to the Treasury initially as "cash in vault" against which no gold certificates were outstanding, and thus had no effect on either Federal Reserve or member bank reserves or on the money supply. However, the Secretary could, as he wished, issue gold certificates against the gold profit and thus acquire additional deposits at the Federal Reserve which he could spend at will. In effect, he had acquired extensive central banking powers. By expending these funds to purchase foreign exchange, government securities, or other assets he could create additional bank reserves.

Many Federal Reserve officials, and others outside the System, feared that the Secretary would use this power aggressively, thus usurping the monetary management powers of the Federal Reserve and negating its policies. Federal Reserve officials discussed the possibility of decreasing the Treasury's power by selling to it, in exchange for the gold profit, a large part of the System's holdings of government securities. Most Federal Reserve officials were intrigued by the proposal but worried about two consequences of such an action: the loss of earnings to the Reserve banks, whose other earning assets were falling; and the decrease in their ability to take restrictive actions at a later date because of the depletion of their securities portfolio. In fact, no such action was taken, and the Secretary proved to be more "cooperative" than Federal Reserve officials had dared hope. He did keep the Federal Reserve aware of his monetary powers and did on occasion expend some of the funds to help stabilize the government securities market and for other purposes. In general, however, these actions were small and were taken in cooperation with the Federal Reserve. Exceptions will be noted later.

Facilitation of Treasury financing and maintenance of orderly conditions in markets for government securities were important considerations in Treasury and Federal Reserve policies during this period. Many, both within and outside government, feared that the Treasury would encounter serious financing difficulties, especially in its long-term financing, because of its large and continuing deficits and perhaps also because of a "loss of confidence in the dollar." Such fears proved to be unfounded. The Treasury easily met all of its financing needs, mostly with new issues with maturities of five years or more, and at declining rates of interest. (See Table 19-6.) Interest rates began to fall early in 1934 and continued downward through the end of 1936. Yields on long-term government bonds averaged 3.5 percent in January 1934; by the end of 1936 they were down to about 2.5 percent. Yields on shorter-term issues fell even more.

In the face of this happy turn of events, Federal Reserve and Treasury officials continued to believe that they should intervene from time to time to maintain orderly conditions in the market for government securities. Despite their general upward trend, prices of these securities did fall on occasion. For example, in February 1935, when the Supreme Court was considering the gold-clause cases and its decision was still in doubt, the market became disturbed and the prices of government securities without gold clauses fell relative to the prices of those containing gold clauses. The FOMC discussed

the responsibility of the Federal Reserve for the status of the government security market in view of the fact that under recent conditions the government securities market had become a dominating factor in the money market . . . .

It was generally agreed that it was neither possible nor desirable to peg the prices of government securities at any point, but that it might be desirable in certain conditions to ease movements in either direction.[5]

Moreover, the rapidity and extent of the rise of prices of government securities, and especially of prices of the longer-term issues, created apprehensions in both the Treasury and the Federal Reserve that the rise might become too rapid and would be followed by price declines, which would both injure investors and complicate later Treasury financing. They agreed that both price increases and price decreases should be "cushioned" on occasion.

Though Federal Reserve officials pledged their cooperation in maintaining an orderly market for government securities, they were highly reluctant to do so by changing the total size of the System's portfolio. They were unwilling to make net sales because these might be interpreted as a move toward restriction and might elicit both an adverse public reaction and a fall of bond prices. They were also highly reluctant to make net purchases, both because these were not needed to increase bank reserves and because they might be interpreted as a shift toward an even more expansionary policy. Only once during this period did the Federal Reserve change the total size of its portfolio; it made net purchases of $96 million in April 1937 when prices of government securities had fallen following the increase of member bank reserve requirements in March. On all other occasions when it attempted to

[5]Minutes of the FOMC, February 5, 1935.

TABLE 19-6

Yields on U.S. Government Securities, 1934-1941
(January figures, percent per annum)

	1934	1935	1936	1937	1938	1939	1940	1941
Long-term bonds	3.50	2.79	2.65	2.68	2.56q	2.36	2.21	1.95
3-5-year tax-exempt notes	3.11	1.29	1.11	1.40	0.83	0.59	0.50	0.46
3-month Treasury bills (Dealer's quotations)	0.72	0.17	0.17	0.28	0.07	0.05	0.04	0.13

Source: Board of Governors of the Federal Reserve System, *Banking and Monetary Statistics*, Washington, D.C., 1943, pp. 460-471.

TABLE 19-7

Member Bank Reserve Requirements, 1936-1937
(percent of deposits)

Class of deposits and bank	June 21, 1917–August 15, 1936	August 16, 1936–February 28, 1937	March 1, 1937–April 30, 1937	May 1, 1937–April 15, 1938
On net demand deposits				
Central reserve city	13	19 1/2	22 3/4	26
Reserve city	10	15	17 1/2	20
Country	7	10 1/2	12 1/4	14
On time deposits, all member banks	3	4 1/2	5 1/4	6

Source: Board of Governors of the Federal Reserve System, *Banking and Monetary Statistics*, Washington, D.C., 1943, p. 400.

exert a stabilizing influence it did so by shifting the maturity composition of its portfolio, switching from shorts to longs or vice versa. In switching from short to long maturities, Federal Reserve officials had to overcome their long-standing prejudice in favor of short maturities.[6] However, they derived some solace from the fact that earnings were higher on the longer maturities.

Such actions by the Federal Reserve were usually taken in cooperation with the Treasury. For example, the FOMC and the Treasury agreed in July and October 1936 that purchases at times of weakness in the securities market would be divided equally between the FOMC and funds available for investment by the Treasury. In December, members of the FOMC found themselves in general agreement on these principles:

> It is the duty of the Reserve System to determine at any period of weakness whether the market is sufficiently disorderly to justify intervention from this broad standpoint, and that at times of disturbing weakness when intervention is justified it would appear desirable to consult with the Treasury, indicating the intention of the Committee to operate in the markets and its willingness (a) to make all the necessary purchases itself, (b) to operate 50/50 with the Treasury, or (c) to keep out of the market entirely in case the Treasury expresses a desire to make all the purchases itself in order to employ funds which may be on hand for investment.[7]

EXCESS RESERVES AND THEIR INFLATIONARY POTENTIAL

The most controversial actions taken by the Federal Reserve during this period were its two increases of member bank reserve requirements. The first increase, which became effective on August 16, 1936, increased by half legal reserve requirements against all classes of deposits at member banks. The second increase, half of which became effective on March 1, 1937 and the other half on May 1, raised these requirements to the limit permitted by law. (See Table 19-7.) These actions were not taken lightly or hastily. The first one occurred only after more than a year of discussion within the System, after consultation with and approval by the Treasury, and after careful study of both the size and distribution of excess reserves in the banking system. The purpose was not to slow down the current rate of increase of bank credit and the money supply nor to raise interest rates. Rather, the purpose was to remove from the banking system some part of the excess reserves that were currently "serving no useful purpose" but which might later serve as a basis for undesired inflation. Yet it is probably true, as many have alleged, that the second increase of reserve requirements played at least a minor role in precipitating the recession of 1937-1938.

Federal Reserve officials became concerned about the inflationary potential of excess reserves at least as early as the spring of 1935, when excess reserves had risen above $2 billion. At a meeting of the Governors' Conference on May 28, it was

---

[6]For data concerning the maturity composition of the Federal Reserve portfolio, see *Banking and Monetary Statistics,* pp. 343-344.

[7]Minutes of the Executive Committee of the FOMC, December 21, 1936.

voted to be the sense of the Conference that no action is necessary or desirable at this time, but that the problem of controlling excess reserves is one which will require the utmost courage and ingenuity when the time comes for action. It was generally conceded that whatever action on the part of the Reserve System is determined upon should be taken well in advance of any credit inflationary tendency, and that action should not be postponed until statistics indicate a definite trend toward such inflation.[8]

At a meeting on October 22-24, 1935, the FOMC decided that the time for preventive action was approaching. It was the

unanimous opinion of the Committee that the primary objective of the System at the present time is still to lend its efforts towards the furtherance of recovery .... In these circumstances, the Committee was unanimously of the opinion that there is nothing in the business or credit situation which at this time necessitates the adoption of any policy designed to retard credit expansion.

But the Committee cannot fail to recognize that the rapid growth of bank deposits and bank reserves in the past year and a half is building up a credit base which may be very difficult to control if undue credit expansion should become evident. The continued large imports of gold and silver serve to increase the magnitude of that problem. Even now actual reserves of member banks are more than double their requirements, and there is no evidence of a let-up in their growth. That being so, the committee is of the opinion that steps should be taken by the Reserve System as promptly as may be possible to absorb at least some of these excess reserves, not with a view to checking some growth of credit, but rather with a view to put the System in a better position to act effectively in the event that credit expansion should go too far.

Two methods of absorbing excess reserves have been discussed by the Committee: (a) the sale of short-term Government securities by the Federal Reserve System, and (b) the raising of reserve requirements.

While the Committee feels that (a), if employed, would have the dual effect of absorbing excess reserves and improving the position of the Reserve banks, nevertheless, there are two risks in this method: first, that it may be a shock to the bond market, inducing sales of securities by banks all over the country; second, that however it may be explained publicly, it may be construed by the public as a major reversal of credit policy, since this method has never been employed except as a means of restraint, which is not desired at this time. A majority of the Committee is opposed to the sale of government securities at this time, believing that its advantages do not now justify the risks involved in this method of dealing with the subject.

There are also risks incident to method (b)—raising reserve requirements. This method of control is new and untried and may possibly prove at this time to be an undue and restraining influence on the desirable further extension of bank credit. The Committee feels, therefore, that before this method of dealing with the problem of excess reserves is employed, it would be wise for the Board of Governors of the Federal Reserve System to make a thorough study, through the 12 Federal Reserve banks, of the amount and location of excess reserves by districts and classes of banks, in order to determine whether, or to what extent, if at all, an increase of reserve requirements might interfere with the extension of loans and investments of member banks.

In view of the monetary powers now possessed by the Treasury, the Committee is impressed with the importance of advising with the Treasury relative to any steps that may be taken by the Reserve System in order as far as possible to insure reasonable coordination of action.

Furthermore, the Committee reocgnizes the possible dangers of the public misunderstanding of any action which may be taken in this matter, and would favor a careful public statement before action is taken.

In making these suggestions to the Board of Governors regarding reserve requirements, the Committee recognizes that it is going somewhat beyond its own immediate

---

[8]Minutes of the Governors' Conference, May 27-28, 1935.

jurisdiction but it has found it impossible to consider open-market operations independently from the whole credit situation and other Federal Reserve policies.[9]

After considering this resolution at a meeting on November 8, the Federal Reserve Board unanimously decided

... to take no action at this time to increase reserve requirements, but that the situation should be watched carefully, so that the Board would be in a position to act whenever developments in the situation indicated that action was necessary.[10]

During the remainder of 1935 and the first months of 1936, Federal Reserve officials continued to discuss both the timing of actions to absorb some of the excess reserves and whether this should be done through Federal Reserve sales of securities or by increases of member bank reserve requirements. At a meeting of the FOMC on December 18, 1935, the committee concluded that

action should be taken as soon as possible without undue risk to absorb a part of these excess reserves as a safeguard against possible dangers, and not as a policy of credit restraint.[11]

However, some members preferred to achieve this by selling securities, while others favored an increase of reserve requirements. After meetings of the FOMC with the Board, the following press release was issued:

The Board of Governors of the Federal Reserve System and the Federal Open Market Committee have given extended consideration to the general business and credit situation and to the recommendation of the Federal Advisory Council and are of the opinion:
   1. That continued improvement has been made in business and financial conditions but that the country is still short of a full recovery.
   2. That the primary objective of the System at the present time is still to lend its efforts to a furtherance of recovery.
   3. That there is at the present time no evidence of overexpansion of business activity or the use of business credit.
   4. That the present volume of member bank reserves, which have been greatly increased by imports of gold from abroad, continues to be excessive, far beyond the present or prospective requirements of credit for sound business expansion.
   Therefore, the special problems created by the continuing excess reserves has had and will continue to have the unremitting study and attention of those charged with the responsibility for credit policy in order that appropriate action may be taken as soon as it appears to be in the public interest.[12]

The first increase of reserve requirements probably would have come earlier in 1936 had it not been for the impending change of membership and reorganization of the Board on February 1. Marriner Eccles, meeting with the FOMC on January 21, observed that "the problem of dealing with excess reserves was probably more of a problem for the future when a new Board

---

[9]*Annual Report of the Board of Governors of the Federal Reserve System,* 1935, pp. 231-233.

[10]*Ibid.,* p. 205.

[11]*Ibid.,* p. 224.

[12]*Ibid.,* pp. 224-225.

had been organized."[13] In fact, the Board delayed until July 14 its decision to raise reserve requirements by 50 percent, the increase to become effective August 16. In a press statement the Board emphasized these points:

1. Excess reserves had risen to nearly $3 billion dollars and were expected to increase further. Moreover, these were widely distributed in the banking system.

2. Even after the increase, excess reserves would amount to about $1.9 billion, by far the highest level ever achieved prior to the recent gold imports.

3. This was not a reversal of the System's easy-money policy.

In the light of recent experience and in view of the fact that after the increase in requirements goes into effect member banks will still have approximately $1.9 billion of excess reserves, the Board is convinced that this action will not affect easy money conditions now prevailing. It does not constitute a reversal of the easy money policy which has been pursued by the System since the beginning of the depression. Rather it is an adjustment to a changed reserve situation brought about through the extraordinary inflow of gold from abroad.[14]

4. This reduction of excess reserves would bring the remaining volume

within the scope of control through the System's open-market portfolio which consists of $2,430 million of United States Government securities. Frequent changes in reserve requirements of member banks should be avoided because they affect all banks regardless of their reserve position. At this time an increase can be made equitably because reserves are widely distributed. Unless large additional increases in reserves occur through gold imports or otherwise, no occasion for further adjustments in reserve requirements is likely to arise in the near future.[15]

This first increase of reserve requirements had no visible effect on monetary and credit conditions. Bank credit and the money supply continued to expand, and interest rates continued downward.

Though excess reserves declined to an average of less than $1.9 billion in the latter half of August, they quickly began to rise again as gold imports and silver purchases continued. They exceeded $2,000 million in October and $2,200 million in November. This renewed growth of excess reserves, together with the prospect of still more increases to come, led the FOMC, at a meeting on November 20, 1936, to discuss the possibility of selling securities or raising reserve requirements again. The committee decided to take no action at the time but to hold another meeting in January to reconsider the matter. In the meantime, on December 21, the Executive Committee of the FOMC, the Board of Governors, and the Secretary of the Treasury had agreed upon a new method of preventing further gold imports from enhancing bank reserves: the Treasury would "sterilize" further changes in the gold stock by putting gold imports into an "inactive gold account." In effect, the Treasury would pay for

[13]Minutes of the FOMC, January 21, 1936.

[14]*Annual Report of the Board of Governors of the Federal Reserve System*, 1936, p. 217.

[15]*Ibid.*, pp. 217-218. The entire press statement appears on pp. 216-218. A table showing the size and distribution of reserves and excess reserves among classes of member banks appears on p. 218.

TABLE 19-8

The Inactive Gold Account of the U.S. Treasury and Changes in the
Monetary Gold Stock, December 1936-April 1938 (in millions of dollars)

End of month	Inactive gold account	Change in inactive gold account during the month	Change in monetary gold stock during the month
1936			
November	0	—	—
December	26	+ 26	+ 64
1937			
January	127	+ 101	+100
February	205	+ 118	+ 78
March	343	+ 138	+138
April	568	+ 225	+225
May	758	+ 190	+191
June	1,087	+ 329	+328
July	1,213	+ 126	+128
August	1,335	+ 122	+121
September	1,209	− 126	+174
October	1,271	+ 62	+ 61
November	1,243	− 28	− 29
December	1,228	− 15	− 14
1938			
January	1,223	− 5	− 4
February	1,201	− 22	+ 20
March	1,183	− 18	+ 19
April	0	−1,183	+ 74

Source: Board of Governors of the Federal Reserve System, *Banking and Monetary Statistics*, Washington, D.C., 1943, pp. 376-377 and 515.

additions to the gold stock by issuing interest-bearing securities rather than by issuing gold certificates to the Reserve banks and then drawing upon the resulting deposits at the Federal Reserve to pay for the gold. Thus changes in the gold stock would not lead to changes in bank reserves. The plan was put into effect on December 22, 1936. From that time until January 1938, almost all changes in the monetary gold stock were offset by changes in the inactive gold account.[16] (See Table 19-8.) For example, between December 23, 1936 and the end of August 1937, the monetary gold stock rose $1,383 million; the inactive gold account rose $1,335 million in the same period. Note that the Treasury continued to sterilize gold imports even after the second and highly controversial increase of reserve requirements that became effective in March and May of 1937. Federal Reserve officials fully approved the Treasury's policy of gold sterilization, but they were not unaware of the fact that the sterilized gold enhanced the power of the Treasury to take expansionary monetary actions at a later date.

Though the Treasury's gold sterilization policy prevented further additions from this source to bank reserves and excess reserves, it did nothing to

---

[16]An exception occurred in September 1937 when the Treasury, at the request of the Federal Reserve, "desterilized" $300 million of gold in order to supply additional reserve funds. It did this by failing to sterilize a $174 million addition to the gold stock and by decreasing its inactive gold account by $126 million.

reduce the existing volume of excess reserves, which averaged nearly $2.1 billion in January 1937. Federal Reserve officials considered these excessive. At a meeting of the FOMC on January 26, Emanuel T. Goldenweiser, economist to the Board of Governors, advocated an increase of reserve requirements by the full amount permitted by law and warned against excessive delays, especially in view of the continuing rise of business activity and prices. John H. Williams, economist for the New York Bank, agreed fully with this position. On January 30 the Board of Governors adopted this recommendation, providing that one-half of the increase would become effective on March 1 and the other half on May 1. In its press release the Board made these principal points:

> By its present action the Board eliminates as a basis of possible credit expansion an estimated $1,500,000,000 of excess reserves which are superfluous for the present or prospective needs of commerce, industry, and agriculture and which, in the Board's judgment, would result in injurious credit expansion if permitted to become the basis of a multiple expansion of bank credit. The Board estimates that, after the full increase has gone into effect, member banks will have excess reserves of approximately $500,000,000, an amount ample to finance further recovery and to maintain easy money conditions. At the same time the Federal Reserve System will be placed in a position where such reduction or expansion of member bank reserves as may be deemed in the public interest may be effected through open-marked operations, a more flexible instrument, better adapted for keeping the reserve position of member banks currently in close adjustment to credit needs.[17]

TABLE 19-9

Federal Reserve Estimate of Ability of Member Banks to Meet Proposed Increase of Reserve Requirements, January 13, 1937

Class of banks	Number of banks	Member Banks with Reserves Insufficient, when Increased by One-half of Balances with Correspondents, to Meet a 33 1/3 Percent Increase in Requirements	
		Number of banks	Additional reserves required (in millions of dollars)
Total	6,367	197	$123
Central reserve city banks			
New York City	37	12	100
Chicago	13	1	9
Reserve city banks	334	16	11
Country banks	5,983	168	2

Source: *Annual Report of the Board of Governors of the Federal Reserve System,* Washington, D.C., 1937, p. 4.

In fact, the volume of excess reserves fell from an average of $2,152 million in February to $1,371 million in March, to $876 million in June and July and to $750 million in August. (See Table 19-1, above.)

Before taking this action, the Board considered a report on the distribu-

---

[17]*Annual Report of the Board of Governors of the Federal Reserve System,* 1937, p. 46.

tion among member banks of excess reserves and of balances with correspondents. It found that both excess reserves and balances with correspondents were widely distributed and concluded that all except a handful of members could meet the full increase of reserve requirements by utilizing their excess reserves and by decreasing their balances with correspondents by no more than 50 percent. (See Table 19-9.) More specifically, the report indicated, that only 197 member banks out of a total of 6,367 would be unable to meet the full increase of reserve requirements by drawing down their excess reserves and reducing by half their balances with correspondents, and that their total reserve deficiency after such actions would be only $123 million. Of these banks, 13 were in New York City and Chicago, and they accounted for $109 million of the projected $123 million reserve deficiency. Federal Reserve officials clearly expected that banks would meet their increased reserve requirements primarily in these ways, and they did not anticipate that banks would curtail their expansion of loans or sell securities, or that interest rates would rise. Their forecasts were wrong. They had repeated a mistake made too often in earlier years; they had again underestimated member bank demands for excess reserves as a source of liquidity.

Interest rates began to rise almost immediately after the first half of the increase of reserve requirements became effective on March 1, and they continued to rise until mid-April, after which time they declined slightly. (See Table 19-10.) In general, the rise of rates was small, but it extended to all maturities and to all types of open-market paper. Officials were especially concerned about the decline of bond prices. For example, prices of long-term government bonds averaged 103.8 percent of par during January and February; in April they averaged only 99.5 percent of par.

Federal Reserve officials were initially inclined to minimize the extent to which the decline of bond prices was attributable to the increase of reserve requirements. For example, Eccles told the FOMC on March 15 that the market situation was

a readjustment brought about by a number of factors, that the Government securities market, particularly the longer-term securities, had shown weakness in part for the reason that the public had begun to feel, even before the Board issued its announcement of a further increase in reserve requirements, that the market for corporate securities was out of line, that some issues had been overpriced during the recent period of extremely low interest rates, and that this weakness in the corporate securities had affected the Government securities market. He referred to the French financial situation, the British armament program and the demand for war materials from other countries, labor troubles and the building of inventories in anticipation of higher prices in this country, which had resulted in unjustified increases in commodity prices, and discussions with respect to the possibility of increased relief expenditures and reduction of social security taxes which might result in a continued unbalanced budget. He felt that this situation, together with some feeling on the part of the public that the Board was moving to stop price inflation which would naturally result in the prices of long-term securities seeking somewhat lower levels.[18]

Harrison and Burgess were in general agreement with these views. Later, how-

---

[18]Minutes of the FOMC, March 15, 1937.

TABLE 19-10

Behavior of Selected Interest Rates in 1937
(monthly averages in percent per annum)

	Jan.	Feb.	March	April	May	June	July	Aug.	Sept.	Oct.	Nov.	Dec.
U.S. government securities												
Long-term bonds	2.47	2.46	2.60	2.80	2.76	2.76	2.72	2.72	2.77	2.76	2.71	2.67
3-5-year tax-exempt notes	1.18	1.22	1.44	1.59	1.48	1.54	1.44	1.45	1.50	1.42	1.31	1.27
Dealers' quotations on 3-month Treasury bills	0.17	0.15	0.38	0.56	0.41	0.36	0.28	0.29	0.31	0.20	0.09	0.11
4- to 6-month prime commercial paper	0.75	0.75	0.75	1.00	1.00	1.00	1.00	1.00	1.00	1.00	1.00	1.00
90-day prime bankers' acceptances	0.22	0.31	0.38	0.56	0.53	0.47	0.44	0.44	0.44	0.44	0.44	0.44
High-grade corporate bonds	3.09	3.24	3.36	3.43	3.36	3.31	3.27	3.25	3.26	3.26	3.22	3.17
High-grade municipal bonds	2.79	2.96	3.19	3.24	3.14	3.11	3.07	3.01	3.18	3.24	3.17	3.15

Source: Board of Governors of the Federal Reserve System, Banking and Monetary Statistics, Washington, D.C., 1943, pp. 451, 460, 471.

ever, Eccles conceded that the decline of excess reserves had been an important factor. He

said that banks have become accustomed for a long time to an extremely large amount of excess reserves, that by the action of the Board this excess has been sharply reduced and that it would take the banks some time to accustom themselves to operating with a smaller amount of excess reserves, as evidenced by the fact that they had sold earning assets rather than reduce their balances with correspondents.[19]

Secretary Morgenthau had been fully informed about the proposed increase of reserve requirements and had discussed it with Roosevelt, and neither disapproved. However, Morgenthau was quite upset by the turn of events. He had no doubt that the decline of security prices was attributable to the increase of reserve requirements, and he was concerned about both the decrease in the prices of government securities and the possibility that further increases of interest rates would impede economic recovery. On March 13,

He indicated a feeling that the Federal Reserve System should take such steps as might be necessary to prevent any further decline in prices. He asked what the Federal Reserve System proposed to do to meet the situation and indicated that, in the event System action was not effective, he would have to consider the use of every authority the Treasury has, including the use of the stabilization fund and the discontinuance of the sterilization of gold imports. He considered it particularly important to prevent the newly issued 2 1/2% bonds from going below par.[20]

Members of the FOMC agreed that they should cooperate in maintaining an orderly market for government securities, but they were unwilling to make a commitment to peg security prices at any fixed level or to increase the total size of the System's portfolio. During the remainder of March they cooperated with the Treasury on approximately a 50-50 basis in maintaining an orderly market. The Treasury bought bonds with funds from its investment accounts, while the Federal Reserve shifted some of its holdings from shorts to longs. During the period March 10-31, the System increased its holdings of bonds by $104 million and reduced its holdings of Treasury notes by $85 million and its holdings of Treasury bills by $19 million.

By the latter part of March, as security prices continued to decline, Secretary Morgenthau became convinced that more vigorous action was required. Eccles agreed, stating that prices of government securities had declined to an unjustified extent and that the System should consider increasing its portfolio by $200-250 million.[21] At the time, however, the Executive Committee of the FOMC did not have this authority, for the directive of March 15 had authorized it to increase or decrease its portfolio by not more than $250 million only "in the event of an emergency arising requiring such action before a meeting of the Federal Open-Market Committee can be held." The latter limitation was removed at a meeting of the FOMC on April 3. At this same meeting Eccles informed the committee that the Secretary of the Treas-

---

19Minutes of the FOMC, April 3, 1937.

20Minutes of the Executive Committee of the FOMC, March 13, 1937.

21Minutes of the Executive Committee of the FOMC, March 23, 1937.

ury was determined to act independently if the Federal Reserve did not co-operate. Members generally agreed that it would be better for the Federal Reserve to buy securities, which it could sell later, rather than have the Treasury pay out gold funds and diffuse responsibility for credit conditions. Purchases began on April 5. Between that date and the end of the month the System purchased $96 million of Treasury bonds. No further purchases were made until after the end of October, and shifts in the maturity distribution of the System's portfolio were not significant during this period.

BANK CREDIT AND THE MONEY SUPPLY

Total loans and investments of member banks rose during all of the three years, 1934-1936. The rise in 1936 was over $3 billion, or 10 percent. (See Table 19-1.) However, they fell during 1937, only slightly during the first half but nearly 3.8 percent for the year as a whole. Why did bank credit first cease to rise and then fall? One hypothesis might be that this behavior reflected a decrease of private demands for bank credit as business activity first grew less rapidly and then declined. This hypothesis may have some validity for the second half of 1937, when member bank loans did decline by $317 million. However, it cannot explain the behavior of bank credit during the

TABLE 19-11

Loans and Investments of All Member Banks
on Call Dates, 1936-1937 (in millions of dollars)

| | | | Investments | | |
| | Total loans and investments | Loans | Total | U.S. government obligations | Other securities |
Call date					
1935					
December 31	29,985	12,175	17,810	12,268	5,541
1936					
March 4	30,288	12,079	18,189	12,444	5,745
June 30	32,259	12,542	19,717	13,672	6,045
December 31	33,000	13,360	19,640	13,545	6,095
1937					
March 31	32,525	13,699	18,826	12,718	6,108
June 30	32,739	14,285	18,454	12,689	5,765
December 31	31,752	13,958	17,794	12,372	5,422
Addenda: Change, December 31, 1935– December 31, 1936	+3,015	+1,185	+1,830	+1,277	+ 549
Change, December 31, 1936– June 30, 1937	− 261	+ 925	−1,186	− 856	− 330
Change, December 31, 1936– December 31, 1937	−1,248	+ 598	−1,846	−1,173	− 673

Source: Board of Governors of the Federal Reserve System, *Banking and Monetary Statistics,* Washington, D.C., 1943, p. 74.

first half of 1937 or for the year as a whole, for bank loans actually increased during these periods. The entire decline was accounted for by decreased bank holdings of investments. Another hypothesis might be that banks decreased their investments because, as the rise of business activity slowed down and then yielded to a decline, banks became more suspicious of the creditworthiness of private debtors. This hypothesis has only limited explanatory power because in fact only one-third of the decrease of bank investments was accounted for by the decline of bank holdings of investments other than obligations of the U.S. Treasury; the latter accounted for two-thirds of the decline.

The decline of bank credit in 1937 probably resulted largely from three forces: (1) The increases of reserve requirements decreased the actual stock of excess reserves below the levels desired by banks for purposes of safety and liquidity. (2) The transition from the stage of rising business activity to recession may have increased the banks' demands for liquidity. (3) Capital losses on securities in the early months of 1937 may have changed expectations concerning the future course of interest rates and created fears of further capital losses.

The behavior of the money supply, defined to include currency and demand deposits, was similar to that of bank credit. After rising 14 percent in 1936, it declined 1 percent in the first half of 1937, about 5 percent in the second half, and 6 percent for the year as a whole.[22]

The role played by this behavior of bank credit and the money supply in precipitating the recession of 1937-1938 is still a disputed subject, as will be indicated in the next chapter.

---

[22]See Milton Friedman and Anna J. Schwartz, *A Monetary History of the United States, 1867-1960*, Princeton University Press, Princeton, 1963, pp. 714-715.

20

The Recession of 1937–1938

When Federal Reserve officials decided, in late January 1937, to increase member bank reserve requirements, and even as they took actions in March and April to maintain orderly conditions in the government securities market, they fully expected that economic recovery, which had been under way since early 1934, would continue. They certainly hoped so, for they realized that output and employment were still far below capacity levels. They did not foresee that a sharp recession was imminent.

THE COURSE OF THE RECESSION

For this recession, as for many others, it is difficult to date upper and lower turning points precisely, partly because of problems of definition, partly because the various indexes reach their peaks or troughs at different times, and partly because even a given index may stay at or near its peak or trough for some time. We shall follow other writers who say that this recession began in May 1937 and ended in June 1938. However, it should be noted that the really sharp and persistent decline began only after August 1937. (See Table 20-1.) Thus the recession was relatively short, lasting only 13 months, even if we date its beginning as early as May 1937. But it was sharp and severe. For example, industrial production, factory employment, and freight-car loadings all fell by at least a quarter. Factory payrolls fell even more, largely because of the increase of part-time unemployment. Contract construction awards fell less, partly because of contracts for public construction.

CAUSES OF THE RECESSION

We shall not attempt to make any original contributions to the already voluminous literature on the causes of this recession and its severity or on the causes of recovery from it.[1] However, in view of the tendency of some econo-

---

[1] See especially Kenneth D. Roose, *The Economics of Recession and Revival: An Interpretation of 1937-38*, Yale University Press, New Haven, 1954.

TABLE 20-1

Some Indexes of Production, Employment, and Trade, 1937-1938
(1923-1925 average = 100)

	Industrial production SA[a]	Construction contracts awarded (value) SA	Factory employment SA	Factory pay-rolls NSA[b]	Freight-car loadings SA
1937					
January	114	63	105	94	80
February	116	62	106	100	82
March	118	56	107	106	83
April	118	53	108	109	84
May	118	56	109	110	80
June	114	61	108	107	78
July	114	67	109	105	80
August	117	62	109	108	79
September	111	56	107	104	78
October	102	52	105	105	76
November	88	56	101	93	71
December	84	61	95	84	67
1938					
January	80	52	90	75	65
February	79	51	89	77	62
March	79	46	87	77	60
April	77	52	85	75	57
May	76	51	84	73	58
June	77	54	82	71	58
July	83	59	83	71	61
August	88	66	85	77	62
September	90	78	87	81	64
October	96	82	88	84	68
November	103	96	90	84	69
December	104	96	92	87	69
Percentage decline, May 1937-June 1938	25%	4%	25%	35%	27%

[a]SA = seasonally adjusted.
[b]NSA = not seasonally adjusted.
Source: Federal Reserve Bulletin, September 1939, p. 804.

mists, and especially of Milton Friedman, to stress so heavily the role of monetary policy, it may be useful to review the situation briefly.

In retrospect, the increase of reserve requirements in the spring of 1937 was a mistake—a mistake stemming from both erroneous economic forecasting and an underestimate of the demands of the banking system for excess reserves. Federal Reserve officials would not have taken this action if they had expected a recession to occur, either because of their own act or for other reasons. To the extent that this monetary action exerted any effect on the economy, it was obviously deflationary. We have already noted that it played a major role in raising interest rates somewhat and in ending the expansion and inducing a contraction of bank credit and the money supply. It probably also affected adversely expectations concerning the future course of interest rates and economic activity.

Yet a questions remains: "Was this monetary action a necessary or sufficient condition for the recession? Would the recession have occurred even if it had not been taken?" My guess is that it would have occurred anyway but that it would have been less severe. "Would the increase of reserve requirements have precipitated a recession even in the absence of other adverse developments not traceable to this monetary action?" I doubt it. At least two other developments are highly relevant: a sharp decrease in the expansiveness of federal fiscal policies and an increase in the "vulnerability" of the private sectors of the economy.

Table 20-2 shows that the federal government's deficit on income and product account rose markedly from $2,571 million in 1935 to $3,629 million in 1936 and then dropped abruptly to only $358 million in 1937. The size of a deficit is not, of course, an accurate indicator of the net impact of fiscal policy on private incomes or aggregate demands for output, partly because its behavior reflects not only the effects of upward or downward shifts

TABLE 20-2

Receipts and Expenditures of the Federal Government on Income and Product Account, Calendar Years, 1935-1938 (in millions of dollars)

	1935	1936	1937	1938
Receipts—Total	3,964	5,024	7,039	6,480
Contributions for social insurance	136	391	1,573	1,734
All other	3,832	4,633	5,464	4,746
Expenditures—Total	6,535	8,653	7,393	8,609
Purchases of goods and services	2,919	4,935	4,664	5,409
Transfer payments to persons	634	2,064	838	1,196
All other	2,982	1,654	1,901	2,004
Deficit on income and product account	2,571	3,629	358	2,129

Source: The National Income and Product Accounts of the United States, 1929-1965, U.S. Department of Commerce, p. 52.

of the government's revenue and expenditure functions relative to GNP but also the "automatic" changes of its revenues and expenditures resulting from changes in the level of GNP. However, we can identify enough "autonomous" or "policy" shifts of the revenue and expenditure functions to justify a statement that the federal government's fiscal policy was considerably more expansionary in 1936 than in either 1935 or 1937.

The increase in the federal government's net contribution from 1935 to 1936 came from two principal sources: an increase of $2,016 million in its purchases of goods and services and an increase of $1,430 million in its transfer payments to persons. The latter, in turn, reflected largely the declaration of a $1,700 million soldiers' bonus in June, of which $1,400 million had been paid out by the end of the year. Thus in 1936 the federal government increased its own demands for output and made sharply larger contributions to private disposable incomes, which helped to support the upsurge of private demands during that year.

Three policy actions largely explain the sharp decrease of the federal government's net contributions in 1937. One was the $1,184 million increase in the public's contributions for social insurance, mainly reflecting the imposition of new social security taxes. Another was the $271 million decrease of federal expenditures for goods and services. The other was a $1,236 million decline of transfer payments to persons, this resulting primarily from the absence of another soldiers' bonus. The decrease of the government's own demand for output, and even more the decrease in its contributions to private disposable income, undoubtedly contributed to both the onset of the recession and its severity.

These conclusions are consistent with those of E. Carey Brown, noted earlier.[2] Brown found that the net contribution of the federal government, measured as a percentage of the full employment level of real GNP, rose from 1.9 percent in 1935 to 2.5 percent in 1936 and then dropped sharply to only one-tenth of 1 percent in 1937. Henry H. Villard has estimated the excess of federal income-increasing expenditures over income-decreasing receipts during this period.[3] (See Table 20-3.) These were $3,043 million in 1935, or an average of $761 million a quarter. In 1936 they were $3,943 million, or $986 million a quarter. Then they dropped to only $833 million in 1937, or $208 million a quarter. Note the sharp decline from an average of more than $1,000 million a quarter during the last three quarters of 1936 to only $374 million in the first quarter of 1937; in the third quarter of that year they amounted to only $55 million. Villard also estimated the *net* income-creating expenditures (income-creating expenditures minus income-decreasing receipts) of all units of government—federal, state, and local. He found that in 1936 these were $4,058 million, or $338 million a month. In 1937 they were only $801 million, or less than $67 million a month. They were only $6.3 million in July and were negative by $66.8 million in August and $46.2 million in November.[4]

TABLE 20-3

Difference Between Federal Income-Creating Expenditures and Income-Decreasing Receipts, by Quarter, 1935-1938 (in millions of dollars)

Year	First quarter	Second quarter	Third quarter	Fourth quarter	Year
1935	745	876	627	795	3,043
1936	644	1,301	1,033	965	3,943
1937	374	231	55	173	833
1938	204	610	756	864	2,434

It is impossible to quantify the effects of this sharp shift of fiscal policies, but they must have been strong, especially in view of the fragility of the expectations of businessmen.

Another element in the situation was referred to earlier as "an increase in the vulnerability of the private sectors of the economy." This statement

---

[2]See Chapter 16, above, especially pp. bbb.

[3]Henry H. Villard, *Deficit Spending and the National Income*, Holt, Rinehart and Winston, Inc., New York, 1941, p. 285.

[4]*Ibid.*, p. 323.

refers to certain developments which made the economy more sensitive to adverse shocks and which might have brought a decrease of output and employment even in the absence of such shocks. One of the most important of these was the high rate of accumulation of business inventories in 1936 and early 1937. We noted earlier that private fixed investment did not revive enough to support a sustained recovery. This type of investment did rise in 1936, but a very substantial part of the rise of total private investment was in the form of net increases in business inventories. The net accumulation of nonfarm business inventories rose from $376 million in 1935 to $2,066 million in 1936. The $973 million increase in the last quarter of 1936 was larger than that during any quarter in the 1920s. Inventories rose further by $306 million and $787 million in the first two quarters of 1937.[5] Current commentators noted that stocks of inventories were rising relative to sales and that some inventory accumulation was in anticipation of cost and price increases or labor troubles.

With their stocks of inventories already built up to such high levels relative to sales, business firms might well have decided to cease buying to add to their inventories, or at least to reduce their rate of inventory accumulation, even if they had continued to expect sales to rise. This decision in itself could have precipitated a decline of output and employment. Certainly a cessation of the rise of sales, or even a slowing down of their expected rate of increase—whether because of more restrictive fiscal or monetary policies or for other reasons—would make existing inventories appear excessive and lead business firms to attempt to reduce them. The very large increase of business inventories during the third quarter of 1937—nearly $1.5 billion—was "undesired"; inventories rose because sales fell faster than business firms could reduce their production or purchases for inventory purposes. This set the stage for a sharp decline of inventories in late 1937 and early 1938, which increased the rapidity of the fall of output and employment. Nonfarm business inventories declined by $2.6 billion in 1938.

Another source of increased vulnerability of business by early 1937 was the rapid rise of costs, primarily because of rising wage rates and increasing prices of raw materials. The significance of this development is hard to assess, but current commentators stated that it made businessmen less optimistic about the profitability of investment.

This brief and incomplete review has not even attempted to settle the controversy over the relative roles of fiscal policy, monetary policy, and other forces in precipitating the recession of 1937–1938 and in making it so severe. At the very least, however, it casts some doubt on the most extreme monetary interpretations. The increase of reserve requirements in the spring of 1937 was clearly a mistake; so was the shift of fiscal policy. Roosevelt later admitted this, saying:

> In the late spring of 1937, the public works program began to taper off too quickly. The new social security taxes were beginning to withdraw some of the funds

---

[5]Roose, *op. cit.*, p. 183.

from private sources. The net Federal contribution to national buying power declined from 4.3 billion dollars in 1936 to 1.1 billion dollars in 1937.[6]

FEDERAL RESERVE POLICIES

The Federal Reserve took no significant policy actions between the end of April 1937 and the third week of August. It did not change the size of its portfolio of government securities nor make significant shifts in the maturity distribution of its portfolio, and it changed neither its discount nor its bill-buying rates. After the adverse reaction of markets to the increase of reserve requirements that became effective on March 1, officials discussed the possibility of rescinding the increase that had already been announced to become effective on May 1, but in the end they decided to allow it to go into effect.

Not until September did economists and officials in the Federal Reserve recognize that a recession had begun. However, they had noted much earlier that the rate of rise of economic activity had subsided. For example, John H. Williams told the FOMC on May 4 that

conditions had undergone change since the meeting of the Committee in March at which time he was fearful that the recovery movement was proceeding too rapidly and that it might turn into disorderly upward movement which might result in price spirals and dislocations which would be distinctly harmful . . . . Since the last meeting of the Committee the movement had leveled out with some reduction in prices both at home and abroad and a more orderly condition had appeared, so that there seemed to be much less likelihood of a runaway movement than was the case a month or so ago.[7]

Goldenweiser added that one reason for the substantial decline of prices of internationally traded goods was a recent rumor that the United States might lower the dollar price of gold. Williams' report to the FOMC on June 9 was in a similar vein. At that time neither he nor Goldenweiser foresaw a recession. Under these conditions, the FOMC saw no need for further actions other than occasional shifts of maturities in its portfolio to prevent disorderly movements of government security prices.

The next easing action was taken in late August, when discount rates were lowered to 1 percent at New York and to 1 1/2 percent at the other Reserve banks. They had been 1 1/2 percent at New York, 2 percent at 10 other Reserve banks, and 1 1/2 percent at Cleveland. The primary reason for these rate reductions was not to combat a recession. Rather, it was to adjust to the reduction of excess reserves in the banking system and to enable banks to meet seasonal increases in demands for credit. Total excess reserves of member banks averaged only $750 million in August, and $321 million of these were in country banks. Excess reserves of members in New York City were only $108 million. Moreover, member bank borrowings from the Federal Reserve, which had not risen above $10 million in 1935 and 1936, averaged

---

[6]Notes subsequently appended to the text of Roosevelt's fireside chat of April 14, 1938. *The Public Papers and Addresses of Franklin D. Roosevelt*, Random House, New York, 1941, Vol. 7, p. 234.

[7]Minutes of the FOMC, May 4, 1937.

$24 million in August 1937. Half of these were made by banks in New York City. The Board gave these reasons for the rate reductions:

> The Board's approval was based upon the view that the reduction of discount rates at this time would assist in carrying out the System's policy of monetary ease and make Federal Reserve bank credit readily available to member banks for the accommodation of commerce, business and agriculture, without encouraging member banks to borrow outside their district or to liquidate their portfolios in order to be in a position to meet the needs of present or prospective borrowers.
>
> The reduction of discount rates, which have had little or no practical effect during the period when excess reserves were abnormally large and widely distributed throughout the System, brings the rates into closer relation with the interest rate structure generally prevailing, and affords to member banks the benefit of rates, on advances made by the Federal Reserve bank, which are in line with those available in the money market . . . .
>
> As a result of the continued progress of the recovery movement, demands of agriculture, industry and commerce for bank accommodation have steadily increased and at the present time are augmented by seasonal requirements, particularly with respect to crop movements . . . .
>
> It is the Board's view, therefore, that at this time the Federal Reserve System can best discharge its public responsibility and promote the continuance of recovery by making it possible for member banks to obtain accommodation from Federal Reserve banks at rates which will encourage them to employ their funds to meet the needs of agriculture, industry and commerce.[8]

On September 14 the Board took another action designed to increase the availability of Federal Reserve loans to member banks: It issued a revised and liberalized regulation governing Federal Reserve discounts and advances. Eccles had long been dissatisfied with the old regulation, which emphasized the legal form of paper rather than its soundness and restricted the types of collateral acceptable to the Reserve banks. The new regulation broadened the types of paper acceptable and emphasized soundness rather than legal form.[9]

The economic outlook was still unclear when the FOMC met on September 11. Goldenweiser

> stated that, while the impetus of recovery had slackened temporarily, there was as yet no evidence of a general decline or recession. In the capital market, . . . there had been a very definite slackening of activity with less refunding than last year and a scarcity of new issues, and the stock market had gone through a pretty severe reaction recently. In the banking situation, the aggregate amount of investments had gone down and the volume of deposits had decreased but not substantially. He was of the opinion that the situation was one where, in terms of short-term developments, there was no danger of the speculative excesses or inflationary developments that were in evidence six months ago, but, where on the contrary there was a possibility that the uncertain situation, partly as a result of the hesitation in the capital market, might lead to a decline in business of indeterminable magnitude.[10]

Williams had thought a recession was unlikely and was still inclined to that view, but he was growing less confident about it and now thought there might be some recession. He pointed to a number of adverse developments: (1) the

---

[8]*Annual Report of the Board of Governors of the Federal Reserve System,* 1937, pp. 53-54.

[9]*Ibid.,* pp. 56-57.

[10]Minutes of the FOMC, September 11, 1937.

sluggish and incomplete recovery of private fixed investment; (2) the accumulation of inventories in the preceding winter and spring because of fears of rising prices and labor troubles; (3) the decline of new orders; (4) the break in the stock market; and (5) the shift of federal fiscal policy.

It seemed clear that if the Administration went forward on the present basis there would be a reduction in this fiscal year in the income-creating expenditures of the Government of $2.5 billion to $3 billion, which is a substantial proportion of national income, and which it had been expected would be replaced by private spending. While he had felt last spring that the time for such replacement had come, there was now a question in his mind whether that situation would materialize fully.[11]

Members of the FOMC agreed that there was no immediate danger of an excessive upsurge in the economy and that a recession might develop. Goldenweiser recommended a policy and outlined alternative methods of carrying it out.

... the System should contemplate at this time a policy of counteracting such seasonal tightening influences as are likely to develop between now and the end of the year as a result of a prospective increase in the demand for currency of approximately $400 million and possibly some increase of reserve requirements owing to the growth of deposits in connection with the autumn trade, which would reduce excess reserves of member banks at the peak of the currency demand to between $300 million and $400 million, while in the New York market excess reserves might be wiped out completely.

He felt that, if it were still the System's policy to maintain a condition of monetary ease for the furtherance and completion of recovery, the System should be prepared to take action to make that policy effective, and if that point were made clear it would be easier to consider the possible courses of action that might be pursued in carrying out that policy. These alternatives in his opinion were

(1) A reduction in reserve requirements.
(2) Action by the System in the open market.
(3) Action by the Treasury to desterilize gold or to modify its policy of gold sterilization, or
(4) A combination of actions by the System and the Treasury.

He was strongly of the opinion that a reduction of reserve requirements had all the vices and none of the virtues of any other policy that could be adopted, that it would be a reversal of the position that changes in reserve requirements should not be utilized except infrequently, and that it would involve the use of an inflexible instrument instead of a flexible one, to meet a seasonal situation.

He also said that action by the Treasury to desterilize a certain amount of gold would be better than the discontinuance of further sterilization, for the reason that in the event the latter course were pursued the extent of the action could not be determined, whereas the desterilization of a given amount of gold would increase reserves of member banks by a definite amount. The objections to desterilization, he said, were that the increase in reserves could not be counteracted except by sales out of the System portfolio, and that action by the Treasury at this time also might be interpreted as violating the principle that the Federal Reserve System has primary responsibility for credit conditions and has adequate instruments for handling it. He then expressed the opinion that the most satisfactory action would be for the System to take such independent action through the medium of open market operations as, in its judgment, was necessary to meet the situation.[12]

---

[11]*Ibid.*

[12]*Ibid.*

After debating the merits of the various alternatives, the FOMC came to two decisions on September 12. (1) The first was to recommend to the Board of Governors that it request the Treasury to desterilize $300 million of gold. The Board voted unanimously to make the request, and the Treasury complied immediately. After doing so, however, the Treasury resumed its policy of sterilizing changes in the gold stock. (2) The second was to authorize its Executive Committee

to purchase in the open market from time to time sufficient amounts of short-term U.S. Government obligations to provide funds to meet seasonal withdrawals of currency from the banks and other seasonal requirements. Reduction of the additional holdings in the open-market protfolio is contemplated when the seasonal influences are reversed or other circumstances make their retention unnecessary.

The purpose of this action is to maintain at member banks an aggregate volume of excess reserves adequate for the continuance of the System's policy of monetary ease for the furtherance of economic recovery.[13]

It was understood that purchases would be made only after the effects of the Treasury's desterilization of $300 million of gold could be observed, and then only to the extent necessary to reach the stated objective. In fact, the System increased its portfolio by $38 million during the 3 weeks following November 3. From that time until June 1939 the size of the System's portfolio remained unchanged at $2,564 million.

The FOMC held its next meeting on November 29. By this time it was obvious that the economy was in recession. However, members of the FOMC decided that the volume of excess reserves, now above $1.1 billion, was sufficient. The Federal Reserve took no further significant policy actions until mid-April 1938, and these were taken as a part of Roosevelt's new recovery program.

THE RECOVERY PROGRAM OF 1938

In a message to Congress on April 14, requesting necessary legislation, Roosevelt announced a new recovery program including both increased government expenditures and loans and expansionary monetary measures. He summarized as follows his requests for new money for government expenditures and loans:[14]

	(In millions)
1. Expenditures from the Treasury for work	
Works Progress Administration	$1,250
Farm Security Administration	75
National Youth Administration	75
Civilian Conservation Corps	50
Public Works Administration	450
Highways	100

---

[13]Minutes of the FOMC, September 12, 1937.

[14]*The Public Papers and Addresses of Franklin D. Roosevelt, op. cit.,* Vol. 7, pp. 229-230.

TABLE 20-4

Member Bank Reserve Requirements,
1938-1941 (percent of deposits)

Class of deposits and bank	May 1, 1937- Apr. 15, 1938	Apr. 16, 1938- Oct. 31, 1941	Nov. 1, 1941-
On net demand deposits			
Central reserve city	26	22 3/4	26
Reserve city	20	17 1/2	20
Country	14	12	14
On time deposits, all member banks	6	5	6

Flood control	37
Federal buildings	25
	$2,062

2. Loans from the Treasury for work	
Farm Security Administration	100
Public Works Administration	550
United States Housing Authority	300
	$ 950

Two actions were proposed to promote monetary expansion:

... the Administration proposes immediately to make additional bank resources available for the credit needs of the country. This can be done without legislation. It will be done through the desterilization of approximately one billion four hundred million dollars of Treasury gold, accompanied by action on the part of the Federal Reserve Board to reduce reserve requirements by about three-quarters of a billion dollars. These measures will make more abundant the supply of funds for commerce, industry and agriculture.[15]

On the next day, April 15, the Board of Governors reduced reserve requirements against all classes of deposits at member banks, thus creating about $750 million of excess reserves. (See Table 20-4.) These new requirements remained unchanged until November 1941.

The Treasury announced that it would desterilize gold held in its inactive account and would not sterilize further changes in the monetary gold stock.[16] Almost immediately it terminated its inactive gold account, which amounted to $1,392 million, adding this amount to its deposits at the Federal Reserve banks. Member banks reserves were not immediately increased by this transfer; they would be increased only as the Treasury expended these deposits to pay expenses, to retire debt held by banks or the public, or for other purposes. Morgenthau told Eccles that he planned to spend all of these funds, and that to speed the process he proposed to retire $50 million of Treasury bills each week

---

[15]*Ibid.*, pp. 227-228.

[16]The Treasury had announced on February 14 that, retroactive to January 1, it would sterilize gold in any quarter of the year only to the extent that net inflows exceeded $100 million. (See *Federal Reserve Bulletin*, March 1938, p. 181.) However, this decision had virtually no practical effect because net inflows between the beginning of the year and mid-April were extremely small.

until further notice as well as $250 million of tax bills maturing in the middle of June. In fact, however, he paid out only about $800 million by the end of July.

Thus, the combined effect of the reduction of reserve requirements and the desterilization of gold by the Treasury was to add about $1.5 billion to the excess reserves of member banks. Total excess reserves had averaged about $1.5 billion in March; in June and July they averaged about $3 billion. This sharp increase of excess reserves was accompanied by a rapid decline of yields on government securities of all maturities. Yields on Treasury bills and on notes with maturities up to two years declined abruptly, both because of the pressure of excess reserves and because the supply of bills was being reduced by the Treasury. Prices of long-term Treasury bonds, which had again risen above par even before these actions were taken, rose so rapidly that some feared the movement would become disorderly and lead to later reaction.

The next meetings of the FOMC after these actions by the Board and the Treasury came on April 21 and 29. At these and later meetings, members of the FOMC faced difficult problems of reconciling two objectives: that of maintaining constant the total size of their portfolio of government securities and that of promoting orderly conditions in the markets for these securities. The problem was complicated by the almost "disorderly" rise of the prices of bonds and the increasing difficulty of replacing maturing securities with bills or other short-term securities at prices which would yield a positive, or even a zero, rate of return.

Members of the FOMC saw no reason to change the total size of their portfolio for the purpose of affecting the reserve and excess reserve positions of the banking system. Net purchases were neither necessary nor desirable in view of the expansionary actions already taken by the Board and the Treasury. On the other hand, even a small net reduction of their total holdings would be viewed as a violation of the government's policy of increasing excess reserves. Eccles told the FOMC on April 21 that

if the System were to allow the bills in its portfolio to run off without replacement, the effect on excess reserves would be practically to offset the reduction in reserve requirements which had been made by the Board of Governors, and he felt that such action would be regarded as in effect nullifying the action of the Board in reducing reserve requirements or as nullifying to an equivalent extent the action of the Treasury in paying off maturing bills as a means of giving effect to the gold desterilization policy, with its consequent increase in the lending power of banks.[17]

W. Randolph Burgess reported increasing difficulty in purchasing short maturities except at negative yields; that is, except at prices representing a "premium over a no-yield basis." At first this applied only to Treasury bills; later it extended to Treasury notes with maturities up to two years. For example, Burgess reported to the FOMC on May 31 that

it had been possible up to the present time to replace all maturing bills with other bills on a better than no-yield basis, but that the replacement of bills was becoming increasingly difficult, and that it appeared that if the present program of the Treasury of issuing only $50 million of bills each week is to be continued it will not be possible to replace maturities with other bills without paying premiums over a no-yield basis. He pointed out

---

[17]Minutes of the FOMC, April 21, 1938.

that the action of the System in replacing maturing bills with other bills had forced other investors to go into the note market, which had contributed to reducing the yield on notes to a point where notes up to nearly two years were on a minus-yield basis, and stated that if replacements were made by purchases of notes, the prices of all issues of notes would be forced still higher.[18]

Similar difficulties were encountered many times during the following years.

In fact, the FOMC kept the size of its total portfolio constant through March 1939. However, it succeeded in doing so only by purchasing more bonds. For example, between the end of May 1938 and the end of March 1939, its holdings of bonds rose by $254 million, these purchases being offset by an equal decrease of its holdings of bills and notes. On December 30, 1938 the FOMC prepared the public for possible future changes in the size of its portfolio.

The Federal Open Market Committee announced, following a meeting today, that weekly statements of the total holdings in the Federal Reserve System's Open Market Account may at times show some fluctuation depending upon conditions in the market affecting the Committee's ability to replace maturing Treasury bills held in its portfolio. The volume of Treasury bills available on the market has declined materially during the year and, owing to the large and increasing demand, such bills are already selling either on a no-yield basis or at a premium above a no-yield basis. It has, therefore, become difficult and in some weeks impossible for the System to find sufficient bills on the market to replace those that mature. Short-term notes are also selling on a no-yield basis and longer-term notes have at times been difficult to obtain. In these circumstances, it may be necessary from time to time to permit bills held in the portfolio to mature without replacement, not because of any change in Federal Reserve policy but solely because of the technical situation in the market. Because no change in Federal Reserve policy is contemplated at this time, maturing bills will be replaced to the extent that market conditions warrant.[19]

After its actions in April 1938, the Federal Reserve took only one further action that might be considered to be an antirecession measure, and this was at least partly for purposes of longer-run reform. The Board of Governors, the FDIC, and the Comptroller of the Currency jointly announced during the summer a revised procedure for bank examination, which liberalized appraisals of bank loans and investments. (1) With respect to bank loans, the old classifications of "slow," "doubtful," and "loss" were eliminated and numerical classifications were introduced. "Under the new designations the principle is clearly recognized that in making loans banks should be encouraged to place emphasis upon soundness and intrinsic value rather than upon liquidity or quick maturity, and the examiners are expected to follow this principle in their examinations."[20] (2) For purposes of appraisal, bank investments were divided into three classes: (a) Stocks and defaulted securities. (net depreciation, based on current prices for these securities, was to be classified as a loss and charged off); (b) securities of investment charac-

[18]Minutes of the FOMC, May 31, 1938.

[19]*Annual Report of the Board of Governors of the Federal Reserve System,* 1938, pp. 83-84.

[20]*Annual Report of the Board of Governors of the Federal Reserve System,* 1938, pp. 37-38. For a fuller explanation of these changes, see pp. 37-39 and 89-93.

ter (on these securities, appreciation or depreciation was to be disregarded and banks were to be allowed to carry them at book value with proper amortization of premiums); (c) securities having distinctly or predominantly speculative characteristics (these were to be valued on the basis of their average market prices during the 18 months preceding the examination, and only 50 percent of any net depreciation was to be taken into account in computing a bank's capital account position).

The introduction of these more liberal examination procedures was constructive and would undoubtedly have been more useful if employed much earlier in the depression. At the very least it would have reduced charges that examiners closed banks that could have survived and that they brought pressure on banks to avoid less liquid types of loans and investments. It might also have increased the willingness of banks to acquire or retain such assets.

RECOVERY

As already indicated, the recession reached its nadir in June 1938 and was followed by recovery. By the end of the year business activity had regained about half of its losses during the period from May 1937 to June 1938. Recovery continued somewhat erratically and sluggishly in 1939 but gained momentum in 1940 and 1941.

Without attempting to explain fully why the recession ended and recovery ensued, we can note three favorable developments: (1) The rapid rate of reduction of business inventories in late 1937 and early 1938 decreased the desire of business firms for further reductions and paved the way for additions to inventories in 1939. (2) Federal fiscal policies became considerably more expansionary. Between 1937 and 1938, the federal government increased its purchases of goods and services by $745 million and its transfer payments by $368 million. (See Table 20-2, above.) E. Carey Brown estimates that the federal government's net contribution rose from only one-tenth of 1 percent in 1937 to 1.2 percent in 1938 and 1.4 percent in 1939. (See Table 16-6, p.bbb.) Henry Villard estimates that the excess of federal income-creating expenditures over its income-decreasing receipts rose from only $833 million in 1937 to $2,434 million in 1938. These increased sharply from $204 million in the first quarter of 1938 to $756 million and $864 million in the third and fourth quarters. (See Table 20-3, above.) (3) Finally, there was a resumption of growth of the money supply. Currency plus demand deposits had decreased by 6.5 percent between March 1937 and May 1938. From this low point it began to rise, and had increased 9 percent by the end of the year.[21] Bank loans and investments also rose, reflecting mainly increases in bank holdings of Treasury obligations.

It seems reasonable to infer that the increases of excess reserves supplied by the Federal Reserve reduction of reserve requirements and the Treasury's desterilization of gold played an important role in reversing the decline of

---

[21]Milton Friedman and Anna J. Schwartz, *A Monetary History of the United States, 1867-1960*, Princeton University Press, Princeton, 1963, p. 715.

bank credit and the money supply. This, in turn, helped reverse the recession, but how the credit should be divided between monetary and fiscal policy remains a debatable question, partly because, for a change, both worked in the same appropriate direction.

21

From Depression to War, 1938–1941

THE GOLDEN AVALANCHE CONTINUES

The expansionary monetary monetary actions of the Federal Reserve and the Treasury in early 1938 to combat the recession had been completed by the middle of that year. From that time through the remainder of the pre war period the reserve position of the banking system was almost completely dominated by an accelerated golden avalanche. The monetary gold stock had risen by $5,847 million between February 1934 and July 1938. It rose another $1,431 million in the remaining months of 1938, $3,102 million in 1939, and $4,272 million in 1940. The total increase between July 1938 and the end of 1940 was $8,905 million. Not until 1941 did the rate of gold inflows decline. (See Table 21-1.) None of this gold inflow was sterilized by the Treasury; all of it was allowed to increase the base of high-powered money.

Table 21-2 shows that the principal factors producing the huge gold inflows during the years 1938-1940, inclusive, were the $3,506 million net

TABLE 21-1

The U.S. Monetary Gold Stock and Member Bank Reserves, 1938-1941
(monthly averages of daily figures, in millions of dollars)

		Monetary gold stock	Member Bank reserves	Excess reserves of Member Banks
1938	July	12,985	8,167	3,026
	December	14,416	8,745	3,226
1939	June	16,028	10,085	4,246
	December	17,518	11,473	5,011
1940	June	19,560	13,596	6,696
	December	21,890	14,049	6,646
1941	June	22,603	13,201	5,351
	October	22,779	13,097	5,001
	December	22,759	12,812	3,390

Source: Board of Governors of the Federal Reserve System, *Banking and Monetary Statistics,* Washington, D.C., 1943, p. 372.

TABLE 21-2

*Major Items in U.S. Balance of International
Payments, 1938-1941 (in millions of dollars)*

	1938	1939	1940	1941	Total for years 1938-1940
Balance on account of goods and services	1,109	888	1,509	1,274	3,506
Net capital movements to the U.S.—Total	416	1,179	728	− 502	2,323
Increase of foreign banking funds in the U.S.	256	993	696	− 305	1,945
Decrease of U.S. banking funds abroad	61	135	159	19	355
Return of U.S. funds from foreign securities	59	110	83	52	252
Foreign purchases of U.S. securities	59	− 89	− 234	− 270	− 265
Inflow of brokerage balances	0	33	23	0	56

Sources: For balance on account of goods and services, Table 19-4 above. For net capital movements, Board of Governors of the Federal Reserve System, *Banking and Monetary Statistics,* Washington, D.C., 1943, p. 564. Changes during years are measured from end of week closest to the end of December.

exports of goods and services and $2,323 million of net capital inflows. By far the largest component of the latter was the $1,945 million net inflow of foreign short-term banking funds. Few, if any, of these funds came to take advantage of higher interest rates in the United States; most were fleeing the mounting political and military disturbances abroad. In fact, the great bulk of them flowed to the United States around the time of four major crises: (1) August-September 1938, the first Czechoslovakian crisis, when war seemed imminent; (2) March and April 1939, the second Czechoslovak crisis, when Germany occupied Bohemia and Moravia; (3) August-September 1939, when World War II began; and (4) the spring of 1940, when Germany invaded Denmark, Norway, and the Low Countries. Net capital movements to the United States slowed down in the latter part of 1940 and 1941 as leading European countries became actively engaged in war and imposed increasingly stringent controls over capital exports. Some—notably Britain—used their dollar claims to pay for American exports.

These huge gold imports were sufficient to cover the increase of currency in circulation that occurred as business activity and incomes rose and to provide very large increases in member bank reserves. The latter, which averaged $8,167 million in July 1938, reached a peak of $14,049 million in December 1940 and then declined slightly in 1941. Banks employed a part of these increased reserves as a basis for expanding their loans and investments and the money supply. Demand deposits plus currency in circulation, which had decreased to $55,569 million in mid-1938, rose 15 percent by the end of 1939, 27 percent by the end of 1940, and 41 percent by the end of 1941. Time deposits at commercial banks rose 7 percent between mid-1938 and the end of 1941. These increases of deposits added to required reserves but since the latter rose far less than actual reserves, excess reserves soared. Excess reserves averaged only a little more than $3 billion in July 1938; they rose to $5 billion in late 1939 and averaged about $6.6 billion in 1940. Though they declined somewhat in 1941, they never fell below $3.3 billion. This huge volume of excess reserves exerted downward pressures on interest rates throughout the period.

During this entire period, the Federal Reserve took only one action whose major purpose or effect was to influence the volume of bank reserves, the cost of bank reserves, or the amount of excess reserves. It raised member bank reserve requirements to the limit permitted by law, effective November 1, 1941. It undertook no open-market operations for the purpose of influencing the supply of bank reserves. Such changes in its portfolio as did occur reflected its difficulty in replacing maturing issues with short-term obligations at a positive or zero yield, or were for the purpose of maintaining orderly conditions in the government securities market. The System did not change its bill-buying rate, and its holdings of bills remained negligible. Discount rates were changed only once; in September 1939 several of the Reserve banks instituted a special discount rate of 1 percent on loans to both member and nonmember banks, if the loans were collateraled by government securities. However, the major purpose of this action was to promote stability in the market for government securities.

In the virtual absence of significant actions for the purpose of general monetary or credit management, Federal Reserve officials devoted most of their attention to three problems: the inflationary potential of the huge volume of excess reserves, maintenance of orderly conditions in the government securities market, and—in the latter part of the period when the rearmament program had become large and was accelerating—problems of Treasury finance and inflation control.

THE PROBLEM OF EXCESS RESERVES

We have already seen that during 1935 and 1936, as excess reserves rose toward $3 billion, both Federal Reserve and Treasury officials became concerned about their inflationary potential, and that this concern led to increases of member bank reserve requirements and to the adoption by the Treasury of a policy of sterilizing additional gold imports. These officials again became concerned about the problem when excess reserves once more exceeded $3 billion before the end of 1938 and then rose to much higher levels, with prospects of more to come. They felt that they should absorb at least a part of this inflationary potential before inflation became imminent and serious. However, they faced difficult problems in determining when and how to do so.

Several considerations counseled delay in reducing excess reserves or even in preventing further increases. One was the slowness and incompleteness of economic recovery in 1939 and even in 1940. Another was the unhappy sequel that had followed the increase of reserve requirements in the spring of

1937. After that experience, neither Federal Reserve nor Treasury officials wished to run the risk of impeding economic recovery or even of being charged with an intent to do so. Still another consideration was the inadequacy of the legal powers of the Federal Reserve, to which we now turn.

Under existing laws, the Federal Reserve and the Treasury had three principal instruments for dealing with the problem of excess reserves: an increase of member bank reserve requirements, sales of earning assets by the Federal Reserve, and actions by the Treasury to sterilize a part of the existing gold stock and further gold inflows. Both Federal Reserve instruments together were not powerful enough to absorb all existing excess reserves. For example, in late 1939, when excess reserves averaged well above $5 billion, large amounts of excess reserves would have remained even if the Federal Reserve had increased member bank reserve requirements to the maximum permitted by law and had sold all of its earning assets, which averaged about $2.7 billion. Federal Reserve officials had several reasons for postponing actions of these types. One, already mentioned, was its reluctance to do anything that might be construed as inimical to economic recovery. Another was that large net sales of their earning assets would leave the Reserve banks with insufficient income to cover their expenses and those of the Board. Still another was that an early use of these powers would leave the Federal Reserve with inadequate ammunition to deal with further additions to bank reserves. For example, in March 1939 Goldenweiser advised the FOMC that it would face serious problems of limiting credit in the future and that it should conserve its remaining powers to be used as a signal of policy change when such a change became desirable.[1]

There remained, of course, the power of the Treasury to control excess reserves by sterilizing gold imports and even a part of the existing monetary gold stock. It could do this by selling its interest-bearing obligations to the public and using the proceeds to retire gold certificates held by the Reserve banks or to increase its deposits at the Reserve banks. No such action was taken; the Treasury did not even sterilize further gold imports. Though the reasons for this inaction are not wholly clear, the Treasury was probably reluctant to take responsibility for reducing excess reserves and perhaps also unwilling to incur the increased interest costs that would be required. Moreover, it may have shared the belief of Federal Reserve officials that, as a matter of principle, it would be undesirable to transfer from the Federal Reserve to the Treasury such great power to regulate monetary and credit conditions.

This situation led to an unprecedented action at the end of 1940; for the first time since the establishment of the Federal Reserve System, the Board of Governors, the presidents of the 12 Federal Reserve banks, and the Federal Advisory Council joined in making a special report to Congress requesting legislation that would restore to the Federal Reserve adequate powers of control.[2] The report recommended a five-point program.

---

[1]Minutes of the FOMC, March 7-8, 1939.

[2]For the full text of the report, see *Federal Reserve Bulletin*, January 1941, pp. 1-2.

TABLE 21-3

Reserve Requirements Proposed on December 31, 1940
(in percent)

Class of bank and deposits	Minimum requirements	Maximum requirements
Demand deposits		
Central reserve city	26	52
Reserve city	20	40
Country	14	28
Time Deposits—all banks	6	12

1. Reserve requirements

   Minimum statutory reserve requirements should be set at the maximum levels currently provided by law, and the Federal Reserve should have power to alter requirements up to double the minimum levels. (See Table 21-3.)

   These requirements would apply to nonmember as well as member banks and could be changed separately for each class of banks. The power to determine reserve requirements and to determine open-market policy should be vested in the same body.

2. Elimination of various potential sources of excess reserves

   Congress should repeal the powers to issue greenbacks, to monetize further amounts of foreign silver, and to issue silver certificates against the accumulated seigniorage on silver.

3. Future gold acquisitions

   Further gold acquisitions should be insulated from bank reserves and bank credit and should later be allowed to affect monetary and credit conditions only after consultation with the FOMC.

4. Debt management policy

   The Treasury should make every effort to sell its securities to the public rather than to increase bank holdings.

5. Fiscal policy

   A larger and larger part of defense expenditures should be met from taxation rather than borrowing.

This report is an interesting indicator of the state of thinking of Federal Reserve officials and of the 12 member bankers who constituted the Federal Advisory Council. However, it led to no action by Congress. In fact, as noted earlier, the only significant action taken during this period to reduce excess reserves was the increase of member bank reserve requirements to the maximum permitted by law, effective November 1, 1941. When this action was announced on September 23, the Secretary of the Treasury and the Chairman of the Board of Governors issued a joint statement:

The Treasury and the Board of Governors will continue to watch the economic situation and to cooperate with other agencies of the Government in their efforts, through priorities, allocations, price regulation, and otherwise, to fight inflation. Recommendations on the question of what additional powers, if any, over bank reserves the Board should have during the present emergency and what form these powers will take will be made whenever the Treasury and the Board, after further consultation, determine that such action is necessary to help in combatting inflationary developments.[3]

The Treasury and the Board continued to watch and made no recommendations for dealing with excess reserves. Thus member banks reserves still exceeded $3.6 billion when the United States entered the war.

PROMOTION OF ORDERLY CONDITIONS IN MARKETS FOR GOVERNMENT SECURITIES

We have already noted that during this period Federal Reserve officials continued to be highly reluctant to show changes in the size of their total portfolio of government securities and that they made virtually no purchases and sales for the purpose of regulating the reserve position of the banking system. Such changes in the size and composition of their portfolio as did occur resulted from the increasing difficulty of replacing maturing issues with short maturities except at prices representing a "premium over a no-yield basis" and from the System's continuing and increasing concern for promoting orderly conditions in markets for government securities. Table 21-4 summarizes both the behavior of the size of the Federal Reserve portfolio and the principal reasons for its changes.

In its statement in December 1938 the FOMC had prepared the public for future changes in the size of its total portfolio, noting that any such changes would reflect no changes of policy but only the difficulty of replacing maturing issues. In fact, it succeeded in replacing all maturing issues up to June 21, 1939, but then allowed $141 million of maturing issues to run off during the next eight weeks. It held no Treasury bills at all after November 1939, and its holdings of other short maturities declined, both absolutely and as a fraction of its total portfolio. (See Table 21-5.) This marked shift from short to long maturities resulted from both the difficulty of acquiring short maturities and the FOMC's efforts to maintain orderly conditions in markets for the longer-term issues.

Members of the FOMC generally approved the principles of current open-market policy as stated by Eccles at a meeting on December 13, 1939.

Open market operations during recent months were not directed toward changing or influencing money rates. The large volume of excess reserves had removed the System so far from contact with the money market that the System's purchases and sales of securities have had little effect on the market and practically no effect on the aggregate volume of available funds. In these circumstances, transactions for the System open market account should continue to be in the direction of maintaining stability in the Government securities market, which in turn reflects itself in the entire capital market.

---

[3]*Annual Report of the Board of Governors of the Federal Reserve System*, 1941, pp. 60-61.

TABLE 21-4

Behavior of the Size of Total Federal Reserve Holdings of
U.S. Government Securities, 1938-1941 (in millions of dollars)

Period	Behavior of total portfolio	Principal reason for change in size, if any
November 24, 1937- June 21, 1939	Constant at $2,564 million.	
June 21, 1939 August 23, 1939	Decrease by $141 million to $2,423 million.	Inability to replace maturing issues with short maturities except at a price representing a premium over a no-yield basis.
August 23, 1939- September 20, 1939	Increase by $403 million to $2,826 million.	Purchase of bonds to cushion the fall occasioned by the outbreak of war in Europe.
September 20, 1939- January 3, 1940	Decrease by $349 million to $2,477 million.	Inability to replace maturing issues with short maturities except at negative yields. Very small sales of bonds to cushion price rise.
January 3, 1940- June 12, 1940	Virtually constant at $2,477 million.	Very small purchases of bonds, only $10 million, at time of German invation of Denmark, Norway, and Low Countries.
June 12, 1940- December 4, 1940	Reduced by $293 million to $2,184 million.	Sales of bonds and notes to cushion their price increases.
December 4, 1940- December 3, 1941	Constant at $2,184 million.	
December 3, 1941- December 31, 1941	Increased by $60 million to $2,254 million.	Purchases to maintain orderly markets at time of U.S. entry into the war.

Source: Data on holdings from Board of Governors of the Federal Reserve System, *Banking and Monetary Statistics.* Washington, D.C., 1943, pp. 391-394. Reasons from various sources, chiefly from Federal Reserve archives.

This does not mean that we should sell for the purpose of preventing interest rates from going down nor does it mean that we should purchase securities in order to hold interest rates at any particular level. It does mean, however, that if there were substantial fluctuations which were the result of a small amount of buying at a time when there was no selling in the market or vice versa or which were the result of other conditions which did not reflect fundamental market trneds the System might go into the market and

TABLE 21-5

Maturities of Government Securities in the Federal Reserve Portfolio on
Selected Dates, 1938-1941 (end-of-month figures, in millions of dollars)

Date	Total	Maturities			
		Within 1 year	1 to 2 years	2 to 5 years	Over 5 years
December 1938	2,564	824	391	589	760
May 1939	2,564	807	350	577	830
December 1939	2,484	243	280	697	1,265
December 1940	2,184	233	182	633	1,136
November 1941	2,184	193	247	477	1,337

Source: Board of Governors of the Federal Reserve System, *Banking and Monetary Statistics,* Washington, D.C., 1943, p. 344.

attempt to exercise an influence toward stability of the market by counteracting such conditions. The System would buy or sell on a sliding scale rather than at a fixed price so that the market would not rise too rapidly when there were few or no selling orders in the market and would not fall too rapidly when there was little or no buying interest present.

It is essential that the System use the open market portfolio in such manner as to make it as effective as possible and at the same time give consideration to the income requirements of the System. It should be recognized also that the System cannot and should not attempt to peg the market on either the up or down side, and that under present conditions, with excess reserves more than twice as large as the entire System portfolio, our responsibility is one of attempting to maintain orderly market conditions rather than of attempting to influence market rates.[4]

Some of these views began to change in 1941 as the rearmament program accelerated and the Treasury's financing needs grew rapidly. Until that time, however, Federal Reserve officials stated repeatedly that the System should not attempt to peg prices and yields on government securities at any particular level, that these should be allowed to adjust to "fundamental market trends," and that only "disorderly movements" should be combatted. The Board emphasized two principal purposes of this policy.

(1) By helping to maintain orderly conditions in the market for United States Government securities the System can exert a steadying influence on the entire capital market, which is an essential part of the country's economic machinery, and disorganization in which would be a serious obstacle to the progress of economic recovery. The market for United States government securities is the only part of the capital market in which the System is authorized by law to operate, and Government securities occupy a vital place in that market.

(2) The System also has a measure of responsibility for safeguarding the large United States Government portfolio of the member banks from unnecessarily wide and violent fluctuations in price. The System cannot and does not guarantee any current prices of government obligations, nor does it undertaken to preserve for member banks such profits as they may have on their government securities, or to protect them against losses in this account. The Government security market, however, has become in recent years the principal part of the money market, and member banks are in the habit of adjusting their cash positions through sales and purchases of United States Government securities . . . . In the enhanced importance of the Government portfolio to member banks, the System sees an additional reason for exerting its influence against undue disturbances in Government security prices.[5]

Public statments did not mention another purpose of the policy—to facilitate Treasury finance. Internal doucments show clearly that the Teasury was deeply interested in the maintenance of an orderly market and that Federal Reserve officials were responsive . However, the type of policy desird by the Treasury prior to 1941 was not incompatible with that directed to the other purposes noted above. During this period, Secretary Morgenthau did not want a policy of inflexible pegging of security prices and yields, or one aimed only at preventing price declines. He wanted an orderly market, and a policy of combatting disorderly price increases as well as disorderly price declines. For example, at a meeting of the FOMC on March 13, 1939,

---

[4]Minutes of the FOMC, December 13, 1939.

[5]*Annual Report of the Board of Governors of the Federal Reserve System,* 1939, pp. 5-6.

Chairman Eccles reported that during the late afternoon of March 10, 1939, Mr. Ransom received a telephone call from the Secretary of the Treasury, the substance of which Mr. Ransom immediately communicated to the Chairman. The Chairman said that the Secretary expressed the view that the Government securities market was going up too rapidly, that he believed something should be done to meet the situation, that he had given the Federal Reserve bank of New York an order to sell $10,000,000 of bonds from the Trust Accounts administered by the Treasury, and that he would like to know if the Federal Reserve System would join with the Treasury in the sale of bonds under an arrangement similar to that under which securities had been purchased in the past by the System and the Treasury when the market was under pressure.[6]

Members of the FOMC believed that such sales would be inappropriate under the circumstances.

It was the general consensus that any action taken in furtherance of a sale of bonds could have only a temporary influence in slowing down an upward movement of the market because the strength of the market was due to fundamental causes which would not be reached by the action suggested.[7]

At a conference with the FOMC,

The Secretary of the Treasury replied that, as he had stated before, he felt the System portfolio should be a flexible one, that action should be taken by the System to slow down a rapidly rising market in the same manner as it had taken action to prevent disorderly conditions on a decline.[8]

As it turned out, the rate of increase of security prices subsided, rendering unnecessary sales by the Federal Reserve or further sales by the Treasury. Morgenthau held similar views when security prices fell at the outbreak of World War II. He did not want pegging at a fixed price or "excessive support" because he wanted "natural conditions" in the market when he offered new issues.[9]

Though the Federal Reserve had exerted its influence toward the maintenance of orderly conditions on earlier occasions, primarily through small shifts of maturities in its portfolio, its largest operations occurred around the time of the outbreak of war in early September 1939. Federal Reserve officials had anticipated the need for such action at least as early as September 1938, at the time of the first Czechoslovak crisis. Harrison told the FOMC on September 15 that in the event that war should break out in Europe the stock exchanges might have to be closed, over-the-counter markets might be demoralized, and panicky disorder might develop in markets for government securities. He felt that the System should develop a program for dealing with such an event.[10] Such a program was largely completed by April 1939 and was officially approved by the FOMC on June 21. Two principal methods were to be used. (1) The Reserve banks would stand ready to lend on government

[6]Minutes of the FOMC, March 13, 1939.

[7]*Ibid.*

[8]*Ibid.*

[9]Minutes of the FOMC, September 18, 1939.

[10]Minutes of the FOMC, September 15, 1938.

securities at par value to both member and nonmember banks. (2) The Federal Reserve and the Treasury would buy government securities to prevent disorderly declines of their prices, but not to peg prices inflexibly. The Executive Committee of the FOMC was empowered to increase its total holdings by not more than $500 million. It was understood that the System and the Treasury would participate equally in purchases until the Treasury had acquired approximately $100 million, which amount it had available in its trust funds, and that thereafter all purchases would be made for the System's account.

Eccles explained

that any purchases by the Treasury after available trust funds were exhausted would have to be with funds from the stabilization fund, which would create in the Treasury an open market portfolio in addition to the System's portfolio, and that this condition would be undesirable for the reason that it would result in lessening the ability of the System to discharge its functions in the field of credit control.[11]

Though the outbreak of war in September 1939 did not bring the panicky conditions that had earlier been anticipated, the Federal Reserve put its stabilization program into effect. The Board announced on September 1 that the Reserve banks would lend to both member and nonmember banks on government securities at par and at rates applicable to member banks. Six of the Reserve banks established a special discount rate of 1 percent for such loans, the same rate as that already prevailing at New York, while the other 5 Reserve banks maintained their rates at 1 1/2 percent. Since banks did not experience drains, the Reserve banks made no loans under this provision. In the meantime, pruchases of securities had begun. The Treasury bought an unknown amount of bonds, presumably no more than $100 million. The Federal Reserve increased its total protfolio by about $400 million between August 30 and September 20, purchasing $397 million of bonds and $66 million of notes while allowing its holdings of bills to decline by $63 million.

The average price of Treasury bonds was allowed to decline from about 108 percent of par in mid-August to approximately par in the third week of September. Then the market rallied without further official support, and the Federal Reserve made small sales to cushion the rise. The German invasion of Norway, Denmark, and the Low Countries in the spring of 1940 evoked such small disturbances in the securities markets that the Federal Reserve bought only $10 million of bonds. Upward pressures on bond prices were so strong during the remainder of 1940 that the Federal Reserve reduced its holdings of notes and bonds by $293 million, but even this action did not prevent the average price of Treasury bonds from rising to 111 percent of par. No further significant purchases or sales were made until America's entrance into the war, when the Federal Reserve purchases of $60 million of bonds and notes were sufficient to maintain orderly conditions.

---

[11]Minutes of the FOMC, April 19, 1939.

TREASURY FINANCE AND INFLATION CONTROL

By mid-1941 economic conditions were changing rapidly in response to accelerating increases in aggregate demands emanating from exports, rising government expenditures for rearmament, and induced increases in private spending for investment and consumption purposes. Though large numbers remained wholly or partially unemployed and large amounts of plant capacity were still underutilized, shortages of some types of skilled manpower and of strategic materials were beginning to appear. Prices had started to rise more rapidly. Moreover, it was expected that the Treasury's borrowing needs would be huge by peacetime standards—probably $13.5 billion during the fiscal year ending June 30, 1942 and $16.5 billion during the following year.. Under these circumstances Federal Reserve officials turned their attention to problems related to inflation control and Treasury finance.

At a meeting on March 17, 1941 the FOMC directed its executive committee, Goldenweiser, and various other staff members to study and report upon methods of inflation control and Treasury financing. They considered various methods of combatting inflation: general monetary and credit restriction, selective credit controls, fiscal policies, Treasury borrowing policies, and direct controls, such as limitations on the use of strategic materials, production orders, rationing, and price controls. All seem to have agreed that general monetary and credit restriction should play no more than a minor role, at least in the near future. At the FOMC meeting on June 10,

Mr. Williams expressed the opinion that we were going through a revolutionary period during which the controls that were being exercised were not merely supplementing central banking policies but were supplanting them, that as long as the present situation existed the System could not do much to restrict the supply of credit and, therefore, finds itself in a secondary or tertiary role, that the question of specific controls of credit required careful exploration, and that although the System could not exercise general monetary controls at this time, it could be of assistance in Treasury financing and legitimately should be should be interested in all questions relating to taxation and borrowing and other control measures. He also said that the accepted method prior to the World War period of preventing inflation, first by the use of monetary controls, second by the use of fiscal policies, and then by direct control measures, had been turned around and the direct control measures were being used first.[12]

In fact, the only general restrictive monetary action taken was the increase of member bank reserve requirements on November 1. Why the System did not even give serious consideration to sales of government securities is not wholly clear. A major, and probably dominating, reason was an unwillingness to permit an increase of interest rates on government securities, but this may have been supplemented by an unwillingness to appear to be jeopardizing the rearmament program and a desire to conserve remaining restrictive powers for later use.

The System did impose one type of selective credit control: For the first time it regulated consumer installment credit. On August 21, acting under the authority of an executive order, the Board issued Regulation W, which

---

[12]Minutes of the FOMC, June 10, 1941.

provided both minimun down payments and maximum periods of repayment. The stated purposes of the regulation were

(a) to facilitate the transfer of production resources to defense industries, (b) to assist in curbing unwarranted price advances and profiteering which tend to result when the supply of such goods is curtailed without corresponding curtailment of demand, (c) to assist in restraining general inflationary tendencies, to support or supplement taxation imposed to restrain such tendencies, and to promote the accumulation of savings available for financing the defense program, (b) to aid in creating a backlog of demand for consumers' durable goods, and (e) to restrain the development of a consumer debt structure that would repress effective demands for goods and services in the post-defense period.[13]

Federal Reserve officials agreed on a cardinal principle of fiscal policy: Taxation should be relied upon to the maximum feasible extent to cover the government's rising expenditures. They also agreed on a major principle of Treasury borrowing: As much as possible, the Treasury should borrow from lenders other than commercial banks. To this end it should offer an array of marketable and nonmarketable securities designed especially to appeal to the various types of nonbank buyers, such as insurance companies, other nonbank financial intermediaries, nonfinancial corporations, and individuals. It should also mount sales campaigns to appeal to such buyers.

What should be the Treasury's interest-rate policies on its borrowings during the emergency, and what should be the role of the Federal Reserve in supporting Treasury policies? Federal Reserve officials debated these questions at length. They seem to have rejected at an early stage one aspect of Treasury financing policy during World War I—the provision of higher interest rates on successive issues. This policy had encouraged buyers to postpone purchases and had imposed inequitable capital losses on purchasers of earlier issues unless these were refunded with issues bearing higher coupon rates. In a memorandum presented to the FOMC for discussion on June 10, Goldenweiser recommended that

a definite rate be established for long-term Treasury offerings, with the understanding that it is the policy of the Government not to advance this rate during the emergency. The rate suggested is 2 1/2 percent. When the public is assured that the rate will not rise, prospective investors will realize that there is nothing to gain by waiting, and a flow into Government securities of funds that have been and will become available for investment may be confidently expected.
. . . It is suggested that the public should be informed as soon as feasible of the Government's decision to finance the defense program at rates not exceeding 2 1/2 percent. The authorities could proceed immediately toward stabilization of the market at around this level.[14]

Note that at this stage Goldenweiser recommended a ceiling only on the long-term bond rate; he made no reference to ceilings on shorter-term issues. By September, however, Federal Reserve officials were discussing the desirability of supporting "a pattern of rates."

At a meeting of the FOMC on September 27, Goldenweiser discussed the alternative courses of action before the System.

---

[13]*Federal Reserve Bulletin*, September 1941, p. 839.

[14]Minutes of the FOMC, June 10, 1941.

(1) To do nothing and let the market rise or fall as it saw fit, which he thought was not a policy that should be seriously considered. (2) To continue the policy that had been pursued during the last three or four years of attempting to maintain orderly market conditions, which implied an underlying conception of a natural market, a conception which he said did not accord with conditions as they exist today. In his opinion the orderly market policy was about as much out of line with reality now as discount rate policy had become some years ago. (3) In the event additional powers were obtained, to proceed to tighten credit controls to a point where excess reserves would almost entirely disappear, a substantial number of banks would be short of funds, and interest rates would be allowed to rise. Such a policy would have to be on the theory that higher interest rates were cheap insurance against inflation. In present circumstances this would not be a feasible policy for the reason that it would increase the cost of government borrowing without being effective in preventing price rises, and it could not be carried out with the approval of other branches of government. It would also raise serious problems about the decline in the capital value of outstanding securities. (4) To adopt a policy under which a pattern of interest rates would be agreed upon from time to time and the System would be pledged to support that pattern for a definite period. The pattern of rates would not need to provide for the same range of fluctuation on all types of rates. It might limit' fluctuations on long-term rates to a narrow range, and permit intermediate and short-term rates to respond more freely to current market influences. This appeared to him to be the wisest and most practicable policy at this time.[15]

He added his opinion that the support that the System might need to give the market would not be on such a scale as to offset such restrictive actions as the System might want to take. Members of the FOMC were favorably inclined toward Goldenweiser's recommendation, though they did not adopt it at that time.

Federal Reserve and Treasury officials and members of their staffs had conferred many times before the next meeting of the FOMC on November 24. At this meeting members moved closer to a commitment to maintain a pattern of rates. It is interesting to note how far Federal Reserve officials had moved toward a policy of pegging a pattern of rates even before America entered the war, and even before it was clear that she would become a belligerent. They had rejected a policy of permitting interest rates to rise on successive Treasury issues. They had agreed that yields on the longest Treasury bonds should not be allowed to rise much, if at all, above 2 1/2 percent. And they had agreed that they should also concern themselves with the pattern of rates on intermediate and short-term issues, though the pattern had not yet been specified and they had not yet committed themselves to support an inflexible and unchanging pattern.

Immediately after America's entrance into the war, the Board announced that the Federal Reserve would ensure that all the needs of war finance would be fully met.

The financial and banking mechanism of the country is today in a stronger position to meet any emergency than ever before.

The existing supply of funds and of bank reserves is fully adequate to meet all present and prospective needs of the Government and of private activity. The Federal Reserve System has powers to add to these resources to whatever extent may be required in the future.

The System is prepared to use its powers to assure that an ample supply of funds is available at all times for financing the war effort and to exert its influence toward

---

[15]Minutes of the FOMC, September 1941.

maintaining conditions in the Government security market that are satisfactory from the standpoint of the Government's requirements.

Continuing the policy which was announced following the outbreak of war in Europe, Federal Reserve Banks stand ready to advance funds on United States Government securities at par to all banks.[16]

The System kept its word; neither the government nor war industries were impeded by any lack of funds or by a rise of interest rates. In contrast to its policies during World War I, the Federal Reserve supplied only a negligible amount of funds by lending to banks and others. It supplied huge amounts by purchasing Treasury securities, increasing its total holdings to $25 billion by the end of the war. By the spring of 1942 it had taken the final step to a policy of inflexible pegging of prices and yields on Treasury obligations of all maturities. The pattern of ceiling rates was three-eights of 1 percent of maturities within 3 months, seven-eights of 1 percent for maturities of 12 months, 2 percent for 10-year maturities, and 2 1/2 percent for the longest maturities. Rates remained within this pattern throughout the war and well into the postwar period. The Federal Reserve achieved this stability by standing ready to purchase all the securities issued by the Treasury that others did not elect to hold. However, in the process it surrendered control over both the size and composition of its portfolio and over the supply of bank reserves and money.

The Federal Reserve's long, frustrating, and largely unsuccessful efforts to combat depression and to induce economic recovery had finally come to an end.

---

[16]*Annual Report of the Board of Governors of the Federal Reserve System,* 1941, p. 1.

22

In Retrospect

Even if judged by lenient standards, American monetary policies during the period 1928-1941 were a failure. Those from early 1928 to the bottom of the depression in 1933 were disastrous, and those in the following years failed to achieve full recovery until they were aided by a rapidly mounting rearmament program.

In the period before March 1933 monetary policies did not fail because the Federal Reserve used its full powers to maintain and restore high levels of output and employment, only to find that its powers were inadequate. They failed because such policies were not even tried. Diverted by a multiplicity of objectives and policy considerations, the Federal Reserve did not direct its full efforts to the promotion of economic stability and recovery. Mistakes in the ranking of objectives were accompanied by mistakes in implementation, which reflected lack of understanding, and even misunderstanding, of the System's powers and of the relationships between its actions and the behavior of the economy.

These mistakes, in turn, can be understood and explained only in the context of the state of economic and political thinking and attitudes of the time, both within and outside the Federal Reserve. Professional economists, lacking a valid and generally accepted theory of income and employment, contributed to the confusion, irresolution, and mistakes. Some did counsel strong positive policies that would still be considered appropriate under the circumstances. However, their advice was countered by that of many others. Liquidationists replied that recovery could come only as a result of "natural liquidation" and warned that "artificial" attempts to halt liquidation would only worsen and prolong the depression. Commercial loan theorists and other accommodationists counseled the Federal Reserve to look to the quality rather than the quantity of credit, to adjust credit to the needs of trade as evidenced by demands for commercial loans, to allow the volume of credit to decline as the needs of trade fell, and to avoid purchasing government securities or other assets that did not qualify as short-term commercial loans. Still others urged the Federal Reserve to maintain its own liquidity and to conserve its resources until economic conditions were propitious for recovery. And may agnostics advised that though positive expansionary policies might do no harm they had little chance of stopping an economic decline once it had begun and even less chance of inducing recovery. Large numbers of economists also advised, especially during the first years of the depression, that the appropriate rule for fiscal policy was that of the annually balanced budget. Economic understanding and thinking were at least as diverse and confused in the Federal Reserve, the government, and the public.

The Federal Reserve Act itself contributed to the confusion and mistakes. Most relevant were its sections suggesting a policy of passivity or accommodation in meeting the needs of trade and those providing favored treatment for commercial loans and discrimination against investment and speculative credit. Attempts to modify or repeal such provisions always drew the ire of the most powerful man in the Congress on monetary and banking matters—the venerable Senator Carter Glass. He and his principal advisor, H. Parker Willis, disapproved of Federal Reserve purchases of government securities, its loans on a wider range of bank assets, and commercial bank investments and loans of a noncommercial character.

Partly because of the state of economic thinking and understanding, but also because of the dominant political philosophy of the time, there was no general consensus that either the government or the Federal Reserve could or should assume heavy responsibility for promoting economic stability. The government itself assumed no such responsibility. Indicative of its state of economic understanding were its actions in 1932, decreasing its expenditures and imposing the largest percentage tax increase in American peacetime history. Nor did the government exert strong pressure on the Federal Reserve to take vigorous stabilizing actions. This policy may have resulted in part from the prevailing concept of the "independence" of the Federal Reserve, but it stemmed basically from the lack of understanding and irresoluteness of the government itself. Large sections of the public did criticize Federal Reserve policies, especially as the deflation ground on, but public pressures were divided and did not provide any consensus of support for any one specific type of policy prescription.

Such were some of the most important conditions of the time that shaped Federal Reserve policies and basically accounted for their failure, at least until 1933. Let us now review more closely a few important aspects of the monetary policies in the three subperiods we have discussed: from early 1928 to the time of the stock-market crash in October 1929, from the stock-market crash to the advent of the New Deal in March 1933, and from March 1933 to the end of 1941.

MONETARY RESTRICTION, 1928-1929

During this period the Federal Reserve attempted to promote three objectives simultaneously: to curb stock speculation by decreasing the supply of credit for this purpose, to maintain high levels of business activity at home, and to maintain the viability of gold standards and economic activity abroad. It failed in all respects. For about 20 months after the restrictive policy was initiated in early 1928, stock speculation continued to rise, supported by increasing amounts of credit particularly from nonbank sources, and then ended in the greatest stock-market crash in the nation's history. In the meantime, the severe restriction of money and credit over a protracted period weakened economic activity both in the United States and abroad and played a role in precipitating the depression.

The policy failed because the Federal Reserve tried to promote the multiple goals which could not be reconciled with the instruments that it used—general credit restriction and "direct action," the latter a type of selective credit control applicable only to member banks currently borrowing from the Federal Reserve. The conflict of objectives could have been resolved in either of two ways: by refusing to allow the use of credit for stock speculation to be a policy consideration, or by devising a new instrument or new instruments capable of dealing with the stock-market problem without jeopardizing other objectives. The government and the Federal Reserve did neither.

At least two lessons can be drawn from this experience. The first, which would be too obvious to mention if Federal Reserve officials and others had not thought otherwise during the period, is that general credit restriction is an inefficient and generally ineffective method of achieving selective credit effects, in the sense of decreasing the supply and increasing the cost of credit for certain specifed purposes without exerting significant similar effects on credit for other uses. A general restrictive policy may indeed have differential impacts on various sectors of the economy, but in a financial system with so many sources and channels and a high fluidity of funds, restrictive effects are likely in virtually all sectors. The belief that general restriction would fall far more heavily on speculation than on "legitimate" business apparently stemmed from notions that only credit in excess of the needs of legitimate trade flowed into speculative uses; that, faced with a shortage of the supply of credit relative to total demands, lenders would first curtail their supply to speculators; and that speculation was more sensitive to credit restriction than were "legitimate" uses.

A second lesson is that a selective control program must apply to virtually all types of important lenders if it is to succeed in reducing the supply of credit for disapproved purposes without also reducing the supply for other purposes. The direct action program of early 1929, which applied only to member banks making speculative loans while borrowing from the Federal Reserve, was basically defective. It made no attempt to curb such lending by member banks not borrowing from the Federal Reserve, by nonmember banks, by other financial intermediaries, by nonfinancial corporations, by individuals, or by others. Huge amounts of speculative credit were supplied by these sources. Moreover, the direct action program was defective even as it applied to borrowing members. A banks was criticized not for borrowing at the Federal Reserve nor for making speculative loans, but for doing both simultaneously. Thus a bank could escape criticism by discontinuing either practice. Some probably did cease to make speculative loans for this reason. However, there is strong evidence that many elected to repay their debts at the Federal Reserve, doing so by selling government securities, acceptances, or other open-market assets and even by marginal reductions of customer loans.

Thus they contributed to the general restriction of credit and rise of interest rates. This experience suggests that if the Federal Reserve is to exercise selective controls, these should be based on powers far broader than the power to regulate access to the discount window.

THE GREAT SLIDE, 1929-1933

Monetary policy did not fail to halt the great slide of output, employment, and prices during this period because vigorous expansionary policies proved ineffective; such policies were not even tried. Policies that permitted the money supply to decline by 25 percent can hardly be called highly expansionary. Why did the Federal Reserve fail to adopt much more expansionary policies? A major reason was the lack of convictions, within the System and outside, that the Federal Reserve should make the promotion of economic recovery its overriding objective and that highly expansionary actions could make valuable contributions to the achievement of this objective. Prior to September 1931 the System was not diverted from this goal by the need to follow restrictive or less expansionary policies in order to promote other objectives. It certainly had no need to restrict credit to discourage excessive exuberance in the stock market, and its freedom to adopt more expansionary policies was not limited by the nation's international reserve or balance-of-payments position. In fact, both the nation's international reserve and the Federal Reserve's gold reserve positions were very comfortable, and the nation's balance of payments was in continuous surplus. This situation changed somewhat during the international crisis of late 1931, with its attendant gold outflows, the latter continuing through the first half of 1932. Even then, however, the Federal Reserve could have followed less restrictive, and even expansionary, policies if it had had the resolute will to do so.

In short, the Federal Reserve was not forced by lack of power to choose the policies that it did; it chose them freely and deliberately. Some of the major reasons for these choices have already been mentioned: ideas that liquidation was necessary to pave the way for recovery, that "aritficial" easing measures would not be helpful and would probably be harmful, that credit should be permitted to adjust to the needs of tread, that expansionary policies could do little or nothing to promote recovery, and so on. Thus, many Federal Reserve officials remained unconvinced that the System should adopt "easy money" policies.

However, even those who favored positive expansionary policies made serious mistakes in defining "easy money" and in evaluating the reserve positions of banks. Some of their most serious mistakes were these: (1) They judged monetary and credit conditions by the behavior of interest rates in the market, and especially by the behavior of rates on the safest and most liquid types of short-term, open-market paper. Thus a decline of market rates was viewed as an indicator of "easier money" which would have expansionary effects, even though the rate decline emanated solely from decreases of demands for credit and was accompanied by reductions in the quantity of money and bank credit. This mistake was compounded by concentrating attention on yields on the safest and most liquid assets, which declined most. Thus some officials could conclude that credit conditions were so easy as to be sloppy, even though the cost of credit to most types of private borrowers was rising and the availability of credit decreasing.

(2) The officials underestimated the demands of the banking system for excess reserves as a source of safety and liquidity. Banks appear to have demanded only very small amounts of excess reserves during the 1920s; any increase over those small amounts was used quickly to repay borrowings at the Federal Reserve or as a basis for expanding bank credit. Federal Reserve officials assumed that this pattern would still hold true in the 1930s, that excess reserves over legal requirements were also in excess of the quantities that banks would demand to hold, and that such a surplus would impel banks to expand their earning assets. However, bank demands for excess reserves rose sharply, so that excess reserves which were very large by historical standards were still deficient relative to bank demands for them. This point will be elaborated later.

(3) Officials overestimated the willingness of member banks to borrow as a basis for lending. Some insisted that there was no need for the Federal Reserve to supply funds through purchases of government securities and bills because member banks could and would borrow to meet the "needs of trade." Because of the tradition against continuous borrowing from the Federal Reserve and also because many of the Reserve banks did not reduce their discount rates relative to market yields on the safest types of earning assets, this process could not have been an adequate substitute for large Federal Reserve purchases in the open market. However, the unwillingness of banks to borrow to maintain or expand their stock of earning assets increased during the depression. As confidence in banks weakened, at least some banks became unwilling to show borrowings on their balance sheets because these might be construed as a sign of weakness. However, their willingness to borrow and lend deteriorated even before this stage was reached, and for many reasons. Several of these relate to the fact that when a bank discounted paper at a Reserve bank it still had to bear the risks on the earning asset. (a) One reason for the decline was reduction of customers' demands for loans. A major motive for borrowing by banks in the 1920s was probably to meet demands for loans by their customers, on whom they relied for deposits and with whom they had other profitable relationships. Thus a major motive for bank borrowing at the Federal Reserve was weakened as customer demands for loans subsided. (b) A second reason was the marked decline of market yields on the safest and most liquid types of earning assets. Discount rates at most of the Reserve banks during most of this period were not low enough to make it profitable for banks to borrow in order to acquire these types of assets. (c) A third was the increasing risks and decreasing liquidity of most other types of earning assets, together with a growing unwillingness among banks to bear additional risks and illiquidity. The margin between promised market yields on such assets and discount rates at the Reserve banks would have had to be large indeed to entice banks into borrowing enough to maintain their holdings of such assets, to say nothing of expanding them. (d) Among other factors which militated against an expansion of member bank borrowings were a shortage of eligible

paper, requirement of excess collateral by most of the Reserve banks, and illiberal policies by some Reserve banks in appraising collateral.

These developments were closely related to the "passion for liquidity," and especially to the sharp increase of demands for money itself and for the safest and most liquid short-term assets, that developed throughout the economy as the deflation of incomes and values continued. The adoption of highly expansionary monetary policies in the earliest stage of the depression might well have prevented the development of this passion. However, such actions were not taken, and the process of deflation created conditions and expectations that enhanced demands for money and for the most liquid types of assets. All types of entities—financial intermediaries, business firms, and households—became less confident that they could rely upon current money receipts as a source of liquidity with which to meet payments. For most of them, borrowing became a less reliable source of liquidity. Moreover, almost all other types of assets—physical assets, stocks, and most types of debt claims—became increasingly inferior bearers of safety and liquidity. Thus preferences and demands shifted sharply toward money and the closest substitutes for money. For commercial banks this meant increased demands for cash in vault, for excess reserves, and for such highly liquid earning assets as short-term Treasury obligations and acceptances issued by the most highly regarded banks.

Such developments account in a large degree for the marked fall of yields on the safest and most liquid types of assets. These fell so much not because of large increases in the total supply of loan funds or because of a sharp decline in the total supply of earning assets available to lenders, but because lenders, including banks, shifted their preferences away from other earning assets and toward those which were safest and most liquid.

Could a highly expansionary Federal Reserve policy have arrested the decline of aggregate demand, output, and employment and induced economic recovery by 1933 even if all other public policies had remained the same and the Federal Reserve had used only its conventional instruments—discount rates, moral suasion, and open-market operations in government securities and acceptances? Actual experience during this period provides no basis for an answer, since no such policy was tried. However, I conjecture that such a policy would have had a good chance of success, although only under two conditions: that it was initiated early in the depression—in 1930 or in the first few months of 1931 at the latest—and that it was so aggressive and extensive as to enable virtually all banks to retire their borrowings at the Federal Reserve and to accumulate very large amounts of excess reserves. This policy would have required far larger open-market purchases by the Federal Reserve. For example, during 1930 the excess reserves of member banks averaged only $55 million, while member bank borrowings averaged $272 million. Thus net free reserves were negative by more than $200 million. In no month during 1930 did excess reserves rise above $74 million or bank borrowings at the Federal Reserve fall below $189 million. During the first half of 1931 excess reserves never rose above $129 million and bank borrowings never fell below $155 million. Net free reserves remained negative. Under these conditions, the banking system almost certainly felt under pressure to contract rather than to expand its loans and investments. Federal Reserve purchases of at least an additional $1 billion of bills and government securities in 1930 or early 1931 could have altered the situation markedly. Such a purchase would have enabled the banks to retire virtually all of their borrowings at the Federal Reserve and to add about $750 million to their reserve balances. At the very least it would have decreased contractionary pressures and it probably would have brought some expansion of bank credit.

There is, of course, no assurance that such an expansionary policy, or even one more aggressive, would have arrested and reversed the decline of aggregate demands for output. Several conditions had become adverse as early as mid-1930. The depression abroad militated against a revival of American foreign lending and against a recovery of foreign demands for American exports. At home, the profitability of private investment had declined. Vacancy rates in housing had risen, and prices of housing had in most cases fallen below current building costs. Excess capacity had also risen in most industries. Despite these adverse developments, I would still conjecture that a really expansionary Federal Reserve policy of the type indicated above would have had a good chance of success if introduced early enough.

However, I am far less optimistic about the probable success of an expansionary monetary policy introduced only in the latter part of 1931 or in 1932, for economic conditions became increasingly adverse as the grinding deflation continued. For one thing, government fiacal policies became more restrictive. The decrease of state and local government expenditures for public works beginning in 1931 and the decrease of federal expenditures and the sharp increase of federal tax rates in 1932 militated against recovery. In the meantime, the entire saving-investment process had deteriorated seriously. (1) Rising amounts of excess capacity in housing and in plant and equipment reduced the expected profitability of new private investment. (2) The shrinking liquidity and solvency of business firms and other private potential spenders for investment purposes decreased their willingness to make new investments, lowered their creditworthiness, and reduced the availability of funds to them. (3) Many forces led banks and other financial intermediaries to increase greatly their demands for money and close money substitutes and to decrease their willingness to acquire most other types of earning assets. Among these were fears of deposit withdrawals, decreased value and liquidity of assets already in their portfolios, and increased risk and illiquidity of most types of new loans and investments.

It is because of such economic developments that I am so pessimistic about the ability of conventional monetary policy alone to reverse the decline of aggregate demands for output if such a policy had been initiated only in the latter part of 1931 or later. Of course, there may have been some amount of excess reserves that would have turned the trick, but it would have had to be massive indeed.

THE ROOSEVELT PERIOD, MARCH 1933–END OF 1941

Though it is valid to say that monetary policy first failed to prevent the depression and then failed to reverse it in the 1928-1933 period because it did not really try, the same conclusion does not hold for the Roosevelt period. The Federal Reserve and the government, especially the latter, took numerous large-scale actions during the period that enabled banks to retire virtually all their debts to the Federal Reserve and to amass huge amounts of excess reserves. Yet output and employment did not again approach full employment levels until after mid-1941, more than eight years after Roosevelt first assumed office. Even with the benefit of hindsight it is impossible to explain precisely why recovery was so incomplete before the rearmament program reached large proportions in 1941. This is partly because so many actions were taken, not only in the area of monetary and fiscal policies but also in many other fields. However, we can note some of the factors that were adverse to recovery.

The recession of 1937-1938 undoubtedly prolonged the depression. Though the period of decline lasted only about a year, from the spring of 1937 to the spring of 1938, it was the autumn of 1939 before business activity again reached the levels achieved in early 1937. Faulty monetary and fiscal policies contributed to the severity of this recession, and may even explain its occurrence. The large decline of federal expenditures from 1936 to 1937 and the imposition of new social security taxes were sharply deflationary. So were monetary policies; the Treasury's continued sterilization of gold and two increase of member banks reserve requirements lowered excess reserves of member banks from $2.9 billion in mid-1936 to only $750 million in August 1937, which served to arrest the increase of the money supply and to induce a decline. Reversals of both fiscal and monetary policies in the spring of 1938 assisted economic recovery, which accelerated in 1940 as both exports and government demands for rearmament purposes rose.

However, we are still confronted by the task of explaining why economic recovery was so slow and incomplete during the four years between March 1933 and the onset of the recession in the spring of 1937. Many forces appear to have contributed. The mutual distrust and animosity that developed between the Roosevelt administration and many sectors of the business community did not create a favorable atmosphere for private investment. Many government actions contributed to this deterioration of relationships—the Securities Act of 1933, the Securities Exchange Act, the breakup of public utility holding companies, public power projects, investigations of financial practices and monopoly, and so on. However desirable these actions may have been on other grounds, they did not create a favorable environment for private investment. I doubt, however, that they were a major obstacle to recovery. Much more important were the nature of government fiscal policies, the continuance of large amounts of excess capacity, the slow process of financial rehabilitation, and delays in taking expansionary monetary actions.

During the four years, 1933-1936, the combined fiscal policies of federal, state, and local governments were strongly expansionary only in 1936. During the other years their net contributions to aggregate demand were smaller than they had been during the years 1930-1932. The expansionary effects of increased federal expenditures were countered by the higher effective tax rates under the Revenue Act of 1932 and by decreased expenditures and higher tax rates by state and local governments. Thus monetary policy was not assisted by strongly expansionary fiscal policies.

Many conditions in the private sectors of the economy were unfavorable to recovery. Excess capacity was widespread in housing and in industry, militating against an early recovery of fixed investment. The solvency and liquidity of great numbers of business firms, farmers, homeowners, local governments, and other debtors were seriously impaired. Banks and other financial intermediaries were laden with frozen assets of uncertain value. Even a vigorous expansionary monetary policy had little chance of success until the positions of debtors and of financial institutions had been rehabilitated. This process proved to be very difficult and time-consuming. It began slowly in 1933, gained momentum in 1934, and was not completed until after 1935. Even then it provided inadequate financial assistance to an important class of debtors—nonfinancial business firms outside agriculture and housing.

Also relevant is the fact that really strong expansionary monetary actions were postponed until 1934. The government's gold and silver policies contributed virtually nothing to bank reserves during 1933. Silver purchases during that year were almost negligible, and the RFC paid for its gold purchases not with newly created money that could augment bank reserves but by issuing interest-bearing debentures. Federal Reserve purchases of about $595 million of government securities and net inflows of currency to the banks did enable member banks to accumulate $766 million of excess reserves by the end of the year and to reduce their borrowings at the Federal Reserve to $117 million. However, in view of the ordeals that banks had been through and their large holdings of depreciated and illiquid earnings assets, this volume of excess reserves was probably still smaller than the amounts they demanded. Excess reserves began to reach very high levels only after January 1934, when the Gold Reserve Act became effective. They exceeded $1.7 billion by mid-1934 and continued to rise to about $4 billion by the end of 1935. In the meantime, banks had repaid virtually all their borrowings at the Federal Reserve. It is impossible to say at what point the banking system came under pressure to expand its total earning assets. However, it was probably no earlier than the spring of 1934.

In view of all these conditions—including the postponement of vigorous expansionary monetary actions until 1934, the absence of a strongly supportive expansionary fiscal policy, and the accumulated effects of more than four years of grinding deflation on the entire financial structure and on the state of expectations—it is hardly surprising that large additions to bank reserves were not quickly translated into proportional increases of bank credit, the money supply and demands for output. Experience during this period can teach us virtually nothing concerning the ability of an aggressively expansionary monetary policy to induce economic recovery if such actions are taken soon after the onset of depression. It can only warn us of the danger of long delays.

On balance, the gold policies of the Roosevelt administration—first the suspension of the redeemability of the dollar in terms of gold and then the gold devaluation of the dollar—had favorable effects, though they were not necessarily superior to available alternatives. (1) The suspension of the redeemability of the dollar in gold increased the freedom of the new administration to adopt more expansionary monetary and fiscal policies without worrying about effects on the balance of payments and the nation's gold reserves. It is unfortunate that the administration did not exploit its new freedom more quickly and aggressively. (2) The decrease in the gold value of the dollar was an effective method of lowering the value of the dollar in exchange markets, thereby raising the dollar prices of American exports. In view of the preceding excessive rise of the dollar in terms of nongold currencies, some decrease was justified. However, the depreciation of the dollar in exchange markets was almost certainly excessive and smacked of "beggar-my-neighbor" policies. From a world point of view, an international agreement on exchange rates would have been preferable, though difficult to achieve. (3) The gold purchase policy did add huge amounts to bank reserves. This was, of course, a crude method of controlling the size of the monetary base, for neither the government nor the Federal Reserve could control either the timing or the amounts of gold purchases. Equally large amounts could have been added to the monetary base with more precision of timing by Federal Reserve purchases of securities or by government issues of fiat money. However, given the state of thinking at the time, it is improbable that either Federal Reserve or government officials would have deliberately created such large additions to the monetary base.

Two favorable things can be said about the silver purchase policy. It added significant amounts to the American monetary base, and it enabled the Treasury to accumulate large stocks of silver which proved highly useful for nonmonetary purposes during World War II. On the other hand, it exerted strong deflationary pressures on silver-standard countries. As a subsidy scheme it was helter-skelter. A minor part of the total subsidy did go to silver mining at home and abroad, but a larger part rewarded speculators in existing stocks of silver and those who withdrew silver from monetary circulation abroad.

CAN IT HAPPEN AGAIN?

Largely because of what we learned from, or at least because of the great depression, it is virtually inconceivable that America will ever again experience a depression of that type, depth, and duration. There is no reason to believe that economic recessions are a thing of the past or that we shall never have a recession deeper and more prolonged than any of those experienced during the generation since World War II. The economy could also be immobilized by bitter class conflict or political instability. However, in the absence of social or political deadlock, the economy should never again be allowed to sink so low or to remain in depression for anything like a dozen years. The conditions that made possible the depth and duration of the great depression have undergone revolutionary changes—changes in our understanding of the determinants of income and employment, in beliefs that serious depressions can be controlled, in concepts concerning the responsibility of government for promoting economic stability, in the balance of political forces, and in the nation's financial structure. Our mistakes in the future should be of a different kind. But the mistakes of the late 1920s and the 1930 are worth reviewing and remembering in a larger sense, for they are agonizing testimony to the costs that can accrue from insisting that new national economic problems be fought with old weapons.

Selected Bibliography

GENERAL

Board of Governors of the Federal Reserve System, Washington, D.C.

Annual Reports
Federal Reserve Bulletin (monthly)
Banking and Monetary Statistics, 1943
All Bank Statistics, 1959

U.S. Treasury

Annual Reports
Treasury Bulletin (monthly)

BOOKS

Barger, Harold, *The Management of Money,* Rand McNally, Chicago, 1964.
Burgess, W. Randolph, *The Reserve Banks and the Money Market,* Harper & Row, New York, 1927.
Chandler, Lester V., *Benjamin Strong, Central Banker,* Brookings, Washington, D.C., 1950.
Clarke, Stephen V.O., *Central Bank Cooperation, 1924-31,* Federal Reserve Bank of New York, New York, 1967.
Clay, Sir Henry, *Lord Norman,* St. Martins, London, 1957.
Cowles Commission for Research in Economics, *Common Stock Indexes,* 1871-1937, Principia Press, Bloomington, Ind., 1938.
Currie, Lauchlin, *The Supply and Control of Money in the United States,* Harvard University Press, Cambridge, Mass., 1934.
Everest, A.S., *Morgenthau, the New Deal and Silver,* Kings Crown Press, New York, 1950.
Friedman, Milton, and Schwartz, Anna J., *A Monetary History of the United States, 1869-1960,* Princeton University Press, Princeton, 1963.

Goldenweiser, Emanuel T., *American Monetary Policy*, McGraw-Hill, New York, 1951.

Gordon, R. A., *Business Fluctuations*, Harper & Row, New York, 1952.

Hansen, Alvin H., *Economic Stabilization in an Unbalanced World*, Harcourt, Brace & World, New York, 1932.

Hardy, Charles O., *Credit Policies of the Federal Reserve System*, Brookings, Washington, D.C., 1932.

Hardy, Charles O., and Viner, Jacob, *Report on the Availability of Credit in the Seventh Federal Reserve District*, U.S. Government Printing Office, Washington, D.C., 1935.

Homer, Sidney, *A History of Interest Rates*, Rutgers Press, New Brunswick, N.J., 1963.

Hoover, Herbert C., *Memoirs: The Great Depression, 1929-1941*, Macmillan, New York, 1952.

Johnson, G. Griffith, *The Treasury and Monetary Policy, 1932-1938*, Harvard University Press, Cambridge, Mass., 1939.

Kimmel, Lewis H., *The Availability of Bank Credit, 1933-1938*, National Industrial Conference Board, New York, 1939.

McKinney, George W., Jr., *The Federal Reserve Discount Window: Administration in the Fifth District*, Rutgers University Press, New Brunswick, N.J., 1960.

Morrison, George R., *Liquidity Preferences of Commercial Banks*, University of Chicago Press, Chicago, 1966.

Myers, William Starr, and Newton, Walter H., *The Hoover Administration: A Documented Narrative*, Scribners, New York, 1936.

National Industrial Conference Board, *The Availability of Bank Credit*, the Board, New York, 1932.

Owens, Richard N., and Hardy, Charles O., *Interest Rates and Stock Speculation*, Macmillan, New York, 1925.

Reeve, Joseph E., *Monetary Reform Movements: A Survey of Recent Plans and Panaceas*, American Council on Public Affairs, Washington, D.C., 1943.

Robbins, Lionel, *The Great Depression*, Macmillan, London, 1934.

Roose, Kenneth D., *The Economics of Recession and Revival: An Interpretation of 1937-38*, Yale University Press, New Haven, 1954.

Roosevelt, Franklin D., *The Public Papers and Addresses of Franklin D. Roosevelt*, Random House, New York, Vols. 1-7.

Schumpeter, Joseph A., *Business Cycles*, McGraw-Hill, New York, 1939, two volumes.

The Twentieth Century Fund, *Debts and Recovery 1929-1937*, the Fund, New York, 1938.

Villard, Henry H., *Deficit Spending and the National Income*, Farrar & Rinehart, New York, 1941.

Wicker, Elmus R., *Federal Reserve Monetary Policy, 1917-1933*, Random House, New York, 1966.

ARTICLES

Brown, E. Cary, "Fiscal Policies in the 'Thirties: A Reappraisal," *American Economic Review,* December 1956.

Fabricant, Solomon, *Profits, Losses and Business Assets, 1929-1934,* Bulletin 55, National Bureau of Economic Research, April 11, 1935.

Miller, Adolph C., "Responsibility for Federal Reserve Policies, 1927-1929," *American Economic Review,* September 1935.

Noyes, C. Reinold, "The Gold Inflation in the United States, 1921-1929," *American Economic Review,* June 1933.

Persons, Charles E., "Credit Expansion, 1920-1929," *Quarterly Journal of Economics,* November 1930.

Villard, Henry H., "The Federal Reserve's Monetary Policy in 1931 and 1932," *Journal of Political Economy,* Vol. 45 (December 1937), pp. 721-39.

CONGRESSIONAL DOCUMENTS

House Banking and Currency Committee

Hearings on H.R. 11806, 70th Congress, 1st Session (May 1928)
Hearings on H.R. 9203, 72nd Congress, 1st Session (February 1932)
Hearings on H.R. 10517, 72nd Congress, 1st Session (March 1932)
Hearings on H.R. 5357, 74th Congress, 1st Session (March 1935)

Senate Banking and Currency Committee

Hearings on S. Res. 71, 71st Congress, 3rd Session (January 1931)
Hearings on S. 2959, 72nd Congress, 1st Session (January 1932)
Hearings on S. 1715 and H.R. 7617, 74th Congress, 1st Session (April-June 1935).

Index

Index